I0625233

ECHOES OF ETERNITY

EXPLORING ANCIENT BABYLON'S RITUALS

VOLUME 2

M.D. RUSOSAK

Copyright © 2023 by Trient Press

All rights reserved. No part of this publication may be reproduced, distributed, or transmitted in any form or by any means, including photocopying, recording, or other electronic or mechanical methods, without the prior written permission of the publisher, except in the case of brief quotations embodied in critical reviews and certain other noncommercial uses permitted by copyright law. For permission requests, write to the publisher, addressed "Attention: Permissions Coordinator," at the address below.

Criminal copyright infringement, including infringement without monetary gain, is investigated by the FBI and is punishable by up to five years in federal prison and a fine of $250,000.

Except for the original story material written by the author, all songs, song titles, and lyrics mentioned in the novel Echoes of Eternity: Exploring Ancient Babylon's Rituals are the exclusive property of the respective artists, songwriters, and copyright holder.

Trient Press
3375 S Rainbow Blvd
#81710, SMB 13135
Las Vegas,NV 89180

Ordering Information:
Quantity sales. Special discounts are available on quantity purchases by corporations, associations, and others. For details, contact the publisher at the address above.
Orders by U.S. trade bookstores and wholesalers. Please contact Trient Press: Tel: (775) 996-3844; or visit www.trientpress.com.

Printed in the United States of America

Publisher's Cataloging-in-Publication data
Ruscsak, M.L.
A title of a book : Echoes of Eternity: Exploring Ancient Babylon's Rituals Volume 2
ISBN
Hard Cover   979-8-88990-129-7
Paper Back   979-8-88990-130-3
Ebook   979-8-88990-131-0

Introduction:

Welcome to Part 2 of Echoes of Eternity: Exploring Ancient Babylon's Rituals, Incantations, Spells, and Unveiling the Shadows. In this section, we will delve deeper into the mystical and spiritual practices of ancient Babylon, allowing us to gain a profound understanding of the fascinating traditions that thrived within this ancient civilization.

In the chapters ahead, we will uncover the secrets and wisdom of Shamanism, Ecospirituality, and Magic as they were practiced in ancient Babylon. These ancient traditions offer a window into the beliefs, rituals, and profound connections that the Babylonians held with the spiritual and natural realms.

Through the exploration of Shamanism in Ancient Babylon, we will discover the pivotal role that shamans played in the Babylonian culture. Their practices, techniques, and rituals allowed them to embark on spiritual journeys, communicate with spirits, and heal the physical and spiritual ailments of their community.

Ecospirituality in Ancient Babylon will introduce us to the deep reverence and spiritual connection that the ancient Babylonians had with the natural world. Their cosmology, nature worship, and rituals honoring the cycles of the seasons and the fertility of the land will provide us with insight into their profound understanding of the interdependence between humans and their environment.

Magic in Ancient Babylon will unravel the mysteries of Babylonian magical practices. We will explore the diverse range of magical rituals, spells, and objects that the Babylonians used to manipulate supernatural forces, protect themselves, seek knowledge, and influence their world. We will also examine the ethical considerations surrounding Babylonian magic and the moral framework within which it operated.

Lastly, in Synthesis and Reflection, we will bring together the knowledge we have gained and reflect on the connections between Witchcraft, Divination, Herbalism, Shamanism, Ecospirituality, and Magic in ancient Babylon. We will explore the legacy and influences of these mystical traditions on later civilizations, as well as their contemporary relevance and adaptation in modern spiritual practices.

Throughout this section, we will engage in critical thinking, discussion, and exploration through the use of examples, problems, and exercises. As We of new-age studies, you will have the opportunity to immerse yourselves in the rich tapestry of ancient Babylonian traditions, opening yourselves to new perspectives and insights that can enrich your personal spiritual practices.

Prepare yourselves for a profound journey into the depths of ancient Babylon, where the echoes of eternity still resonate. Let us embark on this enlightening exploration of Shamanism, Ecospirituality, and Magic in ancient Babylon, uncovering the hidden wisdom and mystical heritage that awaits us.

Chapter 1: Shamanism in Ancient Babylon

I. Introduction to Shamanism in Ancient Babylon

Understanding the Essence of Shamanism

Shamanism, an ancient and profound spiritual practice, played a significant role in the cultural fabric of ancient Babylon. To grasp the essence of shamanism in this context, we must explore its foundational principles and its distinctiveness within the Babylonian civilization.

Shamanism, at its core, is a belief system and practice that recognizes the existence of spiritual dimensions beyond the physical realm. Shamans, as the intermediaries between humans and the spiritual world, possess unique abilities to communicate with spirits, navigate the unseen realms, and harness spiritual forces for healing, divination, and guidance.

The Shamanic Journey

Central to Babylonian shamanism is the shamanic journey, a transformative experience that allows the shaman to enter altered states of consciousness and access the spiritual realms. Through rhythmic drumming, chanting, or other techniques, the shaman achieves a trance-like state, opening the doorway to encounters with deities, ancestral spirits, and supernatural beings.

The shamanic journey serves as a vehicle for personal and collective transformation, healing, and obtaining wisdom. It enables the shaman to retrieve lost soul fragments, seek guidance from the spirit world, and acquire insights that guide their actions within the Babylonian society.

Roles and Functions of Shamans

Shamans in ancient Babylon assumed multifaceted roles within their communities. As healers, they tapped into the spiritual energies and knowledge to address physical, emotional, and spiritual imbalances. Through rituals, chants, and herbal remedies, they sought to restore harmony, offering remedies for ailments and facilitating the well-being of individuals and the community.

Divination was another crucial aspect of Babylonian shamanism. Shamans employed various techniques such as interpreting dreams, reading omens, and casting lots to gain insight into future events and provide guidance to individuals and leaders.

Rituals, Ceremonies, and Tools of the Shaman

Rituals and ceremonies were integral to Babylonian shamanism. These sacred acts served as channels through which shamans connected with the spiritual realm, invoked deities, and conducted healing or divinatory practices. Rituals involved the use of specific gestures, chants, offerings, and sacred objects to create a sacred space and evoke spiritual energies.

Shamans employed a variety of tools in their practices, including drums, rattles, feathers, crystals, and herbs. These objects held symbolic meaning and assisted the shaman in their journeying, communication with spirits, and energy manipulation.

Shamanism and the Natural World

Ancient Babylonians revered the natural world and recognized its intimate connection to spiritual realms. Shamanism in Babylon was deeply intertwined with the cycles of nature, the elements, and the cosmic forces. Shamans drew inspiration from the wisdom of plants, animals, celestial bodies, and natural phenomena, recognizing them as teachers and allies in their spiritual work.

The ecological perspective within Babylonian shamanism emphasized the harmony between humans and the Earth. Through rituals, offerings, and the practice of responsible stewardship, shamans and their communities sought to maintain balance and ensure the flourishing of both human and natural realms.

The Global Tapestry of Shamanism

While Babylonian shamanism had its unique cultural expressions, it is important to recognize the broader tapestry of shamanic traditions across the globe. Siberian shamanism, for example, shares similarities with Babylonian shamanism in terms of journeying and healing practices. Native American shamanism, on the other hand, places a strong emphasis on the relationship with the natural world and animal spirits.

Exploring the diversity and commonalities among different shamanic traditions broadens our understanding of the universal principles underlying shamanism and enriches our appreciation for its multidimensional nature.

Shamanism and Modern Society

Shamanism continues to captivate the modern imagination and has experienced a resurgence in recent times. Many individuals seek shamanic practices to reconnect with their spirituality, find healing, and seek guidance in navigating the complexities of contemporary life. However, it is essential to approach shamanic practices with respect, cultural sensitivity, and ethical considerations, recognizing that authentic shamanic traditions are rooted in specific cultural contexts.

Through critical thinking and ethical exploration, we can discern the appropriate application and adaptation of shamanic principles in contemporary settings while avoiding cultural appropriation and superficial interpretations.

Exploring Shamanic Journeys: Examples, Problems, and Exercises

Example 1: Engage in a guided shamanic journey to the mythical realm of Babylon and reflect on your encounters with spirits, deities, or animal allies. What messages or insights did you receive, and how can you integrate them into your life?

Problem 1: Discuss the ethical implications of utilizing shamanic practices in a modern therapeutic setting. How can shamanic principles be integrated into contemporary healing modalities while respecting cultural origins and ensuring ethical practices?

Exercise 1: Design a personal shamanic ritual that incorporates elements of Babylonian shamanism and discuss the symbolism and intentions behind each step.

Exercise 2: Research and analyze the role of divination in Babylonian shamanism. Practice a divinatory technique, such as dream interpretation or scrying, and reflect on the insights gained.

Conclusion

In conclusion, the introduction to shamanism in ancient Babylon reveals a rich tapestry of beliefs, practices, and spiritual exploration. By understanding the essence of Babylonian shamanism, the role of shamanic journeying, the diverse functions of shamans, the significance of rituals and tools, the connection to the natural world, and its place in modern society, we can appreciate the profound wisdom and transformative potential embedded within this ancient tradition. Through engaging examples, thought-provoking problems, and experiential exercises, We are encouraged to delve deeper into the realm of shamanism, fostering critical thinking, reflection, and respectful engagement with these profound practices.

A. Definition and overview of shamanism

Understanding the Essence of Shamanism

Shamanism is a multifaceted spiritual practice that has been prevalent across cultures throughout human history. It encompasses a profound connection to the spiritual realm, a unique set of practices, and the ability to bridge the gap between the physical and metaphysical worlds. At its core, shamanism is rooted in the belief that everything in the universe is interconnected and that there are hidden dimensions of reality that can be accessed through altered states of consciousness.

The Shamanic Journey

Central to shamanism is the concept of the shamanic journey, a transformative experience that involves entering altered states of consciousness to explore realms beyond ordinary perception. Through various techniques such as drumming, chanting, dancing, or the use of sacred plants, shamans enter into a trance-like state where they communicate with spirits, ancestors, and non-ordinary beings. This journey serves as a vehicle for personal growth, healing, and spiritual guidance.

Roles and Functions of Shamans

Shamans assume multiple roles within their communities, acting as healers, diviners, and spiritual leaders. As healers, they address physical, emotional, and spiritual ailments by restoring balance and harmony to individuals and the community as a whole. Through their intuitive abilities and connection to the spiritual realm, shamans offer guidance, insight, and prophecy, helping individuals navigate the complexities of life and make informed decisions.

Rituals, Ceremonies, and Tools of the Shaman

Rituals and ceremonies are integral to shamanic practices. These sacred acts serve as a bridge between the physical and spiritual worlds, allowing shamans to establish connections with spirits and deities. Rituals may involve offerings, purification rites, invocations, or the use of sacred objects and tools. Such objects can include drums, rattles, feathers, crystals, or herbs, each holding symbolic significance and aiding the shaman's journey and communication with the unseen.

Shamanism and the Natural World

Shamanism recognizes the interconnectedness between humans and the natural world. Ancient wisdom traditions, including those of Babylon and other cultures, emphasize the sacredness of the Earth and the vital role of nature in spiritual practices. Shamans draw inspiration from the elements, plants, animals, and celestial bodies, honoring their inherent wisdom and seeking guidance from these sources to maintain balance and harmony in both the individual and collective realms.

The Global Tapestry of Shamanism

While shamanism manifests differently across cultures, there are common threads that weave through these diverse traditions. For example, Siberian shamanism highlights the importance of journeying to other realms, whereas Native American shamanism focuses on the deep relationship with nature and animal spirits. Exploring the richness and diversity of global shamanic practices allows us to appreciate the universal aspects of shamanism while embracing the unique expressions within each cultural context.

Shamanism and Modern Society

In contemporary society, there has been a resurgence of interest in shamanism. Many individuals seek its transformative potential, recognizing the need for spiritual connection, healing, and personal growth. However, as shamanism is appropriated and adapted in modern contexts, it is essential to approach its practices with respect and cultural sensitivity. It is also important to distinguish between authentic shamanic traditions and contemporary interpretations that may deviate from their original roots.

Exploring Shamanic Journeys: Examples, Problems, and Exercises

Exercise 1: Guided Journey to Meet a Spirit Guide - Engage in a guided meditation to connect with a spirit guide or guardian and reflect on the experience.

Exercise 2: Designing a Personal Shamanic Ritual - Create a ritual that incorporates elements of shamanic practice, such as drumming, visualization, or honoring nature, and reflect on the symbolism and intention behind each step.

Problem 1: Ethical Considerations in Shamanic Healing - Analyze case studies that present ethical dilemmas faced by shamans in their healing practices, encouraging critical thinking and discussion on responsible and culturally sensitive approaches.

Problem 2: Balancing Tradition and Innovation - Discuss the tensions and challenges that arise when adapting shamanic practices to modern contexts, exploring the potential benefits and pitfalls of innovation in contemporary shamanism.

Conclusion

In conclusion, shamanism is a profound spiritual practice rooted in ancient traditions across cultures. It provides a pathway for personal transformation, healing, and spiritual connection through the shamanic journey, rituals, and the deep reverence for the natural world. As we explore the definitions and overview of shamanism, it is crucial to approach these practices with respect, cultural sensitivity, and an open mind. By engaging in examples, problems, and exercises, we can deepen our understanding, develop critical thinking skills, and embrace the wisdom that shamanism offers.

B. Importance of shamanism in ancient Babylonian culture

The Cultural Significance of Shamanism

Shamanism held immense importance within the fabric of ancient Babylonian society. It served as a vital spiritual and healing tradition, providing guidance, rituals, and insights that shaped the lives of individuals and the collective community. Understanding the cultural significance of shamanism in ancient Babylon enables us to appreciate its profound impact on various aspects of Babylonian culture and the individuals within it.

Spiritual and Supernatural Connections

Shamanism in ancient Babylon was deeply rooted in the belief that the physical world was intertwined with the spiritual realm. Shamans acted as intermediaries, forging connections between humans and the divine. They possessed the ability to communicate with spirits, deities, and ancestral beings, allowing for the exchange of wisdom, guidance, and blessings. This spiritual connectivity was a central pillar of Babylonian shamanism, offering individuals and communities a profound sense of belonging and purpose.

Healing and Restoration of Balance

Healing was an essential function of Babylonian shamanism. Shamans used their spiritual insight and connection to the supernatural to address physical, emotional, and spiritual ailments. They sought to restore balance and harmony within individuals and the broader community. Through rituals, chants, herbal remedies, and energy work, they offered relief from afflictions, fostering a sense of well-being and promoting a holistic approach to health.

Divination and Guidance

Divination played a significant role in Babylonian shamanism, providing individuals and leaders with insights into future events, decisions, and potential outcomes. Shamans employed various techniques such as interpreting dreams, reading omens, or consulting oracles to access knowledge from the spiritual realm. The guidance provided by shamans through divination helped individuals navigate challenges, make informed choices, and ensure the prosperity and stability of the community.

Rituals and Ceremonies

Rituals and ceremonies were fundamental components of Babylonian shamanism, offering a framework for spiritual connection and collective participation. These rituals, performed by shamans, encompassed a wide range of practices, from purification ceremonies to seasonal celebrations. Through the power of symbolism, sacred objects, incantations, and precise gestures, rituals in ancient Babylonian culture reinforced social cohesion, expressed reverence for the divine, and invoked spiritual energies for various purposes.

Shamanic Roles and Status

Shamans occupied revered positions within Babylonian society. They were respected spiritual leaders, healers, and advisors, sought after for their unique abilities and wisdom. Shamans often held positions of influence and served as mediators between the divine and human realms. Their status and roles within the community were reinforced by their demonstrated knowledge, efficacy in healing, and the trust bestowed upon them by the people.

Artistic Expression and Symbolism

The influence of shamanism extended beyond spiritual and healing practices; it permeated Babylonian art and symbolism. Depictions of shamans, spiritual journeys, and mythological beings adorned murals, sculptures, and ritual objects, encapsulating the mystical aspects of Babylonian cosmology and the shamanic experience. Art served as a visual language that conveyed the sacred and profound aspects of shamanism, leaving a lasting cultural and artistic legacy.

Exploring the Significance: Examples, Problems, and Exercises

Example 1: Analyze a Babylonian artifact, such as a ritual vessel or a figurine, depicting a shamanic motif. Interpret the symbolism and discuss its significance in the context of Babylonian shamanism.

Problem 1: Explore the counterarguments regarding the importance of shamanism in Babylonian culture. Consider dissenting opinions that question the efficacy or role of shamans within the society, and critically evaluate their validity.

Exercise 1: Imagine you are a Babylonian shaman. Write a journal entry detailing a typical day in your role, describing the rituals, healings, and divinations you perform, and reflecting on the impact of your practices on the community.

Exercise 2: Create a visual representation, such as a drawing or painting, that captures the essence of Babylonian shamanism and its cultural significance. Annotate your artwork, explaining the symbolism and meaning behind each element.

Conclusion

In conclusion, shamanism held a position of utmost importance within ancient Babylonian culture. It provided spiritual connections, healing, guidance, and rituals that shaped the lives of individuals and the collective community. The cultural significance of shamanism in Babylonian society extended beyond the realms of spirituality and healing, influencing artistic expression, social structures, and the overall sense of identity and purpose. Through engaging examples, thought-provoking problems, and experiential exercises, We can delve into the profound impact of shamanism on ancient Babylonian culture and develop a deeper understanding of its cultural, spiritual, and social significance.

C. Key characteristics and roles of Babylonian shamans

Babylonian shamans possessed distinct characteristics and fulfilled important roles within their society. Understanding these key aspects provides insight into the nature of Babylonian shamanism and the significance of shamans within their cultural context.

Spiritual Connection and Abilities:

Babylonian shamans were believed to possess a heightened spiritual sensitivity and the ability to connect with the supernatural realm. They served as intermediaries between humans and deities, spirits, and ancestral beings.

Shamans had the capacity to enter altered states of consciousness, allowing them to journey into the spiritual realms and communicate with divine entities. Their spiritual connections enabled them to access spiritual wisdom, receive guidance, and interact with unseen forces.

Healing and Restoration of Balance:

One of the primary roles of Babylonian shamans was healing. They utilized their spiritual insight and connection to address physical, emotional, and spiritual ailments.

Shamans employed various techniques, such as rituals, chants, herbal remedies, and energy work, to restore balance and harmony within individuals and the community. Their healing practices aimed to alleviate suffering and promote holistic well-being.

Divination and Prophecy:

Babylonian shamans were skilled in divinatory practices, providing individuals and leaders with insights into future events, decisions, and potential outcomes.

Through techniques such as dream interpretation, reading omens, or consulting oracles, shamans accessed spiritual knowledge to guide individuals in navigating challenges, making informed choices, and ensuring the prosperity and stability of the community.

Rituals and Ceremonies:

Shamans conducted a wide array of rituals and ceremonies as part of their spiritual practices. These rituals served as bridges between the human and divine realms and were crucial for spiritual connection and collective participation.

Rituals often involved precise gestures, invocations, offerings, and the use of sacred objects. They were performed to invoke spiritual energies, seek blessings, honor deities, and mark significant events in the community.

Status and Respect:

Babylonian shamans held esteemed positions within their society. They were respected spiritual leaders, healers, and advisors, sought after for their unique abilities and wisdom.

The status and roles of shamans were reinforced by their demonstrated knowledge, efficacy in healing, and the trust bestowed upon them by the community. They played an influential role in shaping social, cultural, and spiritual dynamics.

Overall, Babylonian shamans possessed spiritual gifts, provided healing and guidance, practiced divination, and conducted rituals. They held respected positions within their society, serving as intermediaries between the human and divine realms. Understanding the key characteristics and roles of Babylonian shamans sheds light on the importance of shamanism within ancient Babylonian culture and its impact on the lives of individuals and the community as a whole.

II. Shamanic Practices and Techniques in Babylonian Culture

Welcome to the fascinating realm of Babylonian culture, where the art of shamanism flourished as an integral part of spiritual and healing traditions. In this section, we will explore the rich tapestry of shamanic practices and techniques that were prevalent in ancient Babylon. Through studying these practices, We of new-age studies can gain valuable insights into the role of shamans, their connection with the spiritual realms, and the profound impact they had on the society and individuals they served.

Understanding Shamanism in Babylonian Culture

In this section, we will provide an overview of shamanism and its significance in Babylonian culture. We will learn about the core beliefs and principles that underpin shamanic practices, as well as the role of the shaman as a mediator between the human and spirit worlds. By understanding the cultural context in which shamanism thrived, We can appreciate the deep-rooted spiritual traditions that shaped Babylonian society.

Shamanic Healing and Spiritual Practices

This section delves into the various healing and spiritual practices employed by Babylonian shamans. We will explore the use of trance and altered states of consciousness, ritual purification, and divination as essential tools in the shaman's repertoire. Through examining specific techniques, such as soul retrieval, spirit communication, and energy healing, We will gain a deeper understanding of the transformative powers of shamanic practice.

Ancestral Worship and Spirit Communication

Babylonian shamanism placed great importance on the veneration of ancestors and spirit communication. In this section, We will explore the rituals and ceremonies performed by shamans to connect with ancestral spirits and seek guidance from the spiritual realm. By delving into the practices of necromancy, spirit possession, and mediumship, We will gain insight into the unique ways in which Babylonian shamans communed with the unseen world.

Shamanic Journeying and Otherworldly Realms

Shamans in Babylonian culture embarked on visionary journeys to explore otherworldly realms and receive wisdom from spiritual entities. This section focuses on the techniques and rituals involved in shamanic journeying, as well as the cosmology of the spirit world in Babylonian belief systems. Through the study of these practices, We will gain an appreciation for the profound spiritual experiences and insights that can be accessed through shamanic journeying.

Contemporary Applications and Adaptations

In the final section, we examine the contemporary relevance and adaptations of Babylonian shamanic practices. We will explore how these ancient techniques can be integrated into modern spiritual and healing modalities. By considering ethical considerations and cultural sensitivity, We will learn how to respectfully incorporate Babylonian shamanic elements into their own spiritual practices.

Conclusion:

The study of shamanic practices and techniques in Babylonian culture offers We a unique glimpse into the spiritual heritage of ancient civilizations. By exploring the beliefs, rituals, and transformative practices of Babylonian shamans, We can deepen their understanding of the shamanic tradition and its enduring relevance in contemporary spiritual and healing practices. Through this exploration, We will gain insights and tools to enhance their personal and collective spiritual journeys.

A. Rituals and ceremonies conducted by Babylonian shamans

Babylonian shamans performed various rituals and ceremonies as integral components of their spiritual practices. These rituals served as channels for communication with the divine, invocation of spiritual energies, healing, and the maintenance of balance within the community. Understanding the nature and significance of these rituals provides insights into the richness of Babylonian shamanism.

Purification Rituals:

Purification rituals held great significance in Babylonian shamanism, as they served to cleanse individuals, objects, and spaces of negative energies or spiritual impurities. These rituals were considered essential preparatory steps before engaging in further shamanic practices, as they aimed to restore spiritual balance and create a sacred and purified environment.

Water played a central role in purification rituals, symbolizing its purifying and cleansing properties. The shaman would incorporate the use of water in various ways, such as through ritual baths, ablutions, or the sprinkling of water on individuals or objects. Water was believed to possess the power to wash away impurities and restore spiritual harmony. In these rituals, the shaman would often recite invocations or prayers, invoking the blessings of deities or spirits associated with purification and healing.

In addition to water, incense and sacred herbs were also utilized in purification rituals. The burning of aromatic substances, such as frankincense or myrrh, released fragrant smoke that was believed to have purifying and protective qualities. The shaman would carefully select and prepare these sacred herbs, often combining them with other ingredients to create specific blends for different purposes. As the incense or sacred herbs were burned, the smoke permeated the space, purifying it and creating an atmosphere conducive to spiritual practices.

During these rituals, the shaman would assume the role of a facilitator and guide, leading the participants through the ceremony. With deep knowledge and understanding of the spiritual realms, the shaman would recite invocations, chants, or prayers, invoking the assistance and presence of benevolent spirits or deities. These invocations were believed to invoke divine blessings and protection, ensuring the success and efficacy of the purification ritual.

Gestures and movements were also integral components of purification rituals. The shaman would perform specific gestures or dance movements that symbolized purification and the casting away of impurities. These physical expressions served not only as symbolic representations but also as a means to channel energy and intention, amplifying the potency of the purification process.

By engaging in purification rituals, individuals sought to rid themselves of negative energies, spiritual impurities, or any obstacles that hindered their spiritual growth and well-being. The rituals aimed to create a sacred and sanctified space, free from disruptive influences, allowing individuals to connect more deeply with the spiritual realms and embark on their shamanic journeys with clarity and focus.

In conclusion, purification rituals were integral to Babylonian shamanism, serving as important preparatory steps before engaging in further spiritual practices. Through the use of water, incense, sacred herbs, invocations, and specific gestures, these rituals aimed to cleanse individuals, objects, or spaces of negative energies and spiritual impurities. By purifying and sanctifying the participants or the environment, the shaman created a conducive and harmonious space for spiritual exploration and transformation.

Healing Ceremonies:

Babylonian shamans conducted elaborate healing ceremonies to address physical, emotional, and spiritual ailments. These ceremonies involved a combination of ritualistic practices, energy work, and the use of herbal remedies.

Shamans would chant incantations, perform sacred dances, or utilize ritual objects to facilitate the healing process. They called upon the assistance of deities, ancestral spirits, and other supernatural beings to aid in the restoration of the individual's well-being.

Spirit Communication Rituals:

Shamans utilized rituals to establish communication and seek guidance from the spirit realm. These rituals allowed the shaman to connect with deities, ancestral spirits, and other non-ordinary beings.

The shaman would enter an altered state of consciousness, often induced by rhythmic drumming or chanting, and journey to the spirit realm. Through invocations and offerings, the shaman sought wisdom, prophecy, and messages from the spiritual entities.

Seasonal and Agricultural Celebrations:

Babylonian shamans played a crucial role in seasonal and agricultural celebrations. These ceremonies marked significant periods, such as the planting and harvesting seasons, and aimed to ensure a prosperous and bountiful year.

Shamans would perform rituals to honor deities associated with fertility, growth, and abundance. Offerings of food, libations, and sacred objects were made to express gratitude and seek blessings for a successful harvest or fruitful season.

Initiation Rituals:

Initiation rituals were conducted to mark an individual's entry into shamanic practice or to bestow higher levels of knowledge and authority within the shamanic community.

These rituals involved various elements, such as purification, symbolical death and rebirth, and the transmission of sacred teachings and rituals. Initiation rituals served to validate the shaman's spiritual abilities and prepare them for their roles as healers, diviners, and spiritual guides.

The rituals and ceremonies conducted by Babylonian shamans were diverse and carried deep cultural significance. They fostered spiritual connection, promoted healing and balance, facilitated communication with the spiritual realm, honored deities, and celebrated the cycles of nature. The meticulous performance of these rituals showcased the expertise and spiritual prowess of the shamans, reinforcing their role as intermediaries between the human and divine realms.

1. Description of key rituals and their purposes

Babylonian shamans conducted a range of rituals, each with its unique purpose and significance within the context of their spiritual practices. These rituals served as powerful conduits for spiritual connection, healing, and the maintenance of cosmic harmony. Understanding the key rituals and their purposes provides insights into the profound nature of Babylonian shamanism.

Purification Rituals:

Purification rituals held a central role in Babylonian shamanism, serving as transformative practices aimed at cleansing individuals, objects, or spaces of negative energies or spiritual impurities. These rituals were integral in restoring spiritual balance, creating sacred environments, and preparing individuals for further shamanic practices. The purpose and significance of purification rituals within Babylonian shamanism can be further explored through an in-depth examination of their description and symbolism.

Description of Purification Rituals:

Purification rituals in Babylonian shamanism involved the use of various elements such as water, incense, or sacred herbs, each carrying their own symbolic and purifying qualities. The shaman, as the spiritual guide and facilitator, played a pivotal role in leading and conducting these rituals.

The ritual would typically commence with the shaman reciting invocations or prayers, invoking the presence and assistance of benevolent spirits or deities associated with purification and cleansing. This act of invoking divine presence added a sacred and powerful dimension to the ritual, reinforcing the intention of spiritual purification.

Water, a universal symbol of cleansing and renewal, played a significant role in purification rituals. The shaman might sprinkle or pour water over individuals or objects, symbolizing the washing away of negative energies, impurities, or spiritual stagnation. Water, believed to possess inherent purifying qualities, was considered a transformative force capable of rejuvenating and purifying the spirit, body, and soul.

Incense and sacred herbs were also employed in purification rituals. The shaman would burn specific types of incense or smudge sacred herbs, allowing the fragrant smoke to permeate the space or be wafted over individuals. The aromatic smoke was believed to carry the essence of the plants and possess purifying qualities. This act of smudging or burning incense not only purified the environment but also created a heightened state of awareness and sacredness within the participants.

In addition to the use of purifying elements, the shaman would often employ specific gestures, such as hand movements or symbolic actions, to amplify the transformative power of the ritual. These gestures might include tracing sacred symbols in the air or making specific hand motions that symbolized the dispelling of negativity and the invoking of positive energies.

Symbolism and Significance:

Purification rituals in Babylonian shamanism held profound symbolic meaning. The act of purification represented a process of spiritual cleansing, shedding layers of negative energies or influences that hindered spiritual growth and connection. By purifying the spirit, body, and environment, individuals were prepared for deeper engagement in shamanic practices, as they entered a state of heightened receptivity and spiritual readiness.

Symbolically, these rituals washed away impurities and restored individuals to a state of spiritual purity and balance. The purification process aligned individuals with the natural rhythms of the universe, harmonizing their energies with the cosmic forces at play. It symbolized a return to one's authentic self and a shedding of the burdens that hindered spiritual growth and connection.

Moreover, purification rituals created sacred environments by cleansing and sanctifying physical spaces. This sanctification set the stage for spiritual work, establishing a consecrated space where participants could commune with the divine, access spiritual insights, and engage in transformative experiences.

The symbolic and transformative nature of purification rituals fostered a deep sense of renewal, preparation, and spiritual readiness within individuals and the community. By engaging in these rituals, individuals set the stage for further shamanic practices, ensuring that they entered into the realms of the sacred with clarity, intention, and a purified spirit.

Exercise 1: Reflect on your personal understanding of purification rituals and their significance. Consider instances in your own life where purification practices are employed, such as the use of water or burning of incense. How do these practices create a sense of renewal or spiritual cleansing? Discuss your reflections with a study partner or write a reflective essay.

Problem 1: Explore the potential challenges or limitations of purification rituals. Discuss whether purification rituals can be considered purely symbolic or if they have tangible effects on the psyche or environment. Consider dissenting opinions and alternative perspectives on the efficacy and importance of purification rituals in spiritual practices.

Example 1: Analyze a purification ritual from another cultural or spiritual tradition, such as the Native American smudging ceremony. Compare and contrast its elements, symbolism, and purpose with Babylonian purification rituals. Discuss the universality of purification practices across different cultures and their significance in fostering spiritual connection and well-being.

Healing Ceremonies:

Purpose:

Healing ceremonies held a crucial role in Babylonian shamanism, addressing physical, emotional, and spiritual ailments. These intricate and multifaceted rituals aimed to restore balance, alleviate suffering, and promote holistic healing. By examining the description and components of healing ceremonies, we can gain a deeper understanding of their purpose, techniques, and the intricate connection between the shaman, the individual seeking healing, and the spiritual realm.

Description of Healing Ceremonies:

Healing ceremonies in Babylonian shamanism encompassed a rich array of practices, each contributing to the overall healing process. The shaman, as the conduit between the human and spiritual realms, performed various actions to invoke spiritual forces and facilitate the healing journey.

Chanting incantations was a prominent aspect of healing ceremonies. Through the power of words and sacred sounds, the shaman invoked the assistance of benevolent deities or ancestral spirits, calling upon their healing energies and blessings. The incantations served as potent tools to establish a connection with the divine realm, activating the healing forces and opening pathways for restoration.

Dance was another significant element in healing ceremonies. The shaman would engage in rhythmic and purposeful movements, often accompanied by music or drumming. The dance served as a form of energetic expression, allowing the shaman to channel healing energies and create a heightened state of spiritual awareness. The movements were symbolic, embodying the healing intentions and acting as a catalyst for the transformative process.

Ritual objects were frequently utilized during healing ceremonies. The shaman would employ specific tools or sacred objects with symbolic meanings and energetic properties. These objects acted as amplifiers of intention and conduits for divine energies. For instance, a ritual knife might be used to energetically cut away negative influences or blockages, while a healing wand could be employed to direct and channel healing energies towards the individual.

Herbal remedies played a significant role in Babylonian healing ceremonies. The shaman would utilize their knowledge of medicinal plants and their corresponding properties to prepare remedies for various ailments. These herbal remedies were often ingested or applied externally to facilitate physical healing and alleviate discomfort. The use of herbs combined the natural healing properties of plants with the shaman's spiritual connection, creating a holistic approach to well-being.

Energy work was an essential component of healing ceremonies. The shaman would engage in subtle energy manipulation, often through laying hands on the individual or employing specific techniques such as energy scanning or balancing. This energetic intervention aimed to restore the flow of vital energies, remove energetic blockages, and promote the body's self-healing abilities.

The shaman acted as a bridge between the individual seeking healing and the spiritual realm. Through their deep spiritual connection and ritual expertise, the shaman established a sacred space and channel for the transmission of healing energies. The shaman served as a conduit, facilitating the flow of divine assistance and aligning the individual's energy with the healing forces of the universe.

Symbolism and Significance:

Healing ceremonies in Babylonian shamanism held profound symbolism and significance. The restoration of balance and well-being encompassed not only the physical body but also the emotional and spiritual aspects of the individual. Healing was viewed holistically, recognizing the interconnectedness of the various dimensions of human experience.

The chanting of incantations represented the power of words and sound vibrations in invoking divine assistance and healing energies. The dance movements embodied the transformative power of rhythm and movement, creating a sacred space where healing energies could flow freely. Ritual objects and herbal remedies symbolized the partnership between the natural world and the spiritual realm, harnessing the healing properties of plants and imbuing them with sacred intent.

Healing ceremonies emphasized the shaman's role as a facilitator and healer, merging their spiritual connection and knowledge with practical techniques to bring about healing and well-being. By establishing a connection between the individual seeking healing and the spiritual realm, the shaman channeled divine energies, facilitating restoration and harmony.

Exercise 1: Explore the use of sound and music in healing practices. Reflect on how different types of music or specific sound frequencies can elicit healing responses and create a sense of well-being. Discuss your findings with a study partner or write a reflective essay.

Problem 1: Evaluate the significance of energy work in healing ceremonies. Discuss the potential mechanisms through which energy manipulation and balancing can contribute to physical, emotional, and spiritual healing. Consider alternative perspectives and scientific research on energy healing modalities.

Example 1: Analyze a specific healing ceremony from another cultural or spiritual tradition, such as the Ayurvedic Panchakarma treatment. Compare and contrast its elements, techniques, and symbolism with Babylonian healing ceremonies. Discuss the universality of healing practices across different cultures and their shared emphasis on holistic well-being.

Exploring the Methods: Examples, Problems, and Exercises

Example 1: Observe a modern healing ceremony or practice, such as Reiki or acupuncture, and compare it with Babylonian healing ceremonies. Discuss the similarities and differences in techniques, symbolism, and underlying philosophies.

Problem 1: Discuss the potential ethical considerations and challenges faced by modern practitioners in incorporating ancient healing techniques, such as the use of ritual objects or herbal remedies, into their practice. Analyze the cultural appropriation and respectful integration of traditional healing methods into contemporary approaches.

Exercise 1: Create a healing ritual that incorporates elements from Babylonian shamanism, such as chanting, dance, or the use of ritual objects. Perform the ritual in a safe and sacred space, reflecting on the experience and its impact on your sense of well-being. Consider the intention behind each element and the symbolism involved.

Spirit Communication Rituals:

Spirit communication rituals held a profound purpose within Babylonian shamanism, serving as conduits for establishing contact and seeking guidance from the spirit realm. These rituals facilitated communication with deities, ancestral spirits, and other non-ordinary beings, providing insight, wisdom, and even prophecies. By exploring the description and techniques employed in spirit communication rituals, we can gain a deeper understanding of their purpose, processes, and the invaluable role they played in Babylonian shamanic practices.

Description of Spirit Communication Rituals:

Spirit communication rituals involved the shaman entering an altered state of consciousness, allowing them to journey into the spirit realm and establish communion with spiritual entities. Various techniques were employed to induce this altered state, such as rhythmic drumming, chanting, or other forms of repetitive stimulation.

The shaman would initiate the ritual by creating a sacred space, often through the use of specific rituals, invocations, and offerings. These rituals served as a means of invoking the presence of the spirits, creating an open channel for communication, and establishing a sacred connection between the physical and spiritual realms.

Rhythmic drumming played a significant role in spirit communication rituals. The shaman would skillfully play the drum, producing repetitive beats that entrained the shaman's brainwaves and induced an altered state of consciousness. The steady rhythm served as a vehicle for the shaman's journey, guiding their spirit to traverse the realms of the divine.

Chanting was another technique employed to alter consciousness and facilitate spirit communication. The shaman would engage in repetitive vocalizations, often utilizing sacred syllables or invocations, which acted as powerful tools for attuning to the spiritual frequencies and opening channels of communication.

Once the altered state was achieved, the shaman would embark on a spiritual journey, navigating the spirit realm in search of communion with deities, ancestral spirits, or other non-ordinary beings. Through their spiritual prowess, the shaman would engage in dialogue, receive messages, guidance, or divinatory insights from these entities.

Symbolic offerings played a crucial role in spirit communication rituals. The shaman would offer gifts, such as food, drink, or symbolic objects, as a means of showing respect and creating a reciprocal relationship with the spirits. These offerings symbolized the shaman's willingness to establish a connection and honor the spiritual entities encountered during the journey.

The shaman acted as a mediator and interpreter between the human and spirit realms, relaying messages, guidance, or prophetic insights to the community or individuals seeking answers. The information received during the spirit communication ritual held great significance, as it provided a direct link to the wisdom, knowledge, and divinatory powers of the spirit realm.

Symbolism and Significance:

Spirit communication rituals in Babylonian shamanism were rich in symbolism and held immense significance. They represented a means of transcending the physical limitations and establishing connections with the divine and ancestral realms. By entering an altered state of consciousness and engaging in spiritual journeying, the shaman accessed profound wisdom and sought guidance for individuals or the community.

The rhythmic drumming and chanting created a harmonious resonance that aligned the shaman's consciousness with the vibrational frequencies of the spiritual realms. These techniques facilitated an attunement to the energies and vibrations of the spirit realm, allowing for a deeper level of communication and communion.

The offerings made during the spirit communication ritual symbolized a sacred exchange and reciprocal relationship with the spiritual entities encountered. By giving gifts, the shaman demonstrated reverence and respect, fostering a connection based on mutual trust and cooperation.

The shaman's role as a mediator between the human and spirit realms was crucial. Through their journeying and communication, the shaman served as a conduit for wisdom, guidance, and divinatory insights. This information was invaluable to individuals seeking answers, as it provided direct access to the spiritual realm's profound insights and perspectives.

Exercise 1: Experiment with drumming or chanting techniques to induce an altered state of consciousness. Engage in a spirit communication ritual by setting an intention, establishing a sacred space, and inviting contact with benevolent spirits or guides. Reflect on your experience and any insights or messages received.

Problem 1: Discuss the ethical considerations and potential challenges faced by shamans in interpreting and relaying messages received during spirit communication rituals. Explore the role of the shaman as a mediator between realms and the responsibility that comes with conveying spiritual insights to individuals or the community.

Example 1: Explore the concept of spirit communication in contemporary spiritual practices, such as mediumship or channeling. Compare and contrast these practices with Babylonian spirit communication rituals, discussing similarities, differences, and cultural variations in the methods and beliefs surrounding spirit communication.

Exploring the Methods: Examples, Problems, and Exercises

Problem 1: Analyze the potential benefits and limitations of drumming and chanting as techniques for inducing altered states of consciousness. Discuss the psychological and physiological mechanisms behind these practices and their efficacy in facilitating spirit communication.

Exercise 1: Research and analyze a specific spirit communication ritual from another cultural or spiritual tradition, such as the Tibetan Buddhist practice of Chöd. Compare and contrast its techniques, symbolism, and purpose with Babylonian spirit communication rituals. Reflect on the universal elements and distinct cultural expressions found in spirit communication practices.

Exercise 2: Design your own spirit communication ritual, incorporating elements from Babylonian shamanism while adapting them to your own spiritual beliefs and practices. Consider the use of drumming, chanting, invocations, or offerings. Perform the ritual in a respectful and sacred manner, reflecting on the experience and any insights or messages received.

Seasonal and Agricultural Celebrations:

Seasonal and agricultural celebrations held great significance within Babylonian culture, as they marked important periods such as planting and harvesting seasons. These celebrations were not only a means to honor the deities associated with fertility, growth, and agricultural abundance but also served to ensure the well-being of the community by seeking blessings for a successful harvest or fruitful season. By exploring the purpose and description of these ceremonies, we can gain a deeper understanding of their role in fostering abundance, unity, and gratitude within the Babylonian community.

Description of Seasonal and Agricultural Celebrations:

Seasonal and agricultural celebrations were vibrant and joyous occasions, reflecting the interconnectedness of the community with the cycles of nature. These ceremonies involved a variety of rituals, expressions of gratitude, and communal activities that cultivated a sense of unity and fostered a deep connection with the land and its fertility.

The ceremonies commenced with rituals of gratitude and reverence for the deities associated with fertility, growth, and agricultural abundance. Offerings of food, libations, and sacred objects were presented as acts of appreciation and devotion. These offerings symbolized the community's recognition of the divine forces at work in nature and their gratitude for the sustenance and abundance they provided.

Dancing played a prominent role in these celebrations. The community would come together, engaging in rhythmic and coordinated movements that mirrored the cycles of growth and the energy of the natural world. Dance served as a form of expression, celebrating the life force that permeated the land and invoking the blessings of the deities.

Singing and chanting were also integral to these celebrations. The community would join in harmonious melodies, offering prayers and invocations to the deities associated with agricultural fertility. These melodic expressions connected individuals with the spiritual realm, fostering a sense of collective purpose and attuning to the rhythms of the natural world.

Communal feasting was a cherished element of these celebrations. The abundance of the harvest was shared among the community, strengthening social bonds and reinforcing the interconnectedness of all members. The feast became a symbolic act of unity, gratitude, and shared prosperity, as individuals came together to enjoy the fruits of their collective efforts.

Symbolism and Significance:

Seasonal and agricultural celebrations held deep symbolism and profound significance within Babylonian culture. They represented a harmonious relationship between humans, nature, and the divine forces that governed fertility and abundance.

The rituals of gratitude and offerings expressed the community's acknowledgment of their dependency on the natural world and the divine powers that sustained them. These acts of appreciation deepened the spiritual connection with the land, its resources, and the cycles of growth, fostering a sense of reverence and gratitude for the sustenance it provided.

Dance and music played a pivotal role in these celebrations. Through rhythmic movements and harmonious melodies, individuals connected with the energetic pulse of the natural world, invoking the blessings of the deities and aligning themselves with the flow of life. These expressions of joy and celebration uplifted the community's spirits and reinforced their role as co-creators in the cycles of growth and abundance.

Communal feasting held deep symbolism in these celebrations. It served as a tangible manifestation of shared prosperity and solidarity, as individuals gathered to partake in the abundance provided by the land. The act of eating together symbolized the interconnectedness of the community and the importance of unity in fostering collective well-being.

Exercise 1: Reflect on the significance of communal celebrations in your own culture or spiritual practice. Consider how these celebrations foster a sense of gratitude, unity, and connection with the natural world. Discuss your findings with a study partner or write a reflective essay.

Problem 1: Explore the potential challenges and ethical considerations in modern-day agricultural practices. Discuss the impact of industrialization, climate change, and the commodification of food on the spiritual and communal aspects of seasonal celebrations. Consider alternative approaches to agriculture that prioritize sustainability, community involvement, and honoring the interconnectedness of humans and nature.

Example 1: Analyze a contemporary seasonal celebration or harvest festival from another cultural tradition, such as Thanksgiving or Lammas. Compare and contrast its elements, rituals, and symbolism with Babylonian seasonal and agricultural celebrations. Discuss the universal themes and cultural variations found in these celebrations.

Exploring the Methods: Examples, Problems, and Exercises

Problem 1: Discuss the potential psychological and social benefits of communal feasting in fostering a sense of unity and well-being within a community. Explore the cultural significance of shared meals in different traditions and how they contribute to a sense of belonging and gratitude.

Exercise 1: Design your own seasonal or agricultural celebration, incorporating elements inspired by Babylonian practices. Consider the rituals, offerings, music, and dance that would contribute to a sense of gratitude, abundance, and unity. Reflect on the symbolism and intentions behind each element and the ways in which they connect individuals with nature and the cycles of growth.

Exercise 2: Research the impact of modern agricultural practices on the environment and community well-being. Develop a proposal for sustainable agricultural practices that prioritize the restoration of ecological balance, preservation of biodiversity, and community engagement. Present your findings and recommendations in a written report or a multimedia presentation.

Initiation Rituals:

Initiation rituals held significant purpose within Babylonian shamanism, as they marked a pivotal moment in an individual's journey into shamanic practice or the bestowing of higher levels of knowledge and authority within the shamanic community. These intricate and transformative rituals served to validate the shaman's spiritual abilities, prepare them for their roles as healers and guides, and facilitate their integration into the shamanic community. By exploring the description and significance of initiation rituals, we can gain a deeper understanding of their role in spiritual connection, healing, guidance, and communal well-being within Babylonian shamanism.

Description of Initiation Rituals:

Initiation rituals within Babylonian shamanism were meticulously designed processes that encompassed various elements, each contributing to the transformative journey of the initiate. These rituals represented a symbolic death and rebirth, purifying and transforming the individual's spiritual essence.

Purification played a crucial role in initiation rituals. The initiate would undergo rituals of cleansing and purification, symbolically shedding their former self and purging any impurities or spiritual obstacles. These purification practices prepared the individual for the transformative experiences and the integration of higher spiritual powers.

Symbolic death and rebirth were central to initiation rituals. The initiate would undergo a metaphorical death, representing the dissolution of their former identity and the shedding of old patterns and limitations. This process was followed by a symbolic rebirth, signifying the emergence of the initiate as a new being, spiritually aligned and prepared to embark on their shamanic journey.

The transmission of sacred teachings and rituals was a pivotal component of initiation rituals. The initiate would receive profound knowledge, rituals, and practices passed down through generations, enriching their understanding and abilities as a shaman. These teachings bestowed spiritual power and responsibility upon the initiate, empowering them to fulfill their roles as healers and guides within the community.

Initiation rituals often involved intense visionary experiences and challenges. Through trance states induced by rhythmic drumming, chanting, or other methods, the initiate would journey into the spirit realm, encountering benevolent and malevolent entities. These experiences tested the initiate's courage, spiritual strength, and ability to navigate the realms beyond the ordinary.

The initiates would also receive teachings and guidance from experienced shamans. These teachings imparted spiritual wisdom, techniques, and ethical principles that guided the initiate's path and shaped their role within the shamanic community. The mentorship and guidance provided during initiation rituals fostered a deep sense of reverence, trust, and respect between the initiates and the experienced shamans.

Symbolism and Significance:

Initiation rituals in Babylonian shamanism held profound symbolism and immense significance. They represented a rite of passage, marking the transformation of an individual into a fully initiated shaman, equipped with the spiritual power, knowledge, and authority to serve the community.

The symbolic death and rebirth mirrored the cyclical nature of life and the transformative journey of the initiate. The shedding of old patterns and limitations signified a release from the constraints of the ego and the opening of pathways for spiritual growth, connection, and service.

The transmission of sacred teachings and rituals was a sacred exchange, as the experienced shamans bestowed their accumulated wisdom and power upon the initiates. This transmission ensured the continuity of spiritual traditions, fostering a lineage of shamanic practitioners and preserving the collective knowledge of the community.

The intense visionary experiences and challenges faced during initiation rituals served as tests of the initiate's dedication, courage, and ability to navigate the spiritual realms. These transformative encounters deepened the initiates' connection with the divine, expanded their spiritual capacities, and strengthened their resilience as they ventured into the unknown.

Initiation rituals played a vital role in fostering a deep sense of reverence, trust, and unity within the shamanic community. The meticulous performance of these rituals exemplified the skill, knowledge, and spiritual connection of the shamans. The initiation of new members reinforced the community's faith in the shamanic tradition, fostering a strong bond between initiates and experienced practitioners.

Exercise 1: Reflect on the concept of initiation rituals in your own spiritual or personal growth journey. Consider moments of transformation or rites of passage you have experienced. Discuss the significance of these experiences in shaping your spiritual path and sense of identity.

Problem 1: Explore the potential challenges and ethical considerations in modern-day initiation rituals. Discuss the power dynamics, consent, and responsibility involved in initiating individuals into spiritual practices. Consider how contemporary approaches to initiation can honor tradition while ensuring the well-being and autonomy of the initiates.

Example 1: Analyze a specific initiation ritual from another cultural or spiritual tradition, such as the Native American vision quest. Compare and contrast its elements, symbolism, and purpose with Babylonian initiation rituals. Discuss the universal themes and cultural variations found in initiation practices.

Exploring the Methods: Examples, Problems, and Exercises

Problem 1: Discuss the impact of initiation rituals on individual transformation and community dynamics. Explore how initiation rituals contribute to the cohesion and stability of shamanic communities, as well as the personal growth and development of initiates.

Exercise 1: Design your own initiation ritual, drawing inspiration from Babylonian shamanism while adapting it to your own spiritual beliefs and practices. Consider the elements, symbolism, and challenges that would facilitate transformation and empower the initiates. Reflect on the ethical considerations and intentions behind each component of the ritual.

Exercise 2: Research and analyze the role of initiation rituals in contemporary spiritual and religious practices. Select a specific tradition or organization and explore the initiation processes involved. Discuss the significance of these rituals in fostering spiritual growth, communitycohesion, and the transmission of spiritual knowledge. Reflect on the similarities and differences between contemporary initiation rituals and those practiced in Babylonian shamanism.

2. Use of sacred objects and tools in shamanic practices

Babylonian shamans employed various sacred objects and tools in their shamanic practices. These objects held symbolic significance and assisted in creating a sacred space, invoking spiritual energies, and facilitating communication with the divine. Understanding the purpose and role of these sacred objects and tools provides insights into the depth and intricacy of Babylonian shamanism.

Drums and Rattles:

Purpose: Drums and rattles were essential tools used by Babylonian shamans to induce altered states of consciousness and facilitate shamanic journeying.

Description: The rhythmic beats of drums and rattles created a trance-like state, enabling the shaman to enter altered states of consciousness and access the spiritual realms. The steady rhythm served as a vehicle for the shaman's journey, guiding their spirit to connect with the divine and commune with spirits, deities, and other non-ordinary beings.

Feathers and Fan-like Objects:

Purpose: Feathers and fan-like objects were utilized for energetic clearing, purification, and directing spiritual energies during rituals and healing ceremonies.

Description: Shamans would use feathers or fan-like objects to create gentle air movements, dispersing stagnant energies and clearing the energy field of individuals or sacred spaces. The sweeping motions of feathers or fans symbolized the cleansing and harmonizing of energies, ensuring a conducive environment for spiritual practices and healing.

Crystals and Gemstones:

Purpose: Crystals and gemstones were employed for their energetic properties, acting as conduits for amplifying, focusing, or directing spiritual energies.

Description: Babylonian shamans would select specific crystals or gemstones based on their properties and symbolic significance. These stones would be used in rituals or placed strategically to enhance the energetic vibrations, strengthen intentions, or attune to specific spiritual forces. For example, amethyst may have been chosen for its calming and protective qualities, while carnelian may have been used for vitality and courage.

Herbs and Incense:

Purpose: Herbs and incense played a vital role in Babylonian shamanism for their aromatic and energetic properties, creating a sacred atmosphere, and facilitating connection with spiritual realms.

Description: Babylonian shamans burned specific herbs or incense during rituals to purify the space, invoke specific energies, or enhance spiritual experiences. Different herbs and incense were chosen for their symbolic meanings, spiritual associations, and ability to shift consciousness. The aromatic smoke was believed to carry prayers and intentions to the divine realm and establish a spiritual connection.

Ritual Tools and Implements:

Purpose: Various ritual tools and implements were utilized by Babylonian shamans to symbolically represent their authority, facilitate rituals, and invoke spiritual energies.

Description: These tools could include ceremonial knives, wands, staffs, or amulets, each with its unique symbolism and purpose. For example, a ceremonial knife might be used to make precise cuts during rituals, symbolizing the separation of negative energies or the opening of gateways to the spiritual realm. These objects served as extensions of the shaman's power and were imbued with spiritual significance and intent.

The use of sacred objects and tools in Babylonian shamanic practices deepened the connection to the spiritual realm, amplified energy, and facilitated rituals and healing ceremonies. These objects were carefully selected, based on their symbolic meanings, energetic properties, and their ability to aid in spiritual practices. The intentional use of these sacred objects and tools added layers of symbolism and intention to the shamanic journey, rituals, and spiritual work conducted by Babylonian shamans.

B. Divination and prophecy in Babylonian shamanism

Divination and prophecy were integral components of Babylonian shamanism, providing individuals and leaders with insights into future events, decisions, and potential outcomes. Babylonian shamans employed various techniques and practices to access spiritual knowledge and provide guidance to their community. Understanding the nature of divination and prophecy within Babylonian shamanism sheds light on the significance of these practices and their role in shaping the lives of individuals and the community as a whole.

Dream Interpretation:

Dream interpretation held a central purpose within Babylonian shamanism, providing a means for shamans to gain insights into hidden truths, future events, and receive guidance from the divine realm. Through the analysis of symbols, images, and narratives present in dreams, shamans deciphered the messages conveyed by the spiritual realm. Dream interpretation required a deep understanding of symbolism, cultural context, and knowledge of mythological and cosmological elements. By exploring the purpose and description of dream interpretation, we can gain a deeper appreciation for its role in unraveling the mysteries of the unconscious and guiding individuals toward greater understanding and spiritual growth.

Description of Dream Interpretation:

Dream interpretation was a sophisticated practice within Babylonian shamanism, involving the analysis and deciphering of the symbolism, images, and narratives present in dreams. Shamans served as skilled interpreters, unlocking the hidden messages conveyed by the divine realm through the medium of dreams.

Shamans recognized that dreams held a deeper significance beyond mere random imagery. They believed that dreams were a gateway to the unconscious mind and a means of communication with the spiritual realm. As such, the shaman would guide individuals in understanding the potential impact of their dreams on their lives and provide insights into hidden truths and future events.

To interpret dreams accurately, shamans drew upon a rich repertoire of knowledge, including an understanding of symbolism, cultural context, and mythological and cosmological elements. They recognized that symbols and images in dreams often carried multiple layers of meaning, influenced by the cultural beliefs, myths, and cosmological framework of Babylonian society.

Dream interpretation involved a holistic approach that encompassed both the individual's personal experiences and the broader collective consciousness. Shamans would engage in dialogue with the dreamer, probing for details, emotions, and contextual information that could provide clues to the dream's meaning. By weaving together personal and cultural symbolism, the shaman sought to unravel the deeper significance and guidance contained within the dream.

The shaman's role as an interpreter extended beyond mere analysis. They acted as spiritual guides, helping individuals integrate the insights gained from dream interpretation into their waking lives. The shaman would offer counsel, advice, and guidance based on the messages revealed in the dream, supporting the individual's spiritual growth and navigating life's challenges.

Symbolism and Significance:

Dream interpretation in Babylonian shamanism held profound symbolism and immense significance. It represented a bridge between the conscious and unconscious realms, enabling individuals to access hidden truths, receive divine guidance, and gain insights into their own psyche.

Symbols and images in dreams were considered portals to the spiritual realm and a means of communication from the divine. By deciphering the symbolism present in dreams, shamans unveiled the messages, prophecies, and guidance transmitted by benevolent spiritual entities. This process deepened the individual's connection to the divine and facilitated a greater understanding of their life's purpose and journey.

Dream interpretation also played a role in personal transformation and spiritual growth. The insights gained from dream analysis allowed individuals to gain self-awareness, explore unresolved emotions and conflicts, and embark on a path of healing and self-discovery. By integrating the messages and lessons from dreams into their waking lives, individuals could align themselves with their spiritual purpose and live in harmony with the guidance received.

Exercise 1: Keep a dream journal for one week, recording your dreams upon waking. Reflect on the symbols, images, and narratives present in your dreams. Research the potential meanings and interpretations of these symbols, considering their personal significance and any cultural or mythological connections. Discuss your findings with a study partner or write a reflective essay.

Problem 1: Explore the potential limitations and challenges of dream interpretation. Discuss the subjective nature of dream analysis, the role of personal bias, and the difficulty of accurately deciphering the complex layers of dream symbolism.

Consider alternative approaches to dream interpretation that incorporate multiple perspectives and techniques.

Example 1: Compare and contrast dream interpretation practices in Babylonian shamanism with contemporary approaches, such as those found in psychology or spiritual traditions. Discuss the similarities, differences, and cultural variations in the methods and beliefs surrounding dream interpretation.

Exploring the Methods: Examples, Problems, and Exercises

Problem 1: Analyze the ethical considerations in interpreting and sharing dream interpretations with others. Discuss the potential impacts of dream analysis on individuals' psychological well-being, personal autonomy, and decision-making processes. Explore the responsibility of the shaman in offering guidance and the importance of maintaining confidentiality and respect for the dreamer's experiences.

Exercise 1: Explore different techniques for enhancing dream recall and lucidity, such as keeping a dream journal, practicing relaxation and visualization exercises before sleep, or engaging in mindfulness practices. Experiment with these techniques and reflect on how they impact your dream experiences and your ability to gain insights from them.

Exercise 2: Conduct a comparative analysis of dream interpretation practices from various cultures or spiritual traditions. Select a specific tradition and explore their methods, symbolism, and beliefs surrounding dreams. Discuss the universal themes and cultural variations in dream interpretation and the ways in which they contribute to spiritual growth and self-understanding.

Omen Reading:

Omen reading held a significant purpose within Babylonian shamanism, providing a means for shamans to interpret signs and omens found in natural phenomena or everyday occurrences. Through careful observation and analysis, shamans unveiled insights into the future and guided decision-making processes. Omen reading required a deep understanding of symbolism, a vast corpus of omen texts, and intuitive knowledge. By exploring the purpose and description of omen reading, we can gain a deeper appreciation for its role in providing guidance, foresight, and informed choices within the Babylonian community.

Description of Omen Reading:

Omen reading was a skill honed by Babylonian shamans, allowing them to discern meaning from signs and omens found in natural phenomena or everyday occurrences. Shamans were keen observers, recognizing that these signs held valuable insights into future events and could guide decision-making processes.

The signs and omens could manifest in various forms, such as the flight patterns of birds, the behavior of animals, celestial events, or unusual weather patterns. The shaman would carefully observe these occurrences, noting their timing, location, and any specific characteristics or patterns that stood out.

Interpreting these signs required a deep knowledge of symbolism and a vast corpus of omen texts. Babylonian culture had developed a rich tradition of recording and interpreting omens, providing a framework for understanding their significance. The shaman would draw upon this knowledge and their own intuitive insights to decipher the messages conveyed by the signs.

The process of interpreting omens involved comparing observed signs with established interpretations found in omen texts. These texts cataloged a wide range of omens and their meanings, offering guidance and predictions based on specific observations. The shaman would consider the context, cultural beliefs, and mythological references associated with the particular sign or omen, refining their interpretation accordingly.

Omen reading was not a rigid and formulaic practice but required the shaman's intuition and ability to perceive subtle nuances. Shamans would apply their personal insights and spiritual connection to refine the interpretation of omens, allowing for a more nuanced understanding of the messages conveyed.

Based on their interpretation, shamans would provide guidance and counsel to individuals or leaders facing important decisions. The insights gained from omen reading could help individuals navigate challenges, anticipate potential outcomes, and make informed choices. By aligning their actions with the guidance revealed through omens, individuals could increase their chances of success or mitigate potential risks.

Symbolism and Significance:

Omen reading in Babylonian shamanism held profound symbolism and immense significance. It represented a means of tapping into the wisdom of the divine and the hidden forces that shape the unfolding of events.

The signs and omens found in natural phenomena or everyday occurrences were believed to be messages from the spiritual realm, conveying insights into the future and offering guidance. By interpreting these signs, shamans gained access to hidden knowledge and foresight, enabling them to navigate uncertainty and support the well-being of individuals and the community.

Omen reading played a vital role in decision-making processes. The insights gained from the interpretation of signs and omens allowed individuals to make informed choices, anticipate potential outcomes, and align their actions with the cosmic forces at play. The guidance provided by the shaman offered a sense of reassurance and increased the likelihood of favorable outcomes.

Exercise 1: Reflect on your own experiences with signs and omens in your life. Consider moments when you noticed unusual occurrences or patterns that seemed to convey a deeper meaning or message. Analyze the symbolism and significance of these signs and their potential impact on your decision-making or life events.

Problem 1: Explore the potential limitations and challenges of omen reading. Discuss the subjectivity of interpreting signs and omens, the role of personal bias, and the difficulty of accurately predicting future events based on these observations. Consider alternative approaches to decision-making that balance intuitive insights with rational analysis.

Example 1: Compare and contrast omen reading practices in Babylonian shamanism with contemporary approaches to divination, such as tarot card reading or astrology. Discuss the similarities, differences, and cultural variations in the methods, symbolism, and beliefs surrounding divination practices.

Exploring the Methods: Examples, Problems, and Exercises

Problem 1: Analyze the ethical considerations in providing guidance based on omen readings. Discuss the responsibility of the shaman in offering advice and the potential impact of their interpretations on individuals' lives and decision-making processes. Explore the importance of empowering individuals to make their own choices while still honoring the insights gained from omen reading.

Exercise 1: Engage in a practical exercise of omen observation. Spend a day or a week actively observing natural phenomena or everyday occurrences, noting any signs or omens that stand out to you. Reflect on their potential meanings and interpretations based on your own intuition and knowledge. Discuss your observations with a study partner or write a reflective essay.

Exercise 2: Research and analyze the role of divination practices in different cultures or spiritual traditions. Select a specific tradition and explore their methods, symbolism, and beliefs surrounding divination. Discuss the universal themes and cultural variations in divination practices and the ways in which they contribute to guidance, decision-making, and personal growth.

Casting Lots:

Casting lots held a significant purpose within Babylonian shamanism, providing a divinatory practice through which individuals sought answers to specific questions or received insights into future events. By using a set of marked objects, such as stones or sticks, shamans engaged in the act of casting lots to interpret the arrangement or patterns formed. This practice allowed individuals to seek clarity, receive guidance, and make decisions based on divinely guided responses. By exploring the purpose and description of casting lots, we can gain a deeper understanding of its role in divination and the quest for guidance within Babylonian shamanism.

Description of Casting Lots:

Casting lots involved the use of a set of marked objects, typically stones or sticks, each representing a specific meaning or answer. The shaman would hold the marked objects in their hand, focusing their intention and energy on the question or situation at hand.

The act of casting lots entailed throwing or drawing the marked objects onto a surface or arranging them in a designated pattern. The resulting arrangement or patterns formed by the lots were then interpreted by the shaman to provide guidance and insights.

The interpretation of the cast lots required the shaman's expertise in recognizing the significance of the positions, arrangement, or patterns formed. Each marked object held its own meaning or symbolism, which contributed to the overall interpretation. The shaman drew upon their knowledge and intuitive insights to decipher the messages conveyed through the cast lots.

Casting lots allowed individuals to seek clarity and guidance in making decisions. By posing a specific question or focusing on a particular area of concern, individuals sought divinely guided responses through the interpretation of the lots. The insights gained from casting lots provided valuable information that could aid in navigating challenges, anticipating future events, or understanding the underlying dynamics of a situation.

Symbolism and Significance:

Casting lots in Babylonian shamanism held profound symbolism and immense significance. It represented a means of accessing divine wisdom and receiving guidance in the face of uncertainty or dilemmas.

The marked objects used in casting lots carried symbolic meanings that were imbued with spiritual significance. Each object represented a specific aspect or answer, allowing the shaman to tap into the spiritual realm and draw forth insights from the divine.

The act of casting lots was seen as a way to engage in a dialogue with the spiritual forces at play. It was believed that the arrangement or patterns formed by the lots were influenced by these unseen forces, allowing individuals to receive divinely guided responses to their questions or concerns.

Casting lots served as a tool for decision-making and seeking clarity in various aspects of life. Whether it was choosing between different courses of action, seeking guidance on matters of personal importance, or gaining insights into future events, casting lots provided a means for individuals to make informed choices based on divine guidance.

Exercise 1: Create your own set of marked objects for casting lots. Choose symbols or markings that hold personal significance or resonate with your spiritual beliefs. Experiment with casting the lots and interpreting the resulting arrangements or patterns. Reflect on the insights gained and their potential impact on your decision-making process.

Problem 1: Explore the cultural and historical significance of casting lots in other traditions or divination practices. Select a specific tradition and analyze the methods, symbolism, and beliefs surrounding the casting of lots. Compare and contrast the similarities, differences, and cultural variations in the use of marked objects for divination purposes.

Example 1: Discuss the role of chance and free will in casting lots. Explore the philosophical implications of seeking guidance through the interpretation of randomly cast objects. Reflect on how individuals can balance the insights gained from casting lots with their own agency and personal responsibility in decision-making.

Exploring the Methods: Examples, Problems, and Exercises

Problem 1: Analyze the potential biases and limitations of casting lots as a divinatory practice. Discuss the subjective nature of interpreting the arrangements or patterns formed by the lots and the role of personal intuition in the process. Consider how individuals can approach casting lots with discernment and critical thinking.

Exercise 1: Engage in a practical exercise of casting lots. Create a list of specific questions or situations you would like guidance on. Use your set of marked objects to cast lots and interpret the resulting arrangements or patterns. Reflect on the guidance received and its potential impact on your decision-making or understanding of the situations at hand.

Exercise 2: Research and analyze the role of divination practices using marked objects in different cultures or spiritual traditions. Select a specific tradition and explore their methods, symbolism, and beliefs surrounding this form of divination. Discuss the universal themes and cultural variations in the use of marked objects for seeking guidance, decision-making, and personal growth.

Oracle Consultation:

Consulting oracles held a significant purpose within Babylonian shamanism, providing a means for shamans to gain guidance and prophecy from personified deities or spirit beings. By entering a ritualized state of communication, invoking the presence of the oracle through prayers, invocations, or offerings, shamans sought answers to specific questions or sought guidance on matters of importance to individuals or the community. The responses received from the oracle were then interpreted by the shaman, providing valuable insights into future events, advice, or instructions for actions to be taken. By exploring the purpose and description of consulting oracles, we can gain a deeper understanding of their role in accessing spiritual knowledge, receiving guidance, and shaping the destiny of the community within Babylonian shamanism.

Description of Consulting Oracles:

Consulting oracles involved the shaman's engagement in a ritualized state of communication, establishing a connection with personified deities or spirit beings. Through prayers, invocations, or offerings, the shaman would seek to invoke the presence of the oracle and establish a channel of communication.

The rituals performed by the shaman varied depending on the specific oracle being consulted and the desired purpose of the consultation. The shaman would engage in a sacred space, often within a temple or a designated ritual area, creating an atmosphere conducive to divine communication.

Once the connection with the oracle was established, the shaman would present specific questions or seek guidance on matters of importance to individuals or the community. These questions could range from personal dilemmas to communal concerns, seeking insights into future events, advice on decision-making, or instructions for actions to be taken.

The responses received from the oracle were often conveyed through various means, such as visions, auditory messages, or symbolic manifestations. The shaman would interpret these responses based on their knowledge of the mythological and cosmological framework of Babylonian culture, as well as their own intuitive insights.

Interpreting the oracle's responses required a deep understanding of symbolism, cultural context, and the specific characteristics and attributes associated with the deity or spirit being being consulted. The shaman would draw upon their knowledge and spiritual connection to decipher the messages conveyed, providing valuable insights and guidance.

Divination and prophecy obtained through consulting oracles played a vital role in the lives of individuals and the community. The guidance received helped individuals navigate challenges, make informed decisions, and anticipate future events. For leaders and decision-makers, the insights gained from consulting oracles were of particular significance, as they influenced the shaping of policies, strategies, and the destiny of the community as a whole.

Symbolism and Significance:

Consulting oracles in Babylonian shamanism held profound symbolism and immense significance. It represented a means of accessing spiritual knowledge, receiving guidance, and tapping into the wisdom of deities or spirit beings.

The personification of the oracles as deities or spirit beings represented the belief in their divine nature and their ability to communicate insights from the spiritual realm. Through the consultation of oracles, individuals sought the wisdom and guidance of these divine entities, recognizing their unique connection to the unseen forces that governed the universe.

The rituals performed during the consultation process reflected the sacred nature of the interaction between the shaman and the oracle. The offerings, prayers, and invocations served as acts of reverence and acknowledgement of the oracle's authority and presence.

The interpretations provided by the shaman were influenced by the cosmological beliefs and mythological framework of Babylonian culture. The shaman drew upon their knowledge of the gods and their attributes, as well as the broader understanding of the interconnectedness of the spiritual and physical realms, to make sense of the oracle's responses and provide meaningful guidance.

Exercise 1: Reflect on instances in your own life where you have sought guidance or prophecy from spiritual sources or individuals. Consider the methods used, the insights gained, and the impact on your decision-making or personal growth. Discuss your experiences with a study partner or write a reflective essay.

Problem 1: Explore the potential challenges and limitations of consulting oracles. Discuss the subjective nature of interpreting the oracle's responses, the role of personal bias, and the potential influence of the shaman's own beliefs and experiences on the interpretation process. Consider the ethical considerations in providing guidance based on the oracle's messages.

Example 1: Compare and contrast the practice of consulting oracles in Babylonian shamanism with contemporary approaches to divination or seeking guidance from spiritual sources. Discuss the similarities, differences, and cultural variations in the methods, symbolism, and beliefs surrounding oracular practices.

Exploring the Methods: Examples, Problems, and Exercises

Problem 1: Analyze the role of divination and prophecy in decision-making processes. Discuss the balance between relying on spiritual guidance and exercising personal agency in making choices. Explore the potential benefits and limitations of consulting oracles in shaping personal and communal destiny.

Exercise 1: Engage in a practical exercise of seeking guidance from a spiritual source. Choose a specific question or concern and explore different methods of seeking guidance, such as meditation, prayer, or divination practices. Reflect on the insights gained and their potential impact on your decision-making or understanding of the situation at hand.

Exercise 2: Research and analyze the role of oracular practices in different cultures or spiritual traditions. Select a specific tradition and explore their methods, symbolism, and beliefs surrounding oracles. Discuss the universal themes and cultural variations in the use of oracles for seeking guidance, prophecy, and personal growth.

Conclusion

In conclusion, divination methods employed by Babylonian shamans provided avenues for accessing spiritual knowledge, receiving guidance, and gaining insights into future events. Dream interpretation, omen reading, casting lots, and oracle consultations were integral practices within Babylonian divination. Through engaging examples, thought-provoking problems, and experiential exercises, We can explore the methods of divination used by Babylonian shamans, deepening their understanding of the cultural significance and practical applications of divinatory practices in ancient Babylonian society.

2. Interpretation of signs and omens

In this section, we delve into the fascinating world of interpreting signs and omens— a divinatory practice that allowed the Babylonians to unlock the messages of the universe and gain insights into the workings of the spiritual realm. The interpretation of signs and omens was an essential aspect of Babylonian spiritual traditions, deeply ingrained in their cosmology, and utilized in various aspects of life, from personal decision-making to guiding the destiny of the community.

In this section, we will examine the purpose, methods, and significance of interpreting signs and omens in Babylonian culture. We will explore the intricate process by which shamans and diviners deciphered the hidden meanings behind natural phenomena, everyday occurrences, and the symbolic language of the universe. By understanding the principles underlying this ancient divinatory practice, we can gain valuable insights into the Babylonian worldview and develop our own skills in deciphering signs and omens.

Through a comprehensive analysis of this topic, we aim to foster critical thinking, encourage exploration of diverse perspectives, and provide practical exercises that will enable you, as We of new-age studies, to engage deeply with the subject matter. By combining historical knowledge with contemporary understanding, we strive to shed light on the profound wisdom embedded within the interpretation of signs and omens, allowing you to uncover its relevance and potential applications in your own spiritual journeys.

Section Outline:

The Purpose of Interpreting Signs and Omens: Understanding the underlying motives and objectives behind the Babylonians' engagement with signs and omens. Exploring how this divinatory practice served as a means of gaining insights, making informed decisions, and anticipating future events.

Methods of Interpreting Signs and Omens: Delving into the techniques and approaches employed by Babylonian shamans and diviners to decipher the symbolic language of the universe. Examining the role of observation, knowledge of omens, and the interpretation of patterns and correlations.

The Significance of Signs and Omens in Babylonian Culture: Unveiling the cultural and spiritual significance attached to signs and omens in the Babylonian worldview. Investigating the interplay between the natural world, the divine realm, and human affairs.

Counterarguments and Dissenting Opinions: Presenting alternative viewpoints and critical perspectives on the interpretation of signs and omens. Engaging in a balanced and objective discussion that allows for a comprehensive understanding of this divinatory practice.

Examples, Problems, and Exercises: Providing practical examples, thought-provoking problems, and engaging exercises that will enable you to apply your knowledge, develop your skills, and foster a deeper appreciation for the interpretation of signs and omens. Through these activities, you will sharpen your analytical thinking and expand your ability to perceive the subtle messages woven into the fabric of existence.

By the end of this chapter, you will have acquired a solid foundation in the interpretation of signs and omens, understanding its historical context, its significance in Babylonian culture, and its potential relevance to your own spiritual practices. You will be equipped with the knowledge and tools to engage in critical analysis, form your own interpretations, and explore the depths of the universe's symbolic language.

So, let us embark on this enlightening journey into the interpretation of signs and omens—a gateway to unraveling the mysteries of the universe and gaining profound insights into the interconnectedness of the spiritual and physical realms. Open your mind, sharpen your senses, and prepare to uncover the hidden messages that lie in wait, ready to guide your path.

C. Power of chants, incantations, and spells in Babylonian shamanism

In Babylonian shamanism, the use of chants, incantations, and spells played a significant role in harnessing mystical forces and facilitating spiritual transformation. These powerful verbal expressions held the potential to evoke and channel the energies of the divine realm, enabling shamans to manifest their intentions, invoke deities, ward off malevolent spirits, heal the sick, and bring about desired outcomes. In this section, we explore the purpose, methods, and significance of chants, incantations, and spells in Babylonian shamanism, shedding light on their transformative power and their role in the spiritual practices of ancient Babylon.

Purpose:

The purpose of employing chants, incantations, and spells in Babylonian shamanism was multifaceted. Firstly, they served as vehicles for communication and connection with the divine. Through the recitation of sacred words and phrases, shamans established a direct link between the human and spiritual realms, invoking the presence and aid of deities and ancestral spirits. Secondly, these mystical utterances were believed to possess inherent power and vibrational frequencies capable of influencing the energetic fabric of reality. By using specific words, sounds, and rhythms, shamans sought to harmonize and manipulate the subtle forces at play, aligning them with their intended purposes. Thirdly, chants, incantations, and spells acted as catalysts for personal and collective transformation, inducing altered states of consciousness, activating latent spiritual abilities, and enhancing the shaman's connection to the spiritual realm.

Methods:

The methods employed in the use of chants, incantations, and spells varied depending on the specific intention and desired outcome. Shamans often memorized and recited sacred texts containing prescribed formulas, invocations, and rituals. These texts were passed down through generations, embodying the accumulated wisdom and knowledge of the shamanic tradition. The recitation of these texts was accompanied by specific rhythmic patterns, tonal variations, and gestures, all of which contributed to the overall efficacy of the practice. In addition to established texts, shamans also possessed the ability to spontaneously create chants and incantations, drawing upon their intuitive understanding and connection to the spiritual realm.

Significance:

The significance of chants, incantations, and spells in Babylonian shamanism lay in their transformative power and their ability to shape and influence the fabric of reality. These verbal expressions were regarded as sacred and potent, encapsulating the wisdom, intentions, and vibrational frequencies necessary for manifesting change. Through the repetition and embodiment of these sacred utterances, shamans entered into a state of resonance with the spiritual forces they sought to engage. This resonance acted as a catalyst, allowing the shaman to access heightened states of consciousness, transcend the limitations of the physical realm, and tap into the mystical energies of creation. Chants, incantations, and spells were seen as both practical tools for achieving specific outcomes and as sacred rituals that facilitated the shaman's spiritual growth, alignment, and connection to the divine.

Exercise 1: Engage in a chanting practice. Select a phrase or affirmation that resonates with your personal intention or desired outcome. Explore different rhythmic patterns, tonal variations, and gestures as you recite the phrase. Reflect on the sensations, emotions, and energetic shifts that arise within you during the practice. Discuss your experiences with a study partner or write a reflective essay.

Problem 1: Reflect on the potential ethical considerations and limitations of using chants, incantations, and spells in spiritual practices. Discuss the responsibility and intention behind the use of these powerful techniques, exploring the potential impact on personal empowerment, consent, and the ethical treatment of others.

Example 1: Compare and contrast the use of chants, incantations, and spells in Babylonian shamanism with contemporary practices in witchcraft, Wicca, or other spiritual traditions. Discuss the similarities, differences, and cultural variations in the methods, symbolism, and beliefs surrounding the power of vocal expressions in spiritual practices.

Exploring the Methods: Examples, Problems, and Exercises

Problem 1: Analyze the role of chants, incantations, and spells in personal transformation and manifestation practices. Discuss how the intentional use of specific words, sounds, and rhythms can influence one's energetic state, mindset, and ability to manifest desired outcomes.

Exercise 1: Create your own incantation or spell. Set a clear intention or desire and craft a series of affirmations, words, or sounds that align with your intention. Practice reciting your incantation or spell regularly, observing any shifts in your thoughts, emotions, or external circumstances. Reflect on the effectiveness and transformative power of your practice.

Exercise 2: Research and analyze the historical significance and cultural variations of chants, incantations, and spells in different spiritual traditions. Select a specific tradition and explore its unique methods, symbolism, and beliefs surrounding the power of vocal expressions. Discuss the universal themes and cultural diversities in the use of chants, incantations, and spells for spiritual transformation and manifestation.

By exploring the power of chants, incantations, and spells in Babylonian shamanism, we gain insights into the transformative potential of sound, language, and intention. These practices demonstrate the profound connection between the spoken word and the spiritual realm, highlighting the role of vibrational frequencies in shaping personal and collective realities. Through engaging in the provided exercises and critically reflecting on the ethical implications, you will deepen your understanding of the power of vocal expressions and expand your toolkit for spiritual growth and manifestation.

1. Role of verbal incantations and their significance

Verbal incantations held a crucial role within the spiritual practices of Babylonian shamanism, serving as a powerful means of channeling mystical forces and invoking divine assistance. These sacred utterances, carefully crafted and recited by the shamans, possessed inherent vibrational frequencies that resonated with the spiritual realm, enabling the manifestation of intentions, the invocation of deities, the protection against malevolent forces, and the facilitation of healing and transformation. In this section, we explore the purpose, methods, and significance of verbal incantations in Babylonian shamanism, shedding light on their transformative power and their role in the spiritual practices of ancient Babylon.

Purpose:

The purpose of verbal incantations in Babylonian shamanism was multifaceted and deeply rooted in the belief that words held inherent power. Firstly, these incantations served as a means of establishing a direct connection between the shaman and the divine realm. By reciting sacred words and phrases, shamans invoked the presence and assistance of deities, ancestral spirits, and other non-ordinary beings. Secondly, the vibrational frequencies produced by these verbal expressions were believed to harmonize with and influence the subtle energies of the universe. Through the repetition and resonance of specific sounds, rhythms, and tones, the shaman sought to align these energies with their intended purposes, manifesting their desires and intentions. Thirdly, verbal incantations acted as catalysts for personal and collective transformation, inducing altered states of consciousness, activating dormant spiritual abilities, and enhancing the shaman's connection to the spiritual realm.

Methods:

The methods employed in the use of verbal incantations were diverse and varied depending on the specific intention and desired outcome. Babylonian shamans were well-versed in sacred texts and possessed deep knowledge of the prescribed formulas, invocations, and rituals contained within them. These texts were meticulously crafted over generations, embodying the accumulated wisdom, knowledge, and spiritual power of the shamanic tradition. The recitation of these texts was accompanied by specific rhythmic patterns, tonal variations, and gestures, all of which contributed to the overall efficacy of the practice. Furthermore, Babylonian shamans also possessed the ability to spontaneously create incantations, drawing upon their intuitive understanding and connection to the spiritual realm. Through their deep attunement to the energies at play, they crafted words and phrases that resonated with the intended purpose and invoked the desired spiritual forces.

Significance:

The significance of verbal incantations in Babylonian shamanism lay in their transformative power and their ability to shape and influence the fabric of reality. These sacred utterances were regarded as vehicles through which the shaman could tap into the mystical forces of creation and manifest their intentions. Through the repetition and resonance of specific sounds and words, the shaman established a vibrational harmony that bridged the gap between the physical and spiritual realms. The vibrations emitted by the incantations were believed to affect not only the shaman but also the external environment, influencing the energies at play and bringing about desired changes. Verbal incantations were seen as both practical tools for achieving specific outcomes and as sacred rituals that facilitated the shaman's spiritual growth, alignment, and connection to the divine.

Exercise 1: Engage in a vocalization practice. Select a specific intention or desired outcome and create your own incantation or chant. Experiment with different sounds, rhythms, and tonal variations as you recite the incantation. Reflect on the sensations, emotions, and energetic shifts that arise within you during the practice. Discuss your experiences with a study partner or write a reflective essay.

Problem 1: Reflect on the potential limitations and ethical considerations surrounding the use of verbal incantations. Explore the responsibility and intention behind the use of these powerful techniques, considering the potential impact on personal empowerment, consent, and the ethical treatment of others. Discuss the potential ethical dilemmas that may arise in the practice of verbal incantations and propose ways to address them.

Example 1: Compare and contrast the use of verbal incantations in Babylonian shamanism with contemporary practices in witchcraft, Wicca, or other spiritual traditions. Discuss the similarities, differences, and cultural variations in the methods, symbolism, and beliefs surrounding the power of vocal expressions in spiritual practices.

Exploring the Methods: Examples, Problems, and Exercises

Problem 1: Analyze the role of verbal incantations in personal transformation and manifestation practices. Discuss how the intentional use of specific words, sounds, and rhythms can influence one's energetic state, mindset, and ability to manifest desired outcomes.

Exercise 1: Create your own incantation or chant. Set a clear intention or desire and craft a series of affirmations, words, or sounds that align with your intention. Practice reciting your incantation or chant regularly, observing any shifts in your thoughts, emotions, or external circumstances. Reflect on the effectiveness and transformative power of your practice.

Exercise 2: Research and analyze the historical significance and cultural variations of verbal incantations in different spiritual traditions. Select a specific tradition and explore its unique methods, symbolism, and beliefs surrounding the power of vocal expressions. Discuss the universal themes and cultural diversities in the use of verbal incantations for spiritual transformation and manifestation.

By exploring the role and significance of verbal incantations in Babylonian shamanism, we gain insights into the transformative potential of sound, language, and intention. These practices exemplify the profound connection between words and the spiritual realm, highlighting the ability to channel and direct energy through vocal expressions. Through engaging in the provided exercises and critically reflecting on the ethical considerations, you will deepen your understanding of the power of verbal incantations and expand your repertoire of spiritual tools for personal growth and manifestation.

2. Understanding the use of spells and their intended effects

In Babylonian shamanism, spells held a significant role as potent tools for manifesting specific intentions and invoking desired effects. These carefully crafted verbal formulas contained encoded energies and symbolic representations that aligned with the desired outcomes. Understanding the use of spells in ancient Babylon provides us with insights into the intentional manipulation of spiritual forces and the belief in the power of language to influence reality. In this section, we delve into the purpose, methods, and intended effects of spells in Babylonian shamanism, shedding light on the principles underlying their use and their role in shaping the spiritual practices of ancient Babylon.

Purpose:

The purpose of employing spells in Babylonian shamanism was to bring about specific effects or changes in the physical, emotional, or spiritual realms. These effects varied widely, encompassing healing, protection, love, abundance, fertility, and the removal of obstacles. Spells were seen as a means to interact with and influence the energetic fabric of the universe, engaging with the forces of creation and transformation. Through the use of symbolic language, invocations, and ritualized formulas, shamans aimed to align their intentions with the spiritual forces at play, amplifying their desired effects and bringing about tangible manifestations.

Methods:

The methods employed in the use of spells were rooted in a deep understanding of symbolism, cosmology, and the relationship between the spiritual and physical realms. Babylonian shamans possessed extensive knowledge of sacred texts, incantation rituals, and the use of specific words and phrases to activate desired effects. The recitation of spells often involved rhythmic patterns, tonal variations, and gestures that enhanced the potency of the verbal formulas. These methods served to intensify the energetic resonance of the spells, strengthening their connection to the intended effects. Additionally, written amulets or talismans containing the encoded words and symbols of the spells were often used to amplify their power and ensure their longevity.

Intended Effects:

The intended effects of spells in Babylonian shamanism were diverse and encompassed a wide range of aspects in human life and the natural world. Spells for healing aimed to restore balance and well-being, alleviating physical ailments and emotional distress. Protection spells were employed to ward off malevolent forces, ensuring the safety and security of individuals and communities. Love spells sought to attract or strengthen romantic relationships, while abundance and fertility spells were used to ensure prosperity and bountiful harvests. Each spell was carefully constructed to address specific needs and desires, reflecting the intricate understanding of the interconnectedness between the spiritual and material realms.

Exercise 1: Create your own spell. Set a clear intention or desired outcome, and craft a verbal formula that aligns with your intention. Consider the use of symbolic language, invocations, and rhythmic patterns that resonate with your intention. Practice reciting your spell regularly, reflecting on any shifts in your thoughts, emotions, or external circumstances. Discuss your experiences with a study partner or write a reflective essay.

Problem 1: Reflect on the potential ethical considerations and limitations of using spells in spiritual practices. Discuss the responsibility and intention behind the use of these powerful techniques, exploring the potential impact on personal empowerment, consent, and the ethical treatment of others. Propose ways to approach spellcasting in an ethical and responsible manner.

Example 1: Compare and contrast the use of spells in Babylonian shamanism with contemporary practices in witchcraft, ceremonial magic, or other spiritual traditions. Discuss the similarities, differences, and cultural variations in the methods, symbolism, and beliefs surrounding the use of spells for manifestation and transformation.

Exploring the Methods: Examples, Problems, and Exercises

Problem 1: Analyze the psychological and neurological mechanisms underlying the efficacy of spells in achieving desired effects. Explore the concepts of intention, belief, and the placebo effect, considering how they may contribute to the perceived effectiveness of spells. Discuss the potential benefits and limitations of incorporating spellwork into personal spiritual practices.

Exercise 1: Research and analyze historical examples of spells in different cultures and traditions. Select a specific culture or tradition and explore the diverse range of spells used for different purposes. Examine the symbolism, language, and intended effects of these spells, highlighting the common threads and unique variations across cultures.

Exercise 2: Reflect on the ethical implications of using spells for personal gain or influencing the will of others. Engage in a debate or group discussion on the potential ethical dilemmas surrounding the use of spells and propose guidelines or ethical frameworks to ensure responsible and respectful spellcasting practices.

By understanding the use of spells in Babylonian shamanism, we gain insights into the intentional manipulation of spiritual forces and the belief in the power of language to shape reality. Spells were seen as vehicles for manifestation, enabling the shaman to align their intentions with the energetic fabric of the universe. Through engaging in the provided exercises and critically reflecting on the ethical considerations, you will deepen your understanding of the use of spells and expand your toolkit for personal and collective transformation.

III. Shamanic Journeys and Spirit Communication

Shamanic journeys and spirit communication were integral aspects of Babylonian shamanism, providing a means for shamans to establish contact with the spirit realm, commune with deities, ancestral spirits, and non-ordinary beings, and gain insights, guidance, and divinatory knowledge. These transformative practices allowed shamans to transcend the physical limitations of the material world and navigate the multidimensional realms of consciousness. In this section, we will delve into the purpose, methods, and significance of shamanic journeys and spirit communication in Babylonian shamanism, shedding light on the rich tapestry of spiritual exploration and connection within this ancient tradition.

Purpose:

The purpose of shamanic journeys and spirit communication in Babylonian shamanism was multifaceted. Firstly, these practices allowed shamans to establish direct contact and forge relationships with spiritual entities, including deities, spirit guides, and ancestors. By entering altered states of consciousness, shamans transcended the boundaries of ordinary perception and engaged in interdimensional communication, seeking insights, wisdom, and divinatory knowledge. Secondly, shamanic journeys provided an opportunity for personal transformation, spiritual growth, and the acquisition of sacred knowledge. Through these journeys, shamans expanded their awareness, honed their intuitive abilities, and deepened their connection to the spiritual realms. Thirdly, spirit communication served the broader community by providing guidance, healing, and divination to individuals and the collective, addressing concerns, predicting future events, and facilitating the resolution of challenges.

Methods:

Babylonian shamans employed various methods to embark on shamanic journeys and establish spirit communication. Rhythmic drumming, repetitive chanting, dancing, and other forms of rhythmic entrainment were used to induce altered states of consciousness. By modulating brainwave patterns and altering their neurophysiology, shamans entered a state of trance that facilitated access to non-ordinary realms of perception. Additionally, the use of psychotropic plants or herbal preparations may have been employed to enhance the visionary experiences and facilitate the connection with the spirit realm. The shaman's knowledge of cosmology, mythology, and symbolism played a crucial role in navigating these realms and interpreting the encounters with spiritual entities.

Significance:

Shamanic journeys and spirit communication held great significance in Babylonian shamanism, as they served as gateways to spiritual realms and sources of wisdom and guidance. Through these practices, shamans bridged the gap between the physical and spiritual realms, acting as intermediaries and facilitators of spiritual communication. The insights and messages received during shamanic journeys provided valuable guidance in decision-making, personal growth, and the well-being of individuals and communities. Furthermore, the act of journeying and communing with the spiritual realm reaffirmed the interconnectedness of all existence and cultivated a sense of reverence, respect, and awe for the mysteries of the universe.

Exercise 1: Engage in a shamanic journey visualization. Find a quiet and comfortable space, close your eyes, and visualize yourself embarking on a shamanic journey. Set a clear intention to connect with a spiritual guide or seek guidance on a specific question. Allow the journey to unfold, observing the landscapes, encounters, and messages that arise. Afterward, journal about your experience, reflecting on any insights, symbols, or guidance received.

Problem 1: Discuss the potential challenges and risks associated with shamanic journeys and spirit communication. Explore the importance of proper preparation, grounding, and integration of experiences. Analyze the potential psychological and spiritual implications of engaging in these practices without adequate guidance or support. Propose strategies for maintaining personal safety and well-being while exploring the realms of spirit communication.

Example 1: Compare and contrast the methods and practices of shamanic journeys and spirit communication in Babylonian shamanism with those found in contemporary shamanic traditions, such as Siberian shamanism or Amazonian shamanism. Analyze the similarities, differences, and cultural variations in the techniques, symbolism, and beliefs surrounding these practices.

Exploring the Methods: Examples, Problems, and Exercises

Problem 1: Analyze the psychological and neuroscientific aspects of shamanic journeys and altered states of consciousness. Explore the concepts of neuroplasticity, neurophysiology, and brainwave entrainment, considering how these processes contribute to the transformative and visionary experiences reported during shamanic journeys. Discuss the potential benefits and limitations of incorporating shamanic journey practices into personal spiritual development.

Exercise 1: Research and analyze the accounts of shamanic journeys and spirit communication in ancient Babylonian texts and artifacts. Select a specific text or artifact and examine the descriptions, symbolism, and themes present. Reflect on the cultural context and cosmological beliefs that shaped these practices, drawing connections to contemporary understandings of shamanic journey practices.

Exercise 2: Engage in a group discussion or debate on the role and relevance of shamanic journeys and spirit communication in modern society. Explore the potential benefits, challenges, and ethical considerations of incorporating these practices into personal or collective spiritual and healing frameworks.

By exploring the methods and significance of shamanic journeys and spirit communication in Babylonian shamanism, we gain insights into the profound connection between the human and spirit realms. These practices exemplify the shaman's ability to transcend ordinary consciousness and establish communication with the spiritual dimensions of existence. Through engaging in the provided exercises and critically reflecting on the challenges and implications, you will deepen your understanding of shamanic journeys and spirit communication and broaden your perspectives on the nature of reality and spiritual exploration.

A. Overview of shamanic journeys in ancient Babylon

Shamanic journeys were a fundamental practice in ancient Babylonian culture, allowing shamans to transcend the boundaries of ordinary consciousness and explore the spiritual realms. These transformative experiences served as a conduit for communication with divine beings, ancestral spirits, and non-ordinary entities. In this section, we will provide an overview of shamanic journeys in ancient Babylon, shedding light on their purpose, methods, and significance within the context of Babylonian shamanism.

Purpose:

The primary purpose of shamanic journeys in ancient Babylon was to establish direct contact with the spirit realm and access hidden realms of knowledge, wisdom, and divination. Shamans embarked on these journeys to seek guidance, receive revelations, and obtain insights into the past, present, and future. The spiritual realms were believed to hold a wealth of information and resources that could be tapped into for the benefit of individuals and the community at large. Shamans acted as intermediaries, bridging the gap between the physical and spiritual dimensions and bringing back valuable knowledge to aid in decision-making, healing, and spiritual growth.

Methods:

Shamans employed various methods to facilitate shamanic journeys and enter altered states of consciousness. Rhythmic drumming, repetitive chanting, dancing, and other forms of rhythmic entrainment were used to induce trance-like states. By altering their brainwave patterns and neurophysiology, shamans accessed non-ordinary realms of perception, allowing them to navigate the spiritual dimensions. Additionally, the use of psychotropic plants or herbal preparations may have played a role in enhancing the visionary experiences and deepening the connection with the spirit realm. These methods allowed shamans to explore the hidden realms and establish communication with spiritual entities.

Significance:

Shamanic journeys held great significance in ancient Babylon, serving as a means of spiritual exploration, communion with higher realms, and acquiring sacred knowledge. These journeys were seen as transformative experiences that expanded the shaman's consciousness and connected them to the collective wisdom of the spiritual realms. Through their encounters with divine beings and ancestral spirits, shamans gained insights into the mysteries of the universe, the workings of the cosmos, and the interplay between the physical and spiritual realms. The knowledge and revelations obtained during shamanic journeys empowered shamans to fulfill their roles as healers, advisors, and intermediaries between the human and divine.

Exercise 1: Engage in a guided shamanic journey. Find a quiet and comfortable space, close your eyes, and follow a guided meditation or visualization designed to facilitate a shamanic journey. Set an intention to explore a specific question or seek guidance on a particular issue. Allow yourself to enter a state of relaxation and receptivity, observing the landscapes, encounters, and messages that arise during the journey. Afterward, journal about your experience, reflecting on any insights, symbols, or guidance received.

Problem 1: Discuss the potential psychological and neurological explanations for the phenomenon of shamanic journeys. Analyze the concepts of altered states of consciousness, neuroplasticity, and the role of the brain's default mode network in facilitating visionary experiences. Explore the potential implications of these scientific perspectives on the understanding and interpretation of shamanic practices.

Example 1: Compare and contrast the methods and practices of shamanic journeys in ancient Babylon with those found in other cultures and traditions, such as Siberian shamanism, Native American shamanism, or Ayahuasca ceremonies in the Amazon. Analyze the similarities, differences, and cultural variations in the techniques, symbolism, and beliefs surrounding shamanic journeys.

Exploring the Methods: Examples, Problems, and Exercises

Problem 1: Explore the potential challenges and risks associated with shamanic journeys. Discuss the importance of proper preparation, grounding techniques, and integration practices to ensure the safety and well-being of individuals engaging in these journeys. Analyze the potential psychological and spiritual implications of encountering powerful or challenging experiences during shamanic journeys.

Exercise 1: Research and analyze accounts of shamanic journeys in ancient Babylonian texts and artifacts. Select a specific text or artifact and examine the descriptions, symbolism, and themes present. Reflect on the cultural context and cosmological beliefs that shaped these practices, drawing connections to contemporary understandings of shamanic journey practices.

Exercise 2: Engage in a group discussion or debate on the significance and relevance of shamanic journeys in modern society. Explore the potential benefits, challenges, and ethical considerations of incorporating shamanic journey practices into personal or collective spiritual and healing frameworks.

By exploring the overview of shamanic journeys in ancient Babylon, we gain insights into the profound nature of these spiritual practices and their role in connecting individuals to higher realms of knowledge and guidance. The methods and significance of shamanic journeys exemplify the deep spiritual connection ancient Babylonians had with the unseen realms and the belief in the power of altered states of consciousness for transformative experiences. Through engaging in the provided exercises and critically reflecting on the challenges and implications, you will deepen your understanding of shamanic journeys and broaden your perspectives on the nature of reality and spiritual exploration.

1. Techniques used for entering altered states of consciousness

Entering altered states of consciousness is a fundamental practice in various spiritual traditions, including Babylonian shamanism. These altered states allow practitioners to transcend ordinary awareness and access deeper realms of perception, where they can commune with the divine, receive spiritual insights, and embark on transformative journeys. In this section, we will explore the techniques used by Babylonian shamans to enter altered states of consciousness, providing a comprehensive understanding of these methods and their significance within the context of ancient Babylonian spirituality.

Drumming:

One of the primary techniques employed by Babylonian shamans to induce altered states of consciousness was rhythmic drumming. By playing a drum with a consistent beat, the shaman created a sonic foundation that entrained the brainwaves of both the practitioner and those present in the ceremonial space. This rhythmic entrainment facilitated a shift in consciousness, leading to a state of relaxation, receptivity, and heightened awareness. The steady rhythm of the drum acted as a gateway, guiding the shaman into altered states where spiritual experiences and connections could occur.

Chanting and Vocalization:

The use of vocalization, including chanting, singing, or vocal toning, was another technique utilized by Babylonian shamans to enter altered states of consciousness. Through the repetitive and rhythmic vocalization of sacred sounds and words, the shaman accessed deep states of concentration and resonance. The vibrations produced by vocalization reverberated through the body, activating energy centers and facilitating the flow of spiritual energy. This technique allowed the shaman to attune their consciousness to the frequencies of the spirit realm, creating a bridge between the physical and spiritual dimensions.

Breathing Techniques:

Conscious breathing techniques were also employed to induce altered states of consciousness in Babylonian shamanism. By focusing on slow, deep breaths and regulating the inhalation and exhalation, the shaman engaged in intentional control of their breath, which in turn affected their state of consciousness. The deliberate manipulation of breath patterns helped calm the mind, relax the body, and enhance the flow of life force energy. This technique supported the shaman's ability to enter a trance-like state, facilitating their connection with the spiritual realms.

Psychotropic Plants and Herbal Preparations:

In some instances, Babylonian shamans may have utilized psychotropic plants or herbal preparations to induce altered states of consciousness. These plants, such as ergot, henbane, or poppy, contained psychoactive compounds that could alter perception, induce visions, and enhance spiritual experiences. The shaman's knowledge of specific plant properties, dosage, and preparation methods allowed them to harness the transformative potential of these substances. However, it is important to note that the use of psychotropic plants was not a universal practice among all Babylonian shamans, and their inclusion depended on cultural, geographical, and personal factors.

Exercise 1: Engage in a drumming meditation. Find a comfortable space, sit or lie down, and play a rhythmic drumming track or use a drum if available. Focus your attention on the steady beat, allowing the sound to penetrate your being. Relax into the rhythm, allowing it to guide you into a state of deep relaxation and receptivity. Observe any sensations, images, or insights that arise during the meditation. Afterward, reflect on your experience, noting the impact of the drumming on your consciousness and state of mind.

Problem 1: Compare and contrast the techniques for entering altered states of consciousness in Babylonian shamanism with those found in other cultures and traditions, such as Tibetan Buddhism, Native American shamanism, or Australian Aboriginal practices. Analyze the similarities, differences, and cultural variations in the methods used to induce altered states and their significance within each tradition.

Example 1: Explore the scientific explanations behind the effectiveness of rhythmic drumming, vocalization, and conscious breathing in inducing altered states of consciousness. Investigate concepts such as brainwave entrainment, resonance, and the influence of these techniques on the autonomic nervous system and brain activity. Discuss the potential benefits and limitations of incorporating these techniques into contemporary spiritual practices and therapeutic modalities.

By understanding the techniques used for entering altered states of consciousness in Babylonian shamanism, we gain valuable insights into the profound connection between spiritual practices and the human mind. These techniques were carefully designed to induce specific states of consciousness, allowing shamans to access deeper realms of perception and engage in transformative spiritual experiences. Through engaging in the provided exercises and critically reflecting on the associated problems, you will enhance your understanding of these techniques and their potential applications in contemporary spiritual and therapeutic contexts.

2.Purpose and goals of shamanic journeys

Shamanic journeys were profound spiritual practices in ancient Babylonian culture, undertaken with specific purposes and goals in mind. These journeys allowed shamans to venture into the depths of the spiritual realms, seeking guidance, knowledge, and transformative experiences. In this section, we will explore the purpose and goals of shamanic journeys, shedding light on the intentions behind these powerful spiritual endeavors.
Purpose:

The primary purpose of shamanic journeys in ancient Babylon was to establish direct contact with the spirit realm and access hidden realms of knowledge, wisdom, and divination. These journeys allowed shamans to transcend ordinary consciousness and engage with divine beings, ancestral spirits, and non-ordinary entities. By venturing into these realms, shamans sought guidance, revelations, and insights into the past, present, and future. The spirit realm was believed to hold a wealth of information and resources that could be tapped into for the benefit of individuals and the community at large.

Through shamanic journeys, shamans acted as intermediaries, bridging the gap between the physical and spiritual dimensions and bringing back valuable knowledge to aid in decision-making, healing, and spiritual growth.

Goals:

Shamanic journeys had several overarching goals, each contributing to the shaman's personal and communal roles as a healer, guide, and spiritual intermediary. These goals included:

Seeking Guidance: Shamans embarked on journeys to seek guidance from spiritual entities. They posed specific questions, sought advice, or sought insights into important matters affecting individuals or the community. By connecting with higher wisdom, shamans could provide valuable counsel and direction to those in need.

Divination and Prophecy: Babylonian shamans utilized shamanic journeys as a means of divination and prophecy. Through encounters with spiritual beings and accessing hidden realms, shamans could gain insight into future events, unravel mysteries, and receive prophetic messages. The ability to foresee potential outcomes and guide individuals and leaders in their decision-making processes was a crucial aspect of the shaman's role.

Healing and Restoration: Shamans engaged in shamanic journeys to access spiritual energies and powers that could facilitate healing and restoration. By entering altered states of consciousness and connecting with the spirit realm, they could channel healing energies, receive instructions for remedies, or bring back spiritual guidance to support the physical, emotional, and spiritual well-being of individuals and the community.

Spiritual Growth and Personal Transformation: Shamanic journeys provided an opportunity for shamans to embark on their own personal spiritual journeys. These experiences often involved encountering challenges, facing inner demons, and gaining profound insights into the nature of reality and the self. By undertaking these transformative journeys, shamans underwent personal growth and spiritual development, enhancing their abilities as healers and guides.

Exercise 1: Reflect on your personal goals and intentions for engaging in shamanic journeys or other transformative spiritual practices. Consider the areas of guidance, healing, personal growth, or connection to higher realms that you seek to explore. Write down your intentions and revisit them before each journey, allowing them to guide your experiences and interpretations.

Problem 1: Discuss the ethical considerations and responsibilities that come with the practice of shamanic journeying. Analyze the potential risks, such as spiritual bypassing, delusion, or misuse of power, that can arise when engaging in these practices without proper understanding, respect, and guidance. Explore ways in which practitioners can approach shamanic journeys with humility, integrity, and accountability.

Example 1: Explore the ways in which the goals and purposes of shamanic journeys in ancient Babylon align with or differ from other shamanic traditions, such as Siberian shamanism, Native American shamanism, or Australian Aboriginal practices. Analyze the cultural, geographical, and historical factors that may have influenced the specific aims and intentions behind these journeys.

By delving into the purpose and goals of shamanic journeys, we gain a deeper appreciation for the transformative potential of these practices. Shamanic journeys in ancient Babylon were driven by the desire for guidance, divination, healing, and personal growth. The attainment of these goals empowered shamans to fulfill their vital roles as spiritual intermediaries, healers, and guides within their communities. Through engaging in the provided exercises and critically reflecting on the associated problem and example, you will broaden your understanding of the purpose and significance of shamanic journeys and deepen your engagement with these profound spiritual practices.

B. Spirit communication and interaction

In Babylonian shamanism, spirit communication and interaction were integral components of the shaman's practice. Through these interactions, shamans established connections with spiritual entities, sought guidance, received messages, and facilitated healing and transformation. In this section, we will explore the nature of spirit communication and the various methods employed by Babylonian shamans to bridge the gap between the physical and spiritual realms.

Understanding Spirit Communication:

In Babylonian shamanism, spirits were seen as intermediaries between the divine realm and the human world. They included deities, ancestral spirits, nature spirits, and other non-ordinary beings. Shamans believed that spirits held knowledge, wisdom, and guidance that could benefit individuals and the community. Spirit communication involved establishing a bridge of understanding and mutual exchange between shamans and these spiritual entities.

Methods of Spirit Communication:

Babylonian shamans employed several methods to engage in spirit communication. These methods included:

Invocation and Offering: Shamans would invoke the presence of specific spirits through prayers, chants, or invocations. They would offer sacred objects, libations, or other offerings as a means of honoring and attracting the attention of the spirits. These rituals created a sacred space and invited the spirits to enter into communication with the shaman.

Ritual Tools and Objects: Ritual tools and objects played a significant role in spirit communication. Shamans utilized items such as drums, rattles, sacred herbs, or ritual masks to enhance their connection with the spiritual realm. These objects acted as conduits for energy and served as focal points for the shaman's intention and attention during the communication process.

Trance States: Shamans entered altered states of consciousness, often induced through rhythmic drumming, chanting, or other techniques, to facilitate spirit communication. In these trance states, the shaman's consciousness shifted, allowing them to enter into a state of receptivity and heightened awareness. This altered state of consciousness created a conducive environment for the shaman to interact with spirits and receive their messages.

Symbolic Interpretation: Communication with spirits often occurred through symbolic means. Shamans would interpret signs, omens, dreams, or visions as messages from the spiritual realm. Through their understanding of symbolism, cultural context, and mythological elements, shamans deciphered the meaning conveyed by the spirits and conveyed it to individuals or the community.

Exercise 1: Engage in a spirit communication exercise using symbolic interpretation. Select an object or image that holds personal significance to you. Reflect on its symbolism and its potential connection to the spiritual realm. Close your eyes, hold the object or image in your mind, and ask the spirits for guidance or a message related to your current situation. Be open to receiving impressions, thoughts, or images that may arise. Afterward, reflect on the experience and consider the insights or guidance received.

Problem 1: Analyze the role of skepticism and critical thinking in the context of spirit communication. Discuss the potential pitfalls and challenges associated with accepting spirit communication at face value. Explore how discernment and skepticism can contribute to a balanced and objective approach to interpreting and evaluating spiritual experiences and messages.

Example 1: Compare and contrast the methods of spirit communication used in Babylonian shamanism with those found in other spiritual traditions, such as African tribal practices, Indigenous Australian cultures, or contemporary mediumship practices. Analyze the similarities, differences, and cultural variations in the techniques and approaches employed to establish communication with spirits.

By understanding the methods and nature of spirit communication in Babylonian shamanism, we gain insights into the profound connections between the physical and spiritual realms. These interactions with spiritual entities allowed shamans to access wisdom, guidance, and transformative energies. Through engaging in the provided exercise and critically reflecting on the associated problem and example, you will deepen your understanding of spirit communication and develop a discerning approach to engaging with the spiritual realm.

1. Connecting with deities and ancestral spirits

In Babylonian shamanism, connecting with deities and ancestral spirits was a central aspect of spiritual practice. These sacred relationships formed the foundation for guidance, protection, and support in the shaman's work. In this section, we will explore the significance of connecting with deities and ancestral spirits, the methods employed to establish these connections, and the benefits derived from such relationships.

The Significance of Connecting with Deities and Ancestral Spirits:

Deities were revered as powerful beings in the Babylonian pantheon, embodying various aspects of the natural and supernatural world. Ancestral spirits, on the other hand, represented the collective wisdom and experiences of the past, offering guidance and support to the living. By establishing connections with these spiritual entities, shamans sought to access their wisdom, gain favor, and invoke their aid in various endeavors. The connection with deities and ancestral spirits allowed the shaman to tap into higher realms of consciousness and receive insights that could benefit individuals and the community.

Methods of Connection:

Babylonian shamans employed several methods to establish connections with deities and ancestral spirits. These methods included:

Ritual Invocation: Shamans would perform specific rituals and invocations to call upon the presence of deities and ancestral spirits. Through prayers, chants, and offerings, they would create a sacred space and invoke the presence of these spiritual entities. The ritualistic nature of the invocations helped to establish a sense of reverence and connection.

Ancestor Veneration: Ancestor veneration played a significant role in Babylonian shamanism. Shamans honored their ancestors through rituals, offerings, and remembrance. By acknowledging and paying respects to their ancestral lineage, shamans sought the guidance and blessings of their forebears, drawing upon their wisdom and experiences.

Sacred Offerings: Shamans made offerings to deities and ancestral spirits as a way of establishing a reciprocal relationship. These offerings could include food, drink, incense, or other symbolic items. The act of offering demonstrated respect, gratitude, and a desire for a mutual exchange of energy and assistance.

Meditation and Prayer: Shamans engaged in meditative practices and prayer to quiet the mind, focus their intentions, and open themselves to the presence of deities and ancestral spirits. Through meditation, they sought a state of heightened awareness and receptivity, creating an inner space for communication and connection.

Exercise 1: Engage in an ancestor veneration exercise. Set up a small altar or sacred space dedicated to your ancestors. Place photographs or objects representing your ancestors on the altar. Light incense or candles, and offer a prayer or heartfelt words of gratitude and remembrance. Take a few moments to reflect on the qualities, strengths, or wisdom that you may have inherited from your ancestors. Notice any sensations, emotions, or insights that arise during this practice.

Problem 1: Discuss the potential challenges and ethical considerations in connecting with deities and ancestral spirits. Analyze the potential risks of appropriating or misinterpreting cultural practices related to deity worship and ancestor veneration. Explore the importance of cultural sensitivity, respect, and understanding in engaging with these spiritual relationships.

Example 1: Compare the methods of connecting with deities and ancestral spirits in Babylonian shamanism with those found in other spiritual traditions, such as African, Indigenous American, or Chinese practices. Analyze the similarities, differences, and cultural nuances in the approaches to establishing relationships with these spiritual entities.

By establishing connections with deities and ancestral spirits, Babylonian shamans accessed profound wisdom, guidance, and support in their spiritual work. These sacred relationships provided a sense of belonging, protection, and empowerment. Through engaging in the provided exercise and critically reflecting on the associated problem and example, you will deepen your understanding of the significance of connecting with deities and ancestral spirits and foster a respectful and meaningful approach to establishing your own spiritual relationships.

2. Rituals for invoking and communicating with spirits

In Babylonian shamanism, rituals played a vital role in invoking and communicating with spirits. These rituals provided a framework for establishing a sacred space, invoking the presence of spiritual entities, and facilitating effective communication. In this section, we will explore the purpose of these rituals, the steps involved in their performance, and the benefits derived from engaging in these practices.

The Purpose of Rituals for Invoking and Communicating with Spirits:

Rituals for invoking and communicating with spirits served multiple purposes in Babylonian shamanism. These rituals were designed to:

Establish Sacred Space: Rituals created a sacred space in which the shaman and participants could connect with the spiritual realm. By creating a distinct environment through specific actions, words, and symbols, rituals helped to set the stage for spirit communication and interaction.

Invoke the Presence of Spirits: Through invocations, prayers, and specific ritual gestures, shamans sought to invoke the presence of specific spirits. These rituals acted as an invitation, drawing the attention and energies of the spirits towards the shaman and the participants.

Facilitate Effective Communication: Rituals provided a structured framework for effective communication with spirits. The use of symbolic objects, gestures, and chants served as a common language between the human and spirit realms, facilitating clearer and more meaningful communication.

Steps Involved in Rituals for Invoking and Communicating with Spirits:

Rituals for invoking and communicating with spirits in Babylonian shamanism typically involved the following steps:

Preparation: The shaman and participants would engage in preparatory actions, such as cleansing rituals or purifications, to create a state of readiness and receptivity. This step ensured that both the physical and spiritual aspects were aligned for the ritual.

Invocation: The shaman would perform invocations, prayers, or chants to invoke the presence of specific spirits. These invocations often included the names and attributes of the spirits, their roles, and their association with specific domains.

Offerings: Offerings, such as food, drink, or sacred objects, were made to the spirits as a gesture of respect, gratitude, and invitation. These offerings acted as a means of establishing a connection and demonstrating the shaman's intention to engage in communication.

Symbolic Actions: Symbolic actions, such as the use of ritual objects, gestures, or movements, played a significant role in these rituals. The shaman would utilize these symbolic actions to create a symbolic language that transcended verbal communication, allowing for a deeper level of interaction.

Communication and Receptivity: Once the presence of the spirits was invoked, the shaman and participants would enter into a state of heightened receptivity and openness. This state allowed for clear reception of messages, insights, and guidance from the spirits.

Exercise 1: Engage in a ritual for invoking and communicating with spirits. Create a sacred space in your preferred setting, using candles, incense, or other symbolic objects. Perform a simple invocation or prayer, calling upon the presence of a spirit or deity that resonates with you. Allow yourself to enter into a receptive state and be open to any impressions, insights, or sensations that arise during the ritual.

Problem 1: Explore the potential challenges and ethical considerations in engaging in rituals for invoking and communicating with spirits. Discuss the importance of intention, respect, and consent in these rituals. Analyze the potential risks of misinterpreting or misusing the information received from spirits and the responsibility that comes with engaging in such practices.

Example 1: Compare and contrast the rituals for invoking and communicating with spirits in Babylonian shamanism with those found in other spiritual traditions, such as Native American, Celtic, or African practices. Analyze the similarities, differences, and cultural variations in the approaches to establishing communication and connection with spirits.

By engaging in rituals for invoking and communicating with spirits, Babylonian shamans established sacred connections and opened channels of communication with the spiritual realm. These rituals provided a structured framework for effective communication, fostering a deeper understanding of the spiritual forces at play. Through engaging in the provided exercise and critically reflecting on the associated problem and example, you will enhance your understanding of the significance and practice of rituals for invoking and communicating with spirits, enabling you to forge meaningful connections in your own spiritual journey.

IV. The Shamanic Healing Tradition in Ancient Babylon

In ancient Babylon, the practice of shamanism encompassed a comprehensive approach to healing, addressing physical, emotional, and spiritual ailments. Shamanic healing rituals aimed to restore balance, alleviate suffering, and promote holistic well-being. In this section, we will explore the purpose and methods of shamanic healing in ancient Babylon, highlighting the profound impact these practices had on individuals and the community.

The Purpose of Shamanic Healing:

Shamanic healing in ancient Babylon served several purposes:

Restoring Balance: It was believed that illness and suffering were often manifestations of imbalance in the individual's body, mind, or spirit. Shamanic healing sought to restore equilibrium by addressing the underlying causes of illness and bringing the individual back into a state of harmony and wholeness.

Alleviating Suffering: Shamanic healers were revered for their ability to alleviate physical pain, emotional distress, and spiritual afflictions. Their interventions aimed to bring relief, comfort, and a sense of well-being to those in need.

Promoting Holistic Well-being: Shamanic healing embraced a holistic approach, recognizing the interconnectedness of the body, mind, and spirit. By addressing all aspects of an individual's being, these healing practices aimed to foster overall health, vitality, and a sense of inner balance.
Methods of Shamanic Healing:

Shamanic healing in ancient Babylon encompassed a range of methods and techniques:

Energy Work: Shamans were skilled in working with energy fields, using their hands, breath, or specialized tools to manipulate and balance subtle energies within the body. This energy work aimed to remove blockages, restore the free flow of energy, and promote healing at a deep energetic level.

Herbal Remedies: Shamanic healers possessed extensive knowledge of medicinal plants and their properties. They would prescribe and administer herbal remedies tailored to the specific needs of the individual, harnessing the healing power of nature to support the body's natural healing processes.

Rituals and Ceremonies: Shamanic healing rituals involved the use of specific symbols, incantations, and ritual objects to facilitate healing. These rituals acted as powerful catalysts for transformation, engaging the individual's belief systems, emotions, and spiritual connections.

Spirit Assistance: Shamans would call upon benevolent spirits or deities associated with healing to assist in the healing process. These spirits were believed to possess profound wisdom, healing powers, and the ability to bring about miraculous transformations.

Exercise 1: Engage in a self-healing practice inspired by ancient Babylonian shamanic healing. Choose a method that resonates with you, such as energy work, herbal remedies, or ritualistic practices. Create a sacred space and dedicate time to engage in the chosen practice, focusing on restoring balance, alleviating any distress, and promoting overall well-being.

Problem 1: Explore the ethical considerations in the practice of shamanic healing. Discuss the importance of informed consent, maintaining boundaries, and respecting cultural beliefs and practices when engaging in healing practices. Analyze the potential risks of misusing or misinterpreting ancient healing techniques and the responsibility of the modern practitioner.

Example 1: Research and compare the principles and methods of shamanic healing in ancient Babylon with other ancient healing traditions, such as Ayurveda, Traditional Chinese Medicine, or Indigenous healing practices. Analyze the similarities, differences, and shared underlying principles in addressing health and well-being.

The shamanic healing tradition in ancient Babylon was a profound and multifaceted approach to healing, addressing the interconnected aspects of body, mind, and spirit. By engaging in the provided exercise and critically reflecting on the associated problem and example, you will deepen your understanding of the purpose, methods, and ethical considerations of shamanic healing. These insights will empower you to apply ancient wisdom in contemporary healing practices and foster holistic well-being in yourself and others.

A. Healing methods and techniques employed by Babylonian shamans

In ancient Babylon, the practice of shamanism encompassed a rich array of healing methods and techniques. Babylonian shamans were revered for their ability to address various ailments, restore health, and promote overall well-being. In this section, we will explore the purpose, principles, and examples of healing methods employed by Babylonian shamans, providing insight into their profound healing practices.

The Purpose of Healing:

The healing methods employed by Babylonian shamans served several purposes:

Restoring Health: The primary purpose of these healing methods was to restore the health and well-being of individuals who were suffering from physical, emotional, or spiritual ailments. Shamans aimed to address the root causes of the illness and facilitate the body's natural healing processes.

Balancing Energies: Babylonian shamans recognized the importance of energetic balance in maintaining health. Their healing methods sought to restore harmonious energy flow within the body, ensuring a state of equilibrium and vitality.

Spiritual Connection: Healing in ancient Babylon was deeply intertwined with spirituality. The goal was not only to alleviate physical symptoms but also to address the spiritual and emotional aspects of the individual. Shamans aimed to foster a deep connection between the individual and the spiritual realm, facilitating profound healing on multiple levels.

Healing Methods and Techniques:

Babylonian shamans employed a variety of methods and techniques to facilitate healing:

Herbal Remedies: Babylonian shamans possessed extensive knowledge of medicinal plants and their properties. They prepared and administered herbal remedies tailored to the specific needs of the individual, harnessing the healing power of nature to support the body's natural healing processes. For example, they used herbs such as myrrh, frankincense, and aloe for their healing properties.

Rituals and Incantations: Rituals and incantations were central to Babylonian healing practices. Shamans would perform specific rituals, often involving the use of sacred objects, incense, and chants, to invoke the assistance of deities or spirits and to direct healing energies toward the individual. These rituals acted as powerful catalysts for healing, engaging the mind, body, and spirit in the healing process.

Massage and Manipulation: Babylonian shamans were skilled in the art of therapeutic touch. They would use massage techniques, manipulation of joints and muscles, and other physical interventions to promote relaxation, alleviate pain, and stimulate the body's self-healing mechanisms.

Energy Work: Shamans recognized the importance of energy flow in maintaining health. They would engage in various forms of energy work, such as laying on of hands, to manipulate and balance the subtle energies within the body. This energy work aimed to remove blockages and restore the free flow of vital energy, facilitating healing at a deep energetic level.

Exercise 1: Engage in a self-healing practice inspired by Babylonian shamanic healing. Choose a method that resonates with you, such as herbal remedies, ritualistic practices, or energy work. Create a sacred space and dedicate time to engage in the chosen practice, focusing on restoring balance, promoting healing, and fostering a sense of well-being.

Problem 1: Reflect on the ethical considerations in the practice of ancient healing methods. Discuss the importance of informed consent, cultural sensitivity, and respect for the individual's autonomy and belief systems when engaging in healing practices. Analyze the potential risks and limitations of employing ancient healing techniques in modern contexts.

Example 1: Research and compare the principles and techniques of Babylonian shamanic healing with other ancient healing traditions, such as Traditional Chinese Medicine or Ayurveda. Analyze the similarities, differences, and shared underlying principles in addressing health and well-being.

By exploring the healing methods and techniques employed by Babylonian shamans, engaging in the provided exercise, and critically reflecting on the associated problem and example, you will gain a deeper understanding of the purpose, principles, and ethical considerations in ancient healing practices. These insights will empower you to integrate ancient wisdom with modern healing approaches, fostering holistic well-being and transformation in yourself and others.

1. Herbal remedies and plant-based medicine

In ancient Babylon, herbal remedies and plant-based medicine played a significant role in the healing practices of shamans. The Babylonians had a deep understanding of the medicinal properties of plants and utilized them extensively to address various ailments and promote well-being. In this section, we will explore the importance, principles, and examples of herbal remedies and plant-based medicine in ancient Babylonian healing.

The Importance of Herbal Remedies:

Herbal remedies held great importance in Babylonian healing practices for several reasons:

Natural Healing: The Babylonians recognized the intrinsic healing properties of plants and their ability to support the body's natural healing processes. They believed that plants possessed vital energies and intelligence that could be harnessed for therapeutic purposes.

Holistic Approach: Herbal remedies offered a holistic approach to healing, addressing not only the physical symptoms but also the emotional, mental, and spiritual aspects of the individual. They viewed health as a state of balance and harmony between these different aspects.

Cultural Significance: Plants held deep cultural and symbolic significance in Babylonian society. The use of herbal remedies was intertwined with their spiritual and mythological beliefs, forming a vital part of their cultural heritage and identity.

Principles of Herbal Medicine:

Babylonian herbal medicine was guided by several key principles:

Individualized Treatment: Herbal remedies were tailored to the specific needs of each individual. Shamans would carefully assess the person's condition, considering factors such as their constitution, symptoms, and overall health. This personalized approach ensured that the chosen herbs and remedies were most effective for the individual's unique circumstances.

Knowledge of Medicinal Plants: Babylonian shamans possessed extensive knowledge of medicinal plants, their properties, and their applications. They understood the importance of plant identification, cultivation, harvesting, and preparation techniques to maintain the potency and efficacy of the remedies.

Holistic Perspective: Babylonian herbal medicine viewed health and well-being from a holistic perspective, considering the interconnectedness of the physical, emotional, mental, and spiritual aspects of the individual. Herbal remedies were chosen not only for their physical healing properties but also for their ability to restore balance and promote overall wellness.

Example of Herbal Remedies:

The Babylonians used a wide range of plants and herbs for healing purposes. Here are a few examples:

Myrrh (Commiphora myrrha): Myrrh was highly valued for its antiseptic and anti-inflammatory properties. It was used topically to treat wounds, infections, and skin conditions.

Frankincense (Boswellia sacra): Frankincense was renowned for its aromatic and medicinal qualities. It was used in incense and as an ingredient in various preparations to promote relaxation, uplift the spirit, and enhance spiritual practices.

Aloe (Aloe vera): Aloe was prized for its soothing and healing properties. It was used topically to treat burns, skin irritations, and wounds.

Exercise 1: Explore the healing properties of a specific plant or herb used in Babylonian herbal medicine. Research its traditional uses, chemical constituents, and potential modern applications. Reflect on how the plant's properties align with the principles of Babylonian healing.

Problem 1: Analyze the challenges and ethical considerations surrounding the integration of ancient herbal remedies into modern healthcare practices. Discuss issues such as standardization, quality control, and potential interactions with modern medications. Reflect on the importance of collaboration between traditional herbalists and modern healthcare practitioners.

Example 1: Compare Babylonian herbal medicine with other ancient herbal traditions, such as Traditional Chinese Medicine or Ayurveda. Analyze the similarities and differences in their principles, practices, and approaches to herbal healing.

By studying herbal remedies and plant-based medicine in ancient Babylon, engaging in the provided exercise, and critically reflecting on the associated problem and example, you will gain a deeper understanding of the rich tradition of herbal healing and its relevance in contemporary healthcare. This knowledge will empower you to harness the healing power of plants and integrate their wisdom into modern healing practices, fostering holistic well-being and vitality.

2. Use of rituals and energy healing

Rituals and energy healing practices were integral components of the Babylonian healing tradition. These practices aimed to restore balance and harmony within individuals and communities by harnessing sacred energies and facilitating spiritual transformation. In this section, we will explore the purpose, principles, and examples of rituals and energy healing in ancient Babylon.

The Purpose of Rituals and Energy Healing:

Rituals and energy healing in Babylonian culture served several key purposes:

Restoring Balance: The primary objective of rituals and energy healing was to restore balance and harmony within the individual's energetic system. It was believed that imbalances or blockages in the flow of vital energies could lead to physical, emotional, and spiritual ailments. Through rituals and energy healing practices, shamans worked to harmonize and restore the natural flow of energies, promoting well-being and vitality.

Transformation and Awakening: Rituals and energy healing served as catalysts for personal and spiritual transformation. By engaging in these practices, individuals could access higher states of consciousness, expand their awareness, and tap into their inner wisdom and potential. The transformative power of rituals facilitated personal growth, self-realization, and the cultivation of spiritual connection.

Connection with Divine Forces: Rituals and energy healing practices provided a means to establish a connection with the divine forces and spiritual realms. Shamans acted as intermediaries, channeling and directing these sacred energies to bring about healing, guidance, and blessings. By engaging in these rituals, individuals could access spiritual guidance, receive insights, and experience a profound sense of interconnectedness.

Principles of Rituals and Energy Healing:

The Babylonian rituals and energy healing practices were guided by several fundamental principles:

Intention and Focus: Rituals and energy healing required clear intention and focused attention. The shaman and participants directed their energy and intention towards a specific goal, such as healing, transformation, or spiritual connection. This focused intention amplified the effectiveness of the rituals and allowed for a deepening of the healing process.

Symbolism and Sacred Objects: Rituals often involved the use of symbols and sacred objects that carried potent energetic vibrations. These symbols and objects served as focal points for energy concentration and facilitation of healing. Examples of sacred objects used in Babylonian rituals include amulets, talismans, and ritual tools.

Energetic Alignment: Rituals and energy healing aimed to align and attune the individual's energy with the higher frequencies of the divine realm. This alignment facilitated the transmission of healing energies and allowed for the release of stagnant or disharmonious energies within the person's energetic field.

Example of Rituals and Energy Healing:

The Babylonians employed various rituals and energy healing practices. Here is an example:

Sacred Sound Healing: Sound played a crucial role in Babylonian rituals and energy healing. Shamans used rhythmic drumming, chanting, and vocal toning to create specific vibrational frequencies that resonated with the energy centers of the body. These vibrations helped to clear energy blockages, restore balance, and induce a state of relaxation and receptivity.

Exercise 1: Engage in a sacred sound healing practice. Experiment with different instruments or vocal techniques to create rhythmic patterns or vocal toning. Observe the effects of sound vibrations on your physical, emotional, and energetic state.

Problem 1: Analyze the scientific perspectives on the effectiveness of rituals and energy healing. Discuss the role of intention, placebo effects, and the influence of belief systems in the healing process. Reflect on the potential benefits of integrating rituals and energy healing practices with modern healthcare modalities.

Example 1: Compare the rituals and energy healing practices in ancient Babylon with those found in other indigenous cultures, such as Native American, African, or Indigenous Australian traditions. Explore the similarities and differences in their approaches, symbolism, and underlying principles.

By studying rituals and energy healing in ancient Babylon, engaging in the provided exercise, and critically reflecting on the associated problem and example, you will gain a deeper understanding of the transformative power of rituals and energy healing. This knowledge will empower you to incorporate these practices into your personal and professional life, fostering healing, balance, and spiritual connection.

B. Shamanic diagnosis and treatment of ailments

In ancient Babylon, the shamanic tradition encompassed not only the spiritual and mystical aspects but also a sophisticated understanding of human health and the treatment of ailments. In this section, we will delve into the methods of shamanic diagnosis and the diverse approaches employed by Babylonian shamans in the treatment of various ailments.

Shamanic Diagnosis:

Shamanic diagnosis in ancient Babylon involved a holistic approach that considered the interplay of physical, emotional, and spiritual factors contributing to illness. The shamans possessed a deep understanding of the intricate connection between the body, mind, and spirit, recognizing that disharmony in one aspect could manifest as illness in another. They utilized various diagnostic techniques to identify the underlying causes of ailments:

Intuitive Insight: Babylonian shamans relied on their heightened intuitive abilities to perceive energetic imbalances and identify the root causes of ailments. Through their deep connection with the spiritual realm, they received insights, visions, and messages that provided valuable diagnostic information.

Divination: Divinatory practices, such as reading omens, interpreting dreams, and casting lots, were employed to gain further insights into the nature and causes of the illness. By analyzing the signs and symbols presented through these divinatory methods, shamans could obtain valuable information for diagnosis and treatment.

Observation and Assessment: Shamans closely observed physical symptoms, behavior, and emotional states to discern patterns and identify imbalances within the individual's energy system. They paid attention to changes in energy flow, color, and texture of the aura, as well as the presence of spiritual intrusions or energetic blockages.

Treatment of Ailments:

Babylonian shamans employed a diverse range of treatment methods to restore balance and facilitate healing. These methods encompassed physical, energetic, and spiritual approaches, reflecting the holistic understanding of health and well-being:

Herbal Remedies: The use of herbs and plants played a significant role in Babylonian shamanic healing. Shamans possessed extensive knowledge of medicinal plants and their properties, utilizing them to create potions, infusions, and poultices. These herbal remedies were administered to address physical symptoms, boost the immune system, and promote overall well-being.

Energy Healing: Babylonian shamans were skilled in manipulating and channeling energy to restore balance and harmony within the individual's energetic system. They employed techniques such as laying on of hands, energy clearing, and balancing the chakras to facilitate the flow of vital energies and remove energetic blockages.

Rituals and Ceremonies: Rituals were performed to address the spiritual and emotional aspects of illness. These ceremonies aimed to invoke spiritual forces, cleanse the energy field, and restore harmony within the individual and their relationship with the divine. Rituals often involved the use of sacred objects, incantations, and invocations to facilitate healing and transformation.

Spiritual Guidance and Counseling: Shamans provided spiritual guidance, counseling, and emotional support to individuals experiencing illness. Through their deep connection with the spiritual realm, shamans offered insights, wisdom, and perspective to help individuals navigate their healing journey and address the underlying spiritual and emotional causes of their ailments.

Exercise 1: Reflect on a personal ailment or health issue you have experienced. Use the techniques of intuitive insight, divination, and observation to gain a deeper understanding of the possible energetic and spiritual causes of the ailment. Consider how this understanding can inform your approach to healing and well-being.

Problem 1: Compare the diagnostic and treatment methods used in Babylonian shamanism with other ancient healing traditions, such as Ayurveda, Traditional Chinese Medicine, or Native American healing practices. Analyze the similarities and differences, and discuss how these diverse approaches contribute to a holistic understanding of health and wellness.

By studying the shamanic diagnosis and treatment methods in ancient Babylon, engaging in the provided exercise, and reflecting on the associated problem, you will gain valuable insights into the interconnectedness of body, mind, and spirit in the context of healing. This knowledge will empower you to approach health and wellness from a holistic perspective and explore integrative approaches that encompass the physical, energetic, emotional, and spiritual dimensions of well-being.

1. Understanding the concept of spiritual illness

In ancient Babylonian culture, the concept of illness extended beyond the physical realm and encompassed the spiritual dimensions of human existence. The Babylonians recognized that spiritual imbalances and disharmony could manifest as physical, emotional, and mental ailments. In this section, we will delve into the concept of spiritual illness in Babylonian belief systems and explore how it influenced their approach to healing and well-being.

Definition and Characteristics of Spiritual Illness:

Spiritual illness in Babylonian culture referred to disturbances or imbalances in the individual's spiritual well-being. It was believed that disruptions in the relationship between the individual and the divine or spiritual realm could lead to various forms of illness. Spiritual illness was characterized by symptoms such as:

Loss of Vitality: Spiritual illness often resulted in a diminished sense of vitality, energy, and enthusiasm for life. Individuals experiencing spiritual imbalance may feel drained, disconnected, or lacking purpose and meaning.

Emotional Turmoil: Spiritual imbalances could give rise to emotional distress, including feelings of sadness, anxiety, anger, or apathy. These emotions were seen as indicators of disharmony within the individual's spiritual self.

Lack of Clarity and Purpose: Spiritual illness could manifest as a sense of confusion, uncertainty, or a loss of direction in life. Individuals may feel disconnected from their true purpose and struggle to find meaning and fulfillment.

Understanding the Causes of Spiritual Illness:

According to Babylonian belief systems, spiritual illness could arise from various sources:

Spiritual Imbalances: Disharmony between the individual and the spiritual realm, including deities and ancestral spirits, could result in spiritual illness. Lack of proper rituals, neglect of spiritual practices, or offenses committed against the divine could disrupt the harmonious relationship and lead to spiritual imbalances.

Spiritual Interference: Babylonians believed that malevolent spirits or supernatural forces could inflict spiritual illness on individuals. These forces were seen as causing disruptions in the energetic and spiritual realms, leading to physical and psychological manifestations of illness.

Karmic Influences: The concept of karma played a role in Babylonian belief systems. It was believed that spiritual illness could be a consequence of past actions or unresolved karmic debts. Individuals experiencing spiritual illness were encouraged to reflect on their actions and seek ways to restore balance and harmony.

Addressing Spiritual Illness:

Babylonian shamans played a crucial role in addressing spiritual illness and restoring spiritual well-being. Their practices included:

Rituals and Offerings: Shamans performed rituals and offered prayers, invocations, and sacrifices to appease the deities and ancestral spirits, seeking their intervention and healing. These rituals aimed to restore balance and harmony in the spiritual realm.

Energy Clearing and Cleansing: Shamans utilized various techniques to clear and cleanse the individual's energetic field, removing spiritual intrusions or negative influences. Energy healing, aura cleansing, and spiritual baths were among the methods employed to address spiritual imbalances.

Soul Retrieval: In cases where spiritual illness was believed to be caused by the loss or fragmentation of the soul, shamans engaged in soul retrieval practices. Through journeying into the spiritual realms, shamans sought to locate and reintegrate the lost aspects of the individual's soul, facilitating healing and wholeness.

Exercise 1: Reflect on moments in your life when you have experienced symptoms of spiritual illness, such as loss of vitality, emotional turmoil, or lack of clarity. Consider possible spiritual imbalances or disturbances that may have contributed to these symptoms. Explore ways in which you can restore balance and harmony within your spiritual self.

Problem 1: Compare the concept of spiritual illness in ancient Babylonian culture with similar concepts found in other ancient healing systems, such as Ayurveda or Traditional Chinese Medicine. Analyze the similarities and differences in their understanding of spiritual imbalances and their approaches to healing.

By studying the concept of spiritual illness in ancient Babylonian culture, engaging in the provided exercise, and reflecting on the associated problem, you will gain valuable insights into the interconnectedness of spiritual and physical well-being. This knowledge will empower you to recognize and address spiritual imbalances in your own life and explore practices that promote holistic healing and spiritual growth.

2. Techniques for identifying and addressing spiritual imbalances

In ancient Babylonian culture, the identification and addressing of spiritual imbalances were fundamental aspects of maintaining holistic well-being. The Babylonians believed that spiritual imbalances could manifest as physical, emotional, and mental ailments, and thus, it was crucial to identify and address these imbalances to restore harmony and promote overall health. In this section, we will explore some of the techniques employed by Babylonian shamans to identify and address spiritual imbalances.

Technique 1: Divination and Spiritual Diagnosis

Babylonian shamans utilized divinatory practices to gain insights into the spiritual realm and diagnose spiritual imbalances. They employed various forms of divination, such as dream interpretation, omen reading, and casting lots, to receive guidance and identify the underlying spiritual causes of illness. For example, interpreting symbols and narratives in dreams allowed shamans to discern hidden truths and messages from the divine realm. By understanding the significance of omens and signs in natural phenomena, they could determine the presence of spiritual influences affecting an individual's well-being. Divinatory practices helped shamans uncover the root causes of spiritual imbalances and guide their subsequent healing interventions.

Technique 2: Energy Assessment and Aura Reading

Babylonian shamans were skilled in assessing the energetic and aura fields of individuals to identify spiritual imbalances. They believed that disruptions in the flow of spiritual energy could lead to disharmony and illness. By observing the colors, patterns, and intensity of an individual's aura, shamans could gain insights into the energetic imbalances present. They would also use their intuitive abilities to sense blockages or disturbances within the energetic field. Through this assessment, shamans could pinpoint areas of spiritual imbalance and target their healing efforts accordingly. Techniques such as aura cleansing, energy clearing, and chakra balancing were employed to restore the harmonious flow of spiritual energy.

Technique 3: Ancestral and Past-Life Healing

The Babylonians recognized the influence of ancestral and past-life experiences on an individual's spiritual well-being. They believed that unresolved issues or traumas from previous generations or past lives could contribute to present-day imbalances. To address these imbalances, Babylonian shamans engaged in ancestral and past-life healing practices. They would enter altered states of consciousness to journey into the spiritual realms, seeking guidance and insights from ancestral spirits and accessing past-life memories. By bringing awareness to these unresolved issues and facilitating their healing, shamans aimed to restore balance and promote spiritual well-being.

Exercise 1: Reflect on your own life and experiences. Are there recurring patterns or challenges that you believe may stem from spiritual imbalances? Use divinatory tools, such as tarot cards or rune stones, to gain insights into the underlying spiritual causes of these patterns. Alternatively, practice aura meditation to assess the state of your energetic field and identify areas that may require attention and healing.

Problem 1: Research and compare the techniques used for identifying and addressing spiritual imbalances in ancient Babylonian culture with those found in other indigenous healing traditions, such as Native American spirituality or African shamanism. Analyze the similarities and differences in their approaches and evaluate the effectiveness of these techniques in promoting spiritual well-being.

By exploring the techniques for identifying and addressing spiritual imbalances in ancient Babylonian practices, engaging in the provided exercise, and reflecting on the associated problem, you will gain a deeper understanding of the interconnectedness between spiritual and physical health. This knowledge will empower you to recognize and address spiritual imbalances in your own life and guide you towards practices that promote healing, growth, and spiritual alignment.

V. Cultural and Social Context of Shamanism in Ancient Babylon

In the ancient civilization of Babylon, shamanism held a prominent role in the religious, social, and cultural fabric of the society. Shamanism, an ancient spiritual practice found in various cultures around the world, encompassed a wide range of beliefs and practices centered around the interaction between the human and spiritual realms. In this section, we will delve into the cultural and social context of shamanism in ancient Babylon, exploring the significance of this spiritual tradition within the broader Babylonian culture.

Historical Background

To fully understand the cultural and social context of shamanism in ancient Babylon, we must first explore the historical background of the civilization. The city of Babylon, located in Mesopotamia (modern-day Iraq), was a thriving hub of civilization during the second and first millennia BCE. Known for its advanced knowledge in various fields such as astronomy, mathematics, and literature, Babylon was also home to a rich spiritual heritage. The Babylonians worshiped a pantheon of deities and engaged in elaborate religious practices, with shamanism playing a significant role alongside other religious traditions.

Role of the Shaman in Babylonian Society

Within Babylonian society, the shaman held a unique and revered position. The shaman, also known as the "asipu" or "apkallu," served as a spiritual intermediary, bridging the gap between the human and divine realms. They possessed deep knowledge of the spiritual and natural worlds, acting as healers, diviners, and guides. The shaman's ability to communicate with deities, ancestral spirits, and other non-ordinary beings allowed them to provide vital services to the community, including healing, divination, and spiritual guidance.

Rituals and Ceremonies

Shamanic rituals and ceremonies were integral to Babylonian society. These rituals were conducted to address various needs, such as healing, protection, and ensuring favorable outcomes in agricultural endeavors. Babylonian shamans performed complex and intricate rituals, utilizing a combination of chants, incantations, invocations, and sacred objects. Through these rituals, the shaman established connections with the spiritual realm and invoked divine forces to bring about desired outcomes. Examples of Babylonian rituals include purification ceremonies, spirit communication rituals, and seasonal celebrations.

Community and Belief Systems

Shamanism in ancient Babylon was deeply intertwined with the communal and belief systems of the society. The Babylonians viewed the spiritual realm as an integral part of their daily lives, seeking the guidance and assistance of spiritual beings in various aspects, including personal well-being, fertility, and protection. The shaman, as a trusted and respected figure, played a crucial role in maintaining the spiritual well-being of the community and ensuring its prosperity.

Conclusion:

Understanding the cultural and social context of shamanism in ancient Babylon provides us with valuable insights into the significance of this spiritual tradition within the broader Babylonian culture. The role of the shaman, the performance of rituals and ceremonies, and the communal beliefs surrounding spiritual practices all contributed to a rich and complex tapestry of spiritual life in ancient Babylon. By delving into these cultural and social aspects, we gain a deeper appreciation for the role of shamanism in shaping the spiritual landscape of this ancient civilization.

Exercise 1: Research and compare the cultural and social contexts of shamanism in ancient Babylon with those in other ancient civilizations, such as Ancient Egypt or Ancient Greece. Identify similarities and differences in their beliefs, practices, and societal roles of shamans.

Problem 1: Discuss the potential challenges faced by Babylonian shamans in a society where other religious practices coexisted. Analyze how the cultural and social dynamics of ancient Babylon influenced the perception and acceptance of shamanism within the broader religious framework.

By exploring the cultural and social context of shamanism in ancient Babylon, engaging in the provided exercise, and reflecting on the associated problem, you will gain a comprehensive understanding of how shamanism operated within the complex cultural and social dynamics of the Babylonian civilization. This knowledge will deepen your appreciation for the role of shamanism as a significant spiritual tradition and enable you to critically analyze its place within different cultural contexts.

A. Relationship between shamanism and religious beliefs in Babylon

Shamanism, as a spiritual tradition, coexisted alongside other religious practices in ancient Babylon. In this section, we will explore the relationship between shamanism and the broader religious beliefs of the Babylonian civilization, shedding light on the intricate dynamics that shaped their spiritual landscape.

Shamanism as a Complementary Practice:

Shamanism in ancient Babylon was not a separate religious system but rather an integral part of the overall religious framework. While Babylonians worshipped a pantheon of deities and engaged in organized rituals, shamanism provided a unique approach to spiritual connection and interaction. Shamans acted as intermediaries between the human and divine realms, complementing the established religious practices by offering specialized services such as healing, divination, and spirit communication.

Incorporation of Shamanic Elements into Official Religion:

The Babylonian religious system integrated certain shamanic elements into its official practices. For instance, certain rituals performed by shamans, such as purification ceremonies and spirit communication rituals, found their place within the established religious calendar. This integration allowed for a more holistic understanding and expression of spirituality, encompassing both organized religious practices and the shamanic approach.

Shamanic Influence on Religious Art and Iconography:

The influence of shamanism on religious art and iconography is evident in Babylonian culture. Depictions of shamans engaged in rituals, wearing distinctive ceremonial attire, and holding sacred objects can be found in various forms of artistic expression. These depictions highlight the significance of shamanism within the visual representation of religious beliefs and practices.

Shared Cosmological Concepts:

Shamanism in ancient Babylon shared certain cosmological concepts with the broader religious beliefs. The Babylonians believed in a hierarchical structure of the spiritual realm, with multiple gods and spirits exerting influence over different aspects of the natural and human world. Shamans, through their spiritual practices, accessed these realms and sought guidance from divine beings, aligning with the cosmological framework of Babylonian religious beliefs.

Interactions and Dialogue between Shamans and Priestly Class:

The relationship between shamans and the priestly class in ancient Babylon was complex. While both groups held distinct roles and functions within the religious hierarchy, there was likely interaction and exchange of knowledge between them. Shamans brought their unique experiences, practices, and insights to the table, enriching the overall understanding of the spiritual realm. Likewise, priests may have acknowledged the efficacy of shamanic techniques and incorporated them into their own practices.

Exercise 1: Compare the relationship between shamanism and religious beliefs in ancient Babylon with another ancient civilization, such as ancient Egypt or ancient Greece. Identify similarities and differences in how shamanic practices were integrated or coexisted with the established religious systems of these cultures.

Problem 1: Explore the potential conflicts or tensions that may have arisen between the shamanic practitioners and the religious establishment in ancient Babylon. Analyze the factors that could have influenced the acceptance or rejection of shamanic practices within the religious framework, and discuss the implications for the shamanic community.

By examining the relationship between shamanism and religious beliefs in ancient Babylon, engaging in the provided exercise, and reflecting on the associated problem, you will develop a comprehensive understanding of how shamanism operated within the broader religious context. This knowledge will enable you to critically analyze the interplay between spiritual traditions and establish connections between different aspects of ancient Babylonian culture.

B. Shamanic practices in Babylonian society

Shamanic practices held a significant role in the religious and spiritual fabric of Babylonian society. In this section, we will explore the diverse range of shamanic practices that were prevalent in ancient Babylon, shedding light on their functions, rituals, and cultural significance.

Shamanic Healing and Spiritual Guidance:

Shamans in Babylon served as healers and spiritual guides, addressing physical, emotional, and spiritual ailments. They employed various techniques such as energy healing, herbal remedies, and divination to restore balance and well-being. Through their unique abilities to connect with the spirit realm, shamans offered insights, guidance, and even prophecy to individuals seeking answers and support.

Rituals for Spirit Communication:

Babylonian shamans conducted rituals to establish communication with deities, ancestral spirits, and non-ordinary beings. By entering an altered state of consciousness through rhythmic drumming, chanting, or other techniques, shamans journeyed to the spirit realm. Offerings, invocations, and specific rituals were performed to invoke the presence of the spirits and establish a channel of communication. Through these rituals, shamans received messages, guidance, and divinatory insights from the spiritual realm.

Divination and Prophecy:

Shamanic divination played a crucial role in Babylonian society. Shamans employed various methods, such as dream interpretation, omen reading, and casting of lots, to gain insights into hidden truths, future events, and receive guidance from the divine realm. Divination provided individuals and leaders with valuable information for decision-making, understanding the future, and navigating their lives in alignment with spiritual forces.

Rituals for Purification and Sacred Space Creation:

Purification rituals were performed by shamans to cleanse individuals, objects, or spaces of negative energies or spiritual impurities. These rituals aimed to restore spiritual balance, create sacred environments, and prepare individuals for further shamanic practices. By using water, incense, or sacred herbs, shamans recited invocations, sprinkled or bathed participants with purifying substances, and employed specific gestures to cleanse and sanctify individuals or spaces symbolically.

Shamanic Journeys and Altered States of Consciousness:

Shamans in Babylon utilized various techniques to enter altered states of consciousness, enabling them to journey into the spirit realm. Rhythmic drumming, chanting, dancing, or specific rituals facilitated this state. Through these practices, shamans accessed spiritual realms, sought guidance, and brought back knowledge and healing energies for the benefit of individuals and the community.

Exercise 1: Reflect on the role of shamanic practices in fostering communal well-being and spiritual connection in Babylonian society. Discuss how these practices contributed to the cohesion and harmony of the community, and explore their impact on individual and collective spiritual growth.

Problem 1: Investigate the potential challenges and ethical considerations faced by Babylonian shamans in their practice. Discuss the balance between personal power and responsibility, potential abuses of shamanic authority, and the importance of maintaining integrity and ethical conduct within the shamanic community.

By studying the diverse range of shamanic practices in Babylonian society, engaging in the provided exercise, and reflecting on the associated problem, you will develop a comprehensive understanding of the functions, rituals, and cultural significance of shamanic practices in ancient Babylon. This knowledge will enable you to critically analyze the impact of shamanism on individuals, communities, and the broader cultural landscape of ancient Babylon.

C. Roles and status of shamans within the community

Shamans held a revered and respected position within Babylonian society, playing vital roles in the religious, spiritual, and social fabric of the community. In this section, we will explore the various roles and the esteemed status that shamans occupied in ancient Babylon.

Spiritual Guides and Healers:

Shamans were considered spiritual guides and healers, responsible for addressing the physical, emotional, and spiritual well-being of individuals and the community as a whole. They possessed specialized knowledge and skills in herbalism, energy healing, divination, and other shamanic practices. Through their abilities to connect with the spirit realm, shamans facilitated healing, provided spiritual guidance, and assisted individuals in navigating life's challenges.

Intermediaries with the Divine:

Shamans served as intermediaries between the human realm and the realm of deities, ancestral spirits, and other non-ordinary beings. They possessed the ability to establish communication and receive messages from the spiritual realm. By conducting rituals, invocations, and divinatory practices, shamans sought guidance and insights from divine entities. They played a crucial role in interpreting signs and omens, offering prophetic insights, and facilitating divine communication for individuals and the community.

Guardians of Rituals and Ceremonies:

Shamans were entrusted with the preservation and performance of sacred rituals and ceremonies within Babylonian society. They conducted ceremonies for seasonal celebrations, agricultural cycles, initiations, and other significant events. Shamans ensured the proper execution of rituals, maintained the sacredness of the ceremonies, and upheld the spiritual traditions of the community. They held the knowledge of sacred chants, invocations, and rituals, passing them down through generations.

Advisors and Problem Solvers:

Shamans served as advisors and problem solvers, offering guidance and solutions to individuals and leaders facing dilemmas or challenges. Their divinatory abilities, knowledge of herbal remedies, and spiritual insights allowed them to assist in decision-making processes, conflict resolution, and the pursuit of harmony within the community. Shamans were sought after for their wisdom and ability to access hidden knowledge.

Cultural Preservers and Teachers:

Shamans played a significant role in preserving and transmitting cultural knowledge, myths, and traditions. They served as repositories of ancient wisdom, passing down rituals, chants, and spiritual practices from one generation to the next. Shamans were responsible for educating apprentices and community members in shamanic practices, ensuring the continuity of spiritual knowledge and the preservation of cultural heritage.

Exercise 1: Reflect on the roles of shamans within Babylonian society and their impact on individual and community well-being. Discuss the importance of spiritual leadership, healing, and guidance provided by shamans in promoting harmony, growth, and cultural continuity.

Problem 1: Analyze the potential challenges and criticisms faced by shamans in their roles within Babylonian society. Consider the balance between personal power and community responsibility, the potential for abuse of authority, and the need for ethical conduct within the shamanic profession.

By studying the roles and status of shamans within the Babylonian community, engaging in the provided exercise, and reflecting on the associated problem, you will gain a comprehensive understanding of the significance of shamans and their contributions to the spiritual, social, and cultural life of ancient Babylon. This knowledge will enable you to critically analyze the complexities and dynamics of shamanic roles and their impact on individuals, communities, and the broader cultural landscape.

VI. Legacy and Influences of Babylonian Shamanism

Babylonian shamanism has left a lasting legacy that continues to shape and influence various aspects of spirituality, healing practices, and cultural traditions. In this section, we will explore the profound impact of Babylonian shamanism and its enduring contributions to different fields.

Spiritual and Healing Practices:

The rich spiritual and healing practices of Babylonian shamanism have had a lasting influence on various spiritual traditions. For example, the concept of spirit communication, divination, and dream interpretation found in Babylonian shamanism can be seen in contemporary practices of mediumship, psychic readings, and intuitive healing. Similarly, the use of herbal remedies and plant-based medicine in Babylonian healing has influenced modern herbalism and alternative medicine practices.

Ritual and Ceremonial Traditions:

The rituals and ceremonies performed by Babylonian shamans have inspired and influenced ceremonial practices in many cultures throughout history. Elements such as chanting, drumming, dancing, and invocations are still present in rituals performed in contemporary spiritual traditions, including Witchcraft, Ecospirituality, and shamanic practices worldwide. The focus on creating sacred space, connecting with divine energies, and honoring ancestral spirits can be traced back to the foundation of Babylonian shamanic rituals.

Divination and Prophecy:

The divinatory practices of Babylonian shamans have had a profound impact on the development of divination systems across different cultures and time periods. The use of symbols, omens, and oracles to gain insights into the future and seek guidance from the spiritual realm can be observed in various forms of divination, such as tarot card readings, astrology, and rune casting. The art of interpreting signs and symbols, which was integral to Babylonian divination, continues to be practiced today.

Mythology and Cosmology:

Babylonian shamanism contributed to the development of mythology and cosmology in ancient Mesopotamia. The stories, myths, and cosmological beliefs of the Babylonians had a profound influence on subsequent mythological systems, including those found in ancient Greece, Egypt, and other civilizations. Elements of Babylonian mythology, such as the gods and goddesses, celestial symbolism, and the concept of the underworld, have resonated throughout history and continue to inspire modern mythological and spiritual frameworks.

Exercise 1: Research and explore the influence of Babylonian shamanism on a specific modern spiritual or healing practice of your choice. Examine the similarities, adaptations, and innovations that have occurred over time and discuss how Babylonian shamanism has contributed to the development and evolution of the chosen practice.

Problem 1: Critically evaluate the potential cultural appropriation and ethical considerations associated with the incorporation and adaptation of Babylonian shamanic practices in modern spiritual and healing traditions. Discuss the importance of cultural sensitivity, respectful engagement, and the need for informed understanding when integrating elements from ancient traditions into contemporary practices.

By studying the legacy and influences of Babylonian shamanism, engaging in the provided exercise, and reflecting on the associated problem, you will gain a comprehensive understanding of the enduring impact of Babylonian shamanism on diverse spiritual, healing, and cultural traditions. This knowledge will enable you to appreciate the historical and cultural significance of Babylonian shamanism while fostering a critical and respectful approach to its influences in modern practices.

A. Influence of Babylonian shamanism on later civilizations

The practices and beliefs of Babylonian shamanism have had a profound influence on later civilizations, shaping spiritual, cultural, and healing traditions across different regions and time periods. In this section, we will explore the significant impact of Babylonian shamanism on the development of various civilizations and the enduring legacy it left behind.

Ancient Greece and Rome:

Babylonian shamanism had a significant impact on the ancient Greek and Roman civilizations. The Greeks were exposed to Mesopotamian culture through trade and contact, which influenced their own religious and mythological beliefs. The concept of divine communication and oracles in Babylonian shamanism greatly influenced the Greek practice of consulting oracles, such as the famous Oracle of Delphi. Additionally, Babylonian cosmological beliefs and astrological practices were assimilated into Greek and Roman astrology.

Mesopotamian Legacy:

The influence of Babylonian shamanism extended within the Mesopotamian region itself. Babylonian culture and religious practices were adopted and adapted by subsequent civilizations that emerged in the area, including the Assyrians and Persians. Elements such as divination, dream interpretation, and ritual practices were incorporated into the religious and spiritual traditions of these civilizations.

Magical and Occult Traditions:

Babylonian shamanism provided a foundation for the development of magical and occult practices in later civilizations. The use of incantations, spells, and rituals for purposes such as healing, protection, and divination found in Babylonian shamanism influenced the magical traditions of ancient Egypt, Greece, and Rome. For example, the Greek Magical Papyri, a collection of magical spells and rituals, exhibits strong Babylonian influences.

Western Esotericism:

Babylonian shamanism contributed to the development of Western esoteric traditions. The mystical and spiritual concepts present in Babylonian cosmology, divination, and spirit communication served as precursors to the mystical systems of Hermeticism, Kabbalah, and Gnosticism. These systems incorporated elements from Babylonian shamanism and fused them with other mystical and philosophical ideas, shaping the foundations of Western esoteric thought.

Exercise 1: Research and explore the influence of Babylonian shamanism on a specific civilization or spiritual tradition of your choice. Examine the historical and cultural connections, identify the specific elements borrowed or adapted, and discuss the impact of Babylonian shamanism on the development and practices of the chosen civilization or tradition.

Problem 1: Discuss the potential challenges and controversies associated with tracing the influence of Babylonian shamanism on later civilizations. Consider factors such as cultural assimilation, adaptation, and reinterpretation of spiritual practices across different time periods and regions. Analyze differing perspectives on the extent and significance of Babylonian shamanism's influence, and critically evaluate the evidence and arguments presented.

By studying the influence of Babylonian shamanism on later civilizations, engaging in the provided exercise, and reflecting on the associated problem, you will gain a comprehensive understanding of the enduring impact and cultural diffusion of Babylonian shamanism. This knowledge will allow you to appreciate the interconnectedness of ancient spiritual traditions and their continued influence on diverse cultures throughout history.

B. Survival of shamanic elements in contemporary cultures

The rich tapestry of shamanic practices has persisted throughout history and continues to thrive in various contemporary cultures around the world. Despite the influence of modernization and globalization, shamanic elements have managed to survive and adapt, demonstrating their enduring relevance and power. In this section, we will explore the survival of shamanic traditions in different cultural contexts and the ways in which they have been integrated into contemporary practices.

Indigenous Cultures:

Many indigenous cultures have successfully preserved their shamanic traditions despite the pressures of modernization. Examples include the indigenous tribes of the Amazon rainforest, Siberian nomadic communities, and Native American tribes. These cultures have safeguarded their shamanic practices through oral traditions, initiation rituals, and the transmission of knowledge from one generation to the next. Shamanic elements, such as healing ceremonies, spirit communication, and connection to nature, remain integral to their cultural and spiritual identity.

Neo-Shamanism:

Neo-shamanism refers to contemporary movements that draw inspiration from traditional shamanic practices and adapt them to modern contexts. It emerged in the latter half of the 20th century as a response to a longing for spiritual connection and a reawakening of indigenous wisdom. Neo-shamanism incorporates various elements, such as journeying, energy healing, and working with plant medicines, into its practices. Examples of neo-shamanic traditions include Core Shamanism and the Foundation for Shamanic Studies, which seek to make shamanic teachings accessible to a broader audience.

Ecospirituality and Earth-Based Traditions:

In the face of environmental challenges, there has been a resurgence of interest in ecospirituality and earth-based traditions. These movements emphasize the interconnectedness between humans and the natural world, drawing inspiration from shamanic practices. Practices such as nature-based rituals, earth-centered ceremonies, and plant spirit communication are integral to these traditions. By honoring and reconnecting with the natural world, individuals seek to restore harmony and balance, fostering a deeper sense of ecological consciousness.

Exercise 1: Research and explore a contemporary culture or spiritual movement that incorporates shamanic elements into its practices. Examine how shamanic traditions are integrated, the specific rituals or techniques employed, and the purpose and significance of these practices within the cultural or spiritual context. Reflect on the ways in which shamanic elements contribute to the overall worldview and spiritual experiences of the community.

Problem 1: Critically analyze the challenges and controversies associated with the adoption and adaptation of shamanic elements in contemporary cultures. Consider issues of cultural appropriation, the commercialization of shamanic practices, and the potential dilution or misrepresentation of indigenous traditions. Reflect on the ethical considerations surrounding the appropriation and adaptation of shamanic elements, and engage in a discussion on the importance of cultural sensitivity and respectful engagement.

By studying the survival of shamanic elements in contemporary cultures, engaging in the provided exercise, and reflecting on the associated problem, you will develop a comprehensive understanding of the ways in which shamanic traditions have evolved and been incorporated into diverse cultural and spiritual contexts. This knowledge will enable you to appreciate the resilience and adaptability of shamanic practices while critically examining the ethical implications and complexities surrounding their contemporary expressions.

C. Relevance and lessons from Babylonian shamanism in the modern world

Babylonian shamanism, with its rich tapestry of rituals, practices, and spiritual beliefs, continues to offer valuable insights and lessons that resonate with the modern world. Despite the passage of time and the evolution of human society, the wisdom and teachings derived from Babylonian shamanism remain relevant in several areas, including personal growth, ecological consciousness, and spiritual connection. In this section, we will explore the relevance of Babylonian shamanism in the modern world and the valuable lessons it offers to individuals and communities today.

Personal Growth and Self-Discovery:

Babylonian shamanism emphasizes the importance of self-exploration, self-awareness, and personal growth. Through practices such as shamanic journeying, dream interpretation, and divination, individuals can gain insights into their inner selves, discover hidden talents, and overcome personal challenges. The techniques used in

Babylonian shamanism can be adapted and applied in contemporary contexts to facilitate personal growth, healing, and self-discovery.

Exercise 1: Engage in a shamanic journey using modern adaptations of Babylonian techniques. Reflect on your experience and document any insights, messages, or personal growth you encountered during the journey. Explore how these insights can be applied to your daily life and personal goals.

Ecological Consciousness and Sustainability:

Babylonian shamanism promotes a deep connection with nature and recognizes the interdependence between humans and the natural world. This ecological consciousness is particularly relevant in today's world, where environmental challenges and the need for sustainable practices are of utmost importance. By embracing the ecological wisdom embedded in Babylonian shamanism, individuals can cultivate a greater sense of responsibility toward the Earth, fostering sustainable living practices and promoting environmental stewardship.

Exercise 2: Conduct research on traditional ecological knowledge within Babylonian shamanism and its relevance to contemporary ecological issues. Reflect on how this wisdom can inform and inspire sustainable actions in your daily life, such as reducing your ecological footprint, supporting local and organic farming practices, and engaging in conservation efforts.

Spiritual Connection and Transpersonal Experiences:

Babylonian shamanism provides a framework for deepening spiritual connection and experiencing transpersonal states of consciousness. The rituals, chants, and divination techniques used in Babylonian shamanism can serve as pathways to accessing higher realms of consciousness and connecting with the divine. In the modern world, individuals seeking spiritual growth and expanded awareness can draw inspiration from these practices to foster their own spiritual connection and engage in transpersonal experiences.

Exercise 3: Explore meditation or other spiritual practices inspired by Babylonian shamanism. Document your experiences and reflections on any spiritual insights, connections, or transcendent states you encounter. Discuss how these experiences can enrich your spiritual journey and provide a deeper understanding of your own spirituality.

By recognizing the relevance and lessons from Babylonian shamanism in the modern world, engaging in the provided exercises, and reflecting on the topics presented, We can integrate the wisdom and practices of Babylonian shamanism into their personal and spiritual lives. Through this process, they will not only expand their understanding of ancient traditions but also cultivate a deeper connection with themselves, the natural world, and the spiritual dimensions of existence.

Problem 1: Analyze and discuss potential ethical considerations related to the appropriation and commercialization of Babylonian shamanism in the modern world. Consider the importance of cultural sensitivity, respect for indigenous knowledge, and the potential impact on the integrity and authenticity of ancient traditions. Engage in a balanced and objective exploration of differing perspectives on these issues.

By critically examining the relevance and lessons from Babylonian shamanism in the modern world, as well as engaging with the provided problem, We will develop a well-rounded understanding of how ancient wisdom can inform and enrich contemporary spiritual practices. They will also develop the critical thinking skills necessary to navigate the complexities and ethical considerations surrounding the incorporation of ancient traditions into the modern context.

Chapter 2: Ecospirituality in Ancient Babylon

In ancient Babylon, the spiritual beliefs and practices of its inhabitants were intricately woven into their relationship with the natural world. The concept of ecospirituality, which recognizes the profound interconnection between spirituality and the environment, finds its roots in the ancient wisdom of Babylonian civilization. In this section, we will delve into the fascinating realm of ecospirituality in ancient Babylon, exploring how the Babylonians' spiritual beliefs and practices were intimately tied to their understanding and reverence for nature.

Understanding Ecospirituality:

Ecospirituality is a concept that recognizes the inherent spiritual significance of the natural world and highlights the interconnectedness between humans and the Earth. It encompasses the belief that the divine or sacred can be encountered and comprehended through a deep connection with the natural world, and that spiritual growth is intricately tied to the preservation and sustainable stewardship of the environment.

In the context of Babylonian cosmology, the notion of ecospirituality was deeply ingrained. Babylonians held a profound reverence for the natural world and perceived it as a sacred manifestation of the divine. Their cosmological beliefs depicted a sacred interconnectedness between the heavens, the Earth, and the underworld, establishing a holistic understanding of the universe.

According to Babylonian cosmology, the celestial bodies, such as the sun, moon, planets, and stars, were regarded as divine entities with immense power and influence. They were seen as celestial deities who guided and shaped human destiny. The movements and positions of these celestial bodies were interpreted as divine messages, offering guidance and insight into human affairs. This understanding fostered a deep appreciation for the celestial realm and its role in the interconnected web of existence.

In addition to the celestial bodies, Babylonians recognized the Earth as a sacred and vital component of their cosmology. The rivers, mountains, forests, and other natural landscapes were revered as dwelling places of spirits and deities. Babylonians believed that these natural elements possessed spiritual energies and were imbued with the presence of divine beings. They considered the Earth as a sacred vessel that sustained and nurtured life, emphasizing the interdependence between humans and the natural world.

The Babylonian culture celebrated rituals and practices that honored the Earth and its natural abundance. These rituals involved offerings, prayers, and acts of gratitude to express reverence for the land, water, and flora. Babylonians recognized the importance of maintaining a harmonious relationship with the environment, understanding that the well-being of both humans and the Earth depended on sustainable coexistence.

The concept of ecospirituality in Babylonian cosmology resonated with the belief that spiritual growth and enlightenment were intimately connected to the preservation and responsible stewardship of the environment. By actively participating in the preservation of the natural world, individuals aligned themselves with divine principles and contributed to the well-being of the larger cosmic order.

The Babylonian understanding of ecospirituality offers a valuable example of how ancient cultures recognized and honored the spiritual significance of the natural world. It demonstrates that a deep connection with nature can serve as a pathway to encountering the divine and nurturing one's spiritual growth. The interplay between celestial entities, earthly elements, and human consciousness in Babylonian cosmology underscores the interconnectedness of all aspects of existence, reinforcing the importance of embracing an ecospiritual perspective in modern times.

In conclusion, ecospirituality, as a concept, acknowledges the spiritual value inherent in the natural world and emphasizes the interdependence between humans and the Earth. Babylonian cosmology exemplifies this understanding, with its recognition of the sacred interconnectedness between celestial bodies and the Earth. The Babylonian culture revered the natural world as a dwelling place of spirits and deities, fostering a deep appreciation for the environment and emphasizing the role of responsible stewardship. By studying Babylonian cosmology, we gain insights into the profound connection between spirituality and the preservation of the Earth, encouraging us to adopt an ecospiritual approach in our own lives.

Babylonian Cosmology and the Sacred Landscape:

Babylonian cosmology provided the ancient civilization with a comprehensive framework for understanding the intricate relationship between the spiritual and natural realms. At the heart of their cosmological beliefs was the recognition of a divine order permeating the cosmos, with each element contributing to the harmonious functioning of the universe. This worldview deeply influenced the Babylonians' perception of the natural world, which they regarded as a sacred manifestation of the divine.

In Babylonian cosmology, the universe was seen as a complex system where celestial bodies, earthly landscapes, and the spiritual realm were interconnected. The celestial bodies, such as the sun, moon, planets, and stars, were considered celestial deities, each with their own distinct powers and attributes. The movements and positions of these celestial entities were believed to influence the course of human events and shape the destiny of individuals and nations. By observing and interpreting celestial phenomena, such as eclipses and planetary alignments, the Babylonians sought to discern the will and intentions of the gods.

The natural landscapes of Babylon, including mountains, rivers, and trees, held immense spiritual significance in the cosmological framework of the Babylonians. They believed that gods and goddesses resided in specific natural features, and these divine entities were approached and revered through rituals and offerings conducted at these sacred sites. Mountains were seen as the abodes of the gods, serving as portals between the earthly and divine realms. Rivers, like the mighty Euphrates River, were regarded as sacred lifelines that nourished the land and sustained life. They were considered physical embodiments of divine forces, carrying the blessings and powers of the gods.

Trees, too, were considered sacred in Babylonian cosmology. The Babylonians believed that trees served as conduits of spiritual energy, acting as intermediaries between the earthly and divine realms. They attributed specific qualities and powers to different types of trees, associating them with particular gods or goddesses. It was common for the Babylonians to engage in rituals and ceremonies under the shade of sacred trees, seeking spiritual guidance and invoking the presence of divine forces.

This intricate interplay between the spiritual and natural realms in Babylonian cosmology reflected the deep reverence and respect the Babylonians had for the natural world. They recognized the Earth as a sacred domain intricately connected to the divine, viewing its various elements as conduits of spiritual energy and divine presence. By engaging with and honoring these natural features, the Babylonians sought to maintain the harmony and balance within the cosmos and establish a harmonious relationship between humanity and the gods.

Studying Babylonian cosmology provides us with valuable insights into the profound connection between the spiritual and natural realms in ancient civilizations. It demonstrates how the Babylonians perceived the natural world as a sacred manifestation of the divine, intertwining their spiritual practices and beliefs with their interactions with the environment. This understanding encourages us to foster a deep reverence for the natural world and recognize the interconnectedness of all life. By embracing the wisdom of Babylonian cosmology, we can cultivate a sense of awe and appreciation for the sacredness of the Earth, fostering a harmonious relationship between humanity and the natural world.

Rituals and Practices Celebrating Nature:

Babylonian culture was deeply rooted in a profound reverence for the natural world. Recognizing the inherent spiritual value of the Earth and its cycles, the Babylonians developed rich rituals and practices to honor and celebrate the interconnectedness between humanity and the environment. These rituals served multiple purposes, including invoking the blessings of deities, ensuring prosperous harvests, and fostering a harmonious relationship between humans and the natural world.

One prominent example of a Babylonian ritual that celebrated the interconnectedness of spirituality and the natural world was the Akitu festival. This annual festival, held in honor of the god Marduk, marked the beginning of the agricultural year and the renewal of cosmic and earthly cycles. The Akitu festival spanned several days and included a series of elaborate ceremonies and rituals, each carrying its own symbolic significance.

During the Akitu festival, the Babylonians engaged in acts of purification and renewal. They cleansed themselves and their surroundings, symbolizing the removal of impurities and the preparation for a fresh start. The ritualistic practices involved the use of water, incense, and sacred herbs to purify and sanctify the participants or the environment. Through these purification rituals, the Babylonians sought to restore spiritual balance and create a harmonious space in which the natural and spiritual realms could intermingle.

The Akitu festival also involved the performance of sacred dances, chants, and invocations. These activities were aimed at invoking the blessings of the gods and goddesses, and fostering a strong spiritual connection with the natural world. By engaging in rhythmic movements and reciting sacred words, the participants sought to align themselves with the cosmic forces and channel divine energies into their lives. This ritualistic practice emphasized the deep belief in the interconnectedness between humans, the divine, and the natural world.

In the context of modern ecospirituality, the Akitu festival offers valuable insights and inspiration. It reminds us of the importance of acknowledging and honoring the cycles of nature, and the role of rituals in cultivating a deep spiritual connection with the Earth. As an exercise, We can research the Akitu festival and analyze its significance in celebrating the interconnectedness of spirituality and the natural world. They can reflect on the various elements of the ritual and explore how they can be adapted and integrated into modern ecospiritual practices.

For example, We may consider incorporating purification rituals using water, incense, or sacred herbs into their personal rituals to cleanse and sanctify themselves and their sacred spaces. They can explore the use of sacred dances or invocations to deepen their connection with the natural world and invoke the blessings of the divine. By adapting and integrating elements of the Akitu festival, We can enrich their own ecospiritual practices and foster a greater sense of harmony, reverence, and interconnectedness with the Earth.

Studying Babylonian rituals and practices that celebrated the natural world provides us with a deeper understanding of the profound connection between spirituality and the environment in ancient cultures. It encourages us to reflect on our own relationship with the natural world and consider how we can incorporate rituals and practices that honor and celebrate the interconnectedness of spirituality and nature. By drawing inspiration from Babylonian culture, we can cultivate a greater sense of harmony, reverence, and stewardship towards the Earth in our modern ecospiritual journeys.

Sacred Texts and Ecological Wisdom:

Babylonian civilization produced a wealth of sacred texts that contain allegorical narratives conveying profound ecological wisdom and ethical principles related to human stewardship of the Earth. Among these texts, the Enuma Elish and the Atrahasis Epic stand out as remarkable examples that shed light on the Babylonians' understanding of their relationship with the natural world. These texts serve as invaluable sources of ecological knowledge and provide insight into the ethical considerations associated with living in harmony with nature.

The Enuma Elish, also known as the Babylonian Creation Epic, presents a cosmogonic account of the origins of the universe. Within its poetic verses, the text portrays a complex interplay between the divine and natural realms. It emphasizes the divine order and the interconnectedness of cosmic forces, as well as the vital role of each element in maintaining the equilibrium of the natural world. The Enuma Elish underscores the significance of respecting the natural order and the consequences of disrupting it.

Similarly, the Atrahasis Epic recounts the story of the Great Flood and the subsequent re-establishment of human civilization. This epic narrative illustrates the Babylonians' understanding of the delicate balance between humans and the environment. It highlights the consequences of environmental degradation and serves as a cautionary tale about the need for responsible human stewardship. The text emphasizes the importance of living in harmony with nature and preserving the delicate balance between human development and ecological well-being.

The allegorical narratives found in these sacred texts provide timeless lessons and ethical principles that are highly relevant to contemporary environmental challenges. By studying these texts, We can gain insights into the ecological wisdom of ancient Babylonian culture and apply this wisdom to address modern environmental issues.

To engage We in critical thinking and discussion, Problem 1 prompts them to explore the potential conflicts between urbanization and ecological values in ancient Babylon. We are encouraged to analyze the urban development of Babylon and its impact on the natural environment. They can consider the tensions that may have arisen between the expanding city and the preservation of ecological balance. This problem invites We to think deeply about the challenges associated with urbanization and the potential conflicts that arise when urban development neglects ecological considerations.

Furthermore, We are prompted to formulate strategies to address these challenges based on the principles of ecospirituality. By considering the principles of interconnectedness, respect for nature, and responsible stewardship, We can develop innovative approaches to reconcile modern urban development with ecological values. This problem encourages We to think critically, explore alternative perspectives, and propose practical solutions that align with the principles of ancient Babylonian ecospirituality.

By studying Babylonian sacred texts and engaging with the provided problem, We not only gain a deeper understanding of the historical foundations of ecospirituality but also develop the necessary skills to apply these principles to contemporary environmental challenges. They become equipped to navigate the complexities of the modern world, incorporating ecological wisdom and ethical considerations in their personal and professional lives. Through this exploration, We can contribute to the preservation and sustainable stewardship of the Earth, inspired by the ecological insights of ancient Babylonian culture.

A. Definition and understanding of ecospirituality

Ecospirituality is a multifaceted concept that encompasses the intersection of spirituality and environmental awareness. It recognizes the intrinsic value of the natural world and emphasizes the interconnectedness between humans, the Earth, and the divine. In this section, we will explore the definition and understanding of ecospirituality, its key components, and its relevance in the context of ancient Babylon.

Defining Ecospirituality:

Ecospirituality can be defined as a worldview and a way of life that recognizes the sacredness of the natural world and seeks to cultivate a harmonious relationship between humans and the Earth. It encompasses spiritual beliefs, practices, and values that promote environmental stewardship, ecological mindfulness, and reverence for all living beings.

Example: In ancient Babylon, ecospirituality was ingrained in the cultural fabric, where people recognized the interconnectedness of their spiritual beliefs with the rhythms and cycles of nature. They understood that the Earth was not merely a resource to exploit, but a sacred manifestation of the divine.

Interconnectedness and Unity:

At the heart of ecospirituality lies the recognition of the interconnectedness and unity of all life forms. It acknowledges that humans are an integral part of the web of life and that our actions reverberate throughout the natural world. Ecospirituality encourages individuals to cultivate a deep sense of respect, gratitude, and responsibility towards the Earth and its diverse ecosystems.

Example: Babylonian cosmology depicted the interconnectedness between the celestial, terrestrial, and subterranean realms. This cosmological understanding emphasized the interdependence of various elements and the importance of maintaining balance and harmony within the natural order.

Nature as Sacred:

Ecospirituality recognizes the sacredness inherent in the natural world. It views nature not merely as a physical realm, but as a source of inspiration, wisdom, and spiritual connection. Ecospiritual practices often involve immersing oneself in nature, observing its patterns, and experiencing a profound sense of awe and reverence.

Exercise 1: Engage in a nature observation exercise. Choose a natural setting, such as a forest, river, or garden, and spend time observing and reflecting on the intricate interconnectedness of the ecosystem. Document your observations and write a reflective essay on the spiritual insights and connections you have gained from this experience.

Environmental Stewardship:

Ecospirituality emphasizes the importance of environmental stewardship and responsible custodianship of the Earth. It calls for conscious and sustainable practices that minimize harm to the environment, promote ecological restoration, and support the well-being of all species.

Problem 1: Analyze the potential conflicts between economic development and ecological values in modern society. Investigate industries and practices that contribute to environmental degradation and explore alternative approaches that align with the principles of ecospirituality. Discuss the challenges and opportunities in integrating sustainable practices into economic systems.

Through exploring the definition and understanding of ecospirituality, We will gain a comprehensive understanding of this holistic worldview. They will recognize the interconnectedness between spirituality and the natural world and develop a deep appreciation for the sacredness of nature. By engaging in the provided exercise and problem, We will have the opportunity to apply their knowledge, cultivate a personal connection with nature, and critically analyze the challenges and possibilities of integrating ecospirituality into contemporary environmental practices.

B. Importance of the natural world in ancient Babylonian culture

The ancient Babylonian culture held a deep reverence for the natural world, considering it integral to their spiritual and everyday lives. In this section, we will explore the significance of the natural world in ancient Babylonian culture, its role in religious beliefs, societal practices, and the cultivation of a harmonious relationship between humans and nature.

Spiritual Significance:

In ancient Babylonian culture, the natural world occupied a central place in their spiritual beliefs and practices. The Babylonians held a profound reverence for the natural elements, recognizing their inherent sacredness and spiritual significance. They believed that these elements were not merely physical entities but were inhabited by divine beings, each carrying its own unique spiritual energy and power. Through their worship and rituals, the Babylonians sought to honor and connect with these divine forces, acknowledging their role as creators and sustainers of the world.

The Babylonians worshipped a diverse pantheon of gods and goddesses, each associated with specific aspects of nature. These deities represented the various forces and phenomena found in the natural world, including rivers, mountains, celestial bodies, and more. For the Babylonians, these deities were not distant or abstract figures but were intimately connected to the Earth and its elements. They believed that the gods and goddesses actively influenced and governed these natural realms, ensuring the harmony and balance of the universe.

One prominent example of a deity with a strong association to the natural world is Marduk, the Babylonian god of fertility and agriculture. Marduk was worshipped for his vital role in ensuring bountiful harvests and agricultural abundance. The Babylonians recognized the Earth's ability to provide sustenance and nurture humanity, and they attributed this fertility and abundance to the influence of Marduk. By honoring and offering prayers to Marduk, the Babylonians sought to maintain a harmonious relationship with the natural world, expressing gratitude for the Earth's generosity and seeking blessings for their agricultural endeavors.

This example illustrates the deep spiritual connection that the Babylonians forged with the natural world. Their belief in the divine presence within nature not only affirmed their interconnectedness with the Earth but also acknowledged the Earth's inherent capacity to sustain and provide for humanity. By recognizing and revering the spiritual essence of the natural elements, the Babylonians embraced a holistic worldview that emphasized the interdependence between humans and the environment.

Studying the spiritual significance of the natural world in ancient Babylonian culture allows We to explore the profound relationship between spirituality and nature. It provides insights into the Babylonians' deep appreciation for the Earth's sacredness and their understanding of humanity's interconnectedness with the natural world. This knowledge can inspire We to cultivate a greater reverence for the environment and develop a more profound sense of responsibility as stewards of the Earth. By reflecting on the Babylonians' spiritual practices and beliefs, We can gain a broader perspective on humanity's relationship with nature and explore ways to integrate these insights into their own spiritual journeys and environmental consciousness.

Agricultural Practices:

Agriculture formed the backbone of ancient Babylonian society, playing a central role in sustaining the population and shaping the cultural, economic, and social dynamics of the civilization. The Babylonians recognized the inherent connection between the natural world and their agricultural practices, understanding that the success of their crops relied on the fertility of the land and the availability of water.

The geographical location of Mesopotamia, between the Tigris and Euphrates rivers, provided the Babylonians with fertile lands ideally suited for agriculture. The annual flooding of these rivers deposited nutrient-rich sediments onto the surrounding plains, creating a fertile soil for crop cultivation. The Babylonians ingeniously harnessed this natural advantage, developing advanced irrigation systems to effectively manage water resources and maximize agricultural productivity.

Babylonian irrigation systems were a testament to their understanding of the importance of water management in sustaining their agricultural practices. The construction of canals, channels, and reservoirs allowed for the controlled distribution of water to fields, ensuring a consistent water supply for crops throughout the year. These irrigation systems played a crucial role in mitigating the effects of unpredictable rainfall patterns, allowing the Babylonians to cultivate a variety of crops and reduce the risks of drought and crop failure.

The effectiveness of Babylonian irrigation systems in supporting agricultural development cannot be understated. By efficiently utilizing water resources, the Babylonians were able to cultivate larger areas of land and achieve higher crop yields.

This, in turn, enabled them to sustain a growing population, support trade and economic activities, and establish thriving urban centers.

The success of Babylonian agriculture and its irrigation systems had far-reaching impacts on the social structure of the civilization. A surplus of agricultural produce created the foundation for a specialized labor force, as individuals could devote themselves to other pursuits beyond farming. This led to the development of complex social hierarchies, with artisans, merchants, priests, and rulers emerging alongside the agrarian communities.

Exercise 1: Research Babylonian irrigation systems and their impact on agricultural development. Write a report analyzing the techniques used, their effectiveness, and the role of these systems in sustaining the population and shaping the social structure of ancient Babylon.

In this exercise, We are encouraged to delve into the intricacies of Babylonian irrigation systems. They will explore the engineering techniques employed by the Babylonians, such as canal construction, water diversion, and reservoir management. We will analyze the effectiveness of these techniques in supporting agricultural productivity, examining the role of irrigation systems in sustaining the population and facilitating societal growth. Additionally, We will reflect on the impact of these systems on the social structure of ancient Babylon, considering how the availability of food surplus contributed to the emergence of specialized professions and the development of urban centers. This exercise fosters critical thinking skills, research proficiency, and an understanding of the intricate relationship between natural resources, agricultural practices, and societal evolution.

Observing Natural Phenomena:

The ancient Babylonians possessed a deep reverence for the natural world and recognized the intricate connections between celestial phenomena, earthly events, and the human experience. Through careful observation of natural phenomena and celestial events, they sought to gain insights into the future, comprehend their position in the cosmos, and make informed decisions in various aspects of life.

The Babylonians engaged in the study of astronomy, diligently observing the movements of the stars, planets, and other celestial bodies. They meticulously recorded these observations and developed a sophisticated system of celestial knowledge that encompassed both scientific and spiritual aspects. Babylonian astronomers recognized patterns and cycles in celestial movements, allowing them to predict celestial events such as eclipses, planetary conjunctions, and solstices.

Astrology, a discipline closely linked to astronomy, held significant importance in Babylonian culture. The Babylonians believed that celestial events and the positions of celestial bodies exerted a profound influence on human affairs and destiny. They developed complex astrological systems that associated specific celestial configurations with various aspects of life, such as personal characteristics, relationships, and societal events. By consulting astrological charts and interpretations, individuals sought guidance and insight into their future and made decisions aligned with the perceived cosmic influences.

Beyond celestial observations, the Babylonians keenly observed the natural world and its patterns. They recognized the changing seasons, the behavior of animals, and the flow of rivers as indicators of natural cycles and the passage of time. By closely studying these natural phenomena, they could make predictions about agricultural conditions, plan for the timing of important events, and navigate their daily lives in harmony with nature.

The example of Babylonian astrology exemplifies the close relationship between the natural world and spiritual beliefs. By interpreting celestial events and their impact on human affairs, the Babylonians integrated the cosmic and earthly realms, emphasizing the interconnectedness of all things. Their observations and beliefs in astrology were not limited to individual fate but were also extended to the well-being of society, as they believed that the alignment of celestial forces influenced broader events and the fate of nations.

In understanding the Babylonians' keen observations of nature and celestial events, We gain insight into the rich tapestry of their spiritual and scientific worldview. They recognize the significance placed on natural phenomena as sources of knowledge and guidance. By exploring the example of Babylonian astrology, We can critically examine the role of astrology in ancient Babylonian society and reflect on the ways in which the observation of celestial and natural phenomena can inform personal and collective decision-making processes.

Through studying the natural and celestial world as the Babylonians did, We gain a deeper appreciation for the interconnectedness of the cosmos and the human experience. They develop an understanding of how ancient civilizations sought to understand and navigate the world around them, and they can reflect on the relevance of these practices in contemporary times. Ultimately, this exploration encourages We to cultivate a sense of wonder, curiosity, and respect for the natural world and its profound influences on human life..

Symbolism and Mythology:

The natural world served as a rich source of symbolism and inspiration in Babylonian mythology and religious rituals. Various animals, plants, and natural phenomena were endowed with symbolic meaning and were incorporated into religious ceremonies and mythological narratives.

Problem 1: Choose a significant animal or natural element from Babylonian mythology, such as the serpent or the river. Research its symbolic significance and its role in religious rituals or stories. Write an essay analyzing the cultural and spiritual significance of the chosen element and its relevance in contemporary ecospiritual practices.

The ancient Babylonian culture revered the natural world, recognizing its spiritual, agricultural, and symbolic importance. Through the exercises and problems provided, We can explore the ways in which the natural world influenced the beliefs, practices, and social structures of ancient Babylon. They can also reflect on the lessons and insights that ancient Babylonian culture offers in cultivating a deep connection with the natural world in contemporary ecospiritual practices.

C. Relevance of ecospirituality in contemporary society

In this section, we will explore the relevance of ecospirituality in contemporary society and its potential to address pressing environmental and spiritual concerns. Drawing inspiration from the ancient Babylonian culture's deep connection with nature, we will examine how ecospirituality can provide guidance, inspire sustainable practices, and foster a harmonious relationship between humans and the natural world.

Addressing Environmental Challenges:

In contemporary society, the Earth faces an array of pressing environmental issues, ranging from climate change and biodiversity loss to habitat destruction and pollution. To address these challenges effectively, a holistic approach that integrates spirituality and ecological consciousness is essential. Ecospirituality, with its recognition of the intrinsic value of nature and the interconnectedness of all life, offers a unique perspective and a powerful tool for inspiring individual and collective action in environmental conservation.

Ecospirituality encourages individuals to cultivate a deep spiritual connection with the Earth, recognizing that the natural world is not merely a resource to be exploited but a sacred and interconnected web of life. By developing a sense of reverence and awe for nature, individuals can awaken a profound sense of responsibility and become stewards of the Earth. This spiritual connection serves as a guiding force, shaping attitudes, behaviors, and choices in a way that supports environmental sustainability and the well-being of the planet.

Indigenous communities around the world exemplify the transformative power of ecospirituality in addressing environmental challenges. Drawing upon their rich spiritual traditions and ancestral wisdom, these communities have long recognized the interdependence between humans and the natural world. Their belief systems emphasize the inherent value of nature and the need for harmony and balance in all relationships. As custodians of the land, they have been at the forefront of environmental activism and sustainable practices, advocating for the protection of ecosystems and biodiversity.

For example, Indigenous cultures embrace the concept of "biocentrism," which acknowledges the inherent worth and interconnectedness of all living beings. This perspective rejects the anthropocentric notion that humans are separate from and superior to the natural world. Instead, it highlights the mutual dependencies and responsibilities between humans and other species. By embracing this worldview, Indigenous communities have developed practices and principles that promote sustainable resource management, land conservation, and the preservation of traditional ecological knowledge.

To address specific environmental challenges, such as deforestation or plastic pollution, individuals can draw inspiration from ecospirituality and develop a plan of action that combines ecological principles with spiritual practices. This can involve engaging in acts of ecological restoration, supporting local conservation initiatives, reducing personal ecological footprint, advocating for policy changes, and raising awareness about the interconnectedness of all life.

Problem 1 encourages We to choose an environmental challenge and explore how ecospirituality can provide insights and guidance in addressing the issue. By integrating ecological knowledge and spiritual practices, We can develop a comprehensive plan of action that addresses both the tangible aspects of the challenge and the deeper spiritual dimensions. This problem-solving exercise fosters critical thinking, creativity, and a deepened understanding of the potential of ecospirituality as a catalyst for positive change.

In studying ecospirituality and its application to contemporary environmental challenges, We gain a broader perspective on the relationship between spirituality and ecology. They learn to view environmental issues through a lens of interconnectedness and recognize the potential for personal and collective transformation in their own lives and communities. By embracing ecospirituality, individuals can become agents of change, working towards a more sustainable and harmonious relationship with the Earth.

Cultivating Mindfulness and Reverence for Nature:

In today's fast-paced and technology-driven society, the practice of ecospirituality offers a profound antidote, urging individuals to reconnect with the natural world and cultivate mindfulness. By slowing down, observing the intricate beauty of the Earth, and developing a sense of reverence for all living beings, people can develop a deeper appreciation for the interconnectedness of life and the inherent value of the planet.

In the midst of our busy lives, it is easy to become disconnected from nature. We are often absorbed in screens, surrounded by the constant hum of technology, and consumed by daily responsibilities. However, ecospirituality encourages us to pause and immerse ourselves in the natural world. It invites us to step away from the noise and distractions, allowing ourselves to be fully present and receptive to the wisdom and beauty of the Earth.

An essential aspect of practicing ecospirituality is mindfulness—a state of heightened awareness and non-judgmental attention to the present moment. When we cultivate mindfulness in nature, we begin to notice the intricate details of the environment—the delicate petals of a flower, the rustling of leaves, the rhythmic flow of a river. This focused awareness allows us to appreciate the beauty and interconnectedness of all life forms, fostering a sense of awe and reverence.

Exercise 1 encourages We to spend a day immersed in nature without any electronic devices or distractions. During this time, they are invited to observe and take notes on their experiences. By disconnecting from technology, We have the opportunity to fully engage with their surroundings, sharpen their senses, and deepen their connection to the natural world.

Following the exercise, We are prompted to reflect on their observations and experiences. They are encouraged to explore the potential benefits of mindfulness and reverence in fostering ecospirituality through a personal essay. By reflecting on how this immersive experience affected their connection to nature, We can delve into the transformative power of mindfulness and reverence in deepening their understanding of ecospirituality.

Through the exercise and personal reflection, We develop a firsthand understanding of the benefits of mindfulness and reverence in cultivating a meaningful connection with nature. They gain insight into the potential of ecospirituality to bring about personal transformation, heighten environmental awareness, and foster a sense of responsibility for the well-being of the Earth.

In studying ecospirituality and engaging in mindfulness practices, We not only deepen their understanding of the natural world but also enhance their overall well-being. They develop a greater sense of connectedness, peace, and gratitude, which can positively impact their relationship with themselves, others, and the planet. By embracing ecospirituality and cultivating mindfulness and reverence, individuals contribute to a more harmonious and sustainable coexistence with the Earth.

Ethical Consumption and Sustainable Living:

Ecospirituality goes beyond a mere spiritual connection with the natural world; it encompasses a deep commitment to ethical consumption and sustainable living practices. It recognizes that our choices and actions have a direct impact on the environment and the well-being of all living beings. By embracing ecospirituality, individuals are encouraged to make conscious decisions that minimize harm to the Earth and foster a harmonious coexistence with nature.

One of the key principles of ecospirituality is ethical consumption. It calls for a shift in our mindset and behavior towards making choices that support the health of the planet and promote social justice. This includes considering the environmental impact of our actions, advocating for sustainable practices, and supporting initiatives that prioritize the well-being of both people and the environment.

In the context of daily life, adopting sustainable living practices can encompass a wide range of actions. For example, individuals can reduce their carbon footprint by using public transportation, cycling, or carpooling instead of relying solely on private vehicles. They can embrace energy conservation by minimizing electricity usage, opting for renewable energy sources, and employing energy-efficient technologies.

Food consumption is another significant aspect of daily life where ecospirituality can be practiced. The example of the Slow Food movement highlights the importance of locally sourced, seasonal, and sustainably produced food. Embracing this principle not only supports local farmers and businesses but also reduces the carbon footprint associated with long-distance transportation and the use of chemical pesticides. It encourages individuals to reconnect with the land, traditional farming practices, and the preservation of culinary traditions.

Example: The Slow Food movement, which originated in Italy, emphasizes the importance of locally sourced, seasonal, and sustainably produced food. It promotes a connection with the land, traditional farming practices, and the preservation of culinary traditions, aligning with the principles of ecospirituality.

Problem 2: Choose a specific aspect of daily life, such as food consumption or transportation, and develop a sustainability plan that incorporates ecospiritual values. Consider the environmental impact, ethical considerations, and personal well-being in your plan.

Healing and Well-being:

Within the realm of ecospirituality, the healing power of nature is acknowledged and embraced. It is recognized that engaging with natural environments, practicing nature-based rituals, and participating in ecotherapy can have profound positive effects on physical, emotional, and spiritual well-being. This holistic approach to well-being emphasizes the interconnection between humans and the natural world, and the profound impact that nature can have on our overall health.

Nature has long been revered as a source of solace, inspiration, and rejuvenation. Scientific research has also provided evidence for the therapeutic benefits of nature. Spending time in natural environments, such as forests, parks, or gardens, has been shown to reduce stress, boost mood, enhance cognitive function, and improve overall well-being. This connection to nature can be particularly powerful in urban settings, where access to green spaces may be limited.

Nature-based rituals are another avenue through which individuals can tap into the healing power of nature. These rituals involve connecting with natural elements, such as water, earth, or fire, and engaging in ceremonial practices that promote harmony and balance. For example, a ritual may involve a guided meditation by a waterfall, a ceremony to honor the cycles of the moon, or a fire ceremony to release negative energies. These rituals not only foster a deeper connection with nature but also provide a space for personal reflection, transformation, and healing.

Ecotherapy, also known as nature therapy or green therapy, is an emerging field that utilizes the healing power of nature as a therapeutic intervention. It involves guided activities and exercises in natural settings, such as walking in the woods, gardening, or animal-assisted therapy. Ecotherapy can be effective in treating a range of mental health conditions, including anxiety, depression, and stress-related disorders. By immersing oneself in nature and engaging in mindful and intentional practices, individuals can experience healing, restoration, and a sense of connection to something greater than themselves.

By incorporating the healing power of nature into ecospirituality, individuals can tap into a profound source of well-being and spiritual nourishment. Engaging with natural environments, participating in nature-based rituals, and exploring ecotherapy practices offer opportunities for personal growth, self-discovery, and the cultivation of a deeper connection with the Earth. This holistic approach to well-being not only benefits individuals on a personal level but also fosters a greater sense of responsibility and stewardship towards the natural world.

Through a combination of scientific understanding, spiritual wisdom, and experiential practices, individuals can cultivate a harmonious relationship with nature and harness its healing energies for their own well-being and the greater good of the Earth. Ecospirituality offers a pathway to honor and celebrate the interconnectedness between humans and the natural world, fostering a sense of belonging, healing, and wholeness in today's fast-paced and interconnected society.

Exercise 2: Engage in a nature-based ritual or activity, such as forest bathing, gardening, or meditating outdoors. Keep a journal documenting your experiences and reflections on the healing and transformative effects of connecting with nature.

Conclusion:

Ecospirituality offers a relevant and meaningful framework for addressing contemporary environmental challenges and fostering a deeper connection with the natural world. By integrating spiritual practices, ethical considerations, and sustainable living, individuals can cultivate a harmonious relationship with nature and contribute to a more sustainable and spiritually fulfilling society. The exercises and problems provided in this section encourage We to explore the practical application of ecospirituality in their own lives and engage in critical thinking about its potential impact on the world.

II. Babylonian Cosmology and Nature Worship

In this section, we will delve into the cosmology and nature worship practices of ancient Babylon, exploring their significance within the context of ecospirituality. The Babylonian civilization held a deep reverence for the natural world, perceiving it as intricately connected to the divine and fundamental to their spiritual beliefs. By understanding their cosmological framework and nature worship rituals, we can gain insights into the Babylonian perspective on the sacredness of the Earth and its relevance in contemporary ecospirituality.

Babylonian Cosmology:

The ancient Babylonians held a unique cosmological perspective that shaped their understanding of the universe and its interwoven realms. According to their beliefs, the cosmos consisted of multiple layers and realms, each playing a vital role in the interconnectedness of existence. This cosmological model provided a framework for comprehending the relationships between the earthly, celestial, and chthonic realms, emphasizing the holistic nature of their worldview.

At the center of Babylonian cosmology was the Earth, which was perceived as a flat disk encompassed by a celestial dome. The Earth was the realm of humans, animals, plants, and the diverse ecosystems that sustained life. It was viewed as a sacred and interconnected part of the cosmic order, intimately linked to the heavens above and the underworld below.

Above the Earth's surface, the Babylonians envisioned the celestial realm, where the celestial bodies resided and moved across the sky. The sun, moon, stars, and planets were believed to be divine entities with immense power and influence over human affairs. The movements and positions of these celestial bodies were closely observed and interpreted as omens and messages from the gods, guiding human destiny and providing insights into the natural and supernatural world.

Beneath the Earth's surface lay the chthonic realm, also known as the underworld. This realm was inhabited by various deities, spirits, and ancestral beings. It represented the realm of the dead and the afterlife, as well as the source of fertility and renewal. The chthonic realm played a significant role in Babylonian rituals and beliefs surrounding life, death, and the cycle of rebirth.

The interconnectedness of these realms was fundamental to Babylonian cosmology. The celestial bodies influenced earthly events, and the underworld served as a bridge between the divine and mortal realms. The natural elements, such as rivers, mountains, and forests, were considered sacred dwelling places of spirits and deities, connecting the earthly realm with the celestial and chthonic realms. This interconnectedness reinforced the idea that all aspects of existence were intertwined and affected by the forces of the cosmos.

By understanding and engaging with their cosmological beliefs, the Babylonians sought to establish a harmonious relationship with the natural and supernatural world. Rituals, prayers, and offerings were performed to honor the deities, seek their favor, and maintain cosmic balance. This holistic approach to cosmology influenced various aspects of Babylonian culture, including religious practices, agricultural rituals, and the arts.

Studying Babylonian cosmology offers valuable insights into how ancient cultures perceived and navigated the complex interconnectedness of existence. It provides a glimpse into their deep reverence for the natural world and their understanding of the intricate relationships between humans, celestial forces, and the spiritual realms. Exploring Babylonian cosmology encourages We to reflect on the profound interconnectedness of our own existence, fostering a deeper appreciation for the intricate tapestry of life and our place within it.

Example: The Enuma Elish, a Babylonian creation myth, describes the formation of the world through the actions of divine beings, such as Marduk. This myth reflects the Babylonian belief in the divine order and the interplay between the natural and spiritual realms.

Nature Deities and Worship:

Nature worship held a significant place in the spiritual practices of the ancient Babylonians. They held a deep reverence for the natural world, attributing divine qualities to various natural elements and celestial bodies. Their belief system acknowledged that the Earth and its phenomena were sacred manifestations of powerful deities, and they engaged in rituals, offerings, and ceremonies to honor and connect with these divine forces.

The Babylonians recognized the inherent divinity within nature and viewed it as a tangible expression of the gods and goddesses they worshipped. They believed that mountains, rivers, forests, and other natural features were inhabited by specific deities, making these places sacred and worthy of veneration. The celestial bodies, such as the sun, moon, stars, and planets, were also regarded as celestial entities with divine attributes, each associated with a particular deity.

Through their nature worship practices, the Babylonians sought to establish a deep spiritual connection with the natural world and its divine inhabitants. Rituals played a crucial role in these endeavors, as they provided a structured means of engaging with the gods and expressing devotion. Offerings of food, drink, and incense were presented to the deities as a sign of respect and to gain their favor and protection.

Ceremonies and festivals dedicated to nature deities were important occasions for the Babylonians to come together as a community and express their collective reverence. These events often involved processions, music, dance, and theatrical performances, creating a vibrant and immersive experience that fostered a sense of unity and shared spiritual connection.

An example of nature worship in Babylonian spirituality can be seen in their veneration of the god Marduk. Marduk was associated with fertility and agriculture, and his worship was central to ensuring bountiful harvests and the prosperity of the land. The Babylonians recognized the divine presence of Marduk in the fertility of the soil, the growth of crops, and the abundance of nature.

By engaging in nature worship, the Babylonians sought to establish a harmonious relationship with the natural world and its divine inhabitants. They understood that by honoring and respecting the sacredness of nature, they could attain the blessings and protection of the deities associated with it.

Studying Babylonian nature worship provides We with insights into the deep reverence ancient cultures held for the natural world. It encourages an appreciation for the interconnectedness of humanity and nature, highlighting the importance of nurturing and preserving the environment. Exploring the practices and beliefs of Babylonian nature worship can inspire We to develop a profound sense of reverence for the natural world and to foster a greater understanding of our own relationship with the divine forces that permeate it.

Example: The Babylonians worshipped Ishtar, the goddess of love, fertility, and war. Ishtar was associated with the planet Venus, symbolizing both the beauty and power of nature. Rituals dedicated to Ishtar involved offerings of flowers, music, and dance, highlighting the connection between human expression and the natural world.

Problem 1: Choose a Babylonian nature deity, such as Ea (god of freshwater) or Nergal (god of the underworld), and research their attributes and associated rituals. Create a visual presentation showcasing the importance of these deities in Babylonian nature worship.

Sacred Landscapes and Sacred Trees:

The Babylonians recognized certain landscapes and trees as sacred, considering them as meeting points between the earthly and divine realms. Sacred mountains, rivers, and groves were believed to be imbued with spiritual energy, serving as sites for rituals, pilgrimages, and spiritual retreats.

Example: The Hanging Gardens of Babylon, one of the Seven Wonders of the Ancient World, exemplify the Babylonian appreciation for nature's beauty and their desire to create a harmonious connection between humans and the natural world.

Exercise 1: Visit a local natural site, such as a park or forest, and observe its features, paying attention to the trees, mountains, or bodies of water present. Reflect on the feelings and thoughts evoked by the natural environment and write a journal entry exploring the significance of sacred landscapes and trees in fostering a sense of connection with the divine.

Ecological Responsibility and Stewardship:

Babylonian nature worship encompassed a sense of ecological responsibility and stewardship. The Babylonians recognized the need to maintain balance and harmony within the natural world, understanding that human actions could affect the well-being of the Earth and its inhabitants.

Exercise 2: Conduct a research project on a contemporary ecological issue, such as deforestation or water pollution. Analyze the Babylonian perspective on ecological responsibility and compare it with modern-day approaches. Develop a proposal outlining practical steps and strategies that integrate ecological responsibility with spiritual principles to address the chosen issue.

Conclusion:

The cosmology and nature worship practices of ancient Babylon offer valuable insights into the interconnectedness of the spiritual and natural realms. By understanding and embracing the Babylonian reverence for nature, contemporary ecospirituality can find inspiration to foster a deeper connection with the Earth and cultivate a sense of ecological responsibility. The examples, problems, and exercises provided in this section encourage We to explore Babylonian cosmology and nature worship in a thoughtful and reflective manner, applying their knowledge to contemporary environmental and spiritual contexts.

A. Overview of Babylonian cosmology

In this section, we will explore the fascinating cosmological beliefs of ancient Babylon and their significance within the framework of ecospirituality. The Babylonians developed a rich and intricate cosmology that reflected their understanding of the universe, the divine forces at work, and the interconnectedness of all existence. By delving into the key elements of Babylonian cosmology, we can gain a deeper appreciation for their worldview and its relevance in contemporary spiritual practices.

The Structure of the Universe:

According to Babylonian cosmology, the universe was composed of multiple realms, each with its own distinct characteristics and divine inhabitants. At the center of their cosmology was the Earth, depicted as a flat disc surrounded by an encircling cosmic ocean.

Example: The Enuma Elish, a Babylonian creation myth, describes the birth of the cosmos through the divine struggle between Marduk, the supreme deity, and the primeval forces of chaos. This myth reflects the Babylonian understanding of the origins and structure of the universe.

The Celestial Realm:

Above the Earth was the celestial realm, consisting of the heavens and the celestial bodies. The Babylonians observed the movements of the stars, planets, and constellations, considering them as divine entities that influenced human affairs.

Example: The Babylonians worshipped Ishtar, the goddess of love and war, who was associated with the planet Venus. They believed that the movements of Venus in the night sky held significance for the fertility of the land and the harmony of human relationships.

Problem 1: Research the Babylonian understanding of celestial bodies and their influence on human affairs. Create a chart or diagram illustrating the associations between specific celestial bodies and aspects of human life, such as love, agriculture, or wisdom.

The Underworld:

Beneath the Earth lay the chthonic realm known as the underworld. This realm was associated with death, the afterlife, and the spirits of the deceased. The Babylonians believed that the souls of the departed journeyed to the underworld, where they continued to exist in a different form.

Example: The goddess Ereshkigal ruled over the underworld and governed the realm of the dead. Rituals and offerings were performed to honor and appease Ereshkigal, seeking her guidance and protection for the souls of the departed.

Exercise 1: Reflect on your beliefs about life after death. Compare and contrast the Babylonian understanding of the underworld with different contemporary spiritual perspectives on the afterlife. Write a reflective essay discussing the similarities and differences and how they influence one's perception of the cycle of life and death.

Divine Hierarchy and Mythology:

Babylonian cosmology involved a complex pantheon of deities, each with their own roles and domains. The gods and goddesses represented different aspects of nature, human experiences, and societal functions. Myths and epic tales provided explanations for the creation of the world, the struggles of the gods, and the origins of humanity.

Example: The Epic of Gilgamesh, one of the oldest surviving literary works, narrates the adventures of Gilgamesh, a legendary hero. This epic reflects the Babylonian understanding of the relationship between humans and the divine, as well as the search for immortality and the quest for wisdom.

Exercise 2: Choose a Babylonian deity and research their attributes, stories, and symbolism. Create a presentation or visual representation that highlights their significance within Babylonian cosmology and explores their relevance in contemporary spiritual practices.

Conclusion:

Babylonian cosmology offers a profound understanding of the interconnectedness of the universe, the divine forces at work, and the role of humans within this cosmic tapestry. By studying their cosmological beliefs, we can gain insights into the Babylonian worldview and appreciate the rich tapestry of their spiritual heritage. The examples, problems, and exercises provided in this section encourage We to engage in critical thinking and reflection, fostering a deeper understanding of Babylonian cosmology and its relevance in modern ecospirituality.

1. Beliefs about the universe and its interconnectedness

In this section, we will explore the Babylonian beliefs about the universe and its interconnectedness, shedding light on their profound understanding of the cosmic web and the spiritual implications it held. The Babylonians viewed the universe as a complex and interdependent system, where the celestial, terrestrial, and chthonic realms were interconnected and influenced by divine forces. By examining their beliefs about the interconnectedness of the universe, we can gain insights into their spiritual worldview and its relevance in contemporary ecospirituality practices.

Cosmic Order and Divine Harmony:

The Babylonians believed that the universe operated according to a divine order and harmony. They perceived the interconnectedness between various realms and entities as crucial to maintaining this cosmic balance. The actions of both humans and deities played a role in sustaining this equilibrium.

Example: The Babylonian Enuma Elish myth portrays the struggle between order and chaos, with the god Marduk establishing order by defeating the primordial forces of Tiamat. This myth illustrates the Babylonian belief in the importance of maintaining cosmic harmony.

Exercise 1: Reflect on the concept of cosmic harmony in your own spiritual beliefs or practices. How does the understanding of interconnectedness and balance influence your relationship with the natural world? Write a personal reflection on the significance of cosmic harmony in your spiritual journey.

Holistic View of Nature:

Babylonians recognized the inherent interconnectedness between nature and the divine. They viewed nature as a reflection of the divine forces and believed that the natural world held spiritual significance. Animals, plants, and natural phenomena were seen as manifestations of divine presence and wisdom.

Example: The Babylonians associated specific deities with natural elements, such as Enlil, the god of the air and wind, and Ninhursag, the goddess of fertility and the earth. They believed that these deities influenced the cycles of nature and played a role in the prosperity of their agricultural endeavors.

Exercise 2: Choose a natural element or phenomenon (e.g., a river, a tree, a thunderstorm) and explore its symbolism and spiritual significance in Babylonian culture. Create a visual representation or write a descriptive essay highlighting the connection between the chosen element and its divine symbolism.

Interconnectedness of Humans and the Cosmos:

Babylonians saw themselves as an integral part of the cosmos, intricately connected to the divine and the natural world. They believed that human actions and rituals had the power to influence the cosmic balance and communicate with the divine forces.

Example: Babylonian rituals and offerings aimed to establish a harmonious relationship between humans and deities, seeking blessings, protection, and guidance. These rituals served as a means of maintaining the interconnectedness between the human and divine realms.

Problem 1: Investigate the rituals and practices associated with establishing a connection between humans and the divine in Babylonian culture. Create a step-by-step guide outlining a ritual or practice that embodies the Babylonian belief in the interconnectedness between humans and the cosmos.

Conclusion:

The Babylonians held a profound understanding of the interconnectedness of the universe, recognizing the intricate relationship between humans, nature, and the divine. Their beliefs about the universe and its interconnectedness continue to resonate in contemporary ecospirituality practices. By exploring Babylonian cosmology and their perspective on the cosmic web, we can deepen our own understanding of our place in the interconnected tapestry of existence. The examples, problems, and exercises provided in this section encourage We to engage critically with the concepts of interconnectedness, fostering a deeper appreciation for the Babylonian worldview and its relevance in modern ecospirituality.

2. Deities associated with nature and the elements

In this section, we will explore the Babylonian deities associated with nature and the elements, delving into their significance and roles within the Babylonian cosmological framework. The Babylonians revered a pantheon of gods and goddesses who were intimately connected to various aspects of the natural world. By examining these deities, we can gain insights into the Babylonian understanding of nature's divinity and its profound influence on their spiritual practices.

Enlil - God of Air and Wind:

Enlil was one of the most prominent deities in the Babylonian pantheon, associated with the forces of air and wind. The Babylonians believed that Enlil controlled the breath of life and the winds that brought rain and fertility to the land.

Example: In the Enuma Elish, Enlil plays a significant role in establishing order and separating the heavens and earth. His association with air and wind symbolizes the life-giving forces necessary for sustaining the natural world.

Exercise 1: Research Enlil's myths and symbols. Create a visual representation or write a descriptive essay that depicts Enlil and his connection to the air and wind. Reflect on how Enlil's role resonates with your own understanding of the importance of air and wind in ecological systems.

Ninhursag - Goddess of Fertility and the Earth:

Ninhursag, also known as Ninmah or Nintu, held a crucial place in Babylonian mythology as the goddess of fertility and the earth. She was believed to be the divine mother who nurtured all life and oversaw agricultural abundance.

Example: Ninhursag's association with the earth and fertility made her a central figure in Babylonian agricultural practices. The Babylonians sought her blessings and performed rituals to ensure the fertility of the soil and the success of their crops.

Exercise 2: Explore the symbols and representations of Ninhursag. Create an artistic rendering or write a research paper that explores Ninhursag's role as the goddess of fertility and the earth. Discuss how her symbolism and rituals might inform modern ecological practices and agricultural sustainability.

Ea - God of Water and Wisdom:

Ea, also known as Enki, was a Babylonian deity associated with the primordial waters and the depths of knowledge and wisdom. He was believed to govern the underground waters, rivers, and oceans, making him a significant figure in water-related aspects of life.

Example: In Babylonian myths, Ea is depicted as the creator of humanity and the bestower of knowledge and wisdom. His association with water symbolizes the life-giving and transformative qualities of this element.

Exercise 3: Investigate the stories and attributes of Ea in Babylonian mythology. Create a comparative analysis between Ea and other water-related deities from different cultures. Discuss the universal significance of water as a symbol of life and its ecological importance.

Conclusion:

The Babylonian pantheon included a multitude of deities associated with nature and the elements, reflecting the deep reverence and recognition of nature's divinity in their spiritual practices. Enlil, Ninhursag, and Ea were just a few examples of the gods and goddesses that embodied the forces and elements of the natural world. By exploring these deities, we can gain a deeper understanding of the Babylonian worldview and its relevance in contemporary ecospirituality practices. The exercises provided in this section encourage We to engage critically with the deities' symbolism and roles, fostering a deeper appreciation for the interconnectedness between the divine and the natural world.

B. Nature worship in ancient Babylon

In this section, we will delve into the practice of nature worship in ancient Babylon, exploring the profound reverence and spiritual significance attributed to the natural world. The Babylonians recognized the divine essence and interconnectedness of nature, and their religious practices reflected a deep bond with the elements, animals, plants, and celestial bodies. By examining their beliefs and rituals, we can gain insights into the ways in which ancient Babylonians sought to commune with and honor the natural world.

Anima Spirits and Sacred Places:

In Babylonian culture, the belief in anima spirits, the spiritual essence present in all aspects of nature, formed the foundation of their nature worship. They attributed consciousness and divine energy to animals, plants, rivers, mountains, and celestial bodies.

Example: The Euphrates River was considered sacred, and the Babylonians believed it housed a guardian spirit. They performed rituals and made offerings to appease and honor the spirit, seeking its blessings for fertility, prosperity, and protection.

Exercise 1: Research sacred places and natural elements revered in ancient Babylonian culture. Choose one and create a presentation or write a reflective essay on its significance. Discuss how the anima spirit concept influenced Babylonian rituals and their relationship with the natural world.

Celestial Worship and Astrology:

The Babylonians were avid astronomers, recognizing the celestial bodies' influence on earthly affairs. They worshipped and studied the movements of the sun, moon, planets, and stars, perceiving them as manifestations of divine power.

Example: The Babylonians developed an intricate system of astrology, associating each celestial body with specific deities and attributing various influences on human lives based on their positions in the sky.

Exercise 2: Explore the connection between celestial worship and astrology in Babylonian culture. Select a celestial body or constellation and research its significance in Babylonian astrology. Write an essay or create a visual presentation discussing how this practice influenced their understanding of the universe and human existence.

Sacred Trees and Plants:

Trees and plants held profound spiritual significance in Babylonian culture. They were seen as symbols of life, fertility, and the connection between the earthly and divine realms.

Example: The date palm tree was highly venerated in Babylonian society. It was associated with the goddess Ishtar and represented abundance, beauty, and renewal. Rituals were performed to honor and seek blessings from the tree.

Exercise 3: Investigate the symbolism and rituals associated with sacred trees and plants in ancient Babylonian culture. Choose a specific plant or tree and create a written or visual presentation that explores its significance and the rituals performed around it. Reflect on the potential modern-day applications of connecting with sacred plants.

Conclusion:

Nature worship played a central role in ancient Babylonian spirituality, with anima spirits, celestial bodies, and sacred trees serving as focal points of reverence and spiritual connection. By recognizing the divine essence in nature and engaging in rituals and observances, the Babylonians sought to cultivate a harmonious relationship with the natural world. The exercises provided in this section encourage We to deepen their understanding of Babylonian nature worship and consider its relevance in contemporary ecospirituality practices. By engaging critically with the beliefs and rituals of ancient Babylon, We can develop a profound appreciation for the interconnectedness of humanity and the natural world.

1. Reverence for sacred landscapes and natural features

In this section, we will explore the profound reverence the ancient Babylonians had for sacred landscapes and natural features. Their belief system acknowledged the intrinsic sacredness of the land, recognizing its connection to the divine and the profound impact it had on their spiritual lives. By delving into their beliefs and practices, we can gain a deeper understanding of their reverence for the natural world and its significance in their culture.

Sacred Mountains and Hills:

The Babylonians attributed great significance to mountains and hills, viewing them as sacred sites imbued with divine power and wisdom. They believed that these elevated landscapes acted as gateways between the mortal realm and the divine realms, serving as conduits for spiritual connection and communication.

Example: The Mountain of Mardu was regarded as a sacred mountain in Babylonian mythology, associated with the god Marduk. It symbolized strength, stability, and the divine presence. Rituals and ceremonies were conducted on its slopes to honor and commune with the gods.

Exercise 1: Research and analyze the cultural and spiritual significance of sacred mountains or hills in ancient Babylonian culture. Reflect on their symbolic meanings and the rituals performed in these sacred spaces. Consider the ways in which contemporary ecospirituality practices can draw inspiration from these ancient beliefs.

Sacred Springs and Rivers:

The Babylonians recognized the spiritual power and life-giving properties of springs and rivers. They considered these flowing bodies of water as sacred sources of nourishment, purification, and divine blessings. They believed that water deities resided within these natural features, and they conducted rituals and ceremonies to honor and seek the blessings of these deities.

Example: The Euphrates River held significant importance in Babylonian culture. It was seen as a sacred waterway, and rituals involving bathing, offerings, and prayers were performed to seek purification, fertility, and divine guidance.

Exercise 2: Investigate the cultural and religious practices surrounding sacred springs and rivers in ancient Babylonian society. Analyze their symbolic meanings and the rituals associated with these natural features. Discuss the potential lessons and practices that can be integrated into modern ecospirituality approaches, emphasizing the importance of water as a sacred element.

Sacred Groves and Gardens:

Babylonians held sacred groves and gardens in high regard as spaces that embodied the harmony and abundance of the natural world. These lush environments were considered sacred, serving as places where the human and divine realms intersected. They were seen as spaces for reflection, spiritual connection, and communion with nature.

Example: The Hanging Gardens of Babylon, one of the Seven Wonders of the Ancient World, was a renowned garden that showcased the grandeur of Babylonian horticulture. It was believed to be a manifestation of the gods' blessings and a testament to human ingenuity.

Exercise 3: Explore the concept of sacred groves and gardens in ancient Babylonian culture. Investigate their cultural significance and the rituals and practices associated with these sacred spaces. Discuss the ways in which modern-day ecospirituality can draw inspiration from these ancient beliefs to foster a deeper connection with nature and promote environmental stewardship.

Conclusion:

The ancient Babylonians held a profound reverence for sacred landscapes and natural features. Mountains, springs, rivers, groves, and gardens were viewed as sources of divine power, wisdom, and abundance. They served as gateways for spiritual connection, purification, and communion with the divine. By studying their beliefs and practices, we gain insights into the importance of recognizing the sacredness of the land and its role in fostering a deeper connection with nature. The exercises provided in this section encourage We to delve into the significance of sacred landscapes and natural features, drawing connections between ancient Babylonian practices and contemporary ecospirituality. Through critical thinking and reflection, We can explore the ways in which reverence for the natural world can inform their own spiritual journeys and promote a sustainable and harmonious relationship with the Earth.

2. Symbolism and spiritual significance of natural elements

In this section, we will explore the symbolism and spiritual significance of natural elements in the ancient Babylonian culture. The Babylonians recognized that the natural world was filled with deep symbolism and held profound spiritual meaning. By understanding the symbolism of these natural elements, we can gain insight into the Babylonians' spiritual beliefs and practices and their connection to the larger cosmic order.

Earth:

The Earth held great significance in Babylonian spirituality. It was viewed as the foundation of life, representing stability, fertility, and grounding. The Babylonians saw the Earth as a nurturing and life-giving force, providing sustenance and serving as the home for all living beings.

Example: In ancient Babylonian creation myths, the Earth was personified as the goddess Ninhursag, known as the "Lady of the Mountains." She symbolized the fertile and nurturing qualities of the Earth and played a crucial role in the cycle of life and regeneration.

Exercise 1: Reflect on the symbolism of the Earth in ancient Babylonian culture. Explore its association with fertility, stability, and grounding. Consider how these symbolic meanings can be integrated into modern ecospirituality practices, emphasizing the importance of honoring and protecting the Earth.

Sky and Celestial Bodies:

The sky and celestial bodies held significant spiritual symbolism for the Babylonians. They recognized the vastness of the cosmos and believed that the movements and positions of celestial bodies influenced human destiny. The sky represented the divine realm and was associated with transcendence and spirituality.

Example: The Babylonians had a deep understanding of astronomy and developed intricate celestial calendars. They attributed divine qualities to celestial bodies such as the Sun, Moon, and planets, viewing them as manifestations of powerful deities.

Exercise 2: Explore the symbolic significance of the sky and celestial bodies in ancient Babylonian spirituality. Investigate their association with transcendence, divinity, and cosmic order. Discuss how contemporary ecospirituality can draw inspiration from these ancient beliefs, fostering a deeper appreciation for the cosmos and our interconnectedness with the universe.

Fire:

Fire held a dual symbolism in Babylonian culture, representing both destruction and purification. It was seen as a powerful force of transformation and renewal. Fire was associated with the divine and was often used in rituals to purify and communicate with the gods.

Example: The Babylonians performed fire rituals, such as the burning of offerings, as a means of connecting with the divine and seeking spiritual purification. Fire was believed to carry prayers and offerings to the gods.

Exercise 3: Reflect on the symbolism of fire in ancient Babylonian spirituality. Explore its associations with transformation, purification, and divine communication. Discuss the ethical considerations and responsible use of fire in modern ecospirituality practices, emphasizing the importance of harnessing its power in a respectful and sustainable manner.

Conclusion:

The natural elements held deep symbolic meaning in ancient Babylonian culture. Earth represented stability and fertility, the sky and celestial bodies symbolized transcendence and divine order, and fire signified transformation and purification. By studying the symbolism of these natural elements, we gain insights into the Babylonians' spiritual beliefs and their connection to the larger cosmic order. The exercises provided in this section encourage We to explore the symbolic significance of natural elements and consider how these ancient beliefs can inform contemporary ecospirituality practices. Through critical thinking and reflection, We can develop a deeper understanding of the interconnectedness between nature and spirituality, fostering a greater sense of reverence and responsibility towards the natural world.

III. Rituals and Ceremonies Honoring the Natural World

In this section, we will explore the rituals and ceremonies practiced by the ancient Babylonians to honor and connect with the natural world. These rituals were an integral part of their ecospirituality, serving as a means of expressing reverence for nature, seeking harmony with the divine, and fostering a deep sense of interconnectedness. By studying these rituals, we can gain insights into the Babylonians' spiritual practices and draw inspiration for our own contemporary ecospirituality.

Seasonal Celebrations:

The ancient Babylonians recognized the cyclical nature of the natural world and celebrated the changing seasons with elaborate rituals. These ceremonies marked important agricultural events, such as planting and harvesting, and were dedicated to various deities associated with fertility and abundance.

Example: The Akitu Festival, held in honor of the god Marduk, was one of the most significant Babylonian festivals. It took place during the spring equinox and involved processions, prayers, and offerings to ensure a bountiful harvest and the renewal of life.

Exercise 1: Research and describe a Babylonian seasonal celebration and its associated deity. Explore the symbolism and rituals performed during the festival. Reflect on how the principles and themes of these ancient rituals can be incorporated into contemporary ecospirituality practices, emphasizing the importance of honoring and harmonizing with the seasonal cycles of nature.

Sacred Offerings and Libations:

Offerings and libations played a central role in Babylonian rituals, serving as acts of devotion and communication with the divine. These offerings included food, drink, incense, and flowers, which were presented at sacred sites or dedicated to specific deities associated with natural elements.

Example: The offering of grain, honey, and wine to the goddess Ishtar, the deity of love and fertility, was a common practice in Babylonian ceremonies. These offerings symbolized the abundance and blessings sought from the goddess.

Exercise 2: Explore the concept of sacred offerings and libations in ancient Babylonian rituals. Discuss the symbolism and significance of specific offerings dedicated to deities associated with the natural world. Reflect on how the act of offering can be incorporated into modern ecospirituality practices, emphasizing the importance of gratitude and reciprocity with nature.

Sacred Processions and Dance:

Babylonian rituals often involved elaborate processions and sacred dances. These activities were performed to honor the gods, seek their blessings, and express devotion to the natural world. Processions would take place in sacred locations, such as temples or natural landscapes, with participants adorned in ceremonial attire.

Example: The Ishtar Gate Procession was a grand Babylonian ritual that celebrated the goddess Ishtar. Participants would march through the streets, accompanied by music and dance, carrying statues and symbols of the deity.

Exercise 3: Reflect on the significance of sacred processions and dance in Babylonian rituals. Discuss how these activities were used to connect with the divine and express reverence for the natural world. Consider incorporating processions or movement-based practices into contemporary ecospirituality, fostering a deeper connection with nature and the divine.

Conclusion:

Rituals and ceremonies were vital components of ancient Babylonian ecospirituality, providing a means of expressing reverence for the natural world and seeking harmony with the divine. Seasonal celebrations, sacred offerings and libations, and sacred processions and dance were all integral parts of their spiritual practices. By studying these rituals, we can draw inspiration for our own contemporary ecospirituality, exploring ways to honor and connect with the natural world. The exercises provided in this section encourage We to delve deeper into the symbolism and practices of Babylonian rituals and consider how these ancient traditions can inform and enrich their own ecospiritual practices today. Through critical thinking and engagement with these rituals, We can deepen their connection to nature and cultivate a greater sense of reverence and harmony with the natural world.

A. Seasonal festivals and agricultural rituals

Seasonal festivals and agricultural rituals were integral to the ancient Babylonian culture and their deep connection with the natural world. These ceremonies celebrated the changing seasons, marked important agricultural events, and honored the deities associated with fertility and abundance. Let us explore the significance of seasonal festivals and agricultural rituals in the context of Babylonian ecospirituality.

Seasonal Festivals:

The Babylonians recognized the cyclical nature of the seasons and celebrated them through elaborate festivals. These festivals were not only occasions for joy and merriment but also served as opportunities to express gratitude for the blessings of nature and seek divine favor for a successful harvest.

Example: The Akitu Festival was a prominent Babylonian festival held during the spring equinox. It was dedicated to the god Marduk and marked the beginning of the agricultural year. The festival included processions, prayers, and offerings to ensure a bountiful harvest and the renewal of life.

Exercise 1: Research and describe a Babylonian seasonal festival of your choice. Explore its significance, rituals, and deities associated with it. Reflect on how the principles and themes of these festivals can be adapted and incorporated into modern ecospiritual practices, emphasizing the importance of honoring the seasons and fostering a deep connection with nature.

Agricultural Rituals:

Agricultural rituals were an essential part of Babylonian culture as they sought to ensure a successful and prosperous harvest. These rituals were performed at different stages of the agricultural cycle and involved offerings, prayers, and symbolic actions to invoke divine blessings and protect the crops from harm.

Example: The "First Fruits" ritual was an agricultural ceremony where the first harvested grains or fruits were offered to the gods. This act of offering symbolized gratitude for the abundance of the land and acknowledged the role of the deities in sustaining life.

Exercise 2: Explore the significance of agricultural rituals in ancient Babylonian culture. Discuss the rituals and practices associated with specific stages of the agricultural cycle, such as planting, cultivation, and harvesting. Reflect on how these rituals can inspire modern ecospiritual practices, emphasizing the importance of sustainable agriculture, ecological stewardship, and gratitude for the Earth's bounty.

Sacred Sites and Landscapes:

Babylonian agricultural rituals often took place in sacred sites and landscapes, which were believed to hold special spiritual significance. These sites included temples, groves, and natural features such as rivers or mountains. The choice of these locations was based on the belief that they were inhabited by divine beings and served as portals between the earthly and spiritual realms.

Example: The Etemenanki, a ziggurat in Babylon, was a sacred site associated with the god Marduk. Agricultural rituals were conducted at the base of the ziggurat, symbolizing the connection between the divine realm and the fertility of the land.

Exercise 3: Reflect on the importance of sacred sites and landscapes in Babylonian agricultural rituals. Discuss how the choice of these locations contributed to the spiritual significance of the rituals and the sense of interconnectedness between humans, nature, and the divine. Consider how sacred sites and natural features can be honored and protected in contemporary ecospirituality, promoting a deeper connection with the land and a reverence for its sacredness.

Conclusion:

Seasonal festivals and agricultural rituals were central to Babylonian ecospirituality, providing a framework for expressing gratitude for the cycles of nature, seeking divine blessings for the harvest, and fostering a deep connection with the land. Through the celebration of seasonal festivals and the performance of agricultural rituals, the ancient Babylonians recognized the interdependence between humans and the natural world. By studying and adapting these rituals, we can draw inspiration for our own modern ecospiritual practices, promoting sustainability, gratitude, and a profound reverence for the cycles of nature. The exercises provided in this section encourage We to engage critically with the principles and practices of Babylonian seasonal festivals and agricultural rituals, facilitating a deeper understanding of their relevance to contemporary ecospirituality and the cultivation of a harmonious relationship with the natural world.

Akitu Festival: Held during the spring equinox (around March-April) to mark the beginning of the agricultural year and honor the god Marduk.

Tashmetum Festival: Celebrated during the summer months (around June-July) to honor the goddess Tashmetum, associated with the abundance of the harvest.

Zagmuk Festival: Held during the winter solstice (around December-January) to celebrate the victory of the god Marduk over chaos and darkness, symbolizing the return of light and fertility.

First Fruits Ritual: Conducted during the harvest season, typically in late summer or early autumn, to offer the first harvested grains or fruits to the gods and express gratitude for the abundance of the land.

Planting Rituals: Various rituals performed at the onset of the planting season (around February-March) to seek blessings for successful sowing and growth of crops.

Harvest Festivals: Celebrated in different months depending on the specific crops being harvested. For example, the Barley Harvest Festival was held in late spring, while the Date Harvest Festival took place in the summer.

Please note that the exact dates of these festivals and rituals may vary based on specific regional and cultural variations within ancient Babylonian society.

1. Celebration of the agricultural cycle and harvests

The ancient Babylonians placed great importance on agriculture, recognizing it as the foundation of their society. The cyclical nature of agricultural seasons and the success of harvests were pivotal for their sustenance and well-being. Consequently, the Babylonians developed elaborate rituals and celebrations to honor the agricultural cycle and express gratitude for the bountiful harvests that ensured their survival. This section will explore the significance of these celebrations and rituals, providing insights into the rich cultural practices of ancient Babylonian society.

Rituals for Seasonal Transitions:

The changing seasons held profound meaning for the Babylonians, as they marked the shifts in the agricultural cycle. During the spring equinox, the Akitu Festival was celebrated to signify the beginning of the agricultural year. This festival, dedicated to the god Marduk, emphasized renewal and fertility. It involved purification ceremonies, processions, and offerings to ensure a prosperous growing season.

Honoring the Planting Season:

The Babylonians recognized the critical importance of the planting season, which determined the success of their crops. They performed rituals to seek divine blessings and protection for the seeds and plants. These rituals included prayers, offerings, and the use of sacred tools or symbols associated with fertility and growth. By engaging in these ceremonies, the Babylonians expressed their hopes for a fruitful harvest.

Festivals During Harvest:

Harvest festivals were the pinnacle of celebration in Babylonian agricultural life. These events were held at different times depending on the specific crops being harvested. For instance, the Barley Harvest Festival took place in late spring, while the Date Harvest Festival occurred in the summer. These festivals were marked by feasting, music, dances, and communal gatherings. Offerings were made to the deities associated with agricultural abundance, expressing gratitude for the successful harvest.

First Fruits Ritual:

The offering of the first fruits of the harvest was a significant act of devotion and thanksgiving. The Babylonians conducted ceremonies where the initial yield of crops, such as grains or fruits, was presented to the gods. This act symbolized the acknowledgment of divine providence and the cycle of giving and receiving. It reinforced the belief that the gods played a vital role in sustaining the agricultural prosperity of the community.

Symbolism and Sacred Imagery:

During agricultural celebrations, the Babylonians incorporated symbolic elements and sacred imagery to deepen their connection with the land and the gods. These symbols often included representations of fertility, growth, and abundance. Examples include the use of statuettes or figurines of deities associated with agriculture, floral adornments, and artistic depictions of crops and animals. These symbols served as reminders of the interconnectedness between nature, the gods, and the well-being of the community.

Conclusion:

The celebration of the agricultural cycle and harvests in ancient Babylon was an integral part of their cultural and spiritual traditions. These rituals and festivities demonstrated the deep reverence the Babylonians held for the land, the deities of fertility and abundance, and the interdependent relationship between humans and nature. By engaging in these celebrations, they not only expressed gratitude for the sustenance provided by the earth but also sought blessings for future harvests. Today, the legacy of these agricultural celebrations reminds us of the profound connection between humanity, the natural world, and the cycles of life and abundance.

Examples, Problems, and Exercises:

Research and describe a specific harvest festival from a different ancient culture and compare it to Babylonian harvest celebrations.

Create a hypothetical planting ritual for a modern agricultural community, incorporating elements of gratitude, symbolism, and connection with nature.

Discuss the significance of the first fruits ritual in different cultural and religious traditions, highlighting similarities and differences with Babylonian practices.

Imagine you are organizing a contemporary harvest festival inspired by Babylonian celebrations. Design an event program that includes activities, performances, and rituals that pay homage to ancient Babylonian agricultural traditions.

Reflect on the importance of agricultural celebrations in promoting ecological awareness and sustainability in modern society. Discuss how reconnecting with the cycles of nature can enhance our relationship with the environment.

2. Offerings and rituals to ensure fertility and abundance

In ancient Babylon, the cultivation of fertile land and abundant harvests were crucial for the prosperity and well-being of the community. The Babylonians believed that through rituals and offerings, they could establish a connection with the divine forces responsible for fertility and abundance. This section will explore the significance of offerings and rituals in ensuring agricultural prosperity, emphasizing their role in invoking blessings, fostering fertility, and securing abundant yields.

Offerings to Agricultural Deities:

The Babylonians believed that specific deities governed various aspects of agriculture, fertility, and abundance. Offerings were made to these deities to seek their favor and assistance. For example, the goddess Ishtar, associated with love, fertility, and harvest, was honored through offerings of flowers, fruits, and libations. The god Nabu, linked to writing, wisdom, and fertility, received offerings of clay tablets inscribed with prayers for agricultural prosperity.

Rituals for Rain and Irrigation:

Water was essential for the growth of crops, and the Babylonians recognized its importance in ensuring fertility. Rituals were performed to invoke rain and secure adequate irrigation for the fields. These rituals often involved processions, prayers, and the offering of sacred objects or symbols associated with water, such as vessels or images of water deities. By performing these rituals, the Babylonians sought to ensure sufficient moisture for the crops, fostering their growth and abundance.

Sacred Marriage Rites:

The concept of the sacred marriage, or hieros gamos, played a significant role in Babylonian rituals for fertility and abundance. It involved the symbolic union of a god and a goddess, representing the harmonious union of masculine and feminine energies. These rituals were believed to generate cosmic energies that stimulated fertility in both the natural world and human society. The ceremonies were often accompanied by feasting, music, and dances, and were considered vital in promoting agricultural productivity and prosperity.

Offerings to Ancestral Spirits:

The Babylonians believed that the spirits of ancestors played a role in ensuring the fertility of the land and the continuity of the community. Offerings were made to honor these ancestral spirits and seek their blessings. These offerings included food, drinks, and other items representing the bounty of the harvest. By recognizing and honoring their ancestors, the Babylonians expressed their gratitude and sought their continued support for agricultural abundance.

Rituals for Soil Fertility:

To ensure the fertility of the soil, the Babylonians performed rituals and made offerings directly to the earth itself. These rituals involved the pouring of libations, the scattering of seeds or grains, and the use of sacred tools or symbols associated with agriculture. Through these acts, the Babylonians sought to nurture the soil, inviting its productive powers and ensuring the success of their agricultural endeavors.

Conclusion:

The Babylonians deeply believed in the importance of offerings and rituals to ensure fertility and abundance in their agricultural practices. Through these acts, they sought the favor of deities, invoked the powers of water, celebrated the sacred union of energies, honored ancestral spirits, and nurtured the soil. These rituals and offerings represented their profound connection with the natural world and their commitment to fostering agricultural prosperity. By engaging in these practices, they expressed their gratitude for the bountiful gifts of the land and sought to maintain harmony between humans, nature, and the divine forces that governed fertility and abundance.

Examples, Problems, and Exercises:

Research and describe a specific offering or ritual from a different ancient culture aimed at ensuring fertility and abundance. Compare and contrast it with Babylonian practices.

Design a ritual or ceremony for contemporary agricultural communities to honor and ensure fertility and abundance. Consider the use of symbols, offerings, and invocations that align with modern sensibilities and beliefs.

Discuss the role of sacred marriages or hieros gamos in different religious and spiritual traditions. Explore their significance in promoting fertility and abundance beyond agricultural contexts.

Reflect on the importance of ancestral connection in contemporary agricultural practices. Discuss ways in which modern farmers and communities can incorporate ancestral rituals or offerings to foster fertility and abundance.

Investigate the role of music and dance in Babylonian agricultural rituals. Explore the potential benefits of incorporating music or movement in modern agricultural ceremonies to enhance fertility and abundance.

Reflect on the ethical implications of using offerings and rituals to ensure fertility and abundance in the context of sustainable agriculture. Discuss how such practices can be adapted to align with ecological principles and promote long-term environmental stewardship.

B. Sacred sites and pilgrimage

In ancient Babylon, the concept of sacred sites and pilgrimage held great significance in the spiritual and cultural practices of the society. These sites were considered sacred due to their association with divine beings, powerful energies, or historical events. Pilgrimage, the act of journeying to these sacred sites, was seen as a transformative experience that deepened one's connection with the divine, fostered personal growth, and strengthened communal bonds. This section will explore the importance of sacred sites and pilgrimage in ancient Babylon, emphasizing their spiritual significance, rituals, and transformative nature.

Definition and Significance:

Sacred sites in ancient Babylon were places imbued with spiritual energy, often associated with specific deities or divine manifestations. These sites included temples, shrines, natural landmarks, and historical locations. They served as focal points for worship, prayer, rituals, and community gatherings. Pilgrimage to these sites was considered an act of devotion, providing an opportunity for individuals to connect with the divine and experience spiritual renewal.

Pilgrimage Practices:

Pilgrimage in ancient Babylon involved a structured set of rituals and practices. These included purification rituals, offerings, prayers, and participation in communal ceremonies. Pilgrims often traveled in groups, sharing their experiences and supporting each other on the journey. The act of pilgrimage itself was seen as a transformative process, allowing individuals to transcend their everyday lives and enter a sacred space where they could seek spiritual enlightenment and receive divine blessings.

Major Sacred Sites:

Several sacred sites were revered in ancient Babylon. The city of Babylon itself held great religious significance, housing temples dedicated to various deities such as Marduk, Ishtar, and Nabu. The Etemenanki, a ziggurat dedicated to Marduk, was a prominent pilgrimage destination. The sacred city of Nippur, with its temple dedicated to Enlil, attracted pilgrims from far and wide. The Ishtar Gate in Babylon was another important site associated with the goddess Ishtar and was believed to serve as a gateway between the earthly realm and the divine.

Symbolism and Rituals:

Sacred sites were often adorned with symbolic imagery and architectural elements that reflected the beliefs and cosmology of ancient Babylon. These included sacred symbols, carvings, statues, and elaborate temple structures. Rituals performed at these sites involved offerings, prayers, and acts of devotion. Pilgrims participated in ceremonies led by priests, seeking guidance, blessings, or divine intervention in their lives.

Transformative Nature of Pilgrimage:

Pilgrimage was seen as a transformative experience, allowing individuals to deepen their spiritual connection and gain insights into their own lives. The physical journey represented an inner journey of self-discovery, healing, and personal growth. Pilgrims often returned with a renewed sense of purpose, inspired to live in alignment with their spiritual values and share their experiences with the larger community.

Conclusion:

Sacred sites and pilgrimage played a significant role in the religious and spiritual practices of ancient Babylon. They provided a means for individuals to connect with the divine, seek spiritual guidance, and experience personal transformation. The rituals, symbolism, and communal aspects of pilgrimage fostered a sense of unity and shared spirituality among the participants. Today, the concept of sacred sites and pilgrimage continues to hold relevance in various spiritual traditions, serving as a reminder of our deep connection to the sacred and the transformative potential of embarking on a sacred journey.

Examples, Problems, and Exercises:

Research and describe a sacred site from a different ancient civilization and compare its significance with a sacred site in ancient Babylon.

Design a pilgrimage itinerary to visit sacred sites in ancient Babylon, including the rituals and practices that would be conducted at each site.

Discuss the psychological and spiritual benefits of pilgrimage. How does the act of journeying to a sacred site contribute to personal growth and transformation?

Reflect on the role of pilgrimage in contemporary spirituality. Explore the reasons why individuals embark on pilgrimages today and the transformative experiences they seek.

Investigate the impact of pilgrimage on local communities and economies. Discuss the positive and negative effects of increased tourism to sacred sites.

Reflect on the ethical considerations surrounding the preservation and management of sacred sites. Discuss ways in which sacred sites can be protected while still allowing access for pilgrimage and spiritual practices.

1. Importance of specific locations in nature

In various spiritual and mystical traditions, specific locations in nature hold immense significance due to their energetic qualities, spiritual symbolism, and connection to the natural world. These places, often referred to as power spots, sacred sites, or vortexes, are believed to possess unique qualities that promote healing, spiritual growth, and a deepened connection with the divine. This section explores the importance of specific locations in nature, highlighting their role in various fields such as witchcraft, divination, herbalism, shamanism, ecospirituality, and magic. We will delve into the reasons behind their significance and the ways in which they are utilized for spiritual practices and personal transformation.

Energy and Vibrational Significance:

Specific locations in nature are believed to radiate distinct energy and vibrations that can impact individuals who visit or engage with them. These energies are often attributed to geological features, such as mountains, caves, waterfalls, or forests, which are considered to amplify and concentrate spiritual energy. For example, certain mountains may be considered gateways to the spiritual realms, while bodies of water are associated with cleansing and emotional renewal. The vibrational qualities of these locations are believed to enhance meditation, healing, and spiritual experiences.

Spiritual and Symbolic Connections:

Many specific locations in nature hold deep spiritual and symbolic connections to ancient beliefs, mythologies, and cultural traditions. For instance, caves have been revered as sacred spaces since prehistoric times, representing the womb of the Earth and a gateway to the underworld. Sacred groves, dedicated to nature deities, were places of worship and communion with the natural world. Mountains have often been associated with divine realms, enlightenment, and spiritual ascension. These symbolic connections enhance the spiritual significance of these locations, inviting individuals to engage with their inherent power and wisdom.

Healing and Transformation:

Specific locations in nature have long been regarded as sites of healing and transformation. The natural environment, untouched by human intervention, is believed to possess restorative qualities that promote physical, emotional, and spiritual well-being. People seek out these locations to rejuvenate, find solace, and experience profound healing. The serenity of a forest, the rejuvenating power of a hot spring, or the cleansing properties of a waterfall are examples of the therapeutic benefits offered by specific natural sites.

Rituals and Practices:

Specific locations in nature often serve as settings for rituals, ceremonies, and spiritual practices. Practitioners may engage in meditation, prayer, energy work, divination, or spellcasting to harness the unique energies of these sites. For example, witches may gather in a sacred grove to connect with nature spirits, perform rituals, or seek guidance from the natural world. Shamans may journey to power spots to communicate with spirits or conduct healing ceremonies. These rituals and practices deepen the spiritual connection to the location and amplify the intended effects of the practitioner's work.

Environmental Stewardship and Conservation:

The importance of specific locations in nature extends beyond individual and collective spiritual experiences. The preservation and conservation of these sites play a crucial role in maintaining ecological balance and protecting biodiversity. As individuals engage with these locations, it becomes essential to promote environmental stewardship, practicing responsible and sustainable approaches to ensure their long-term viability and protection for future generations.

Conclusion:

Specific locations in nature hold great importance in various spiritual and mystical traditions. These sites, with their unique energetic qualities, symbolic connections, and transformative potential, provide individuals with opportunities for spiritual growth, healing, and connection with the natural world. Engaging with these locations through rituals, practices, and reverence fosters a deeper understanding of our interconnectedness with the Earth and its sacred landscapes. It is through this connection that individuals can cultivate a sense of awe, respect, and environmental stewardship, ensuring the preservation and continuation of these sacred places for generations to come.

Examples, Problems, and Exercises:

Visit a specific location in nature that holds personal significance to you and reflect on the energetic qualities and symbolic connections you perceive. Share your experience with the class.

Research a specific location in nature that is revered in a particular spiritual tradition (e.g., Stonehenge, Mount Kailash). Discuss its significance, associated rituals, and the transformative experiences people seek there.

Explore the role of specific locations in nature in herbalism and plant-based medicine. Investigate how certain environments or ecosystems support the growth of specific medicinal plants and their healing properties.

Discuss the ethical considerations related to visiting and engaging with specific locations in nature. How can individuals ensure respectful and sustainable practices when interacting with these sites?

Create a guided meditation or visualization exercise centered around a specific location in nature. Encourage We to explore the energetic qualities and transformative potential of the site through their imagination and sensory experience.

Reflect on the impact of human activities on specific locations in nature. Discuss the challenges of balancing spiritual practices and reverence with environmental conservation efforts.

Examine the role of specific locations in nature in divination practices, such as scrying or geomancy. Explore how the natural environment influences the interpretation of signs and symbols during divinatory processes.

2. Pilgrimage rituals and practices

Pilgrimage, a sacred journey to a specific destination, holds deep spiritual significance across various cultures and religious traditions. It is a transformative experience that allows individuals to connect with the divine, seek personal growth, and deepen their faith. This section explores the rituals and practices associated with pilgrimage, drawing examples from fields such as witchcraft, divination, herbalism, shamanism, ecospirituality, and magic. We will delve into the motivations behind pilgrimages, the preparation and rituals involved, and the transformative effects they can have on individuals.

Motivations for Pilgrimage:

Pilgrimages are driven by various motivations, including seeking spiritual enlightenment, expressing devotion or gratitude, seeking healing or guidance, or fulfilling a religious obligation. In the context of witchcraft, individuals may embark on pilgrimages to connect with the energies of sacred sites or commune with nature spirits. Herbalists may undertake pilgrimages to gather specific medicinal plants or visit locations associated with healing traditions. Understanding the motivations behind pilgrimages helps contextualize the rituals and practices involved.

Preparation for Pilgrimage:

Pilgrims often engage in preparatory rituals and practices before embarking on their journey. These may include purifying oneself through cleansing baths, fasting, prayer, or meditation. In some traditions, pilgrims may also seek guidance through divination or consult spiritual practitioners for advice. Adequate physical preparation, such as gathering supplies and ensuring fitness, is also essential for a successful pilgrimage. Preparing oneself mentally, emotionally, and spiritually allows the pilgrim to fully engage with the transformative potential of the journey.

Rituals and Practices during Pilgrimage:

Pilgrimage rituals and practices vary depending on the specific tradition and destination. Common practices include walking specific routes, circumambulating sacred sites, offering prayers or dedications, making offerings or donations, participating in group ceremonies, and engaging in personal introspection and reflection. In witchcraft, pilgrims may create talismans or perform rituals at specific points along the journey. Herbalists may conduct plant blessings or perform healing ceremonies at sacred sites. These rituals and practices serve to deepen the pilgrim's connection with the sacred, foster personal transformation, and honor the spiritual significance of the destination.

Sacred Sites and Destinations:

Pilgrimage destinations hold immense spiritual significance. These can include holy mountains, ancient temples, sacred wells, or natural landscapes associated with mythologies or religious traditions. For example, in shamanism, pilgrims may journey to power spots or sacred mountains to connect with spirits and gain insight. Each destination carries unique energies and symbolism, which influence the pilgrim's experience and the rituals performed. Understanding the history and cultural context of these sites enhances the pilgrim's reverence and engagement with the sacred.

Transformative Effects of Pilgrimage:

Pilgrimage has the potential to bring about profound personal transformation. Through the rituals, practices, and encounters with the sacred, pilgrims often experience spiritual awakening, a deepening of faith, emotional healing, and a heightened sense of connection with the divine and the natural world. The physical challenges, encounters with fellow pilgrims, and the sacredness of the journey contribute to a sense of unity, humility, and personal growth. Pilgrimage becomes a catalyst for self-discovery and spiritual evolution.

Conclusion:

Pilgrimage is a powerful spiritual practice that transcends cultural and religious boundaries. The rituals and practices associated with pilgrimage provide a framework for individuals to connect with the sacred, seek personal growth, and deepen their spiritual understanding. By understanding the motivations, preparations, rituals, and transformative effects of pilgrimage, We can explore the diverse ways in which this ancient practice continues to shape and inspire individuals in various spiritual traditions today.

Examples, Problems, and Exercises:

Research and describe a famous pilgrimage site or route from a specific tradition (e.g., Camino de Santiago, Kumbh Mela). Discuss the rituals, practices, and transformative effects associated with this pilgrimage.

Reflect on a personal pilgrimage experience or create a hypothetical pilgrimage itinerary. Discuss the motivations, rituals, and transformative effects you envision for yourself or others.

Explore the role of divination in pilgrimage preparations. How can divinatory practices guide pilgrims in their journey and enhance their spiritual experiences?

Analyze the ethical considerations related to pilgrimage, such as cultural appropriation, environmental impact, or the commodification of sacred sites. Discuss ways in which pilgrims can approach these challenges responsibly and respectfully.

Create a guided visualization exercise for We, simulating a pilgrimage experience to a specific sacred site. Encourage We to engage their senses, emotions, and imagination to connect with the transformative power of pilgrimage.

Investigate the role of pilgrimage in contemporary witchcraft practices. How do modern witches incorporate pilgrimage as a means of connecting with natural energies and deepening their spiritual practice?

Discuss the potential psychological and emotional benefits of pilgrimage. How can the act of embarking on a sacred journey contribute to personal healing, growth, and self-discovery?

IV. Ethics and Sustainability in Babylonian Ecospirituality

Babylonian ecospirituality encompassed a profound reverence for the natural world and a deep understanding of humanity's interconnectedness with the environment. This section explores the ethical principles and sustainable practices inherent in Babylonian ecospirituality, highlighting the wisdom and lessons that can be drawn from this ancient tradition. By examining the ethical considerations and sustainable approaches of the Babylonians, We can gain insights into how to apply these principles to modern-day ecological challenges.

Harmony with Nature:

Babylonian ecospirituality recognized the interconnectedness and interdependence of all beings in the natural world. The Babylonians understood that the well-being of humans was intricately linked to the health and balance of the environment. They believed in living in harmony with nature, respecting its cycles and rhythms. This perspective emphasized the need to maintain a balanced relationship with the land, animals, and plants.

Stewardship and Conservation:

Babylonian ecospirituality emphasized the concept of stewardship, acknowledging humanity's responsibility to care for and protect the Earth. They recognized that humans were entrusted with the task of safeguarding the natural resources and ensuring their sustainable use for future generations. Conservation practices, such as sustainable agriculture, water management, and responsible hunting and fishing, were integral to their ecological worldview.

Respect for Biodiversity:

The Babylonians held a deep respect for biodiversity and the intrinsic value of all living beings. They understood the importance of preserving the diverse ecosystems and the delicate balance of species within them. This reverence for biodiversity was reflected in their agricultural practices, where they cultivated a wide variety of crops and utilized herbalism to maintain ecological balance and promote healing.

Rituals and Offerings:

Babylonian ecospirituality involved rituals and offerings to express gratitude and reverence for the natural world. These rituals were performed to honor the deities associated with nature, seek their blessings, and ensure the fertility and abundance of the land. Through these practices, the Babylonians sought to maintain a reciprocal relationship with the Earth, recognizing that humans were dependent on the gifts of the natural world.

Ethical Considerations:

Babylonian ecospirituality encompassed ethical considerations that guided human behavior towards the environment. These included principles such as non-exploitation, fairness, and reciprocity. For instance, in hunting and fishing practices, the Babylonians observed limitations to prevent over-harvesting and respected seasonal cycles to ensure the sustainability of animal populations. They understood the importance of sharing resources equitably within their communities.

Lessons for Contemporary Society:

The ethics and sustainability principles of Babylonian ecospirituality offer valuable lessons for addressing modern environmental challenges. By examining their practices, We can explore ways to incorporate sustainable agriculture, responsible resource management, and conservation efforts in their own lives. Babylonian ecospirituality encourages a shift in mindset that recognizes our interconnectedness with the natural world and the need for conscious and ethical actions to preserve and restore the environment.

Examples, Problems, and Exercises:

Research and discuss Babylonian agricultural practices, highlighting their sustainable approaches and their relevance to contemporary organic farming methods.

Analyze the ethical considerations and practices of Babylonian hunters and fishermen, exploring how their principles can be applied to modern wildlife management and sustainable fishing practices.

Engage in a group discussion on the concept of stewardship in Babylonian ecospirituality and how it can inform modern approaches to environmental conservation and land management.

Investigate the Babylonian rituals and offerings associated with nature worship. Design a contemporary eco-ritual or offering that expresses gratitude and reverence for the natural world.

Reflect on personal lifestyle choices and consumer habits in light of Babylonian ecospirituality. Identify ways to align personal values with sustainable practices, such as reducing waste, supporting local and organic agriculture, and conserving resources.

Explore potential challenges in applying Babylonian ecospirituality principles in modern society. Discuss possible solutions and strategies for overcoming these challenges, considering cultural, economic, and social factors.

Collaborate with local environmental organizations or community gardens to develop a sustainable agriculture project inspired by Babylonian practices. Document the process, challenges, and outcomes to reflect on the practical applications of Babylonian ecospirituality in contemporary contexts.

A. Concept of harmony and balance in Babylonian culture

The concept of harmony and balance was fundamental to Babylonian culture, permeating various aspects of their society, including religion, philosophy, and everyday life. This section explores the profound significance of harmony and balance in Babylonian culture, highlighting its influence on diverse fields such as Witchcraft, Divination, Herbalism, Shamanism, Ecospirituality, and Magic. By understanding the principles and practices associated with harmony and balance in ancient Babylon, We can gain insights into the importance of equilibrium in their own lives and the world around them.

Cosmic Balance:

The Babylonians believed in the existence of a cosmic balance that governed the universe. They perceived the world as a delicate equilibrium between opposing forces, such as light and darkness, order and chaos, and life and death. Maintaining this cosmic balance was essential for the stability and prosperity of society and the natural world.

Divine Harmony:

Babylonian religious beliefs centered around the idea of harmony between the gods and humans. They believed that by appeasing the gods through rituals and offerings, they could maintain a harmonious relationship and ensure their favor and protection. Deviations from religious practices were seen as disrupting this divine harmony and could result in calamities and misfortunes.

Social and Moral Harmony:

Harmony extended to interpersonal relationships and ethical conduct within Babylonian society. The Babylonians emphasized the importance of fairness, justice, and respect for others. They believed that by adhering to moral principles and treating others with equity, harmony could be achieved within communities, fostering cooperation and societal well-being.

Natural Balance:

The Babylonians recognized the interconnectedness and interdependence of the natural world. They understood the need to maintain a harmonious relationship with the environment to ensure the sustainability of resources and the balance of ecosystems. Sustainable agricultural practices, responsible resource management, and conservation efforts were integral to their worldview.

Achieving Personal Balance:

Individuals were encouraged to seek balance within themselves, harmonizing their physical, emotional, and spiritual aspects. Babylonian practices such as divination, herbalism, and shamanism aimed to restore inner equilibrium and promote overall well-being. Rituals, meditation, and introspection were employed to achieve personal balance and align with the rhythms of the universe.

Lessons for Contemporary Life:

The concept of harmony and balance in Babylonian culture offers valuable lessons for modern individuals. By striving for equilibrium in personal relationships, ethical decision-making, and interactions with the natural world, individuals can contribute to a harmonious and sustainable society. Learning from Babylonian practices can inspire We to cultivate balance within themselves and foster a deeper connection with the world around them.

Examples, Problems, and Exercises:

Explore the role of balance in Babylonian divination practices. Study the techniques used, such as reading celestial omens or interpreting dreams, and reflect on how the pursuit of balance enhances the accuracy of divination outcomes.

Discuss the ethical considerations of balance in Babylonian society. Analyze a specific moral dilemma and present arguments from multiple perspectives, considering the principles of fairness, justice, and societal harmony.

Research Babylonian herbalism and its focus on restoring balance and healing. Create a project showcasing the therapeutic properties of specific herbs and their ability to promote balance within the body and mind.

Engage in a guided meditation or ritual inspired by Babylonian practices to achieve personal balance. Reflect on the experience and share insights on how it contributes to overall well-being and connection with the natural world.

Investigate the impact of modern lifestyle choices on ecological balance. Design a campaign or educational program that promotes sustainable practices, highlighting the Babylonian emphasis on maintaining harmony with the environment.

Examine the challenges faced in maintaining balance in contemporary society. Analyze the impact of technological advancements, social inequalities, or environmental degradation on the pursuit of harmony and propose strategies to address these challenges.

Collaborate with local organizations or community groups to create a public art installation representing the concept of balance and harmony. Reflect on the symbolism and cultural significance of the artwork, drawing parallels to Babylonian art and symbolism.

1. Understanding the interconnectedness of all beings

The concept of interconnectedness lies at the heart of various spiritual and philosophical traditions, including those found in Babylonian culture. This section explores the profound understanding of the interconnectedness of all beings in fields such as Witchcraft, Divination, Herbalism, Shamanism, Ecospirituality, and Magic in Ancient Babylon. By delving into this concept, We can gain insights into the intricate web of relationships that shape our world and the significance of nurturing harmony and balance within it.

Holistic View of the Universe:

Babylonian culture recognized that everything in the universe, both living and non-living, was interconnected. They perceived a profound unity in the natural world, where all beings, from humans to animals, plants, and celestial bodies, were intertwined in a complex tapestry of existence. This holistic view fostered a deep sense of respect and reverence for all life forms.

Interdependence and Mutual Influence:

The Babylonians understood that every being and element in the universe relied on one another for survival and flourishing. Just as plants depended on the sun for nourishment and growth, humans relied on the earth's resources for sustenance. This interdependence highlighted the intricate relationships and mutual influence that sustained the interconnected web of life.

Cosmic Order and Harmony:

Central to Babylonian cosmology was the belief that maintaining cosmic order and harmony was essential for the well-being of all beings. Any disruption in this delicate balance, whether through human actions or cosmic forces, could have far-reaching consequences. Rituals, prayers, and offerings were performed to restore harmony and align with the cosmic order.

Sacredness of Nature:

In Babylonian culture, nature was considered sacred and imbued with spiritual significance. The rivers, mountains, and forests were not merely physical landscapes but were seen as living entities connected to the divine. This recognition of the sacredness of nature nurtured a deep sense of stewardship and responsibility towards the environment.

Ecological Awareness and Responsibility:

The understanding of interconnectedness in Babylonian culture fostered ecological awareness and a sense of responsibility towards the natural world. Babylonians recognized the impact of their actions on the environment and sought to live in harmony with nature. Sustainable agricultural practices, conservation efforts, and respect for wildlife were integral to their way of life.

Lessons for Contemporary Life:

The concept of interconnectedness has profound implications for modern individuals and society. By recognizing and embracing the interconnected nature of all beings, We can develop a deep sense of empathy, compassion, and environmental consciousness. This understanding encourages responsible actions, promotes sustainability, and fosters a sense of global interconnectedness.

Examples, Problems, and Exercises:

Conduct a meditation or reflective exercise to cultivate a sense of interconnectedness with nature. Observe and journal about the connections you feel with various elements of the natural world, such as plants, animals, and the environment.

Analyze the impact of human activities on the interconnectedness of ecosystems. Choose a specific environmental issue and explore its repercussions on various life forms and ecological systems. Propose strategies for mitigating the negative effects and restoring balance.

Investigate Babylonian divination practices and their understanding of the interconnectedness of cosmic forces and human destiny. Compare these practices to other divination systems, such as Tarot or Runes, and discuss how they convey the idea of interconnectedness.

Research traditional herbal remedies in Babylonian culture and their recognition of the interconnectedness between plants, humans, and healing. Prepare a presentation highlighting specific plants and their medicinal properties, emphasizing their role in restoring balance and promoting well-being.

Engage in a community service project focused on environmental conservation and restoration. Collaborate with local organizations to clean up natural habitats, plant trees, or promote sustainable practices, emphasizing the interconnectedness of all beings in preserving ecosystems.

Examine the ethical implications of recognizing interconnectedness in personal relationships and social interactions. Discuss how embracing the idea of interconnectedness can promote empathy, respect, and understanding among individuals from diverse backgrounds.

Reflect on the concept of interconnectedness and its application in personal spiritual practices. Write a reflective essay discussing how recognizing the interconnectedness of all beings enhances one's spiritual journey and connection with the divine.

2. Respect for the natural order and ecosystems

In Babylonian culture, there was a deep-rooted reverence for the natural order and ecosystems that shaped the world. This section explores the importance of respecting the natural order and ecosystems in various fields such as Witchcraft, Divination, Herbalism, Shamanism, Ecospirituality, and Magic in Ancient Babylon. By understanding and honoring the intricate balance and interdependence within ecosystems, We can develop a profound appreciation for the wisdom inherent in nature and the significance of preserving and nurturing the natural world.

Interconnectedness of Ecosystems:

Babylonians recognized that ecosystems were intricate networks where every component played a vital role. They understood that each element, from the smallest organism to the largest ecosystem, contributed to the overall balance and functioning of the natural world. This understanding emphasized the interconnectedness of all life forms and the delicate harmony required for ecosystems to thrive.

Stewardship and Responsibility:

Respect for the natural order involved a sense of stewardship and responsibility towards the environment. Babylonians believed that humans were entrusted with the care and preservation of the Earth and its ecosystems. They acknowledged that their actions had direct consequences for the well-being of the natural world and future generations.

Sustainable Resource Management:

Babylonians practiced sustainable resource management to ensure the longevity of ecosystems and the availability of essential resources. They recognized the importance of conserving natural resources, implementing agricultural practices that maintained soil fertility, and avoiding overexploitation of plants and animals. By practicing sustainable resource management, they sought to maintain the delicate balance within ecosystems.

Rituals and Offerings:

Rituals and offerings were performed as acts of respect and gratitude towards nature and the natural order. These practices were aimed at nurturing the relationship between humans and the environment, acknowledging the reciprocal relationship between humans and the ecosystems that sustained them. Rituals and offerings expressed gratitude for the abundance provided by nature and sought blessings for the continued well-being of ecosystems.

Observing and Learning from Nature:

Babylonians believed that observing and learning from nature held valuable lessons for human life and society. They studied natural patterns, such as the migration of birds, the behavior of animals, and the cycles of celestial bodies, to gain insights into the rhythms and wisdom of the natural world. This knowledge guided their decision-making and fostered a deeper understanding of the interconnectedness of all beings.

Examples, Problems, and Exercises:

Conduct a field trip to a local natural habitat or ecological reserve. Observe the ecosystem, identify different organisms, and reflect on the interdependencies within the ecosystem. Discuss the potential threats to the ecosystem and propose strategies for its preservation.

Research Babylonian agricultural practices and their emphasis on sustainable farming. Compare these practices with modern industrial agriculture and discuss the implications for ecosystem health and long-term sustainability.

Explore the concept of biomimicry, where humans derive inspiration from nature's designs and processes to solve human challenges. Research examples of biomimicry in modern technology and discuss how it reflects the respect for the natural order and ecosystems.

Conduct a debate or discussion on the ethical considerations of resource extraction and its impact on ecosystems. Analyze different viewpoints and perspectives, considering economic, social, and environmental factors.

Reflect on personal consumption habits and their implications for ecosystems. Identify areas where you can make sustainable choices to reduce your ecological footprint and preserve the natural order.

Engage in a community project focused on restoring or preserving a local ecosystem. Collaborate with local organizations to clean up water bodies, plant native species, or create awareness campaigns about environmental conservation.

B. Practices promoting sustainability and environmental stewardship

In the realm of new-age studies, promoting sustainability and environmental stewardship is of paramount importance. This section explores various practices from fields such as Witchcraft, Divination, Herbalism, Shamanism, Ecospirituality, and Magic in Ancient Babylon that foster a sense of responsibility towards the environment and promote sustainable living. By engaging in these practices, We can develop a deep connection with nature and actively contribute to the well-being of the planet.

Conservation of Natural Resources:

One of the fundamental practices promoting sustainability is the conservation of natural resources. This involves using resources judiciously, reducing waste, and striving for efficient and responsible consumption. We can adopt practices like energy conservation, water conservation, and waste reduction to minimize their environmental footprint and ensure the long-term availability of resources.

Organic and Regenerative Agriculture:

Organic and regenerative agricultural practices prioritize the health of ecosystems, soil fertility, and biodiversity. We can explore techniques such as permaculture, companion planting, and organic farming methods to cultivate food in harmony with nature. By avoiding synthetic pesticides and fertilizers and embracing sustainable farming practices, they contribute to the health of ecosystems and promote sustainable food production.

Renewable Energy Adoption:

Transitioning to renewable energy sources, such as solar, wind, and hydroelectric power, is a crucial step towards sustainability. We can explore the benefits of renewable energy, assess their energy consumption patterns, and seek ways to incorporate renewable energy solutions into their lifestyles. This could involve installing solar panels, supporting community renewable energy projects, or advocating for renewable energy policies.

Waste Reduction and Recycling:

Addressing waste management is essential in promoting sustainability. We can learn about the principles of reduce, reuse, and recycle to minimize waste generation. They can practice responsible waste management by segregating and recycling waste, composting organic matter, and opting for reusable alternatives to single-use items. By adopting a circular economy mindset, they contribute to the conservation of resources and reduction of landfill waste.

Environmental Advocacy and Activism:

Engaging in environmental advocacy and activism empowers We to be catalysts for change. They can raise awareness about pressing environmental issues, participate in local initiatives, and advocate for policy changes that prioritize sustainability. By joining environmental organizations, attending rallies, or organizing educational events, We can actively contribute to the promotion of sustainability and environmental stewardship.

Examples, Problems, and Exercises:

Conduct a waste audit in your living space or local community. Analyze the types of waste generated and propose strategies to reduce, reuse, and recycle effectively.

Research traditional ecological knowledge and practices from different cultures, such as herbalism or indigenous farming techniques. Compare these practices with modern industrial approaches and discuss their potential for sustainable resource management.

Engage in a community garden project where We grow their own food using organic and regenerative practices. Reflect on the benefits of such practices for biodiversity, soil health, and personal well-being.

Organize a workshop or seminar on renewable energy, inviting experts to discuss the benefits and challenges of transitioning to renewable energy sources. Encourage discussions on practical steps We can take to embrace renewable energy in their lives.

Conduct a case study on a successful environmental advocacy campaign. Analyze the strategies used, the impact achieved, and the challenges faced. Develop a plan for an advocacy campaign addressing a local environmental issue of importance.

Participate in a beach or park cleanup initiative. Reflect on the importance of preserving natural spaces and discuss ways to prevent pollution and protect ecosystems.

Note: Adapt the examples, problems, and exercises to suit the specific context and resources available to We. Encourage critical thinking, creativity, and practical application of sustainable practices. By actively engaging in these activities, We can develop a holistic understanding of sustainability and become agents of positive change in the world.

1. Conservation and responsible resource management

Conservation and responsible resource management are integral aspects of sustainable living and environmental stewardship. This section explores the importance of conserving natural resources, reducing waste, and adopting responsible practices across various fields, including Witchcraft, Divination, Herbalism, Shamanism, Ecospirituality, and Magic in Ancient Babylon. By understanding the principles and techniques of conservation, We can actively contribute to the preservation and sustainable use of Earth's resources.

Importance of Conservation:

Conservation refers to the careful preservation, protection, and sustainable use of natural resources, including water, energy, forests, wildlife, and biodiversity. It recognizes the finite nature of these resources and aims to ensure their availability for future generations. Conservation plays a crucial role in maintaining ecological balance, promoting sustainable development, and mitigating the impacts of climate change.

Water Conservation:

Water is a precious resource that requires responsible management. We can learn about water conservation practices such as reducing water usage, capturing rainwater, and practicing efficient irrigation techniques. They can explore methods like xeriscaping, which involves using native plants that require less water, and implementing water-saving technologies in homes and communities.

Energy Conservation:

Energy conservation involves reducing energy consumption and optimizing energy efficiency. We can explore practices such as using energy-efficient appliances, improving insulation in buildings, and adopting renewable energy sources. They can also learn about the importance of behavioral changes, such as turning off lights and electronics when not in use, to minimize energy waste.

Forest and Wildlife Conservation:

Forests and wildlife are essential components of Earth's ecosystems. We can study the importance of forest conservation in maintaining biodiversity, mitigating climate change, and supporting indigenous cultures. They can explore sustainable forestry practices, reforestation efforts, and the protection of wildlife habitats. Understanding the interconnectedness of ecosystems and the role of forests in maintaining a healthy planet is crucial for responsible resource management.

Sustainable Agriculture and Food Systems:

Agricultural practices have a significant impact on the environment. We can explore sustainable agriculture techniques such as organic farming, agroforestry, and permaculture. They can learn about regenerative practices that prioritize soil health, biodiversity, and ecosystem resilience. Understanding the impacts of industrial agriculture and the benefits of sustainable food systems empowers We to make informed choices about their food consumption.

Examples, Problems, and Exercises:

Conduct a water audit in your home or community. Analyze water usage patterns and propose strategies to reduce consumption, such as installing water-efficient fixtures or implementing rainwater harvesting systems.

Research a local conservation project focused on preserving endangered wildlife or protecting natural habitats. Analyze the project's objectives, strategies, and outcomes, and present your findings to the class.

Calculate the carbon footprint of a typical household and identify potential areas for energy conservation. Develop an energy-saving plan that includes practical steps to reduce energy consumption and promote renewable energy sources.

Analyze the environmental impacts of conventional agriculture versus sustainable farming methods. Compare the use of synthetic fertilizers and pesticides with organic alternatives, and discuss the implications for soil health, water quality, and biodiversity.

Organize a tree planting event in your community, involving local residents and organizations. Reflect on the importance of trees in sequestering carbon dioxide, improving air quality, and supporting wildlife habitats.

2. Rituals and guidelines for ethical interactions with nature

Rituals and guidelines for ethical interactions with nature form an essential aspect of various practices, including Witchcraft, Divination, Herbalism, Shamanism, Ecospirituality, and Magic in Ancient Babylon. These rituals and guidelines help individuals establish a harmonious relationship with the natural world, fostering respect, gratitude, and responsible stewardship. This section explores the significance of ethical interactions with nature and provides insights into rituals and guidelines that promote sustainable and respectful engagement with the environment.

Understanding Ethical Interactions with Nature:

Ethical interactions with nature involve recognizing the intrinsic value of all living beings and ecosystems and treating them with respect and reverence. It acknowledges the interconnectedness of life and the interdependence between humans and the natural world. Ethical guidelines provide a framework for responsible behavior, ensuring the preservation of biodiversity, ecological balance, and the well-being of future generations.

Rituals for Connection and Reverence:

Rituals serve as powerful tools for establishing a deep connection with nature and expressing reverence for its diverse manifestations. Examples include:

Rituals for the Four Elements: Engage in rituals that honor and connect with the four elements—earth, air, fire, and water. These rituals can involve offerings, meditation, chanting, and visualization exercises to cultivate a sense of interconnectedness and harmony.

Full Moon and New Moon Ceremonies: Participate in ceremonies that align with the lunar cycles to honor the moon's influence on tides, fertility, and spiritual energy. These rituals may involve meditation, divination practices, and setting intentions for personal growth and environmental healing.

Guidelines for Sustainable Harvesting and Gathering:

Ethical interactions with nature involve responsible harvesting and gathering practices to ensure the sustainability of plant and animal resources. Guidelines may include:

Respect for Plant Life: Learn to identify and harvest plants sustainably, considering factors such as plant maturity, abundance, and the impact on surrounding ecosystems. Use ethical harvesting techniques, such as selective pruning or gathering fallen leaves and branches.

Mindful Animal Interactions: Observe ethical guidelines when interacting with animals in their natural habitats. Respect their boundaries, avoid disturbing nesting sites or breeding areas, and refrain from exploiting or harming them for personal gain.

Gratitude and Reciprocity:

Expressing gratitude and practicing reciprocity are fundamental aspects of ethical interactions with nature. These practices cultivate a sense of appreciation and acknowledge the gifts received from the natural world. Examples include:

Offerings and Sacred Exchange: Engage in rituals that involve offering gratitude and thanks to nature through acts of giving. This may include leaving offerings of food, water, or symbolic items at sacred sites or creating personal altars to honor the elements and natural forces.

Environmental Service: Engage in community service activities that contribute to the well-being of the environment. This can include participating in ecological restoration projects, volunteering for environmental organizations, or advocating for sustainable practices in local communities.

Examples, Problems, and Exercises:

Create a ritual for honoring the four elements and perform it in a natural setting. Reflect on the experience and its impact on your connection with the natural world.

Research traditional indigenous practices for sustainable harvesting and gathering of plant resources. Compare these practices with modern approaches to identify common principles and areas for improvement.

Design a gratitude ceremony that acknowledges the gifts of nature and expresses appreciation for the interconnectedness of all beings. Consider incorporating elements such as music, dance, poetry, or visual art to enhance the ritual experience.

Analyze the ethical dilemmas surrounding the commercialization of natural resources, such as the wild-harvesting of medicinal plants. Discuss potential solutions and ways to promote sustainable practices within the industry.

Engage in a local environmental service project, such as organizing a community cleanup or participating in a tree planting event. Reflect on the importance of giving back to nature and its impact on personal well-being and environmental consciousness.

V. Cultural and Social Context of Ecospirituality in Ancient Babylon

Understanding the cultural and social context in which ecospirituality emerged in Ancient Babylon provides valuable insights into the beliefs, practices, and worldview of the people of that time. This section explores the cultural and social factors that shaped ecospirituality in Ancient Babylon, shedding light on the religious, economic, and ecological dimensions of their society. By delving into this context, we can better comprehend the significance and relevance of ecospirituality in Ancient Babylonian culture.

Religious Beliefs and Practices:

Religion played a central role in Ancient Babylonian society, influencing their perspectives on the natural world. The Babylonians worshiped a pantheon of gods and goddesses associated with various aspects of nature and celestial bodies. Examples include Marduk, the supreme god of the Babylonian pantheon, who represented the power of creation and order, and Ishtar, the goddess of fertility and love. These deities were revered and honored through rituals, prayers, and offerings, reflecting a deep sense of spiritual connection with the natural world.

Cosmology and Divine Order:

Ancient Babylonians held a cosmological worldview that perceived the universe as an interconnected and harmonious system. They believed in the existence of celestial realms, with each celestial body and natural element having a specific role and influence. The cosmology of Ancient Babylon emphasized the balance and harmony of the cosmos, with humans acting as stewards in maintaining this delicate equilibrium.

Relationship with the Land and Agriculture:

Agriculture formed the backbone of Ancient Babylonian society, and their connection to the land was profound. The fertile lands between the Tigris and Euphrates rivers allowed for abundant harvests, and agricultural practices were imbued with spiritual significance. Babylonian farmers recognized the cycles of nature and conducted rituals and ceremonies to ensure fertility, bountiful harvests, and the well-being of their crops. This close relationship with the land reflected a deep understanding of the interdependence between humans and nature.

Economic and Environmental Considerations:

Ancient Babylon was a thriving civilization with a complex economy that relied on agriculture, trade, and craftsmanship. The prosperity of the society was closely tied to the availability and sustainable use of natural resources. Babylonians recognized the importance of responsible resource management, implementing systems to prevent overexploitation and protect the environment. For example, they established regulations for land use, irrigation practices, and the preservation of wildlife.

Social and Community Dynamics:

Ecospirituality in Ancient Babylon was not only a personal practice but also had broader implications for social cohesion and community well-being. Rituals and ceremonies were often conducted collectively, fostering a sense of shared responsibility for the natural world. The interconnectedness of humans, nature, and the divine was a fundamental aspect of their cultural fabric, influencing social norms, ethics, and the perception of human-environment relationships.

Examples, Problems, and Exercises:

Analyze the role of specific deities in Ancient Babylonian ecospirituality, such as Ishtar and Marduk. Investigate their attributes, symbols, and associations with nature, and discuss their significance in promoting reverence for the natural world.

Compare and contrast the cosmological beliefs of Ancient Babylon with other ancient civilizations, such as Ancient Egypt or Ancient Greece. Explore similarities and differences in their understanding of the interconnectedness of the universe.

Research and discuss the economic and environmental challenges faced by the Ancient Babylonians in maintaining a sustainable society. Consider the implications of resource depletion, population growth, and the need for responsible land management.

Examine the social structures and community practices that supported ecospirituality in Ancient Babylon. Explore how rituals and ceremonies fostered social cohesion, ethical values, and a sense of collective responsibility for the environment.

Reflect on the relevance of Ancient Babylonian ecospirituality in contemporary society. Discuss how their perspectives on the interconnectedness of humans and nature can inform modern approaches to sustainability, environmental ethics, and community engagement.

A. Integration of ecospirituality into everyday life

The integration of ecospirituality into everyday life involves applying the principles and practices of ecospirituality in a practical and meaningful way. It entails developing a deep connection with nature, cultivating environmental awareness, and making conscious choices that promote sustainability and a harmonious relationship with the natural world. This section explores how individuals can integrate ecospirituality into their daily lives, highlighting its potential to enhance well-being, foster ecological consciousness, and inspire positive change.

Cultivating Mindfulness in Nature:

One key aspect of integrating ecospirituality into everyday life is developing mindfulness in nature. This involves immersing oneself in natural environments, engaging the senses, and cultivating a deep appreciation for the beauty and interconnectedness of the natural world. Through practices such as nature walks, meditation in natural settings, or engaging in mindful gardening, individuals can enhance their connection with nature and experience a sense of awe and reverence.

Sustainable Living Practices:

Integrating ecospirituality into everyday life involves adopting sustainable living practices that align with the principles of ecological harmony and conservation. This may include reducing consumption, practicing waste reduction and recycling, conserving energy and water, and supporting local and organic food sources. By making conscious choices that minimize environmental impact, individuals can embody their ecological values and contribute to the preservation of the planet.

Rituals and Ceremonies:

Rituals and ceremonies play a significant role in integrating ecospirituality into daily life. These rituals can range from simple acts of gratitude and reverence for nature to more elaborate ceremonies honoring specific natural elements or celestial events. For example, individuals may create personal rituals to mark the changing seasons, perform rituals before harvesting from their gardens, or participate in community ceremonies that celebrate the interconnectedness of all beings.

Connection with Sacred Spaces:

Sacred spaces, both natural and human-made, provide an opportunity for individuals to deepen their connection with the divine and the natural world. Integrating ecospirituality involves visiting and engaging with sacred sites, such as ancient forests, mountains, or bodies of water, to experience their inherent spiritual energy and gain inspiration for environmental stewardship. Engaging in practices such as meditation, prayer, or energy work in these sacred spaces can enhance the integration of ecospirituality into everyday life.

Engaging in Community and Activism:

Integrating ecospirituality into everyday life extends beyond personal practices to include engagement with the community and activism for environmental causes. By participating in local environmental initiatives, supporting conservation organizations, and advocating for sustainable policies, individuals can amplify the impact of their personal ecospiritual practices. This engagement fosters a sense of collective responsibility and creates opportunities for broader societal change.

Examples, Problems, and Exercises:

Keep a nature journal to document observations and reflections during mindful walks or time spent in natural settings. Discuss the ways in which this practice enhances your connection with nature and promotes ecospirituality.

Explore sustainable living practices within your daily routine. Develop a personal sustainability plan that includes actions such as reducing energy consumption, practicing mindful consumption, and supporting local and organic food sources.

Create a personal ritual or ceremony that honors a natural element or celestial event. Reflect on the symbolism and significance of the chosen element, and discuss how incorporating this ritual into your daily life can deepen your ecospiritual connection.

Visit a local sacred site or natural landmark and engage in a mindful practice such as meditation or reflection. Discuss the impact of this experience on your connection with the natural world and your understanding of ecospirituality.

Engage in a community environmental initiative or join an environmental organization. Reflect on the importance of collective action in promoting ecospirituality and discuss how your involvement contributes to the integration of ecospirituality into everyday life.

1. Influence on agriculture, architecture, and city planning

The influence of spiritual and esoteric beliefs on various aspects of society, including agriculture, architecture, and city planning, is an essential component of understanding the interconnections between spirituality and the physical world. In ancient civilizations like Babylon, these influences shaped the way people interacted with their environment, fostering sustainable agricultural practices, inspiring architectural marvels, and influencing the layout of cities. This section explores the profound impact of spiritual beliefs on agriculture, architecture, and city planning in ancient Babylon and their relevance to modern-day practices.

Agriculture:

In ancient Babylon, spiritual beliefs played a pivotal role in agricultural practices, ensuring the fertility of the land and bountiful harvests. The Babylonians believed in the existence of deities associated with agriculture, such as Ishtar, the goddess of fertility, and Nisaba, the goddess of grain. Rituals and offerings were conducted to seek their blessings and protection. Farmers followed specific planting and harvesting cycles aligned with celestial events, such as the rising of certain stars, to ensure successful crop yields. These practices promoted a sense of reverence for the land and its natural cycles, and they hold valuable lessons for sustainable agricultural practices today.

Example: Research the agricultural rituals and practices in ancient Babylon and discuss their significance in promoting fertility and abundance. Explore how these practices can be adapted and integrated into modern sustainable farming methods.

Architecture:

The spiritual beliefs and cosmology of ancient Babylon heavily influenced architectural design and construction. The Babylonians regarded architecture as a means to connect the earthly realm with the divine. Temples and ziggurats, towering structures with multiple levels, served as sacred spaces and focal points for religious rituals. The design of these structures incorporated symbolic elements representing the cosmic order and the sacred geography of the universe. The Babylonians believed that the arrangement and proportions of these buildings facilitated communication with the gods and ensured cosmic harmony. The architectural achievements of ancient Babylon continue to inspire contemporary designers and architects, emphasizing the importance of sacred and harmonious spaces.

Example: Analyze the architectural features of the ziggurats in ancient Babylon and discuss their symbolic significance. Explore how modern architects incorporate spiritual and symbolic elements in their designs to create sacred spaces or promote a sense of harmony and connection with the natural environment.

City Planning:

In ancient Babylon, spiritual beliefs influenced the layout and design of cities. The city of Babylon itself was constructed with intention, reflecting the cosmological order and the principles of harmony and balance. The city's central axis aligned with celestial bodies and sacred mountains, and it was divided into distinct districts and quarters dedicated to specific deities or functions. Water management systems, such as canals and irrigation networks, were integral to the city's design, ensuring the sustenance of agricultural lands and the well-being of its inhabitants. The integration of spiritual beliefs in city planning emphasized the interconnectedness between the natural and built environments and fostered a sense of communal and cosmic order.

Example: Investigate the city planning principles of ancient Babylon and discuss how they reflect the spiritual beliefs of the time. Compare these principles with contemporary approaches to sustainable urban planning and discuss the potential benefits of integrating spiritual and ecological considerations in modern city design.

Problems and Exercises:

Visit a local farm or agricultural project that incorporates sustainable practices. Interview the farmers or project managers to explore the spiritual or philosophical foundations that guide their approach to agriculture. Reflect on how these beliefs contribute to sustainable land management and agricultural practices.

Conduct a research project on a prominent architectural structure that incorporates spiritual or esoteric elements. Analyze its design, symbolism, and the intention behind its construction. Discuss the impact of such elements on the users and the surrounding environment.

Select a city known for its sustainable urban planning initiatives. Investigate how spiritual or ecological considerations have influenced its design and layout. Evaluate the success of these initiatives in promoting a harmonious relationship between humans and the natural world.

Organize a discussion or debate on the integration of spirituality and ecological considerations in agriculture, architecture, or city planning. Encourage We to present different perspectives and engage in critical thinking regarding the benefits and challenges associated with incorporating these elements into modern practices.

2. Relationship between spirituality and societal values

The connection between spirituality and societal values is a fundamental aspect of human culture and civilization. Throughout history, spiritual beliefs have influenced the development of moral frameworks, ethical systems, and social norms. In ancient Babylon, spirituality played a crucial role in shaping the values and behaviors of individuals and communities. This section explores the intricate relationship between spirituality and societal values in Babylonian culture, highlighting the impact of spiritual beliefs on moral principles, social structures, and interpersonal relationships.

Moral Principles:

In Babylonian society, spirituality provided a foundation for moral principles and ethical conduct. The belief in divine beings and cosmic forces instilled a sense of accountability and responsibility among individuals. Spiritual teachings emphasized virtues such as justice, compassion, honesty, and respect for others. These moral principles guided the behavior of individuals in their interactions with fellow humans, animals, and the natural world. For example, the Code of Hammurabi, a Babylonian legal code, reflected the influence of spiritual beliefs in promoting fairness and social harmony.

Example: Discuss the moral principles derived from Babylonian spirituality and their relevance to contemporary ethical systems. Analyze how these principles align with or differ from other moral frameworks, such as those found in modern religions or philosophical systems.

Social Structures:

Spiritual beliefs in ancient Babylon influenced the organization of society and social hierarchies. The priesthood played a significant role in religious rituals and acted as intermediaries between humans and the divine. They held positions of authority and contributed to the maintenance of social order. Additionally, Babylonian spirituality emphasized communal values and the importance of collective well-being. Concepts of reciprocity, communal responsibility, and mutual support were integral to the social fabric, fostering a sense of unity and interdependence among individuals.

Example: Examine the social structures and hierarchies in ancient Babylon and discuss how spiritual beliefs influenced the distribution of power and roles within society. Compare these structures with contemporary societal systems and evaluate the impact of spiritual or religious influences on social organization.

Interpersonal Relationships:

Spirituality in ancient Babylon promoted harmonious interpersonal relationships based on principles of respect, empathy, and cooperation. Individuals were encouraged to cultivate virtues such as kindness, forgiveness, and gratitude in their interactions with others. Rituals and ceremonies provided opportunities for communal gatherings, fostering social bonds and a sense of belonging. Spirituality also played a role in familial relationships, guiding expectations of filial piety, marital fidelity, and parental responsibilities.

Example: Reflect on the role of spirituality in shaping interpersonal relationships in ancient Babylon and consider its relevance to modern-day relationships. Explore how spiritual or ethical teachings can enhance communication, empathy, and conflict resolution in personal and professional contexts.

Problems and Exercises:

Conduct a comparative analysis of moral principles derived from different spiritual or religious traditions, including ancient Babylonian beliefs. Discuss the similarities and differences among these moral frameworks and their implications for personal and societal values.

Organize a panel discussion on the influence of spirituality on social structures. Invite experts from various disciplines to explore the impact of spiritual beliefs on societal hierarchies, social inequalities, and the distribution of power in different historical and cultural contexts.

Design a research project investigating the role of spirituality in interpersonal relationships. Survey individuals from diverse backgrounds about the influence of spiritual beliefs on their attitudes and behaviors in relationships. Analyze the findings to identify common themes and patterns.

Engage in a group discussion on the ethical challenges posed by the integration of spirituality and societal values. Encourage We to present different perspectives and debate the potential benefits and limitations of incorporating spiritual beliefs in shaping social norms and values.

B. Roles and status of spiritual leaders in promoting ecospirituality

In the realm of ecospirituality, spiritual leaders play a crucial role in guiding and inspiring individuals to cultivate a deep connection with nature and promote sustainable practices. These leaders, whether in the fields of witchcraft, divination, herbalism, shamanism, or magic, have the responsibility of advocating for the well-being of the natural world and encouraging their followers to live in harmony with the environment. This section explores the roles and status of spiritual leaders in ancient Babylon and contemporary society, highlighting their influence in promoting ecospirituality and fostering a sense of environmental stewardship.

Guardians of Sacred Knowledge:

In ancient Babylon, spiritual leaders were the custodians of sacred knowledge, possessing wisdom and insights into the interconnection between humans, nature, and the spiritual realm. They were revered for their deep understanding of the natural world and its mystical aspects. Spiritual leaders were responsible for interpreting signs and omens, conducting rituals to honor nature, and providing guidance on sustainable practices. Their role as repositories of wisdom and spiritual guidance contributed to the development and preservation of ecospiritual traditions.

Example: Analyze the role of spiritual leaders in ancient Babylonian culture, such as the Chaldean priests, in preserving ecological knowledge and promoting sustainable practices. Discuss the rituals and ceremonies they performed to maintain a harmonious relationship with nature.

Moral Exemplars and Ethical Teachers:

Spiritual leaders serve as moral exemplars, demonstrating through their own actions the values and principles of ecospirituality. They model a deep reverence for the natural world and demonstrate ethical behaviors that prioritize sustainability, conservation, and respect for all beings. Through their teachings and guidance, they encourage their followers to adopt eco-friendly lifestyles, make conscious choices about resource consumption, and engage in activities that protect and nurture the environment.

Example: Investigate the teachings and practices of modern spiritual leaders in various ecospiritual traditions. Examine how they promote ethical behavior, environmental stewardship, and sustainable living. Explore their efforts in raising awareness about pressing ecological issues and encouraging collective action.

Community Leaders and Catalysts for Change:

Spiritual leaders hold positions of influence within their communities, making them effective catalysts for change. They have the ability to inspire and mobilize individuals towards collective action in safeguarding the environment. By organizing community initiatives, workshops, and ceremonies, they create spaces for individuals to reconnect with nature, deepen their understanding of ecological interdependencies, and actively contribute to environmental conservation efforts.

Example: Explore the role of contemporary spiritual leaders in mobilizing communities for environmental causes. Investigate how they establish networks and collaborations with organizations and individuals working towards sustainability. Discuss the impact of their efforts in raising ecological consciousness and promoting sustainable practices within their communities.

Problems and Exercises:

Conduct interviews or research case studies on influential spiritual leaders who have made significant contributions to ecospirituality. Analyze their teachings, practices, and the impact of their work on environmental awareness and sustainability.

Organize a panel discussion on the role of spiritual leaders in promoting ecospirituality. Invite practitioners from different traditions to share their experiences and perspectives on the responsibilities and challenges they face in inspiring environmental stewardship.

Engage in a group debate on the potential conflicts and tensions that may arise when spiritual leaders advocate for environmental causes. Discuss differing viewpoints and explore strategies for addressing these conflicts while maintaining the integrity of spiritual teachings.

Design a community project in which We collaborate with local spiritual leaders to organize an ecospiritual event or initiative. Evaluate the impact of the project on community engagement, ecological awareness, and behavior change towards sustainable practices.

1. Priesthood and their connection to nature

In ancient Babylon and various contemporary spiritual traditions, the priesthood holds a significant role in bridging the gap between the spiritual and natural realms. As intermediaries between humans and the divine, priests and priestesses were entrusted with the responsibility of maintaining a harmonious relationship with nature and upholding the sacred connection between humans and the natural world. This section delves into the role of the priesthood in ancient Babylon and explores their connection to nature and the environment, emphasizing the relevance of their practices in modern ecospirituality.

Spiritual Mediators:

Priests and priestesses served as spiritual mediators, facilitating communication between humans and the divine forces that governed the natural world. They possessed specialized knowledge and rituals that allowed them to access and interpret the will of the gods or spirits. Through their rituals and ceremonies, they sought to establish a balance and harmony between humans, nature, and the supernatural realm. Their connection to nature was a vital aspect of their role, as they recognized the divine presence and influence within the natural elements.

Example: Analyze the role of the priestesses of Ishtar, the Babylonian goddess of love and fertility, and their connection to the cycles of nature. Discuss how their rituals and practices honored the interconnectedness between human fertility, agricultural fertility, and the changing seasons.

Guardians of Sacred Sites:

Priests and priestesses were often the guardians of sacred sites in ancient Babylon. These sites, which could be natural landscapes, springs, groves, or specific geographical locations, held spiritual significance and were believed to be inhabited by deities or ancestral spirits. The priesthood maintained and cared for these sites, ensuring their sanctity and preserving the spiritual energy associated with them. They facilitated rituals and ceremonies at these sacred locations, fostering a deep connection between the community, the natural environment, and the divine.

Example: Explore the role of contemporary spiritual leaders in safeguarding and revitalizing sacred sites. Discuss their efforts to preserve natural landscapes, protect biodiversity, and engage in land restoration projects in collaboration with local communities and environmental organizations.

Rituals of Nature Worship:

Priesthoods in ancient Babylon performed rituals and ceremonies that celebrated and honored the natural world. These rituals often revolved around agricultural cycles, celestial events, and seasonal changes. By engaging in these rituals, the priesthood acknowledged the interdependence of humans and nature, expressing gratitude for the gifts of the earth and seeking blessings for abundance and fertility. The rituals acted as reminders of the sacredness of the natural world and encouraged the community to live in harmony with nature.

Example: Examine the rituals and practices of modern-day priestesses and priests in various spiritual traditions, such as witchcraft or shamanism. Discuss their role in conducting ceremonies that promote ecological awareness, sustainable agriculture, and the restoration of ecosystems. Explore how these rituals reinforce the connection between spirituality, community, and the natural environment.

Problems and Exercises:

Study the rituals performed by ancient Babylonian priests and priestesses, such as the Akitu festival, and their significance in honoring the agricultural cycle. Analyze how these rituals fostered a sense of ecological awareness and community cohesion.

Research and compare the practices of contemporary spiritual traditions that emphasize the priesthood's connection to nature. Discuss similarities and differences in their approaches to honoring the natural world and promoting environmental stewardship.

Engage in a role-playing activity where We take on the roles of priests and priestesses, conducting a symbolic ritual that expresses gratitude for nature and emphasizes the interconnectedness of all beings. Reflect on the experience and discuss the insights gained.

Conduct interviews or research case studies on modern spiritual leaders who act as stewards of sacred sites or engage in ecological restoration projects. Analyze their motivations, challenges, and the impact of their work on community engagement and ecological conservation.

2. Educators and guides in environmental ethics

Within the realm of environmental ethics, educators and guides play a crucial role in promoting awareness, understanding, and practical application of ethical principles in relation to the environment. They act as facilitators, imparting knowledge, encouraging critical thinking, and guiding individuals and communities toward sustainable practices and responsible stewardship of the Earth. This section explores the significance of educators and guides in environmental ethics, drawing examples from diverse fields such as witchcraft, divination, herbalism, shamanism, and ecospirituality.

Knowledge and Awareness:

Educators and guides in environmental ethics possess a deep understanding of ecological systems, the interconnectedness of all living beings, and the impact of human actions on the environment. They provide knowledge about environmental issues, including the depletion of natural resources, climate change, pollution, and loss of biodiversity. Through their teachings, they raise awareness about the ethical implications of these issues and the urgent need for sustainable practices.

Example: Examine the role of herbalism practitioners in educating communities about the sustainable use of medicinal plants. Discuss how they emphasize the importance of ethical harvesting, cultivation, and preservation of plant species to ensure long-term ecological balance and the continuation of traditional healing practices.

Ethics and Values:

Educators and guides in environmental ethics instill values that promote responsible environmental behavior. They encourage individuals to develop a deep sense of respect, empathy, and interconnectedness with the natural world. They teach the principles of sustainability, conservation, and ecological justice, highlighting the importance of considering the long-term consequences of our actions on future generations and the wider ecosystem.

Example: Explore the teachings of eco-spiritual leaders who emphasize the concept of Earth as a living entity with intrinsic value and rights. Discuss how these teachings inspire individuals to adopt an ecological worldview and prioritize the well-being of the Earth in their decision-making processes.

Practical Application:

Educators and guides in environmental ethics provide practical guidance on how to translate ethical principles into tangible actions. They offer strategies for sustainable living, including energy conservation, waste reduction, organic farming, and eco-friendly consumer choices. They empower individuals to make informed decisions and take steps toward reducing their ecological footprint.

Example: Analyze the role of environmental guides in shamanic traditions, who teach techniques for connecting with nature and seek guidance from the spirits to understand how human actions impact the natural world. Discuss how these practices can inspire individuals to adopt more sustainable lifestyles and advocate for environmental protection.

Problems and Exercises:

Conduct research on prominent environmental educators and guides, such as eco-philosophers, indigenous elders, or environmental activists. Analyze their teachings, writings, and actions, and discuss their impact on environmental ethics and advocacy.

Organize a workshop or seminar led by an environmental educator or guide. Explore topics such as sustainable agriculture, eco-spirituality, or ethical consumerism. Engage in discussions and activities that promote critical thinking and practical application of environmental ethics.

Create a project that promotes environmental awareness in your community. Develop educational materials, such as brochures or online resources, to raise awareness about local environmental issues and provide practical solutions for sustainable living.

Collaborate with local organizations or environmental experts to conduct field trips or site visits that highlight sustainable practices and the importance of environmental ethics. Reflect on the experiences and discuss the lessons learned.

VI. Legacy and Influences of Babylonian Ecospirituality

The ancient civilization of Babylon left a profound legacy in various fields, including ecospirituality. Babylonian ecospirituality was deeply rooted in their connection with nature, reverence for the divine, and recognition of the interdependence between humans and the natural world. This section explores the lasting influences of Babylonian ecospirituality on contemporary spiritual practices and environmental philosophies.

Influence on Witchcraft and Magic:

Babylonian ecospirituality has had a significant impact on the practices of witchcraft and magic. The Babylonians believed in the power of rituals, incantations, and spellwork to interact with the natural forces and seek divine assistance. Many modern witchcraft traditions draw inspiration from Babylonian magical practices, incorporating elements such as sacred symbols, herbalism, and divination techniques.

Example: Investigate the use of Babylonian-inspired symbols and sigils in contemporary witchcraft rituals. Discuss how these symbols are believed to connect practitioners with the natural world and channel spiritual energies for various purposes, such as healing, protection, and manifestation.

Influence on Shamanism:

Babylonian ecospirituality has also influenced shamanic practices, which emphasize communication with spirits and the natural world. Babylonian shamans sought guidance and healing from the spirits of animals, plants, and celestial beings. Contemporary shamanic traditions often incorporate elements of Babylonian cosmology and ritual practices, such as journeying to spiritual realms, working with power animals, and performing sacred ceremonies.

Example: Explore the role of Babylonian mythology and deities in contemporary shamanic journeying practices. Discuss how shamans connect with the energy and wisdom of Babylonian gods and goddesses during trance states to gain spiritual insight and healing.

Influence on Ecospirituality and Earth-based Religions:

Babylonian ecospirituality has left a lasting impact on modern ecospiritual movements and Earth-based religions. The recognition of the sacredness of the Earth, the interconnectedness of all beings, and the practice of honoring the cycles of nature can be traced back to Babylonian beliefs. These ideas are foundational to ecospirituality, which seeks to forge a spiritual connection with the Earth and advocate for its preservation.

Example: Examine the role of Babylonian ecospirituality in the emergence of contemporary Earth-based religious movements, such as modern Paganism and nature-centered spiritualities. Discuss how these traditions draw inspiration from Babylonian cosmology, rituals, and reverence for the natural world.

Influence on Environmental Ethics and Sustainability:

The principles of Babylonian ecospirituality, including respect for nature, responsible resource management, and harmony with the environment, have contributed to the development of environmental ethics and sustainability practices. Concepts such as ecological balance, stewardship, and the consideration of long-term consequences find resonance in contemporary environmental movements.

Example: Investigate how Babylonian perspectives on resource management and the preservation of biodiversity have influenced modern environmental ethics. Discuss the incorporation of Babylonian principles into sustainable development practices, conservation efforts, and the pursuit of ecological justice.

Problems and Exercises:

Conduct research on a contemporary spiritual practice or environmental movement that shows clear influences from Babylonian ecospirituality. Analyze the similarities and differences between the two, considering cultural context and adaptations to modern beliefs and practices.

Explore the use of Babylonian-inspired rituals and symbols in modern ecospiritual practices. Create a visual representation of a ritual or symbol inspired by Babylonian ecospirituality and present its significance and intended effects.

Organize a panel discussion or debate on the legacy of Babylonian ecospirituality in modern spiritual practices and environmental philosophies. Assign We different perspectives to argue for or against the influence of Babylonian ecospirituality, encouraging critical thinking and evidence-based arguments.

Write a reflective essay on the personal relevance and resonance of Babylonian ecospirituality in your own spiritual beliefs or environmental practices. Discuss how elements of Babylonian ecospirituality have influenced your understanding of nature, your sense of interconnectedness, and your commitment to environmental stewardship.

A. Influence of Babylonian ecospirituality on later civilizations

The profound spiritual and ecological insights of Babylonian ecospirituality had a far-reaching influence on later civilizations. The concepts of reverence for nature, interconnectedness, and sustainable practices propagated by the Babylonians left a lasting legacy that shaped the beliefs, rituals, and environmental attitudes of subsequent cultures. This section explores the significant impact of Babylonian ecospirituality on various civilizations throughout history.

Influence on Ancient Greek Philosophy:

Babylonian ecospirituality played a pivotal role in shaping the philosophical ideas of ancient Greece. The Greeks, particularly the pre-Socratic philosophers, were influenced by the Babylonians' holistic worldview and recognition of the interconnectedness of all beings. The concept of harmony with nature, central to Babylonian thought, found expression in Greek notions such as the balance of opposites in Heraclitus' philosophy and the cosmic order in Pythagorean teachings.

Example: Analyze the influence of Babylonian ecospirituality on the philosophy of Anaximander, an ancient Greek thinker who proposed the idea of a universal order and a cyclical nature of life. Compare Anaximander's cosmological views to Babylonian cosmology, highlighting the shared concepts of interconnectedness and cyclical processes.

Influence on Indigenous Wisdom Traditions:

Babylonian ecospirituality also left its imprint on indigenous wisdom traditions across the globe. Indigenous cultures that maintained a deep connection with their natural surroundings incorporated elements of Babylonian ecospirituality into their own spiritual practices. The recognition of nature's sacredness, rituals honoring the land and its resources, and the belief in the inherent wisdom of the natural world can be traced back to Babylonian influences.

Example: Explore how Babylonian ecospirituality influenced indigenous cultures such as Native American tribes, Australian Aboriginal communities, or African traditional religions. Investigate the shared beliefs and practices related to the sacredness of nature, ancestral connections, and ecological stewardship.

Influence on Medieval European Mysticism:

The legacy of Babylonian ecospirituality persisted into the medieval period and influenced the development of mystical traditions in Europe. Mystical movements such as Christian mysticism, Kabbalah, and Sufism embraced the principles of interconnectedness, divine immanence in nature, and the pursuit of unity with the cosmos. These ideas can be traced back to Babylonian notions of the sacredness of the Earth and the divine presence in all aspects of creation.

Example: Examine the influence of Babylonian ecospirituality on the writings of mystics like Meister Eckhart or the teachings of Kabbalistic scholars. Analyze their mystical interpretations of nature and the resonance of Babylonian ideas in their works.

Influence on Modern Ecological Movements:

Babylonian ecospirituality continues to inspire contemporary ecological movements and environmental activism. The recognition of humanity's interdependence with the natural world, the call for sustainable practices, and the spiritual connection to the Earth find echoes in modern environmental philosophies. The influence of Babylonian ecospirituality can be seen in movements advocating for environmental justice, conservation, and the preservation of biodiversity.

Example: Investigate the influence of Babylonian ecospirituality on prominent environmental thinkers or organizations. Discuss how their ideas and initiatives align with Babylonian principles, focusing on specific examples like ecofeminism, deep ecology, or indigenous environmental movements.

Problems and Exercises:

Research and present a case study on a specific civilization or cultural group that demonstrates clear influences of Babylonian ecospirituality. Explore their spiritual beliefs, rituals, and ecological practices, and highlight the similarities and differences between their adaptations and the original Babylonian concepts.

Create a visual timeline illustrating the transmission of Babylonian ecospirituality across different civilizations and time periods. Include key events, figures, and cultural exchanges that contributed to the dissemination and transformation of these ideas.

Debate the extent to which Babylonian ecospirituality influenced the development of specific religious or philosophical traditions. Assign We different perspectives to argue for or against the direct impact of Babylonian ecospirituality, supporting their arguments with historical evidence.

Write an essay discussing the contemporary relevance of Babylonian ecospirituality in addressing pressing environmental issues. Reflect on how Babylonian principles can inspire sustainable practices, social activism, and the promotion of ecological balance in the modern world.

B. Resurgence of ecospiritual practices in modern times

In recent decades, there has been a notable resurgence of ecospiritual practices as individuals and communities seek to reconnect with the natural world and address pressing environmental challenges. Drawing inspiration from ancient wisdom traditions, such as witchcraft, divination, herbalism, shamanism, and magic in Ancient Babylon, modern ecospirituality embraces a holistic approach that combines spiritual beliefs, ecological awareness, and sustainable living. This section explores the factors contributing to the resurgence of ecospiritual practices in modern times and their significance in addressing environmental issues.

Environmental Crises and Ecospiritual Awakening:

The escalating environmental crises, including climate change, habitat destruction, and biodiversity loss, have sparked an ecospiritual awakening among individuals concerned about the fate of the planet. The recognition of humanity's interdependence with nature and the understanding that ecological balance is vital for our collective well-being have led many to explore ecospiritual practices as a means of fostering a deeper connection with the Earth.

Example: Analyze the role of environmental activism in the resurgence of ecospirituality. Explore how environmental movements, such as the global climate strikes, have contributed to the increased interest in ecospiritual practices as a response to the urgency of environmental challenges.

Integration of Indigenous Wisdom:

Modern ecospirituality incorporates indigenous wisdom and practices that have long emphasized the interconnectedness of all beings and the sacredness of nature. By honoring indigenous perspectives and engaging in cross-cultural dialogue, individuals and communities are reawakening to ancient traditions and integrating them into contemporary spiritual practices.

Example: Examine the incorporation of indigenous wisdom into modern ecospiritual practices. Explore the adoption of indigenous rituals, such as smudging, vision quests, or plant medicine ceremonies, and discuss the importance of cultural respect and sensitivity in these practices.

Deep Ecology and Ecopsychology:

Deep ecology and ecopsychology are influential frameworks that promote the merging of ecological awareness with spirituality. Deep ecology emphasizes the intrinsic value of all life forms and encourages a shift in consciousness to view humans as part of an interconnected web of life. Ecopsychology explores the relationship between human well-being and the natural environment, recognizing the psychological and spiritual benefits of connecting with nature.

Example: Discuss the principles of deep ecology and ecopsychology and their integration into ecospiritual practices. Explore the concepts of biocentrism, ecological self, and eco-spirituality within these frameworks.

Ecospiritual Practices in Everyday Life:

One of the defining characteristics of the resurgence of ecospirituality is the integration of spiritual practices into daily life. Mindfulness in nature, sustainable gardening, eco-friendly rituals, and conscious consumption are examples of how individuals are incorporating ecospirituality into their everyday routines, fostering a sense of interconnectedness and environmental stewardship.

Example: Provide practical exercises and activities that We can engage in to incorporate ecospiritual practices into their daily lives. These may include nature meditation, sustainable gardening, eco-friendly rituals, or mindful consumption practices.

Problems and Exercises:

Reflect on personal experiences of ecological awakening and discuss how they have influenced your interest in ecospirituality. Share insights gained from engaging with nature and reflect on the role of spirituality in fostering a deeper connection with the environment.

Conduct research on a specific ecospiritual practice or movement, such as permaculture, earth-based spirituality, or ecofeminism. Present your findings, including the principles, rituals, and guiding philosophies associated with the chosen practice or movement.

Organize a group discussion on the challenges and controversies surrounding the integration of indigenous wisdom into modern ecospirituality. Encourage We to explore diverse perspectives and engage in respectful dialogue.

Design a community project that combines ecospirituality with environmental activism. Develop a plan for engaging local communities in ecological restoration, sustainable practices, or awareness campaigns, incorporating elements of ecospiritual beliefs and rituals.

C. Lessons and inspiration from Babylonian ecospirituality

Babylonian ecospirituality offers valuable lessons and inspiration for modern practitioners seeking to deepen their connection with the natural world. Drawing from the rich traditions of witchcraft, divination, herbalism, shamanism, and magic in Ancient Babylon, this section explores the teachings and practices that can guide individuals in their journey towards ecological consciousness and sustainable living.

Interconnectedness and Harmony:

One of the fundamental lessons from Babylonian ecospirituality is the recognition of the interconnectedness and harmony between humans, nature, and the divine. Babylonian cosmology viewed the natural world as a reflection of the divine order, emphasizing the interdependence and balance among all beings. This perspective encourages us to cultivate a sense of reverence and responsibility towards nature.

Example: Analyze the concept of interconnectedness in Babylonian ecospirituality and its parallels with other ancient and modern belief systems, such as indigenous cosmologies or deep ecology. Discuss the implications of embracing interconnectedness for our relationship with the environment.

Rituals as Sacred Practices:

Babylonian ecospirituality employed rituals as sacred practices to honor and communicate with the natural world. Rituals served as a means to express gratitude, seek guidance, and restore harmony within the ecosystem. By engaging in ritualistic practices, modern practitioners can deepen their connection with nature and develop a greater appreciation for its wisdom and healing powers.

Example: Explore the role of rituals in Babylonian ecospirituality and their relevance in contemporary ecospiritual practices. Provide examples of ritualistic practices, such as nature ceremonies, seasonal celebrations, or offerings, and discuss their significance in fostering a sense of interconnectedness and ecological stewardship.

Wisdom of Nature and Herbalism:

The Babylonians held a profound respect for the wisdom and healing properties of the natural world. Herbalism, the study and use of medicinal plants, was an integral part of their ecospiritual practices. By understanding the properties and energies of different plants, modern practitioners can tap into the wisdom of nature and promote holistic well-being.

Example: Discuss the significance of herbalism in Babylonian ecospirituality and its relevance in modern herbal medicine and alternative healing practices. Explore the principles of plant energetics, such as the Doctrine of Signatures, and their application in herbalism today.

Sustainable Agriculture and Land Stewardship:

Babylonian ecospirituality recognized the importance of sustainable agriculture and responsible land stewardship. The agricultural practices of Babylon, such as irrigation systems and land management techniques, demonstrate an understanding of the need for balance between human needs and the preservation of ecosystems. These principles can inspire modern practitioners to adopt regenerative farming methods and promote sustainable land use.

Example: Examine the agricultural practices of Ancient Babylon and their relevance in modern sustainable farming, permaculture, or community-supported agriculture (CSA) movements. Discuss the lessons learned from Babylonian agricultural techniques and their application in addressing contemporary food and ecological challenges.

Problems and Exercises:

Conduct research on a specific aspect of Babylonian ecospirituality, such as their understanding of celestial bodies and their influence on agriculture or the role of sacred landscapes in their spiritual practices. Present your findings and discuss their relevance in contemporary ecospiritual perspectives.

Organize a workshop on Babylonian-inspired rituals and practices for connecting with nature. Develop a guided meditation or ceremony that incorporates elements from Babylonian ecospirituality, encouraging participants to reflect on their relationship with the environment.

Analyze the ethical considerations of integrating Babylonian ecospiritual teachings into modern practices. Discuss the potential challenges and conflicts that may arise from adopting ancient traditions and highlight the importance of cultural respect and sensitivity.

Reflect on the lessons learned from Babylonian ecospirituality and develop a personal action plan for implementing sustainable practices in your daily life. Consider areas such as waste reduction, energy conservation, conscious consumerism, or supporting local and organic agriculture.

Chapter 3: Magic in Ancient Babylon

Magic has been an integral part of human culture for millennia, and one of the earliest known civilizations to have practiced a sophisticated system of magical beliefs and rituals is Ancient Babylon. Situated in Mesopotamia, the land between the Tigris and Euphrates rivers, Babylon flourished as a center of intellectual and spiritual pursuits.

In this section, we will delve into the fascinating world of Babylonian magic, exploring its historical and cultural context, its connection to other fields such as witchcraft, divination, herbalism, shamanism, and ecospirituality, and its enduring influence on magical practices throughout history.

Historical and Cultural Context:

To understand Babylonian magic, we must first examine the historical and cultural context in which it emerged. Ancient Babylon was a cosmopolitan society known for its advancements in various fields, including astronomy, mathematics, and literature. Magic played a central role in their religious and social life, with rituals and spells performed to communicate with the divine, protect against malevolent forces, and seek guidance for personal and communal well-being.

Magical Beliefs and Practices:

Babylonian magic encompassed a wide range of beliefs and practices. They believed in a complex pantheon of gods and goddesses who controlled different aspects of the natural and supernatural realms. The rituals and incantations performed by priests and practitioners aimed to tap into the power of these deities, as well as manipulate cosmic forces and spirits to achieve desired outcomes.

Magical Techniques and Tools:

Babylonian magic employed various techniques and tools to facilitate its practice. Rituals often involved the use of sacred objects, such as amulets, statues, and figurines, which were believed to embody protective or healing energies. Divination, the practice of foretelling the future or gaining insight, was another significant aspect of Babylonian magic, utilizing methods like astrology, dream interpretation, and omen reading.

The Role of Magic in Babylonian Society:

Magic held a significant place in Babylonian society, influencing areas such as medicine, law, and agriculture. It was believed that magical practices could cure illnesses, provide legal remedies, and ensure successful harvests. The priests, who were the custodians of magical knowledge, played a crucial role in performing rituals and providing guidance to the community.

Example: Explore the historical and cultural factors that contributed to the development of Babylonian magic, examining its connections to the wider Mesopotamian religious and social context. Discuss the influence of neighboring civilizations on Babylonian magical practices and the role of magic in maintaining social order and religious beliefs.

Problems and Exercises:

Research and analyze a specific aspect of Babylonian magic, such as the role of incantations in ritual practices or the use of amulets for protection. Present your findings and discuss the significance of your chosen topic within Babylonian magical traditions.

Develop a guided meditation or visualization exercise inspired by Babylonian magical beliefs and practices. Guide participants in connecting with the energies of Babylonian deities or cosmic forces, encouraging them to explore their own magical potentials.

Compare and contrast Babylonian magical practices with those of other ancient civilizations, such as Egyptian or Greek magic. Discuss the similarities and differences in their beliefs, rituals, and magical tools, highlighting the unique contributions of Babylonian magic to the broader magical tradition.

Reflect on the ethical considerations of practicing Babylonian magic in the modern world. Discuss the importance of cultural sensitivity and the potential challenges of integrating ancient magical practices into contemporary contexts. Engage in a group discussion on the responsibilities and limitations of modern practitioners in relation to cultural heritage.

A. Overview of magic in ancient Babylonian culture

Magic in ancient Babylonian culture held a significant place, intertwining with religious, social, and everyday life. The Babylonians believed in the existence of a complex supernatural realm inhabited by gods, demons, and spirits, and they sought to interact with these entities through magical rituals and practices. In this section, we will provide an overview of magic in ancient Babylonian culture, exploring its historical context, key beliefs, practices, and the role of magical practitioners.

Historical Context:

Ancient Babylon, located in Mesopotamia (modern-day Iraq), flourished as a major civilization from the 18th to the 6th century BCE. Babylonian magic emerged within the broader Mesopotamian context, influenced by neighboring cultures such as the Sumerians and Assyrians. As one of the earliest known civilizations, Babylon developed a rich magical tradition that left a lasting impact on subsequent magical practices.

Beliefs and Concepts:

Babylonian magic was rooted in a complex cosmology and religious worldview. The Babylonians believed in the existence of multiple gods and goddesses who governed various aspects of life and nature. They saw magic as a means of establishing communication with these deities, seeking their favor, protection, and guidance. Magic was also believed to have the power to influence natural forces, combat malevolent spirits, and affect the destinies of individuals and communities.

Magical Practices and Rituals:

Babylonian magical practices involved a wide range of rituals, spells, and divinatory techniques. Rituals were performed by trained priests or individuals knowledgeable in the magical arts. They included the recitation of incantations, the use of magical objects and symbols, and the performance of specific gestures and actions. Divination played a prominent role, with methods such as astrology, dream interpretation, and the examination of animal entrails used to gain insights into the future or seek divine guidance.

Magical Practitioners:

In Babylonian society, individuals with specialized knowledge and skills in magic played significant roles as magical practitioners. These practitioners included priests, who acted as intermediaries between humans and the gods, and diviners, who used various techniques to interpret signs and omens. The priesthood held privileged access to sacred texts and rituals, and their expertise was sought after for matters related to healing, protection, and spiritual guidance.

Example: Explore the historical development of Babylonian magic, tracing its roots back to the Sumerian civilization and its subsequent evolution within Babylonian society. Discuss the influence of other neighboring cultures on Babylonian magical practices and the ways in which magic was integrated into religious ceremonies and everyday life.

Problems and Exercises:

Select a specific aspect of Babylonian magic, such as the use of amulets or the practice of astrology, and research its significance and symbolism in Babylonian culture. Present your findings and discuss the potential applications of this aspect of magic in modern spiritual practices.

Design a hypothetical Babylonian magical ritual for a specific purpose, such as fertility or protection. Provide a step-by-step guide, including the necessary preparations, materials, and invocations, and explain the underlying beliefs and intentions behind each component.

Compare and contrast Babylonian magic with magical practices in other ancient civilizations, such as Egyptian or Greek magic. Identify similarities and differences in their beliefs, rituals, and cosmologies, and discuss the possible cross-cultural influences and exchanges between these traditions.

Reflect on the ethical considerations of practicing Babylonian magic in the modern world. Discuss issues such as cultural appropriation, respectful engagement with ancient traditions, and the responsible use of magical practices. Engage in a group discussion on the potential benefits and challenges of incorporating ancient magical systems into contemporary spiritual paths.

Note: When exploring Babylonian magic, it is essential to approach the subject with cultural sensitivity and respect. Acknowledge that our understanding of Babylonian magical practices is based on historical texts and archaeological evidence, which may present gaps and uncertainties. Emphasize the importance of studying ancient traditions within their historical and cultural context and avoid appropriating or misrepresenting Babylonian culture and beliefs.

B. Significance and purpose of magical practices

Magical practices have played a significant role throughout human history, serving various purposes across different cultures and belief systems. In this section, we will explore the significance and purpose of magical practices, drawing examples from diverse fields such as witchcraft, divination, herbalism, shamanism, and magic in ancient Babylon. We will delve into the underlying principles and motivations behind engaging in magical practices and examine their impact on individuals, communities, and spiritual growth.

Personal Empowerment and Transformation:

One of the primary purposes of magical practices is to empower individuals and facilitate personal transformation. Engaging in rituals, spells, and other magical techniques allows individuals to connect with their inner power and access hidden potentials. Through focused intention and the manipulation of energies, practitioners seek to manifest their desires, overcome obstacles, and enhance their spiritual growth. For example, in witchcraft, spellcasting rituals aim to harness personal energy and align it with specific intentions, thereby promoting self-empowerment and personal transformation.

Connection with the Divine and Spirituality:

Magical practices often serve as a means of establishing a connection with the divine or higher spiritual realms. By engaging in rituals, prayers, and invocations, individuals seek to communicate with gods, goddesses, ancestors, or spirit guides. These practices facilitate a sense of spiritual communion, offering guidance, protection, and support from the spiritual realm. Shamanic journeying, for instance, involves entering altered states of consciousness to connect with spirit allies and receive wisdom and healing.

Healing and Well-being:

Magical practices have long been associated with healing and well-being, addressing physical, emotional, and spiritual ailments. Herbalism, for example, utilizes the medicinal properties of plants and herbs to promote healing and balance within the body. Divination practices, such as tarot readings or scrying, can provide insights into the underlying causes of ailments or life challenges, offering guidance for restoration and well-being.

Nature and Ecological Harmony:

Magical practices often emphasize a deep connection with nature and the pursuit of ecological harmony. Many traditions recognize the interconnectedness of all beings and the importance of living in harmony with the natural world. Ecospirituality, for instance, encourages individuals to cultivate reverence for nature, adopt sustainable practices, and engage in rituals that honor the Earth. By aligning with the natural rhythms and cycles, practitioners seek to restore balance and promote ecological well-being.

Example: Explore the significance of magical practices in ancient Babylonian culture, where magic served as a means to communicate with the gods, influence natural forces, and navigate the complexities of life. Discuss how these practices reflected the Babylonians' worldview and spiritual beliefs, and how they contributed to their overall well-being and societal harmony.

Problems and Exercises:

Reflect on your own spiritual path or personal beliefs and identify a specific magical practice that aligns with your values and intentions. Explain its significance to you and discuss how it contributes to your personal growth and well-being.

Research and analyze different cultural perspectives on magical practices, such as the European witchcraft tradition, Native American shamanism, or African spiritual systems. Compare and contrast their purposes, methods, and underlying philosophies, highlighting the diversity of magical practices across cultures.

Conduct an interview or engage in a discussion with a practitioner of magical traditions, such as a witch, diviner, or herbalist. Explore their motivations for engaging in magical practices and the transformative effects they have experienced. Analyze the similarities and differences between their perspectives and your own.

Analyze potential ethical considerations and challenges associated with magical practices, such as issues of consent, cultural appropriation, and the responsible use of power. Engage in a group discussion to explore different viewpoints and develop strategies for navigating these ethical complexities.

Note: While discussing magical practices, it is important to approach the topic with cultural sensitivity and respect. Recognize the diversity of magical traditions and the complexity of their historical and cultural contexts. Avoid generalizations or stereotypes and be mindful of the potential misrepresentation or appropriation of cultural practices. Always conduct research and engage in discussions with respect for the traditions and the individuals involved.

C. Relationship between magic and religious beliefs

The relationship between magic and religious beliefs is a complex and multifaceted subject that has been explored throughout human history. In this section, we will examine the interplay between magic and religious beliefs, drawing examples from various fields such as witchcraft, divination, herbalism, shamanism, and ecospirituality. We will analyze the similarities, differences, and potential conflicts between magical practices and religious traditions, providing a comprehensive understanding of their relationship.

Overlapping Concepts and Practices:

Magic and religious beliefs often share common concepts and practices. Both involve engaging with unseen forces, supernatural beings, or divine entities. For instance, rituals performed in witchcraft and religious ceremonies frequently incorporate elements such as incantations, prayers, offerings, and the use of sacred symbols or objects. Divination practices, such as tarot reading or scrying, may be employed both as a means of seeking guidance from higher powers and as a tool for magical spellcasting.

Different Perspectives and Approaches:

While magic and religious beliefs may share certain practices, they can have distinct perspectives and approaches. Religious beliefs often involve organized systems of faith, established dogmas, and institutional structures, providing a framework for worship, moral codes, and communal rituals. In contrast, magical practices are often more individualistic and personalized, emphasizing personal empowerment, intention setting, and direct interaction with spiritual forces. However, it is important to note that these distinctions are not absolute and can vary across different magical and religious traditions.

Integration and Syncretism:

In some cases, magical practices and religious beliefs can intertwine and syncretize, creating hybrid traditions. This integration may occur when practitioners incorporate magical techniques into their religious rituals or when religious beliefs influence the purpose and methods of magical practices. For example, in certain shamanic traditions, the shaman acts as both a religious mediator and a magical practitioner, utilizing spiritual connections and employing magical techniques to heal and divine the future.

Conflicts and Controversies:

While there can be harmony and coexistence between magical practices and religious beliefs, conflicts and controversies may also arise. Some religious traditions consider certain magical practices as incompatible with their core tenets or as acts of heresy. Historical examples include the persecution of witches during the European witch trials, where magical practices were viewed as sinful and in opposition to Christian doctrines. Such conflicts often arise due to differences in belief systems, power dynamics, cultural norms, and interpretations of divine will.

Example: Explore the relationship between magic and religious beliefs in ancient Babylonian culture, where magic was intricately woven into religious practices and cosmological beliefs. Discuss the role of priests as both religious leaders and magical practitioners, and how the Babylonians perceived the influence of divine entities in magical workings. Examine the interdependence between religious rituals and magical techniques in the context of temple ceremonies and divinatory practices.

Problems and Exercises:

Compare and contrast the role of magic in different religious traditions, such as the use of ritual magic in Western occultism and the magical practices within indigenous spiritual systems. Analyze how these practices align with or diverge from the religious beliefs and structures within their respective contexts.

Conduct research on the historical perspectives of different religious traditions toward magic, including both positive and negative attitudes. Analyze the factors that contribute to these perspectives and discuss how they have influenced the relationship between magic and religious beliefs.

Engage in a group discussion or debate exploring the potential conflicts and controversies that can arise when integrating magical practices with religious beliefs. Consider the ethical implications, cultural sensitivities, and the potential impact on individuals and communities.

Reflect on your own beliefs and experiences. Discuss how your personal spiritual or religious beliefs intersect with or influence your engagement with magical practices. Consider the ways in which these practices enhance or challenge your understanding of spirituality and its relationship to the divine.

I. Unveiling the Mysteries of Babylonian Magic

In this section, we will embark on a journey to uncover the enigmatic world of Babylonian magic. Drawing upon a wide range of fields, including witchcraft, divination, herbalism, shamanism, and ecospirituality, we will delve into the rich tapestry of Babylonian magical practices. By examining historical sources, archaeological discoveries, and scholarly interpretations, we aim to shed light on the intricate rituals, spells, and beliefs that characterized Babylonian magic.

Historical Context and Cultural Significance:

To understand Babylonian magic, it is essential to explore its historical context and cultural significance. The ancient city of Babylon, located in Mesopotamia, was renowned for its advanced civilization and sophisticated belief systems. Magic played a vital role in Babylonian society, serving as a means of connecting with the divine, seeking protection, influencing events, and understanding the forces of the natural and supernatural realms.

Magical Techniques and Practices:

Babylonian magic encompassed a diverse array of techniques and practices. These included the recitation of incantations, the creation and use of magical objects such as amulets and talismans, the performance of rituals and sacrifices, the interpretation of omens and signs, and the employment of herbal remedies and potions. Through these methods, practitioners sought to harness and manipulate cosmic energies, spirits, and deities to achieve desired outcomes.

Divine Entities and Supernatural Forces:

Central to Babylonian magic were the beliefs in divine entities and supernatural forces. The pantheon of Babylonian gods and goddesses, such as Marduk, Ishtar, and Ea, held significant influence over magical workings. Practitioners invoked these deities through prayers and offerings, establishing a connection between the mortal and divine realms. Additionally, belief in spirits, demons, and celestial bodies played a crucial role in understanding the underlying principles of Babylonian magic.

Magical Texts and Incantations:

One of the key sources of knowledge about Babylonian magic is the collection of magical texts and incantations that have survived to this day. These texts, such as the "Enuma Elish" and the "Shurpu Series," provide insights into the spells, rituals, and invocations employed by Babylonian magicians. By studying these texts, modern researchers and practitioners can gain a deeper understanding of the techniques and beliefs that shaped Babylonian magical practices.

Example: Explore the concept of sympathetic magic in Babylonian magical practices. Discuss how the principles of "like attracts like" and the use of sympathetic objects and rituals were employed to influence desired outcomes. Analyze specific examples of sympathetic magic found in Babylonian magical texts and rituals, such as the use of figurines, images, and symbolic actions.

Problems and Exercises:

Examine the role of divination in Babylonian magic and its relationship to the broader belief systems of the time. Analyze different divinatory techniques, such as hepatoscopy (divination by examining the liver) and astrology, and discuss how they were integrated into magical practices.

Research the use of herbalism in Babylonian magic. Identify specific plants and their associated magical properties and discuss their application in rituals, spells, and healing practices.

Engage in a comparative analysis of Babylonian magic with magical practices in other ancient civilizations, such as Ancient Egypt or Ancient Greece. Explore commonalities and differences in magical beliefs, techniques, and cultural contexts.

Reflect on the ethical considerations surrounding the study and practice of Babylonian magic in the modern age. Discuss the challenges of interpreting and adapting ancient magical practices within contemporary cultural and ethical frameworks.

A. Beliefs about the existence and manipulation of supernatural forces

In this section, we will explore the fascinating realm of beliefs held by various cultures regarding the existence and manipulation of supernatural forces. Drawing upon examples from witchcraft, divination, herbalism, shamanism, ecospirituality, and magic in ancient Babylon, we will delve into the intricate tapestry of human understanding and interaction with the supernatural.

Conceptualizing the Supernatural:

The belief in supernatural forces has been deeply ingrained in human history and spans across cultures and civilizations. These forces are often perceived as entities or energies that exist beyond the realm of the physical world, transcending the boundaries of what can be perceived by the five senses. Supernatural forces may include deities, spirits, energies, and other non-physical entities that possess unique powers and influences.

Dualism and the Balance of Forces:

Many belief systems propose a dualistic understanding of the supernatural, where opposing forces or energies coexist and interact. These forces can be conceptualized as light and dark, good and evil, or masculine and feminine. The balance between these forces is often seen as essential for harmony and well-being. Examples of this duality can be found in the concepts of yin and yang in Chinese philosophy or the notions of white and black magic in witchcraft traditions.

Interaction with Supernatural Forces:

Believers often seek to interact with supernatural forces through various means, such as rituals, prayers, invocations, and offerings. These practices aim to establish a connection with the supernatural realm and to seek assistance, guidance, protection, or empowerment. Examples include the use of divination tools, such as tarot cards or runes, to gain insights from higher powers or the performance of rituals and spells to invoke specific deities or spirits.

Manipulating Supernatural Forces:

Within certain belief systems, the manipulation of supernatural forces is considered a significant aspect of magical practices. This involves harnessing and channeling the energies or powers associated with these forces to bring about desired outcomes. Practices may include spellcasting, the creation and use of talismans or amulets, or the employment of herbs and other natural substances believed to possess specific magical properties.

Example: Discuss the belief in elemental forces in different spiritual traditions. Explore how these forces, such as earth, air, fire, and water, are perceived as fundamental building blocks of the universe and how they are incorporated into various magical practices. Provide examples from witchcraft, shamanism, and ancient Babylonian magic to illustrate different approaches to understanding and working with elemental energies.

Problems and Exercises:

Research the concept of animism and its association with the belief in supernatural forces. Discuss how animistic beliefs are reflected in different cultures and how they shape human interaction with the natural world.

Investigate the role of ancestors and ancestral spirits in different belief systems. Explore how ancestral veneration and communication practices are utilized to establish connections with supernatural forces and seek guidance or support.

Compare and contrast the approaches to supernatural forces in different cultural contexts, such as African, Native American, and Celtic traditions. Identify similarities and differences in beliefs, practices, and cultural interpretations.

Reflect on the ethical considerations surrounding the manipulation of supernatural forces. Discuss potential consequences, both positive and negative, that may arise from engaging in magical practices and interacting with supernatural entities.

B. Role of magic in daily life and society

In this section, we will explore the multifaceted role of magic in daily life and society. Drawing upon examples from witchcraft, divination, herbalism, shamanism, ecospirituality, and magic in ancient Babylon, we will delve into how magic influences various aspects of human existence and shapes social dynamics.

Healing and Well-being:

Magic has long been associated with healing practices and maintaining well-being. Throughout history, practitioners of different magical traditions have utilized spells, rituals, and herbal remedies to address physical, emotional, and spiritual ailments. For example, in herbalism, plants with specific properties are used to create potions or ointments believed to promote healing. Likewise, shamans employ spiritual journeys and energy healing techniques to restore balance and harmony.

Protection and Defense:

Magic often serves as a means of protection and defense against negative influences, malevolent forces, or undesirable events. Amulets, talismans, and protective spells are employed to ward off harm and create a shield of spiritual or energetic protection. In ancient Babylon, magical incantations and rituals were used to guard against evil spirits and supernatural threats. Similarly, practices such as witchcraft incorporate spells and rituals to create a protective barrier around individuals or their living spaces.

Divination and Guidance:

The practice of divination is integral to many magical traditions, allowing individuals to seek guidance and insight into their lives. Divination methods such as tarot readings, astrology, scrying, and rune casting are utilized to gain clarity about the past, present, and future. Divination serves as a tool for decision-making, self-reflection, and understanding one's path. It provides a means to navigate life's challenges and make informed choices based on spiritual guidance.

Rituals and Celebrations:

Magic infuses rituals and celebrations with spiritual significance and deeper meaning. Ceremonies and rituals mark important life events such as births, weddings, and funerals, invoking magical practices to enhance the transformative power of these transitions. Seasonal festivals and lunar cycles are honored through magical rituals, aligning individuals with natural rhythms and cycles. By engaging in magical rituals, individuals connect with their spirituality, commune with deities or spirits, and foster a sense of belonging and community.

Example: Discuss the role of magic in ancient Babylonian society and how it influenced various aspects of daily life. Explore the use of magic in agricultural practices, fertility rites, protection against malevolent forces, and the integration of magic in the social, religious, and political spheres. Provide examples from cuneiform texts and archaeological findings to illustrate the importance of magic in Babylonian society.

Problems and Exercises:

Investigate the role of magic in contemporary witchcraft practices and its impact on personal empowerment and self-transformation. Analyze how modern witches incorporate magical rituals and spells into their daily lives and how these practices contribute to their spiritual growth.

Explore the intersection of magic and social activism. Research how magical practices are utilized as tools for promoting social justice, environmental stewardship, and community healing. Discuss the ethical considerations and challenges that arise in combining magic with social and political action.

Reflect on the role of magic in personal and collective empowerment. Discuss how magical practices can foster a sense of agency, resilience, and interconnectedness. Explore the potential benefits and limitations of relying on magic as a transformative tool in contemporary society.

Examine the cultural and societal perception of magic in different time periods and regions. Compare and contrast the acceptance or suppression of magical practices and beliefs and analyze how these perceptions influence the role of magic in society.

C. Influence of magical practices on various aspects of Babylonian culture

Magical practices held significant influence over various aspects of Babylonian culture, permeating the realms of religion, governance, medicine, agriculture, and daily life. By exploring the interplay between magic and these domains, we gain insight into the profound impact of magical beliefs and rituals on Babylonian society.

Religion and Spiritual Beliefs:

Magic played a pivotal role in Babylonian religion, intertwining with the worship of deities and the veneration of spirits. The Babylonians believed that by invoking divine forces through rituals and spells, they could establish a connection with the divine realm and elicit favorable outcomes. Magical practices were intricately linked to religious ceremonies, where priests and priestesses performed incantations, made offerings, and conducted rituals to communicate with the gods and seek their blessings.

Example: Analyze the Enuma Elish, the Babylonian creation myth, and discuss how magical elements are incorporated into the narrative. Explore the role of magic in the rituals and ceremonies dedicated to deities such as Marduk, Ishtar, and Nabu.

Governance and Political Power:

Magical practices were entwined with the exercise of political power in Babylonian society. Kings and rulers sought the assistance of skilled magicians, known as "asipu" or "baru," who possessed the knowledge and expertise to perform magical rituals for the benefit of the state. These rituals aimed to secure the protection of the gods, ensure the prosperity of the kingdom, and safeguard against malevolent forces.

Example: Investigate the role of the "asipu" in Babylonian court records and royal inscriptions. Examine the rituals performed to legitimize the king's authority and establish divine favor, such as the "tupšarru" rituals.

Medicine and Healing Practices:

Magic played a crucial role in Babylonian medical practices, which blended empirical observations with spiritual beliefs. Ancient Babylonian physicians, known as "asû," believed that illness and disease were caused by supernatural forces or imbalances in the body, mind, and spirit. They employed magical spells, incantations, and herbal remedies to heal ailments, ward off evil spirits, and restore health.

Example: Study the "Diagnostic Handbook" of the Babylonian physician Esagil-kin-apli and analyze the magical aspects of the diagnostic and treatment methods described. Explore the belief in the supernatural causes of diseases and the role of magical incantations in the healing process.

Agriculture and Harvest:

Magical practices were deeply intertwined with agricultural rituals and fertility rites in Babylonian culture. Farmers and agricultural communities relied on magical ceremonies and offerings to ensure bountiful harvests, fertility of the land, and protection against crop failure or pests. These rituals were performed to appease agricultural deities and harness their power to nurture the earth and promote abundant growth.

Example: Examine the Babylonian agricultural calendar and identify the rituals and magical practices associated with each stage of the agricultural cycle. Discuss the importance of festivals such as the Akitu festival and the role of magic in ensuring successful harvests.

Problems and Exercises:

Investigate the counterarguments and dissenting opinions regarding the efficacy and ethical implications of magical practices in Babylonian society. Engage in a critical analysis of skeptical viewpoints and explore alternative explanations for the perceived effects of magic.

Compare and contrast magical practices in Babylonian culture with those in other ancient civilizations such as Ancient Egypt, Greece, or India. Analyze the similarities and differences in the role of magic and its influence on various aspects of society.

Reflect on the modern-day implications of magical practices inspired by ancient Babylonian traditions. Discuss the ethical considerations and potential benefits and challenges of incorporating magical rituals into contemporary spiritual or new-age practices.

Conduct a research project on the archaeological evidence of magical objects, texts, or artifacts found in ancient Babylonian sites. Analyze the cultural significance of these discoveries and their contribution to our understanding of magical practices in Babylonian culture.

II. Types of Magical Practices and Rituals

Magical practices and rituals in ancient Babylon were diverse and multifaceted, encompassing a wide range of techniques, beliefs, and objectives. These practices served various purposes, including protection, healing, divination, and spiritual communion. By exploring the different types of magical practices and rituals in Babylonian culture, we can gain a deeper understanding of their significance and the methods employed to harness supernatural forces.

Incantations and Spells:

Incantations and spells were fundamental components of Babylonian magic. These verbal formulae, recited with precision and accompanied by specific gestures or actions, were believed to invoke the power of supernatural beings and influence the natural and spiritual realms. Incantations often incorporated sacred names, symbolic language, and rhythmic patterns to channel energies and manifest desired outcomes.

Example: Analyze the "Maqlû" series of incantations, which focused on countering malevolent forces and removing curses. Explore the structure and content of these incantations, identifying the specific deities invoked and the objectives sought through their recitation.

Talismans and Amulets:

Talismans and amulets held great importance in Babylonian magical practices. These objects, often made of materials such as clay, metal, or stone, were inscribed with magical symbols, names of deities, or powerful incantations. They were believed to possess protective or healing properties and were worn or carried as personal charms to ward off evil, enhance fertility, or promote well-being.

Example: Investigate the use of cylinder seals as magical talismans in Babylonian culture. Examine the symbols and motifs depicted on these seals and discuss their connection to specific magical beliefs and practices.

Divination and Prophecy:

Divination was a central aspect of Babylonian magical practices, employed to gain insights into the future or uncover hidden knowledge. Various divinatory techniques were utilized, including the interpretation of celestial phenomena, the examination of animal entrails, and the observation of natural signs and omens. By deciphering these signs, the Babylonians sought guidance in making important decisions or understanding the intentions of the gods.

Example: Explore the practice of extispicy, which involved the examination of animal liver and other entrails to interpret omens. Analyze the symbolic significance of different features and anomalies observed in the organs and discuss how these signs were interpreted by the diviner.

Ritual Offerings and Sacrifices:

Ritual offerings and sacrifices played a crucial role in Babylonian magical rituals. These acts of devotion were performed to establish a connection with deities and seek their favor or protection. Offerings could include food, drink, flowers, incense, or symbolic representations of desired outcomes. Sacrifices, involving the ritual killing of animals, were conducted to appease deities, cleanse impurities, or fulfill vows.

Example: Examine the "Akitu" festival, a significant Babylonian celebration, and analyze the rituals and magical practices associated with it. Discuss the purpose and symbolism of the offerings and sacrifices made during this festival and their role in ensuring the renewal of cosmic order.

Problems and Exercises:

Compare and contrast the types of magical practices and rituals in ancient Babylon with those in other ancient civilizations, such as Egypt, Greece, or Mesopotamia. Analyze the similarities and differences in their objectives, techniques, and cultural contexts.

Research and present a case study on a specific Babylonian magical text, such as the "Enuma Anu Enlil" or "Maqlû" series. Analyze the structure, content, and intended use of the text, and discuss its significance in Babylonian magical practices.

Engage in a critical analysis of the ethical implications of certain magical practices, such as the use of curses or love spells. Discuss the potential consequences and ethical considerations associated with the manipulation of supernatural forces.

Reflect on the modern-day adaptation and reinterpretation of Babylonian magical practices in contemporary spiritual or new-age contexts. Investigate how these practices have been integrated into modern belief systems and discuss their relevance and effectiveness in the present-day.

A. Protective magic and warding off evil

In ancient Babylonian culture, the belief in malevolent forces and the need for protection against them was deeply ingrained. Protective magic played a significant role in safeguarding individuals, homes, and communities from harmful influences and evil spirits. This section explores the various methods and rituals employed by the Babylonians to ward off evil and ensure personal and collective well-being.

Amulets and Talismans:

Amulets and talismans were widely used as powerful protective devices in Babylonian magical practices. These objects, often crafted from materials such as clay, metal, or stone, were inscribed with symbols, incantations, or the names of protective deities. The belief was that wearing or carrying these amulets would provide a shield against negative energies and evil spirits.

Example: Examine the use of the "Lamassu" as a protective amulet in Babylonian culture. Analyze the symbolism and imagery depicted on these winged bull or lion statues and discuss their role in guarding entrances and deterring malevolent forces.

Incantations and Spells:

Incantations and spells were recited as a means of invoking the assistance and protection of benevolent deities and supernatural beings. These verbal formulae were believed to possess the power to ward off evil spirits, break curses, and create protective barriers. The recitation of these incantations often accompanied specific rituals and actions.

Example: Study the "Evil Eye" incantations, which aimed to counteract the harmful effects of the evil eye, a belief prevalent in ancient Babylonian culture. Analyze the structure and content of these incantations, including the use of sacred names and symbolic language, to understand how they served as protective measures.

Rituals of Purification:

Purification rituals were performed to cleanse individuals and spaces from negative influences and spiritual impurities. These rituals involved the use of sacred substances, such as water, salt, or incense, and often incorporated prayers and invocations to purify the body, mind, and environment.

Example: Explore the "Ablution Ritual" used for personal purification in Babylonian culture. Investigate the specific steps involved in this ritual, including the symbolic significance of washing with water and the recitation of prayers, and discuss how it was believed to protect against malevolent forces.

Guardians and Apotropaic Symbols:

Babylonian culture also employed various symbols and figurines to ward off evil and protect against negative energies. These symbols were often placed at thresholds, entrances, or in key locations to deter malevolent spirits. Guardians, such as the winged deities "Lamassu" and "Apkallu," were depicted as powerful protectors and were believed to watch over individuals and their homes.

Example: Analyze the use of apotropaic symbols, such as the "Hamsa" hand, in Babylonian protective magic. Discuss their symbolism and function as a means of deflecting evil influences and promoting well-being.

Problems and Exercises:

Research and present a case study on a specific protective magical ritual or object in Babylonian culture. Discuss its purpose, symbolism, and historical context, and analyze its effectiveness in warding off evil.

Engage in a comparative analysis of protective magical practices in ancient Babylon with those found in other cultures, such as ancient Egypt or Greece. Discuss the similarities and differences in their approaches to warding off evil and protecting against negative energies.

Reflect on the role of protective magic in modern-day spiritual or new-age practices. Investigate how ancient Babylonian techniques have been adapted and incorporated into contemporary belief systems and discuss their relevance and effectiveness in the present day.

Explore the ethical considerations surrounding the use of protective magic. Discuss potential ethical dilemmas, such as the unintended consequences of manipulating supernatural forces, and consider the balance between personal protection and respect for the free will and autonomy of others.

1. Rituals and spells for personal protection

In ancient Babylonian culture, the belief in the existence of malevolent forces and the need for personal protection was deeply ingrained. To ensure their well-being and safeguard against harm, individuals in Babylonian society turned to a variety of rituals and spells specifically designed for personal protection. This section explores some of the rituals and spells used by the Babylonians to ward off negative energies and promote personal safety and security.

Rituals for Personal Cleansing and Protection:

Babylonian culture placed great importance on personal cleansing as a means of purifying the body and the spirit. Rituals involving the use of sacred substances, such as water, salt, and incense, were performed to cleanse individuals from negative influences and to establish protective barriers around them. These rituals often incorporated prayers and invocations to invoke the assistance of benevolent deities.

Example: Explore the "Salt Cleansing Ritual" in Babylonian magic, where individuals would perform a ritual purification by sprinkling salt on their bodies and reciting protective incantations. Analyze the symbolic significance of salt as a purifying agent and discuss the intended effects of this ritual on personal protection.

Protective Amulets and Talismans:

Amulets and talismans were common forms of personal protection in Babylonian culture. These objects, typically made from materials such as clay, metal, or stone, were inscribed with symbols, incantations, or the names of protective deities. They were worn or carried by individuals as a means of warding off evil and providing a constant source of protective energy.

Example: Investigate the use of the "Eye of Horus" as a protective amulet in Babylonian magic. Examine its symbolism and discuss the belief that it provided a shield against the evil eye and other malevolent forces.

Spells for Personal Protection:

Spells and incantations were essential tools in Babylonian magical practices. Specific spells were recited or written down to invoke the assistance of deities and supernatural beings for personal protection. These spells often contained symbolic language, sacred names, and ritual actions to create a protective barrier around the individual.

Example: Study the "Personal Protection Incantation" in Babylonian magic, which aimed to create a shield of spiritual energy around the individual. Analyze the structure and content of the incantation, including the use of powerful words and invocations of deities, to understand its purpose and intended effects.

Rituals for Warding Off Evil Spirits:

Babylonians believed in the presence of malevolent spirits that could cause harm and bring misfortune. Rituals were performed to ward off these evil spirits and protect individuals from their negative influence. These rituals often involved the use of fire, sacred herbs, and specific gestures or movements.

Example: Explore the "Fire Cleansing Ritual" used for personal protection in Babylonian culture. Investigate the role of fire as a purifying element and analyze the specific steps involved in the ritual, including the symbolic actions performed to ward off evil spirits.

Problems and Exercises:

Select a specific ritual or spell for personal protection in Babylonian culture and analyze its components, including the use of sacred substances, invocations, and symbolic gestures. Discuss its effectiveness based on historical evidence and cultural context.

Compare and contrast the rituals and spells for personal protection in Babylonian culture with those found in other ancient civilizations, such as ancient Egypt or Greece.

Analyze the similarities and differences in their approaches to personal protection and discuss the underlying cultural and religious beliefs.

Reflect on the ethical considerations associated with the use of personal protection rituals and spells. Discuss potential ethical dilemmas, such as the boundaries between personal autonomy and the manipulation of supernatural forces, and consider the role of informed consent in magical practices.

Research and present a case study on a modern-day practice or adaptation of Babylonian personal protection rituals and spells. Discuss its origins, significance, and effectiveness in contemporary spiritual or new-age contexts.

2. Use of amulets and talismans

Amulets and talismans hold a significant place in various cultural and spiritual practices, including those found in Babylonian culture. These objects are believed to possess inherent powers or energies that can provide protection, good fortune, and other desired outcomes. This section explores the use of amulets and talismans in Babylonian culture, their significance, and their role in magical and spiritual practices.

Definition and Purpose:

Amulets and talismans are objects imbued with specific qualities or energies that are believed to provide various benefits to the wearer or bearer. In Babylonian culture, amulets and talismans were used as protective charms against evil spirits, diseases, misfortune, and other negative influences. They were seen as conduits for accessing the power of deities or supernatural forces, enabling individuals to enhance their personal well-being and navigate the challenges of life.

Example: Discuss the purpose of amulets and talismans in Babylonian culture by examining specific examples such as the "Seal of Shamash," a talisman associated with the Babylonian sun god. Analyze the symbolism and significance of this talisman and its intended effects on the wearer's spiritual and physical protection.

Materials and Symbolism:

Amulets and talismans in Babylonian culture were made from various materials, including clay, metal, stone, or even natural objects like herbs and animal parts. These materials were chosen based on their symbolic properties and associations with specific deities or spiritual concepts. The choice of materials and the symbols inscribed or represented on the amulets played a crucial role in channeling the desired energies or invoking the protection of particular deities.

Example: Explore the use of the "Eye of Marduk" amulet in Babylonian culture. Discuss the significance of the eye symbol and its connection to the god Marduk, and analyze how this amulet was believed to provide protection against evil forces.

Protective Properties and Ritual Use:

Amulets and talismans were believed to possess protective properties, acting as a shield against malevolent forces. The rituals surrounding their creation and activation were essential in harnessing their powers. These rituals often involved invocations, prayers, or specific actions performed by priests or individuals themselves. By consecrating and activating the amulets or talismans through these rituals, they were thought to become potent sources of protection and spiritual support.

Example: Investigate the rituals associated with the creation and activation of the "Falcon Amulet" in Babylonian culture. Discuss the symbolic representation of the falcon and its association with protective deities, and analyze the ritual steps involved in consecrating and empowering the amulet for its intended purpose.

Problems and Exercises:

Research and analyze the use of amulets and talismans in other ancient civilizations, such as ancient Egypt or Greece. Compare and contrast their purposes, materials used, and symbolism, and discuss the cultural and religious significance of these objects.

Select a specific amulet or talisman from Babylonian culture and analyze its symbolic meaning, materials used, and intended protective properties. Discuss its historical context and the cultural beliefs associated with its use.

Reflect on the role of personal belief and intention in the effectiveness of amulets and talismans. Discuss different perspectives on the nature of their power, including the psychological, energetic, and spiritual aspects.

Explore the modern-day use of amulets and talismans in various spiritual or new-age practices. Investigate their adaptation and reinterpretation in contemporary contexts and discuss the reasons for their continued popularity.

B. Divinatory and oracular magic

Divinatory and oracular magic played a significant role in the ancient Babylonian culture, providing a means for individuals to gain insights, guidance, and foresight into various aspects of life. This section explores the practice of divinatory and oracular magic in Babylonian society, including its methods, tools, and the beliefs associated with seeking supernatural knowledge.

Definition and Purpose:

Divinatory and oracular magic refers to the use of magical practices and rituals to access insights and knowledge from supernatural sources. It involves seeking answers to questions, predicting the future, and gaining guidance or advice. In Babylonian culture, divinatory and oracular magic was employed to navigate uncertainties, make informed decisions, and gain a deeper understanding of the divine will.

Example: Provide an example of divinatory and oracular magic in Babylonian culture, such as the consultation of a seer-priestess, known as an "En-Priestess," who would use various techniques to communicate with the gods and interpret their messages. Describe the purpose of this practice and its significance in Babylonian society.

Methods and Techniques:

Babylonian divinatory and oracular magic employed a range of methods and techniques to access supernatural knowledge. These included the interpretation of celestial omens, the examination of entrails or other natural objects, and the use of divinatory tools such as clay tablets inscribed with symbols. These methods were believed to enable individuals to communicate with the divine realm and receive guidance or insights.

Example: Explore the practice of hepatoscopy, which involved the examination of the liver of sacrificial animals as a means of divination. Explain the belief that the liver served as a medium for the gods to communicate their will, and discuss the complex system of interpreting various signs and features found in the liver.

Role of Diviners and Priests:

Divination in Babylonian culture was often performed by specialized individuals known as diviners or priests. These individuals possessed specific knowledge and skills to interpret the signs, symbols, and messages received from the gods. They acted as intermediaries between the human realm and the divine, guiding individuals in seeking answers to their questions and concerns.

Example: Discuss the role of diviners and priests in Babylonian society, using the example of the "Astrologer-Priests of Marduk" who interpreted celestial omens. Explore their training, social status, and the responsibilities they held in providing guidance and predictions based on their divinatory practices.

Problems and Exercises:

Investigate the use of other divinatory methods in ancient Babylonian culture, such as the interpretation of dreams or the casting of lots. Compare and contrast these methods with the ones discussed in this section, examining their purpose, techniques, and cultural significance.

Choose a specific divinatory tool or technique used in Babylonian culture, such as a clay tablet with divinatory symbols. Research its significance and the process involved in using it for divination. Discuss its role in seeking guidance from the gods and its connection to the broader belief system.

Explore the ethical considerations and limitations of divinatory and oracular magic in Babylonian culture. Discuss potential challenges or pitfalls in relying on supernatural knowledge for decision-making and how individuals in ancient Babylon navigated these complexities.

Reflect on the role of divination in contemporary spiritual practices. Investigate the ways in which divinatory and oracular methods have been adapted and utilized in modern divination systems such as tarot reading or astrology. Discuss the similarities and differences between ancient Babylonian divination and modern divinatory practices.

1. Techniques for seeking knowledge of the future

In the realm of magic and divination, the ancient Babylonians developed various techniques to seek knowledge of the future. These techniques were employed to gain insight, foresight, and guidance regarding forthcoming events. This section explores some of the prominent techniques utilized in Babylonian culture to obtain knowledge of the future.

Astrology:

Astrology played a central role in Babylonian divination and the quest for future knowledge. Babylonian astrologers observed celestial phenomena, particularly the movements and positions of celestial bodies such as the sun, moon, planets, and stars.

They believed that these celestial events held profound symbolic significance and could offer insights into future events and their implications for individuals and society.

Example: Discuss the significance of celestial omens in Babylonian astrology, such as the appearance of comets or the position of planets. Explain how astrologers interpreted these celestial events to predict and analyze various aspects of human life, including personal fortunes, political developments, and natural disasters.

Dream Interpretation:

Dreams were considered a channel through which the divine communicated with mortals in Babylonian culture. Dream interpretation held significant importance in seeking knowledge of the future. Babylonians believed that dreams conveyed messages and omens from the gods, providing glimpses into upcoming events and guiding individuals in decision-making.

Example: Explore the practice of dream incubation in Babylonian culture, where individuals sought prophetic dreams by sleeping in sacred spaces or performing specific rituals before sleep. Discuss the methods employed by Babylonian priests to interpret dreams and their role in providing guidance and predictions based on these dreams.

Oracle Consultation:

Oracles were revered sources of divine knowledge in Babylonian society. Individuals sought guidance and future insights by consulting with oracles, who acted as intermediaries between the human and divine realms. Oracles were believed to possess the ability to communicate with the gods and provide answers to specific questions or concerns.

Example: Examine the role of the seer-priestess in Babylonian culture, who served as an oracle and performed rituals to communicate with the gods. Describe the process of oracle consultation, including the preparation of the seer-priestess, the questioner's role, and the interpretation of the divine messages received.

Divination by Rituals and Objects:

Babylonians practiced divination through rituals and objects, seeking knowledge of the future by observing signs, symbols, and patterns in their surroundings. This included methods such as the interpretation of animal behavior, the examination of the liver of sacrificial animals (hepatoscopy), and the casting of lots.

Example: Discuss the use of casting lots, such as drawing marked sticks or stones, to obtain guidance and insights into the future. Explain how diviners interpreted the resulting patterns or sequences to provide predictions and advice.

Problems and Exercises:

Research and compare the techniques of seeking knowledge of the future in Babylonian culture with those of other ancient civilizations, such as ancient Greece or Egypt. Analyze similarities, differences, and cultural contexts.

Explore the ethical considerations and limitations of seeking knowledge of the future through these techniques. Discuss potential challenges, biases, and interpretations that could impact the accuracy and reliability of the information obtained.

Engage in practical exercises related to these techniques. For instance, practice dream journaling to enhance dream recall and interpretation skills. Reflect on personal experiences and discuss how dream symbolism and imagery can offer insights into future events.

Reflect on the contemporary relevance and applications of these ancient techniques. Investigate how elements of Babylonian divination and future knowledge-seeking are incorporated into modern practices such as astrology, dream analysis, or the use of divination tools like tarot cards.

2. Interpretation of signs, symbols, and dreams

In the realm of magic and divination, the interpretation of signs, symbols, and dreams played a crucial role in ancient Babylonian culture. The Babylonians believed that these elements carried hidden messages and insights into the future, allowing individuals to gain a deeper understanding of their circumstances and make informed decisions. This section delves into the principles and methods employed in interpreting signs, symbols, and dreams in Babylonian magic.

Signs and Omens:

Babylonians closely observed the natural world and everyday occurrences for signs and omens that could reveal divine messages. They believed that certain events or phenomena held symbolic meaning and could foretell future events or indicate the gods' will. These signs ranged from celestial events and atmospheric phenomena to the behavior of animals and the occurrence of unusual events in daily life.

Example: Explore the interpretation of celestial signs, such as the appearance of comets, eclipses, or unusual planetary alignments, and how they were perceived as indicators of impending events. Discuss the importance of observing animal behavior, such as the flight patterns of birds or the movement of snakes, and how these observations were interpreted to uncover hidden messages.

Symbolism in Rituals and Objects:

Babylonian magical rituals often incorporated symbolic elements, such as specific objects, gestures, or incantations, which were believed to hold deeper meaning. The interpretation of these symbols involved understanding their inherent properties, cultural significance, and connections to specific deities or realms of existence.

Example: Discuss the symbolic significance of objects used in Babylonian magical rituals, such as the staff, the figurines of deities, or the use of specific colors and materials. Explain how the context and intention of these symbols influenced their interpretation and the resulting magical effects.

Dream Interpretation:

Dreams held great importance in Babylonian culture as a means of communication between humans and the divine realm. Babylonians believed that dreams conveyed messages, omens, and guidance from the gods, offering insights into personal and collective futures. The interpretation of dreams involved understanding the symbolism and narrative elements present in the dream.

Example: Explain the techniques and principles of Babylonian dream interpretation. Explore common dream symbols and their associated meanings, such as encountering specific animals or interacting with deities in dreams. Discuss the role of professional interpreters and their expertise in analyzing dream narratives to uncover hidden messages and provide guidance.

Contextual Analysis:

Interpreting signs, symbols, and dreams in Babylonian magic required a contextual analysis that considered various factors such as the individual's personal circumstances, the cultural context, and the specific question or concern at hand. It involved examining the broader cultural and religious framework to grasp the underlying meanings and implications of the signs and symbols.

Example: Engage We in analyzing and interpreting Babylonian symbols and signs in different contexts. Provide examples of specific situations, such as a person seeking guidance on matters of love, fertility, or political affairs, and discuss how the interpretation of signs and symbols would vary depending on these contexts.

Problems and Exercises:

Analyze the similarities and differences between Babylonian methods of interpreting signs, symbols, and dreams and those found in other ancient civilizations, such as ancient Egypt or Greece. Explore how cultural and religious factors influenced the interpretation practices.

Engage in practical exercises to develop skills in interpreting signs, symbols, and dreams. Encourage We to keep a dream journal and analyze the recurring themes, symbols, and emotions present in their dreams. Discuss the potential messages or insights these dreams may hold.

Investigate the influence of Babylonian interpretation practices on contemporary divinatory and mystical traditions. Explore how elements of Babylonian symbolism and dream interpretation are incorporated into practices such as tarot reading, rune casting, or the analysis of synchronicities.

Discuss the ethical considerations and limitations of interpreting signs, symbols, and dreams. Encourage We to critically reflect on the potential biases, subjective interpretations, and cultural influences that may impact the accuracy and reliability of interpretations.

C. Love and fertility magic

Love and fertility have always been significant aspects of human existence, and ancient Babylonian culture was no exception. The Babylonians developed various magical practices aimed at attracting love, fostering harmonious relationships, and promoting fertility. This section explores the principles, rituals, and spells employed in love and fertility magic in ancient Babylon.

Love Magic:

Babylonian love magic was centered around the desire to attract a specific individual or to enhance existing romantic relationships. These practices involved rituals, spells, and talismans designed to invoke the assistance of deities associated with love and desire, such as Ishtar, the goddess of love and fertility.

Example: Explore the rituals performed by Babylonian practitioners to enhance their personal attractiveness and charm. Discuss the use of perfumes, oils, and adornments to invoke the favor of Ishtar and other love deities. Provide examples of love spells and incantations used to enchant and captivate desired partners.

Relationship Harmony:

In addition to seeking romantic love, Babylonians valued harmonious relationships within marriages and families. Love magic rituals were also employed to restore peace, resolve conflicts, and promote mutual affection and understanding between partners.

Example: Discuss the rituals and practices aimed at reconciling estranged couples or resolving marital disputes. Explore the use of talismans or charms to encourage marital harmony and strengthen the bond between partners. Provide examples of love incantations or prayers that were recited to invoke the blessings of love deities.

Fertility Magic:

Fertility was highly prized in ancient Babylonian society, as the ability to bear children ensured the continuity of the family line and the prosperity of the community. Fertility magic encompassed rituals and spells to promote successful conception, safe pregnancies, and healthy childbirth.

Example: Explore fertility rituals performed by couples desiring to conceive. Discuss the role of deities like Ishtar and Tammuz in fertility rituals and their association with reproductive powers. Explain the use of fertility charms, amulets, and herbal remedies believed to enhance fertility and ensure a successful pregnancy.

Sacred Prostitution:

Sacred prostitution was an integral part of Babylonian culture, particularly in the worship of Ishtar. The practice involved sexual rituals performed by temple priestesses as a means to ensure fertility and divine blessings for the community.

Example: Analyze the role of sacred prostitution within the context of love and fertility magic in ancient Babylon. Discuss differing perspectives on this practice, acknowledging counterarguments and dissenting opinions. Explore its societal implications and the controversies surrounding its ethical aspects.

Problems and Exercises:

Research and present a case study on a specific love or fertility ritual from ancient Babylon. Describe the ritual in detail, including the specific steps, objects used, and the underlying beliefs and symbolism associated with it.

Engage in a group discussion on the ethical considerations surrounding the use of love and fertility magic. Explore the potential consequences of manipulating another person's emotions or interfering with their free will. Discuss ethical guidelines that practitioners should adhere to when performing love or fertility spells.

Explore the presence of love and fertility magic in contemporary new-age practices. Investigate how elements of Babylonian love and fertility magic are incorporated into modern-day rituals, such as love spells, fertility treatments, or relationship enhancement techniques.

Analyze the portrayal of love and fertility magic in ancient Babylonian literature, such as myths, poems, or magical texts. Identify common themes, symbols, and archetypes related to love and fertility. Discuss their significance in understanding the cultural and spiritual beliefs of the time.

Remember to approach the study of love and fertility magic with sensitivity, respect, and a critical lens. Acknowledge the diversity of perspectives and engage in open-minded discussions to foster a comprehensive understanding of these ancient practices.

1. Spells and rituals to attract love and enhance fertility

In ancient Babylonian culture, spells and rituals played a significant role in attracting love and enhancing fertility. These practices were designed to harness the powers of deities associated with love and fertility, such as Ishtar and Tammuz. This section explores the techniques, symbols, and rituals used in Babylonian magic to attract love and promote fertility.

Love Spells:

Love spells were employed to attract the attention and affection of a desired individual. These spells often involved the use of incantations, charms, and symbolic actions to invoke the assistance of love deities and influence the emotions of the targeted person.

Example: Explore a specific love spell from ancient Babylonian texts and analyze its components. Discuss the use of specific words, gestures, and materials in the spell, as well as the intended effects. Engage We in a discussion on the ethical considerations of love spells, including the importance of consent and personal boundaries.

Fertility Spells:

Fertility spells aimed to enhance the chances of conception, ensure a healthy pregnancy, and promote the successful birth of a child. These spells incorporated rituals, prayers, and the use of specific objects believed to possess fertility-enhancing properties.

Example: Describe a fertility spell from ancient Babylonian sources and explain its underlying symbolism and purpose. Discuss the role of deities associated with fertility, such as Ishtar and Tammuz, in these rituals. Encourage We to research and present additional fertility spells from different cultures to compare and contrast practices.

Rituals for Love and Fertility:

Rituals were performed to create a sacred and conducive environment for attracting love or promoting fertility. These rituals often included specific actions, such as lighting candles, making offerings, or engaging in purification practices, to connect with the spiritual forces associated with love and fertility.

Example: Provide a step-by-step guide to a Babylonian ritual for attracting love or enhancing fertility. Include details such as the necessary materials, specific actions, and the intended outcome. Discuss the significance of each step and encourage We to reflect on the psychological and symbolic aspects of the ritual.

Symbols and Talismans:

Symbols and talismans were used in love and fertility magic as potent tools to enhance their effectiveness. These symbols often represented aspects of love, such as hearts or flowers, or fertility, such as seeds or eggs. Talismans were believed to carry the power of the deities and could be worn or placed in specific locations to attract love or ensure fertility.

Example: Present a collection of symbols and talismans associated with love and fertility magic in ancient Babylonian culture. Explain the significance of each symbol and its connection to the desired outcome. Encourage We to create their own love or fertility talismans and explain the reasoning behind their choices.

Problems and Exercises:

Design a love spell or fertility ritual that integrates elements from ancient Babylonian practices while adapting them to contemporary ethical considerations. Justify your choices and explain how you would ensure the well-being and autonomy of all parties involved.

Research the scientific and psychological aspects of love and fertility. Analyze the potential psychological mechanisms that may explain the effectiveness of love spells or fertility rituals. Present counterarguments from a scientific perspective and discuss the role of belief and intention in these practices.

Engage in a group discussion on the cultural and historical context of love and fertility magic. Compare and contrast ancient Babylonian practices with similar practices in other cultures. Discuss how societal values and beliefs influence the development and perpetuation of these magical traditions.

Reflect on the ethical considerations surrounding the use of spells and rituals for love and fertility. Explore the potential risks and unintended consequences of manipulating emotions or interfering with natural processes. Discuss guidelines for responsible and ethical magical practices.

Remember to approach the study and practice of love and fertility magic with respect, cultural sensitivity, and a critical mindset. Encourage We to engage in thoughtful discussions and critical thinking to deepen their understanding of these ancient practices and their modern-day interpretations.

2. Use of aphrodisiacs and potions

In the realm of ancient Babylonian magic, the use of aphrodisiacs and potions was a common practice to enhance desire, passion, and sexual potency. These substances were believed to possess magical properties that could arouse and intensify feelings of love and attraction. This section explores the historical context, ingredients, and methods of preparing aphrodisiacs and potions in Babylonian culture.

Historical Context:

The use of aphrodisiacs and potions can be traced back to ancient civilizations, including Babylon. These substances were regarded as powerful tools to stimulate passion and enhance sexual experiences. Their application was rooted in the belief that certain natural substances possessed properties that could affect the human body and mind, aligning with the principles of sympathetic magic.

Example: Provide an overview of the historical and cultural context surrounding the use of aphrodisiacs and potions in Babylonian society. Discuss the significance of love, romance, and sexuality in ancient Babylonian culture and its influence on magical practices.

Ingredients and Preparation:

Aphrodisiacs and potions in Babylonian magic were typically made from a variety of natural ingredients, including herbs, spices, and other substances believed to possess sensual and stimulating properties. These ingredients were often combined in specific formulas and prepared through methods such as grinding, blending, or steeping.

Example: Explore the ingredients commonly used in Babylonian aphrodisiacs and potions, such as saffron, ginger, cinnamon, and various aromatic herbs. Explain the potential properties of each ingredient and how they were believed to enhance desire and pleasure. Provide a step-by-step guide on the preparation of a Babylonian aphrodisiac or potion, including the specific measurements and instructions.

Rituals and Intentions:

The use of aphrodisiacs and potions in Babylonian magic was often accompanied by rituals and intentions to amplify their effects. These rituals involved the recitation of incantations, the creation of sacred space, and the invocation of deities associated with love and fertility. The intentions behind the use of these substances were to attract a desired partner, deepen emotional connection, and enhance sexual experiences.

Example: Describe a ritualistic framework for the use of aphrodisiacs and potions in Babylonian magic. Discuss the specific rituals and gestures performed during the application of these substances. Encourage We to reflect on the significance of intention, visualization, and the power of suggestion in the context of love and sexuality.

Problems and Exercises:

Research the scientific basis of aphrodisiacs and their potential effects on human physiology and psychology. Analyze the chemical components of commonly used aphrodisiacs and their potential impact on sexual desire and performance. Present counterarguments from a scientific perspective and discuss the role of placebo and psychological factors in the effectiveness of aphrodisiacs.

Engage in a group discussion on the cultural and ethical considerations surrounding the use of aphrodisiacs and potions. Explore different cultural perspectives on enhancing sexual experiences and the potential implications for consent and personal boundaries. Discuss guidelines for the responsible and respectful use of aphrodisiacs in modern contexts.

Explore the symbolism and psychological aspects of aphrodisiacs and potions. Discuss how the use of these substances can serve as a catalyst for self-discovery, exploration of desires, and deepening intimacy within consensual relationships. Encourage We to reflect on their own beliefs and attitudes towards love, sexuality, and the use of magical aids.

Create a personal aphrodisiac or potion recipe that integrates elements from ancient Babylonian practices while considering contemporary ethical considerations and accessibility of ingredients. Justify your ingredient choices and explain the intended effects of the mixture. Engage in a group tasting and discussion of the experiences and perceptions of the prepared concoctions.

Remember to approach the study and practice of aphrodisiacs and potions with respect, cultural sensitivity, and a critical mindset. Encourage We to engage in thoughtful discussions, critical thinking, and self-reflection to deepen their understanding of these ancient practices and their modern-day interpretations.

D. Curse and revenge magic

In the realm of ancient Babylonian magic, the practice of curse and revenge magic held a significant place. This section explores the historical context, methods, and ethical considerations surrounding the use of curses and revenge spells in Babylonian culture. It delves into the intentions, techniques, and potential consequences associated with these practices.

Historical Context:

The use of curses and revenge magic in ancient Babylon can be traced back to a time when belief in supernatural powers and the ability to influence events through magical means were deeply ingrained in the culture. Curses were seen as a way to invoke divine forces to bring harm, misfortune, or punishment upon individuals or groups perceived as deserving.

Example: Discuss the historical context of curse and revenge magic in ancient Babylon, highlighting its prevalence and significance in social, political, and personal contexts. Explore the role of curses in ancient legal systems, conflicts, and personal disputes, and their connection to notions of justice and retribution.

Intentions and Techniques:

The intention behind curse and revenge magic was often driven by a desire to seek justice, protection, or to retaliate against perceived wrongdoings. Babylonian practitioners believed that through specific rituals, invocations, and spells, they could harness supernatural forces to direct harm or misfortune towards their intended targets.

Example: Provide an overview of the techniques and rituals involved in curse and revenge magic in ancient Babylon. Explain the use of specific symbols, incantations, and gestures employed to amplify the desired effect. Discuss the belief in the power of words, intentions, and the symbolism associated with curses.

Ethical Considerations and Consequences:

The practice of curse and revenge magic raises important ethical considerations. While some proponents argue that it serves as a form of justice or protection, others argue against the use of such practices due to potential harm and the negative karmic consequences associated with causing intentional harm to others.

Example: Present counterarguments and dissenting opinions regarding the use of curse and revenge magic. Discuss ethical considerations, including the potential for unintended consequences, the role of personal responsibility, and the importance of ethical guidelines in magical practices. Encourage critical thinking and reflection on the potential ramifications of using curses and revenge spells.

Problems and Exercises:

Engage in a group discussion on the ethical implications of curse and revenge magic. Analyze case studies where curses were employed in ancient Babylonian society and their impact on individuals and communities. Debate the moral implications of seeking justice through magical means and explore alternative methods of conflict resolution.

Research and present a comparative analysis of curse and revenge magic in different ancient civilizations. Explore similarities and differences in practices, beliefs, and cultural attitudes towards revenge and justice. Discuss how cultural and historical contexts shape the perception and application of these magical practices.

Engage in a reflective exercise on personal values and ethical boundaries. Discuss scenarios where curse and revenge magic might be considered, and evaluate the ethical considerations and potential consequences of such actions. Encourage We to contemplate alternative approaches to resolving conflicts and seeking justice.

Explore the concept of protection and self-defense in magical practices. Discuss methods and rituals that focus on personal empowerment, shielding, and neutralizing negativity without causing harm to others. Compare and contrast these protective techniques with curse and revenge magic, emphasizing the importance of ethical considerations.

Remember that the exploration of curse and revenge magic should be approached with caution and an understanding of its historical context. Encourage We to develop a critical mindset, evaluate ethical implications, and consider alternative approaches to conflict resolution and justice-seeking within magical and spiritual practices.

1. Practices for inflicting harm on enemies or seeking justice

Within the realm of magical practices, there exist rituals and spells specifically designed to inflict harm on enemies or seek justice in various ancient cultures, including Babylon. This section explores the historical context, methods, and ethical considerations surrounding these practices, shedding light on their intentions, techniques, and potential consequences.

Historical Context:

The use of magical practices to inflict harm or seek justice on enemies dates back to ancient times when societies believed in supernatural forces and sought ways to address grievances or protect themselves. In Babylonian culture, these practices were often tied to notions of retribution, balancing the scales of justice, and asserting personal power.

Example: Discuss the historical context of practices for inflicting harm on enemies or seeking justice in ancient Babylon. Highlight their prevalence in legal systems, personal disputes, and social hierarchies. Explore examples from ancient texts and artifacts that illustrate the cultural significance and utilization of these practices.

Intentions and Techniques:

Magical practices for inflicting harm on enemies or seeking justice involved specific rituals, incantations, and tools to channel supernatural forces towards desired outcomes. Practitioners aimed to protect themselves, rectify perceived wrongs, or achieve a sense of justice through the manipulation of metaphysical energies.

Example: Provide an overview of the intentions and techniques employed in practices for inflicting harm on enemies or seeking justice. Discuss the use of symbolic objects, such as poppets, effigies, or written spells, as tools for directing harm or influencing the course of events. Explore the belief in the power of intention, visualization, and ritual performance.

Ethical Considerations and Consequences:

The practice of inflicting harm on enemies or seeking justice through magical means raises important ethical considerations. While some argue that these practices serve as a form of self-defense or redress, others express concerns about causing harm and the potential for unintended consequences.

Example: Present counterarguments and dissenting opinions regarding the ethical implications of practices for inflicting harm on enemies or seeking justice. Explore the concept of personal responsibility, the potential for unintended collateral damage, and the importance of considering alternative methods of conflict resolution. Encourage critical thinking and reflection on the ethical boundaries of magical practices.

Problems and Exercises:

Engage in a group discussion on the ethical implications of practices for inflicting harm on enemies or seeking justice. Analyze case studies from ancient Babylonian culture and other civilizations where these practices were employed. Debate the moral implications of using magic to address personal grievances and explore alternative methods of conflict resolution.

Research and present a comparative analysis of practices for inflicting harm on enemies or seeking justice across different cultures and historical periods. Examine similarities and differences in techniques, beliefs, and cultural attitudes towards seeking justice through magical means. Discuss how societal and cultural contexts shape the perception and application of these practices.

Engage in a reflective exercise on personal values and ethical boundaries. Discuss scenarios where practices for inflicting harm on enemies or seeking justice might be considered, and evaluate the ethical considerations and potential consequences of such actions. Encourage We to contemplate alternative approaches to addressing conflicts and seeking justice within magical and spiritual practices.

Explore the concept of justice and personal empowerment in magical practices. Discuss rituals and techniques that focus on healing, self-protection, and positive transformation rather than causing harm. Compare and contrast these practices with those aimed at inflicting harm on enemies, emphasizing the importance of ethical considerations and alternative approaches to seeking justice.

Remember that the exploration of practices for inflicting harm on enemies or seeking justice should be approached with caution and an understanding of their historical context. Encourage We to develop critical thinking skills, evaluate ethical implications, and consider alternative approaches to conflict resolution and justice-seeking within magical and spiritual practices.

2. Understanding the ethics and consequences of such magic

When delving into magical practices that involve inflicting harm on enemies or seeking justice, it is crucial to examine the ethical considerations and potential consequences associated with these actions. As We of new-age studies, it is important to approach these topics with sensitivity, critical thinking, and a comprehensive understanding of the potential impact of one's actions. This section explores the ethical dimensions and potential consequences of engaging in magic with the intention of causing harm or seeking justice.

Ethical Considerations:

a. Respect for Free Will: One ethical concern revolves around the concept of free will. Practitioners must reflect on the implications of using magic to manipulate the lives or decisions of others. It raises questions about personal autonomy, consent, and the potential infringement upon another person's rights.

b. Harm and Responsibility: Engaging in practices that cause harm prompts We to evaluate the consequences of their actions. They must consider whether the potential harm inflicted aligns with their moral principles and whether they are willing to take responsibility for the repercussions.

c. Karmic Balance: Many belief systems emphasize the concept of karma, which posits that one's actions have consequences that reverberate throughout their life and beyond. We should contemplate the potential karmic implications of using magic to cause harm or seek justice, as it may impact their own well-being and spiritual growth.

Potential Consequences:

a. Unintended Outcomes: Engaging in magic with the intent to cause harm or seek justice can lead to unintended consequences. The intricate web of cause and effect in the metaphysical realm is complex, and one must consider the potential ripple effects that may arise from their actions.

b. Energy and Emotional Investment: Magical practices for inflicting harm or seeking justice often require significant emotional investment and energy. We should reflect on the potential toll these practices may have on their own well-being, as well as the emotional and energetic residue that may linger after performing such rituals.

c. Interpersonal and Social Ramifications: Engaging in harmful magic may strain relationships, create conflicts, or perpetuate cycles of revenge. We must consider the wider implications on interpersonal dynamics, community cohesion, and societal harmony.

Problems and Exercises:

Ethical Reflection: Engage in personal reflection on the ethical considerations of engaging in magic for harmful purposes or seeking justice. Write an essay discussing your stance on the ethics of such practices, considering the principles of free will, harm, responsibility, and karmic balance. Support your arguments with references to philosophical and ethical frameworks.

Case Studies: Analyze historical or fictional case studies that involve the use of magic for inflicting harm or seeking justice. Evaluate the ethical dilemmas faced by the individuals involved and explore the consequences of their actions. Discuss alternative approaches to conflict resolution and justice-seeking within magical and spiritual practices.

Group Discussion: Organize a group discussion on the potential consequences of engaging in magic for harmful purposes or seeking justice. Encourage We to share their perspectives, concerns, and insights. Explore the role of personal intention, emotional investment, and the dynamics of energy exchange in these practices.

Alternative Approaches: Research and present alternative approaches to addressing conflicts and seeking justice within magical and spiritual practices. Explore practices that focus on healing, restoration, and personal transformation rather than causing harm. Discuss the ethical considerations and potential benefits of these alternative approaches.

Remember, as We of new-age studies, it is essential to approach magical practices with a deep understanding of the ethical implications and potential consequences. Encourage critical thinking, respectful discussion, and reflection on personal values to develop a well-rounded understanding of the ethics and consequences associated with engaging in magic for harmful purposes or seeking justice.

III. Magical Objects and Incantations

In the realm of magic, practitioners often employ various tools, artifacts, and incantations to enhance their rituals and harness the desired energies. These magical objects and incantations serve as potent symbols and conduits through which practitioners can focus their intention and tap into the subtle forces of the universe. This section explores the significance, types, and functions of magical objects and incantations in various traditions, including witchcraft, divination, herbalism, shamanism, ecospirituality, and magic in Ancient Babylon.

Magical Objects:

Magical objects are physical items imbued with symbolic meaning and believed to possess special powers or energies. They are utilized as tools to enhance rituals, amplify intentions, and connect with the spiritual realms. Here are some examples of magical objects:

a. Athame: A ritual knife or dagger, often associated with witchcraft. It is used to direct energy, create sacred space, and carve symbols into objects or candles.

b. Wand: A long, slender object typically made of wood, used for directing and channeling magical energy. Wands are often associated with spellcasting and invocation.

c. Amulets and Talismans: Small objects worn or carried for protection or to attract specific energies. They can be made of various materials and may contain symbols, herbs, or gemstones.

d. Tarot Cards: A deck of symbolic cards used for divination and accessing intuitive wisdom. Each card represents archetypal energies and can offer insights into past, present, and future events.

Incantations:

Incantations, also known as spells or chants, are vocal or written expressions of intention and invocation. They use specific words, sounds, and rhythms to create a focused and resonant energy that aligns with the desired outcome. Here are examples of incantations:

a. Invocation: A ritualistic prayer or invocation to call upon deities, spirits, or elemental forces for assistance, guidance, or protection.

b. Spells for Intention: A carefully crafted series of words spoken or written with the intention of manifesting a desired outcome, such as love, abundance, or healing.

c. Affirmations: Positive statements repeated to reinforce a particular belief or desired state of being. Affirmations are used to reprogram the subconscious mind and align with desired outcomes.

d. Chants and Mantras: Repeated sounds or syllables with a rhythmic pattern, often used to induce a trance-like state, promote focus, or attune to specific energies.

Problems and Exercises:

Artifact Exploration: Select a magical object from a specific tradition (e.g., wand in witchcraft, rattle in shamanism). Research its history, symbolism, and uses. Write a report or create a presentation exploring its significance and how it is employed in rituals and magical practices.

Incantation Crafting: Create an original incantation or spell for a specific purpose, such as protection, healing, or manifestation. Explain the words chosen, the rhythmic pattern, and the intention behind each phrase. Perform the incantation during a ritual and reflect on the experience.

Comparative Analysis: Compare and contrast the use of magical objects and incantations in two different traditions (e.g., Ancient Babylonian magic and modern witchcraft). Analyze the similarities and differences in the symbolism, purposes, and techniques employed.

Personal Talisman: Create a personal talisman or amulet infused with intention and symbolism. Use materials, colors, and symbols that resonate with your desired outcome. Reflect on the process and the energy you imbued into the talisman.

As practitioners of new-age studies, it is crucial to approach magical objects and incantations with respect, knowledge, and intention. Understanding the symbolism, purpose, and cultural context behind these tools and practices enables We to deepen their connection to the mystical realms and cultivate their magical abilities effectively. Remember, the power of magical objects and incantations lies not solely in the physical items or words themselves but in the intention, focus, and energetic resonance they evoke.

A. Role of sacred objects in Babylonian magic

In the mystical practices of ancient Babylon, sacred objects played a significant role in the realm of magic. These objects were considered powerful conduits for connecting with divine energies, invoking deities, and harnessing the forces of the cosmos. This section explores the role of sacred objects in Babylonian magic, their symbolism, and their functions within the spiritual and magical practices of the time.

Statues and Idols:

Statues and idols were central to the worship and magical rituals in ancient Babylon. These sacred representations of deities served as focal points for devotion, offerings, and communication with the divine. They were believed to embody the presence and power of the gods and goddesses they represented. For example, the statue of the god Marduk, the chief deity of Babylon, held a prominent place in the city's main temple, the Esagila. It was revered as a symbol of protection, prosperity, and divine authority.

Amulets and Talismans:

Amulets and talismans held a vital role in Babylonian magic for their protective and empowering properties. These objects, often made of various materials such as stone, metal, or clay, were inscribed with symbols, prayers, or magical formulas. Amulets were worn or carried by individuals as a means of warding off evil spirits, illness, or misfortune. They were believed to possess the power to repel negative forces and attract positive energies. For example, the Babylonian crescent-shaped amulet known as the "Horns of Ishtar" was thought to offer protection and fertility.

Magical Tools and Instruments:

Babylonian magic practitioners employed specific tools and instruments to perform rituals and spells. These objects served as extensions of their intention and facilitated the manipulation of energies. Examples include:

a. Ritual Knives: Similar to the athame in modern witchcraft, ritual knives were used to inscribe symbols, cut objects, or direct energy in sacred ceremonies.

b. Incense Burners: Incense played a crucial role in Babylonian magic as it was believed to carry prayers and offerings to the divine realm. Incense burners were used to release fragrant smoke during rituals, creating an atmosphere of sacredness and connection.

c. Divination Tools: Objects such as clay models or oracle bones were used for divination and seeking guidance from the gods. These objects were inscribed with symbols or questions, and their arrangement or interpretation provided insights into the future or spiritual guidance.

Problems and Exercises:

Research Project: Select a specific sacred object from Babylonian magic, such as an amulet or an idol, and investigate its historical significance, symbolism, and cultural context. Analyze its role in rituals and its association with specific deities or magical practices.

Ritual Design: Design a ritual incorporating sacred objects inspired by Babylonian magic. Consider the intention, symbolism, and appropriate use of objects such as statues, amulets, and ritual tools. Describe the steps, words, and gestures involved in the ritual.

Comparative Analysis: Compare the use of sacred objects in Babylonian magic with other ancient cultures, such as Egyptian or Greek. Explore similarities and differences in symbolism, function, and cultural context.

Object Empowerment: Choose a personal object and consecrate it as a sacred tool or talisman for a specific purpose. Research the appropriate symbols, rituals, or incantations to infuse the object with your intention. Reflect on the experience and the energetic connection you establish with the object.

By understanding the role of sacred objects in Babylonian magic, We of new-age studies can gain insights into the rich tapestry of ancient mystical traditions. These objects serve as powerful reminders of the human quest for connection with the divine and the belief in the transformative power of ritual and symbolism. Through respectful exploration and engagement with these sacred objects, We can deepen their understanding of the profound impact of material culture on spiritual practices.

1. Magical tools, amulets, and idols

In the realm of magic, the use of tools, amulets, and idols has been prevalent across various spiritual and mystical traditions throughout history. These objects serve as important aids in connecting with spiritual forces, harnessing energy, and manifesting desired outcomes. This section explores the significance and functions of magical tools, amulets, and idols in different mystical practices, including witchcraft, divination, herbalism, shamanism, and the ancient Babylonian tradition.

Magical Tools:

Magical tools are instruments utilized by practitioners to focus their intention, direct energy, and perform rituals or spells. Each tool carries its own symbolic meaning and purpose. Here are some examples of magical tools found in different traditions:

a. Wand: A wand is a long, slender object often made of wood or metal. It is used to channel and direct energy during rituals or spellcasting. Wands are associated with the element of air and are believed to amplify the practitioner's intentions.

b. Athame: The athame is a ritual knife typically with a black handle and a double-edged blade. It symbolizes the element of fire and is commonly used in ceremonial magic to cast circles, inscribe symbols, or direct energy.

c. Chalice: The chalice is a sacred cup or goblet used for holding liquids during rituals, such as water, wine, or herbal concoctions. It represents the element of water and is associated with the feminine energies of the divine.

Amulets:

Amulets are objects imbued with magical properties and worn or carried as a form of protection, luck, or empowerment. They are believed to possess specific energies or qualities that align with the wearer's intentions. Amulets can be made from various materials, such as gemstones, metals, herbs, or symbols. Some common examples of amulets include:

a. Protective Amulets: These are designed to ward off negative energies, evil spirits, or harm. For instance, the ancient Eye of Horus symbol in Egyptian mythology was used as a protective amulet against the "evil eye."

b. Luck Amulets: These are believed to attract good fortune and positive outcomes. A popular example is a four-leaf clover, associated with luck and abundance.

Idols:

Idols are sacred objects or representations of deities that are worshipped and venerated in religious or spiritual practices. They serve as focal points for devotion, prayer, and connection with the divine. In ancient Babylonian culture, idols played a significant role in religious ceremonies and magical rituals. Examples of idols include statues, figurines, or icons depicting gods and goddesses.

Problems and Exercises:

Tool Activation: Select a magical tool of your choice and research its symbolism, history, and traditional use. Reflect on its significance and the intention behind its design. Perform a personal ritual to activate the tool, infusing it with your energy and intention.

Amulet Creation: Create your own amulet for a specific purpose, such as protection, love, or abundance. Select the materials and symbols that resonate with your intention and research corresponding magical properties. Document the process and journal your experiences and observations while using the amulet.

Comparative Analysis: Choose a specific magical tool, amulet, or idol from different mystical traditions, such as Egyptian, Norse, or Celtic. Compare and contrast their symbolism, cultural context, and functions within the respective traditions.

Ethical Considerations: Research and discuss the ethical implications of using magical tools, amulets, and idols. Explore the potential benefits and risks associated with their use, and consider the importance of respect, intention, and cultural sensitivity when engaging with these objects.

By exploring the role of magical tools, amulets, and idols in various mystical practices, We of new-age studies can deepen their understanding of the symbolism, significance, and practical applications of these objects. Through critical thinking and engagement, We can develop a nuanced appreciation for the relationship between material objects and spiritual practice, while also exploring their own personal connections to these tools and symbols.

2. Symbolism and significance of specific objects

In the realm of spiritual and magical practices, specific objects hold deep symbolism and significance, representing various concepts, energies, and spiritual connections. These objects often carry cultural, historical, and mythological associations, making them potent tools for personal and collective transformation. This section explores the symbolism and significance of specific objects in diverse fields such as witchcraft, divination, herbalism, shamanism, and ancient Babylonian magic.

Cauldron:

The cauldron is a symbol of transformation and rebirth in many mystical traditions. It represents the feminine energy, the element of water, and the womb of creation. In witchcraft, the cauldron is associated with brewing potions, performing rituals, and scrying. It signifies the blending of energies and the potential for alchemical change.

Pentacle:

The pentacle is a five-pointed star enclosed within a circle. It is a powerful symbol representing the elements of earth, air, fire, water, and spirit. In witchcraft and other magical practices, the pentacle is used as a tool for protection, manifestation, and invoking elemental energies. It symbolizes the interconnectedness of the elements and the harmonious balance within nature.

Crystal:

Crystals hold significant symbolism and energetic properties based on their composition, color, and structure. Each crystal is believed to embody specific energies and can be used for healing, manifestation, and spiritual work. For example, clear quartz is often associated with clarity, amplification, and spiritual connection, while amethyst is associated with spiritual awakening and intuition.

Ankh:

The ankh is an ancient Egyptian symbol resembling a cross with a loop at the top. It represents life, fertility, and eternal existence. The ankh is often associated with deities and used in rituals for protection, healing, and connecting with the divine. It embodies the idea of eternal life and the eternal cycle of birth, death, and rebirth.

Runes:

Runes are ancient symbols used in divination and magical practices originating from the Norse tradition. Each rune carries specific meanings and associations, representing concepts such as strength, protection, abundance, and transformation. By casting or drawing runes, practitioners seek guidance and insight into various aspects of life.

Problems and Exercises:

Symbolic Exploration: Select an object of personal significance, such as a piece of jewelry, a talisman, or a natural element like a feather or a stone. Reflect on its symbolism, personal meaning, and the energy it holds for you. Write a journal entry exploring your connection to this object and its role in your spiritual or magical practice.

Comparative Analysis: Choose two different symbols from diverse traditions, such as the Celtic triskelion and the Hindu Om symbol. Research their cultural, historical, and mythological significance. Compare and contrast their symbolism, exploring common themes and unique cultural contexts.

Object Activation Ritual: Design a ritual to activate the symbolic power of an object. Consider the elements, symbols, and intentions associated with the object. Create a step-by-step ritual outline, including cleansing, consecration, and charging of the object with your intentions.

Personal Symbol Creation: Design your own symbolic object or talisman that represents an aspect of your spiritual journey or personal growth. Consider the materials, colors, and shapes that resonate with your intentions. Explain the symbolism and meaning behind your creation.

By delving into the symbolism and significance of specific objects, We of new-age studies can deepen their understanding of the intricate relationships between objects, spirituality, and magic. Through critical analysis, personal exploration, and creative exercises, We can develop a richer appreciation for the power and transformative potential of these objects in their own spiritual and magical practices.

B. Power of incantations and spells

Incantations and spells are fundamental tools in various magical traditions, including witchcraft, divination, herbalism, shamanism, and ancient Babylonian magic. These verbal or written formulas harness the power of language, intention, and symbolism to manifest desired outcomes, influence energies, and connect with higher realms. This section explores the profound power of incantations and spells, providing insights into their mechanics and guiding We in their practical application.

Language and Vibrational Energy:

Language plays a crucial role in incantations and spells. Specific words, phrases, and sounds are carefully chosen for their vibrational energy and resonance. Ancient languages, such as Latin, Hebrew, or Sanskrit, are often employed due to their perceived potency. Additionally, the rhythm, cadence, and repetition of words contribute to the energetic impact of an incantation or spell.

Intention and Focus:

Intention is the driving force behind any effective incantation or spell. It is the conscious direction of energy towards a specific outcome. The practitioner's focus, clarity, and emotional alignment with the intention enhance the potency of the incantation. Visualization, concentration, and mindfulness techniques are often employed to amplify the practitioner's focus and intention.

Symbolism and Correspondences:

Incantations and spells frequently incorporate symbolic elements, such as colors, elements, herbs, crystals, and planetary or astrological associations. These correspondences enhance the effectiveness of the incantation by aligning it with specific energies and archetypal forces. For example, using a red candle in a love spell can symbolize passion and desire, while burning sage for purification aligns with the element of air and the removal of negative energies.

Ritual and Ceremony:

Many incantations and spells are performed within ritual and ceremonial contexts. These rituals create a sacred space and provide a structured framework for the practitioner's intention and energy. Rituals often involve cleansing, casting a protective circle, invoking deities or elemental forces, and incorporating specific gestures or movements. The ritualistic aspect enhances the practitioner's focus, intention, and connection with the spiritual realm.

Ethics and Responsibility:

The power of incantations and spells carries great responsibility. Practitioners must consider the ethical implications and potential consequences of their actions. The Wiccan Rede, "An' it harm none, do what ye will," emphasizes the importance of working with positive intentions and not causing harm. Practitioners should exercise discernment, respect for free will, and consider the potential karmic effects of their spells.

Problems and Exercises:

Spell Crafting: Choose a specific intention or desired outcome, such as protection, healing, or attracting abundance. Research correspondences, symbols, and rituals associated with your chosen intention. Design a spell incorporating incantations, symbolism, and ritual elements. Write down the complete spell, including the words of the incantation and the specific actions involved.

Energetic Experimentation: Select a simple incantation or affirmation. Practice reciting it daily for a specific duration, such as one week. Keep a journal noting any shifts, synchronicities, or changes in your life during this period. Reflect on the potential influence of the incantation on your mindset, energy, and experiences.

Ethical Dilemma: Engage in a class discussion or debate on the ethical considerations of using incantations and spells. Discuss the potential consequences of manipulating energy and influencing outcomes. Explore different perspectives, considering arguments for and against the use of magic for personal gain or influencing others.

Historical Analysis: Research the historical use of incantations and spells in a specific culture or time period, such as ancient Egypt, medieval Europe, or indigenous traditions. Write a research paper exploring the cultural significance, context, and beliefs surrounding these practices. Analyze how they reflect the worldview and spiritual beliefs of the culture studied.

By understanding the mechanics and significance of incantations and spells, We can harness the power of language, intention, and symbolism to enhance their magical practices. Through exploration, practice, and critical analysis, We can develop a deeper appreciation for the transformative potential of incantations and spells, while also cultivating ethical awareness and responsibility in their magical endeavors.

1. Words of power and their pronunciation

In various magical traditions, including witchcraft, divination, herbalism, shamanism, and ancient Babylonian magic, the use of specific words of power holds significant importance. These words are believed to possess inherent vibrations, energies, and transformative qualities. Pronunciation plays a crucial role in unlocking the true potential of these words. This section explores the concept of words of power and provides guidance on their pronunciation for optimal efficacy in magical practice.

Significance of Words of Power:

Words of power, also known as sacred words, incantations, or mantras, are believed to hold inherent energy and vibrational resonance. These words are considered potent vehicles for directing and manifesting specific intentions, connecting with spiritual forces, and accessing higher realms of consciousness. The selection of words of power is often based on their historical usage, symbolic meanings, and their alignment with the practitioner's intention.

Phonetic Pronunciation:

The accurate pronunciation of words of power is vital for their effective use. Phonetic pronunciation refers to pronouncing the words in a specific manner, following established rules of pronunciation. Some magical traditions emphasize the importance of pronouncing words precisely as they were historically spoken, such as the reconstructed pronunciation of ancient Egyptian or Babylonian languages. Others focus on the energetic intent behind the words, allowing flexibility in pronunciation.

Oral Transmission and Tradition:

In many magical systems, words of power are transmitted orally from teacher to student, emphasizing the importance of lineage and tradition. The transmission of precise pronunciation ensures the continuity and integrity of the magical practice. We often receive instruction and guidance from experienced practitioners, studying the phonetic nuances and subtleties of each word to maintain the intended energetic resonance.

Practice and Experimentation:

To master the pronunciation of words of power, We are encouraged to engage in regular practice and experimentation. Start by selecting a specific word of power or mantra from a chosen tradition. Research the historical pronunciation and meaning of the word, as well as any associated rituals or practices. Practice reciting the word aloud, paying attention to the sounds, rhythms, and vibrations it produces. Experiment with variations in tone, volume, and speed to explore different energetic qualities.

Adaptation and Personalization:

While the historical pronunciation of words of power is valuable, practitioners also have the flexibility to adapt and personalize their pronunciation based on their own energetic resonance and cultural context. Intent and focus are crucial factors, allowing practitioners to infuse the words with their own unique energy and connection. Trusting one's intuition and sensitivity to energy can lead to powerful personal experiences and results.

Problems and Exercises:

Pronunciation Workshop: Organize a pronunciation workshop where We practice and refine the pronunciation of words of power from different traditions. Assign each student a word or mantra to research and present to the class. Engage in group discussions on the significance of accurate pronunciation and the impact it has on the energetic resonance of the words.

Comparative Analysis: Select two or more words of power from different traditions or cultures. Research their historical pronunciation and compare the phonetic nuances and meanings associated with each word. Write a comparative analysis paper discussing the similarities and differences in pronunciation and the cultural contexts in which they are used.

Personal Pronunciation Practice: Choose a word of power or mantra from a tradition that resonates with you. Spend dedicated time each day practicing its pronunciation, experimenting with different intonations and inflections. Keep a journal documenting your experiences, including any shifts in energy, sensations, or insights that arise during your practice.

Guided Meditation: Create a guided meditation incorporating the repetition of a word of power. Guide We through visualization exercises while softly reciting the word, emphasizing the importance of pronunciation and its impact on their energetic state. After the meditation, facilitate a group discussion on the experiences and insights gained.

By understanding the significance of words of power and their pronunciation, We can harness the transformative potential of language in their magical practices. Through diligent practice, research, and exploration, We can develop their ability to effectively pronounce and utilize words of power, deepening their connection to the energetic forces they seek to engage with.

2. Magical formulas and invocations

In the realm of magical practices, the use of magical formulas and invocations holds significant importance. These formulas, often consisting of specific words, phrases, or chants, are believed to possess inherent power and serve as vehicles for connecting with higher realms, invoking deities or spiritual forces, and manifesting desired outcomes. This section explores the concept of magical formulas and invocations, their structure, and their role in various magical traditions.

Structure of Magical Formulas:

Magical formulas are constructed using carefully selected words, phrases, and rhythms that are believed to align with the intended purpose or desired outcome. These formulas may draw upon sacred languages, such as ancient Egyptian, Hebrew, or Sanskrit, or they may be composed in the practitioner's native language. They often incorporate symbolic language, repetitive patterns, and rhythmic sequences to enhance their effectiveness.

Invocations of Deities and Spiritual Forces:

Magical invocations involve calling upon specific deities, spirits, or elemental forces to seek their assistance, guidance, or blessings. These invocations establish a connection between the practitioner and the invoked entity, establishing a reciprocal relationship and inviting their presence and influence. Different cultures and traditions have their own invocations, each tailored to the specific deities or forces they work with.

Intention and Visualization:

Magical formulas and invocations are infused with intention, which serves as a focal point for directing energy and manifesting desired outcomes. The practitioner's intention, coupled with vivid visualization, enhances the potency of the formula or invocation. By visualizing the desired outcome or the presence of the invoked entity, practitioners strengthen their connection and amplify the energy they channel.

Ritual and Performance:

Magical formulas and invocations are often performed within ritualistic settings to create a conducive environment for the desired energetic shifts. Rituals may involve the use of specific gestures, movements, tools, and symbols to enhance the effectiveness of the formula or invocation. The performance aspect of these practices allows practitioners to immerse themselves fully in the experience, deepening their focus and intention.

Personalized Formulas and Invocations:

While traditional magical formulas and invocations hold cultural and historical significance, practitioners also have the flexibility to create their own personalized formulas and invocations. Drawing inspiration from existing traditions, practitioners can adapt and tailor these practices to their specific needs and spiritual connections. Personalized formulas and invocations allow practitioners to infuse their unique energies and intentions into their magical work.

Problems and Exercises:

Formula Creation: Task We with creating their own magical formula for a specific intention or outcome. Provide guidance on the structure, symbolism, and repetitive patterns commonly used in formulas. Encourage We to reflect on their intention and to consider how each element of their formula contributes to its effectiveness.

Invocation Research: Assign We to research and present on a specific deity or spiritual force from a chosen tradition. Explore the traditional invocations associated with that deity or force, and discuss the significance of the words, phrases, and symbols used. Engage in class discussions on the role of invocations in establishing connections with spiritual entities.

Ritual Performance: Organize a group ritual where We have the opportunity to perform a traditional formula or invocation together. Discuss the experiences and observations from the ritual, highlighting the impact of collective intention and the power of performing these practices in a group setting.

Comparative Analysis: Select two or more traditional magical formulas or invocations from different cultures or traditions. Analyze the similarities and differences in their structures, symbols, and intended outcomes. Discuss the cultural and historical contexts that influence the formulation and usage of these formulas.

By understanding the structure, intention, and performance of magical formulas and invocations, We can effectively incorporate these practices into their magical work. Through research, exploration, and personalization, We can develop a deep connection with these powerful tools, enhancing their ability to manifest desired outcomes and establish connections with spiritual forces.

IV. Ethical Considerations in Babylonian Magic

The practice of Babylonian magic, like any form of spiritual or occult practice, raises important ethical considerations that practitioners must navigate. This section explores the ethical aspects of Babylonian magic, highlighting the significance of intention, responsibility, and the potential consequences of one's actions within this magical system.

Intention and Alignment with Higher Principles:

Ethical considerations in Babylonian magic begin with the practitioner's intention. It is crucial to ensure that one's magical practices align with higher principles such as love, harmony, and respect for the natural world. Practitioners should reflect upon their intentions and motivations to ensure they are rooted in positive values and contribute to the well-being of oneself and others.

Harm None and the Principle of Reciprocity:

Babylonian magic, like many other magical systems, adheres to the principle of "harm none." This principle emphasizes the importance of avoiding the infliction of intentional harm on others. It encourages practitioners to consider the potential consequences of their actions and to act in a responsible and compassionate manner.

The belief in reciprocity further underscores the understanding that one's actions may have consequences that extend beyond immediate outcomes.

Respect for Free Will and Consent:

Respecting the free will and consent of others is an ethical consideration that is particularly relevant in the context of love spells or spells intended to influence the thoughts or actions of others. Practitioners should exercise caution and refrain from attempting to manipulate or control the will of others without their consent. It is essential to recognize and honor the autonomy and agency of individuals.

Environmental and Cultural Considerations:

Babylonian magic, rooted in an ancient civilization, carries with it a connection to specific cultural and environmental contexts. Practitioners should be mindful of the cultural significance and appropriateness of certain practices, symbols, or rituals, especially when borrowing from different cultural traditions. Additionally, there is a responsibility to engage in sustainable and environmentally conscious magical practices that respect and protect the natural world.

Personal Responsibility and Accountability:

Practitioners of Babylonian magic are encouraged to take personal responsibility for their actions and the consequences that may arise from their magical practices. This includes considering the potential effects on oneself, others, and the broader community. Reflecting on one's choices, intentions, and the potential ethical implications of a particular spell or ritual is an essential aspect of maintaining ethical integrity in magical practice.

Problems and Exercises:

Ethical Dilemmas: Present We with various ethical scenarios related to Babylonian magical practices. Encourage them to discuss and analyze the ethical considerations involved in each scenario. This exercise promotes critical thinking and encourages We to apply ethical principles to real-world situations.

Reflective Journaling: Assign We to keep a reflective journal throughout their study of Babylonian magic. In their journal, they should record their thoughts and reflections on the ethical aspects of their own magical practices. Encourage We to explore how their intentions align with ethical principles and how they can incorporate responsible and compassionate actions into their magical work.

Group Discussion: Organize a group discussion where We can openly discuss their perspectives on ethical considerations in Babylonian magic. Encourage them to present and debate different viewpoints, allowing for a comprehensive exploration of the topic. This exercise promotes a deeper understanding of the complexities and diversity of ethical perspectives within the field of magic.

Research and Presentation: Assign We to research and present on a specific ethical issue related to Babylonian magic, such as the ethics of love spells or the ethical use of talismans. We should explore different perspectives, including dissenting opinions, and provide a balanced analysis of the topic. This exercise encourages We to develop their research and critical analysis skills.

By understanding and engaging with the ethical considerations of Babylonian magic, We can cultivate a sense of responsibility, integrity, and respect in their magical practices. Navigating ethical complexities enhances the depth and potency of magical work, fostering a harmonious and conscientious approach to the practice of Babylonian magic.

A. Understanding the moral and ethical framework of Babylonian society

To gain a comprehensive understanding of Babylonian magic, it is essential to explore the moral and ethical framework that shaped the society in which these practices originated. The moral and ethical values prevalent in Babylonian society influenced the beliefs, behaviors, and practices of individuals, including their engagement with magic. This section delves into the moral and ethical principles of Babylonian society, shedding light on the context in which Babylonian magic operated.

Divine Order and Cosmic Harmony:

Babylonian society was deeply rooted in a belief in divine order and cosmic harmony. The Babylonians believed that the gods had established a harmonious order in the world and that it was their duty to maintain and uphold this order. This understanding shaped their moral and ethical framework, emphasizing the importance of living in accordance with divine laws and principles.

Social Hierarchy and Duty:

Babylonian society was hierarchical, with distinct social classes and roles. Each individual had specific duties and responsibilities based on their social position. Upholding these responsibilities was considered a moral obligation. The king, as the representative of the gods on Earth, held a prominent role in maintaining social order and justice.

Justice and Fairness:

Justice was a central tenet of Babylonian society. The concept of justice encompassed fair treatment, adherence to laws, and the resolution of disputes. The Babylonians believed in holding individuals accountable for their actions and sought to establish a just and equitable society. The legal code of Hammurabi, one of the most famous legal codes in ancient history, reflects their emphasis on justice and fair treatment.

Respect for Authority and Tradition:

Babylonian society placed great importance on respect for authority and adherence to traditional customs and practices. The social fabric relied on individuals honoring and respecting their elders, leaders, and religious institutions. Challenging authority or deviating from established traditions was often viewed as morally and socially unacceptable.

Loyalty and Honor:

Loyalty and honor were highly valued in Babylonian society. Individuals were expected to demonstrate loyalty to their family, community, and king. Honor was associated with integrity, honesty, and fulfilling one's obligations. It was seen as a reflection of one's character and played a significant role in maintaining social cohesion.

Compassion and Hospitality:

The Babylonians also emphasized compassion and hospitality towards others. They believed in the importance of extending kindness and assistance to those in need, including strangers and travelers. Compassion and hospitality were seen as expressions of empathy and were highly regarded virtues.

Problems and Exercises:

Comparative Analysis: Assign We to compare and contrast the moral and ethical framework of Babylonian society with that of another ancient civilization, such as Ancient Egypt or Ancient Greece. Encourage We to identify similarities and differences and consider how these frameworks influenced magical practices within each society.

Ethical Dilemmas in Babylonian Society: Present We with ethical dilemmas that individuals in Babylonian society might have faced. Encourage them to analyze the dilemmas from the perspective of the moral and ethical values prevalent in Babylonian society. This exercise promotes critical thinking and a deeper understanding of the societal context in which Babylonian magic operated.

Reflective Essay: Ask We to reflect on how the moral and ethical principles of Babylonian society might have influenced the practice of magic. In their essay, We should explore how these principles shaped the intentions, actions, and responsibilities of practitioners. This exercise encourages We to integrate their knowledge of Babylonian society with their understanding of magic.

Role-Play: Divide We into groups and assign them different roles within Babylonian society. Ask each group to engage in a role-play scenario where they encounter an ethical dilemma. Afterward, facilitate a discussion where We analyze the choices made by each group and explore the ethical considerations involved.

By understanding the moral and ethical framework of Babylonian society, We can gain a deeper appreciation for the cultural context in which Babylonian magic flourished. This knowledge allows for a more nuanced interpretation and analysis of the magical practices and beliefs of ancient Babylonians, fostering a comprehensive understanding of the role of magic in their society.

B. Balancing personal desires with social and cosmic harmony

In the practice of magic, it is crucial to navigate the delicate balance between pursuing personal desires and upholding social and cosmic harmony. The ancient Babylonians recognized the interconnectedness of individuals with the broader community and the cosmic order. This section explores the concept of balancing personal desires with social and cosmic harmony within the context of Babylonian magic.

Understanding Personal Desires:

Personal desires are natural and inherent to human nature. They encompass individual aspirations, goals, and wishes for personal well-being and fulfillment. In the realm of magic, individuals may seek to manifest their desires through various practices, such as spells, rituals, or divination. While acknowledging personal desires, it is important to consider their ethical implications and potential impact on the larger social and cosmic fabric.

Social Interdependence and Responsibility:

Babylonian society emphasized the interdependence of individuals within a communal framework. The well-being and harmony of the community were valued, and each person was expected to contribute positively to the collective welfare. Recognizing this social responsibility is essential when engaging in magical practices. Consideration should be given to how one's desires align with the needs and well-being of the community.

Cosmic Harmony and Divine Order:

Babylonians believed in the existence of a cosmic harmony and divine order, guided by the gods. They viewed the world as an intricately interconnected system where actions had consequences that reverberated through the cosmic web. When pursuing personal desires through magic, practitioners were mindful of maintaining harmony with the greater cosmic order. This involved aligning their intentions with the divine laws and respecting the cosmic balance.

Ethical Reflection and Consideration:

Balancing personal desires with social and cosmic harmony requires ethical reflection and consideration. Practitioners should critically assess the motivations behind their desires, evaluating their potential consequences and ethical implications. This introspective process encourages individuals to align their desires with moral values, such as compassion, integrity, and fairness.

Harmonious Collaboration:

Magic in ancient Babylon often involved collaboration between practitioners, priests, and the divine. Working together with others who share similar intentions and goals fosters a sense of collective responsibility and ensures that personal desires are aligned with broader social and cosmic harmony. Collaborative practices, such as group rituals or communal celebrations, promote unity and reinforce the importance of considering the well-being of the community.

Problems and Exercises:

Ethical Dilemma Analysis: Present We with ethical dilemmas that require balancing personal desires with social and cosmic harmony. Ask them to analyze the dilemmas and propose solutions that strike a balance between individual needs and communal well-being. Encourage We to explore the moral and ethical considerations involved in their decision-making process.

Case Study Examination: Provide We with case studies of historical or contemporary magical practices that highlight the tension between personal desires and social or cosmic harmony. We should analyze the cases, considering the motivations of the practitioners and the potential consequences of their actions. This exercise deepens We' understanding of the complexities involved in balancing personal desires with broader ethical considerations.

Reflective Journaling: Assign We to keep a reflective journal where they document their personal desires and reflect on how these desires align with social and cosmic harmony. Encourage We to explore any conflicts they encounter and reflect on the ethical considerations that arise. This exercise promotes self-awareness and critical reflection.

Group Discussion: Divide We into small groups and assign them different scenarios that require balancing personal desires with social and cosmic harmony. We should engage in group discussions to explore different perspectives, debate the ethical implications, and propose collaborative solutions. Encourage respectful dialogue and the exploration of dissenting opinions.

By encouraging We to grapple with the complexities of balancing personal desires with social and cosmic harmony, they develop a nuanced understanding of the ethical considerations involved in magical practices. This awareness empowers them to engage in magic with greater mindfulness, responsibility, and respect for the interconnectedness of all beings and the cosmic order.

C. Controversial and taboo practices in Babylonian magic

The realm of magic in ancient Babylon encompassed a wide range of practices, some of which were considered controversial or taboo within the cultural and religious context of the time. This section explores the controversial and taboo practices in Babylonian magic, shedding light on their historical significance, ethical considerations, and potential consequences.

Necromancy and Communication with the Dead:

Necromancy, the practice of communicating with the deceased, was a controversial aspect of Babylonian magic. Some practitioners believed that consulting with the spirits of the deceased could provide valuable knowledge and guidance. However, this practice was not universally accepted and was often associated with moral and religious concerns. Critics argued that it could disrupt the natural order and potentially lead to negative spiritual consequences.

Dark Magic and Hexes:

The use of dark magic and hexes, involving the invocation of harmful forces or entities to cause harm to others, was another controversial practice in Babylonian magic. While some individuals may have resorted to these methods out of a sense of revenge or personal gain, they were generally viewed as ethically questionable. Such practices were often discouraged due to the potential harm they could inflict on both the intended target and the practitioner's own spiritual well-being.

Love and Fertility Spells:

Love and fertility spells, while not inherently controversial, could become problematic when used to manipulate the free will or emotions of others. When these spells crossed ethical boundaries by infringing upon personal autonomy or causing harm to individuals involved, they raised moral concerns. The responsible use of such spells required careful consideration of consent, respect for the well-being of all parties involved, and an understanding of the potential consequences.

Divination for Personal Gain:

Divination, the practice of seeking insights or predictions about the future, was a widespread practice in Babylonian magic. However, using divination solely for personal gain or material success was viewed with skepticism and considered ethically questionable. Divination was intended to be a tool for guidance and spiritual growth, and practitioners were expected to approach it with reverence and a genuine desire for wisdom rather than self-serving motives.

Transformation and Shapeshifting:

The concept of transformation and shapeshifting, although intriguing, was surrounded by controversy in Babylonian magic. Some individuals purported to possess the ability to assume the forms of animals or other beings through magical rituals. While such practices were not widely accepted, they captured the imagination and curiosity of some practitioners. Critics questioned the morality and authenticity of these claims, considering them either as illusions or as delving into dangerous territory.

Ethical Considerations and Reflection:

Controversial and taboo practices in Babylonian magic raise important ethical considerations. Practitioners must critically reflect on their intentions, the potential consequences of their actions, and the broader ethical implications. It is crucial to approach these practices with caution, mindful of the potential harm they can cause to oneself and others. The ancient Babylonians valued moral conduct, respect for the divine, and the well-being of the community, providing a framework for responsible magical practice.

Problems and Exercises:

Ethical Debate: Divide We into groups and assign each group a controversial practice in Babylonian magic. Encourage them to engage in a structured debate, with some We arguing in favor of the practice and others presenting counterarguments. This exercise promotes critical thinking, ethical analysis, and respectful dialogue.

Personal Reflection: Ask We to individually reflect on their personal stance regarding controversial practices in magic. Have them write a reflective essay discussing their ethical views and considerations when encountering these practices. Encourage We to explore their reasoning, draw connections to personal values, and consider the potential consequences of such practices.

Case Study Analysis: Provide We with case studies involving controversial practices in Babylonian magic. Ask them to analyze the ethical dilemmas presented, evaluate the motivations and potential consequences, and propose alternative approaches that align with ethical considerations. This exercise enhances We' ethical decision-making skills and their ability to navigate complex moral landscapes.

Cultural and Historical Context: Assign We research projects exploring the cultural and historical context of controversial practices in Babylonian magic. Have them investigate societal norms, religious beliefs, and the prevailing ethical frameworks of the time. This exercise promotes a deeper understanding of the cultural relativism surrounding magical practices and encourages We to critically examine their own beliefs and biases.

By engaging with the controversies and taboos present in Babylonian magic, We develop a nuanced understanding of ethical considerations in magical practices. This knowledge equips them with the ability to navigate these complexities responsibly, aligning their actions with moral values, respect for others, and the preservation of social and cosmic harmony.

V. Cultural and Social Context of Magic in Ancient Babylon

Understanding the cultural and social context in which magic was practiced in ancient Babylon is essential for gaining a comprehensive understanding of this mystical tradition. This section explores the cultural and social factors that influenced the practice of magic in Ancient Babylon, shedding light on the beliefs, values, and societal structures that shaped magical practices.

Religious Beliefs and Cosmology:

Magic in ancient Babylon was deeply intertwined with religious beliefs and cosmology. The Babylonians believed in a complex pantheon of gods and goddesses who controlled various aspects of the world. Magic was seen as a means to interact with and influence these divine forces. The Babylonian religion emphasized the importance of rituals and offerings to maintain cosmic balance and harmony. Magical practices were often integrated into religious ceremonies and performed by priests who were considered intermediaries between the human and divine realms.

Societal Hierarchy and Power Structures:

The hierarchical structure of Babylonian society influenced the practice of magic. Priests, as the religious authorities, held significant power and played a central role in magical rituals and divination. The kings and ruling elite also had access to magical practices and employed them for personal and political purposes. Commoners, while engaging in magical practices on a smaller scale, often sought the assistance of priests for more complex magical needs. The social structure of Babylonian society had a direct impact on the accessibility and utilization of magical knowledge and practices.

Role of Magic in Daily Life:

Magic permeated various aspects of daily life in ancient Babylon. It was believed to have the power to address personal needs, such as health, fertility, love, and protection against evil forces. Babylonians sought magical solutions for ailments, consulted diviners for guidance, and performed rituals to ensure favorable outcomes in their endeavors. Magical practices were integrated into key life events, such as birth, marriage, and death. Magic played a central role in addressing the uncertainties and challenges of daily life, providing individuals with a sense of control and hope.

Cultural Heritage and Traditions:

The practice of magic in ancient Babylon was deeply rooted in cultural heritage and traditions. Babylonians drew upon ancient texts, rituals, and knowledge passed down through generations. Magical practices were shaped by cultural beliefs, symbols, and mythologies unique to Babylonian civilization. The use of specific objects, symbols, and incantations held cultural significance and carried the weight of tradition. Magical practices were not isolated occurrences but were woven into the fabric of Babylonian culture, reinforcing their significance and legitimacy.

Interaction with Other Cultures:

Ancient Babylon was a cosmopolitan city, characterized by trade and cultural exchange with neighboring regions. This interaction influenced the development of magical practices, as ideas and techniques from other cultures were incorporated into Babylonian magic. For example, the influence of Sumerian and Akkadian cultures, as well as later Persian and Greek influences, can be seen in Babylonian magical practices. This cultural exchange enriched Babylonian magic, making it a dynamic and evolving tradition.

By studying the cultural and social context of magic in ancient Babylon, we gain insight into the motivations, practices, and beliefs that shaped this mystical tradition. Understanding the religious, societal, and cultural factors that influenced magical practices enables us to appreciate the complexity and significance of Babylonian magic within its historical and cultural framework.

Problems and Exercises:

Comparative Analysis: Assign We to compare the cultural and social context of Babylonian magic with that of another ancient civilization, such as ancient Egypt or ancient Greece. Have them identify similarities and differences, and discuss the impact of these cultural contexts on magical practices. This exercise fosters comparative analysis skills and encourages We to explore the diverse cultural expressions of magic.

Artifact Analysis: Provide We with images or descriptions of Babylonian magical artifacts, such as amulets, talismans, or clay tablets with incantations. Ask them to analyze the cultural and social significance of these objects, considering their symbolism, materials used, and intended purposes. This exercise enhances We' ability to interpret material culture and understand its contextual relevance.

Social Dynamics and Magic: Divide We into groups and assign them specific social roles in ancient Babylonian society, such as priest, ruler, or commoner. Have each group discuss how their assigned role would influence their access to and use of magical practices. Encourage We to explore the power dynamics and social implications of magic within different societal positions.

Cultural Exchange and Magic: Ask We to research and present on the cultural influences on Babylonian magic, particularly from neighboring civilizations. Have them explore how these influences enriched or transformed Babylonian magical practices. This exercise promotes research skills and encourages We to examine the dynamic nature of magical traditions.

By engaging with the cultural and social context of magic in ancient Babylon, We develop a deeper appreciation for the historical and cultural significance of magical practices. They gain a broader understanding of how magical traditions are shaped by the beliefs, values, and social structures of the societies in which they emerge.

A. Relationship between magic and religious institutions

The relationship between magic and religious institutions in various cultures has been a subject of significant scholarly inquiry. In the context of ancient Babylon, this section explores the dynamic interaction between magic and religious institutions, shedding light on their interdependence and distinct roles within the society.

Complementary Functions:

In ancient Babylon, magic and religion were closely intertwined, with both playing important roles in the lives of individuals and the functioning of society. While magic focused on the practical aspects of manipulating supernatural forces to achieve desired outcomes, religion dealt with broader spiritual and moral concerns. Magic was often employed as a means to interact with the divine and seek divine intervention, complementing the religious rituals and practices performed by the priesthood.

Priestly Involvement in Magic:

The religious institutions in ancient Babylon, particularly the priesthood, held significant influence over magical practices. The priests served as intermediaries between the human and divine realms, possessing specialized knowledge and access to the divine forces. They were often the custodians of magical rituals, incantations, and objects, using them to perform ceremonies, divinations, and healing rituals. The priests' involvement in magic provided legitimacy and ensured the alignment of magical practices with religious beliefs and cultural norms.

Ritual Integration:

Magic and religious rituals often intersected in ancient Babylon. Certain magical practices were integrated into religious ceremonies and festivals, enhancing their spiritual and symbolic significance. For example, during important religious festivals, magical rituals and incantations were performed to ensure the favor of the gods and protect against malevolent forces. These integrated rituals reinforced the connection between magic and religious institutions, emphasizing their shared objectives of maintaining cosmic balance and promoting well-being.

Regulation and Control:

Religious institutions in ancient Babylon played a role in regulating and controlling magical practices within society. The priesthood had the authority to oversee and approve specific forms of magic, ensuring that they adhered to religious principles and societal norms. This regulation aimed to prevent misuse of magic, maintain order, and protect individuals from fraudulent or harmful practices. The involvement of religious institutions in overseeing magical practices underscored the social responsibility associated with the use of supernatural forces.

Limitations and Tensions:

While magic and religious institutions shared a symbiotic relationship, tensions and limitations also existed. Some forms of magic, particularly those associated with personal gain or harmful intentions, were discouraged or condemned by religious authorities. These practices were deemed unethical or went against the moral framework of Babylonian society. The religious institutions provided guidance and set boundaries on the acceptable use of magic, ensuring that it aligned with broader ethical principles and values.

Problems and Exercises:

Analyzing Magical Texts: Provide We with translated excerpts from Babylonian magical texts. Ask them to analyze the language, symbolism, and references to religious elements within the texts. Encourage We to discuss the ways in which magic and religion intersect in these texts and how they reflect the relationship between magical practices and religious institutions.

Ethical Considerations: Divide We into groups and assign each group a specific magical practice, such as love spells or protective rituals. Have each group discuss the ethical considerations associated with their assigned practice from the perspectives of both magic and religious institutions. Encourage We to consider the potential consequences and societal implications of these practices.

Case Study: Present We with a case study involving a conflict between a practitioner of magic and religious authorities in ancient Babylon. Ask them to analyze the motivations, beliefs, and perspectives of the individuals involved, and discuss the potential factors that contributed to the conflict. This exercise encourages We to critically evaluate the complex relationship between magic and religious institutions in a specific historical context.

Comparing Religious Approaches: Assign We to compare the relationship between magic and religious institutions in ancient Babylon with that of another civilization, such as ancient Egypt or ancient Greece. Have them identify similarities and differences, and discuss the influence of cultural and religious factors on the dynamics between magic and religion. This exercise fosters comparative analysis skills and encourages We to explore the diverse manifestations of the relationship between magic and religious institutions.

By examining the relationship between magic and religious institutions in ancient Babylon, We gain insights into the interconnectedness of these practices and the role they played in shaping the spiritual and social fabric of the society. Understanding this relationship contributes to a holistic understanding of Babylonian magic within its cultural and religious context.

B. Role of magicians and priests in Babylonian society

In ancient Babylonian society, magicians and priests held distinct but interconnected roles, playing crucial roles in religious and magical practices. This section explores the roles and functions of magicians and priests, shedding light on their contributions to the social and spiritual fabric of Babylonian society.

Magicians:

Magicians in ancient Babylon were individuals who possessed specialized knowledge and skills in the manipulation of supernatural forces. They were practitioners of magic and utilized various techniques, rituals, and incantations to invoke divine powers, manipulate energies, and influence the natural world. Magicians were sought after for their abilities to heal, provide protection, and bring about desired outcomes in various aspects of life. They were known for their expertise in divination, herbalism, and the casting of spells.

Functions of Magicians:

a. Divination: Magicians often acted as diviners, interpreting signs and omens to gain insights into the future or divine guidance. Through practices such as astrology, scrying, and the interpretation of dreams, they provided individuals with information and predictions about their lives, allowing them to make informed decisions and navigate challenges.

b. Healing and Protection: Magicians were relied upon for their abilities to heal ailments and protect individuals from malevolent forces. They employed rituals, amulets, and herbal remedies to restore health and ward off negative energies. The healing practices of magicians were closely intertwined with religious beliefs and often involved invocations of deities.

c. Spells and Incantations: Magicians were skilled in the art of casting spells and performing incantations. They utilized words of power and ritual actions to influence the natural world, bringing about desired outcomes such as love, fertility, or success. Their use of magical formulas and invocations was believed to harness the forces of the divine and manifest changes in the physical realm.

Priests:

Priests in Babylonian society held esteemed positions within the religious institutions. They acted as intermediaries between the human and divine realms, facilitating communication and worship of the gods. Priests had a deep understanding of religious rituals, cosmology, and the moral code of the society. Their primary function was to maintain cosmic order, ensure the favor of the gods, and provide spiritual guidance to the community.

Functions of Priests:

a. Rituals and Offerings: Priests conducted religious ceremonies and rituals, offering prayers, sacrifices, and libations to the gods. These rituals were performed to maintain harmony between humans and the divine, seeking blessings, forgiveness, and protection. Priests meticulously followed prescribed procedures and incantations, ensuring the correct performance of religious acts.

b. Custodians of Sacred Knowledge: Priests served as custodians of sacred knowledge, including religious texts, magical formulas, and incantations. They preserved and transmitted this knowledge to future generations, ensuring the continuity of religious practices and magical traditions. Their role in preserving and interpreting sacred texts provided a sense of authority and guidance within the religious institutions.

c. Moral and Ethical Guidance: Priests played a crucial role in providing moral and ethical guidance to the society. They enforced religious laws, advised individuals on ethical conduct, and resolved conflicts in accordance with religious principles. Priests acted as spiritual leaders, promoting virtues and guiding individuals on the path of righteousness.

Problems and Exercises:

Research Assignment: Assign We to research famous Babylonian magicians and priests, such as the priestess Enheduanna or the magician Bel-Marduk. Have them present their findings on the lives, contributions, and historical significance of these figures, emphasizing their roles within Babylonian society.

Comparative Analysis: Divide We into groups and assign each group a different civilization (e.g., ancient Egypt, ancient Greece) known for its magical and religious practices. Instruct them to compare the roles and functions of magicians and priests in Babylonian society with those in the assigned civilization. Encourage We to analyze similarities, differences, and potential influences between the cultures.

Class Discussion: Initiate a class discussion on the social status and perception of magicians and priests in ancient Babylonian society. Prompt We to explore questions such as: How were magicians and priests perceived by the general populace? Did they hold positions of power or authority? Were there any social or legal limitations on their activities? Encourage critical thinking and analysis of primary and secondary sources.

Role-Play Activity: Organize a role-play activity where We assume the roles of magicians and priests in ancient Babylon. Provide scenarios involving different societal issues, and ask We to demonstrate how magicians and priests would approach and resolve these issues based on their knowledge, skills, and ethical considerations.

By examining the roles of magicians and priests in Babylonian society, We gain a comprehensive understanding of the intricate relationship between magical practices, religious institutions, and social dynamics. Understanding the contributions and responsibilities of magicians and priests provides valuable insights into the cultural and spiritual landscape of ancient Babylon.

C. Popular beliefs and attitudes towards magic

In ancient Babylon, magic held a significant place in the hearts and minds of the people. This section explores the popular beliefs and attitudes towards magic within the

Babylonian society, shedding light on its cultural significance and the ways in which it shaped the lives of individuals.

Magical Worldview:

Magic was deeply embedded in the Babylonian worldview. People believed that the natural and supernatural realms were interconnected, and that various supernatural forces influenced human lives. They saw magic as a means to tap into these forces and affect the world around them. It was believed that through the use of rituals, spells, and amulets, individuals could invoke divine powers, manipulate energies, and influence their own destinies.

Magical Practitioners:

Magical practitioners, such as magicians and priests, played a central role in Babylonian society. They were regarded as individuals who possessed specialized knowledge and skills to access and harness supernatural powers. These practitioners were sought after for their abilities to provide healing, protection, and guidance in various aspects of life. Their expertise in divination, spells, and incantations gave them a sense of authority and respect within the community.

Cultural Significance of Magic:

a. Religion and Magic: Magic was closely intertwined with religious beliefs and practices in Babylonian society. The Babylonians believed in a pantheon of gods and goddesses who had the power to shape human destinies. Magic was seen as a means to communicate with and seek favor from these deities. Religious rituals often incorporated magical elements, and magical practitioners frequently invoked the names of gods and goddesses in their spells and incantations.

b. Healing and Protection: Babylonians turned to magic for healing and protection against malevolent forces. They believed that illness and misfortune could be caused by supernatural entities or the disruption of cosmic harmony. Magical rituals, amulets, and potions were employed to restore health and ward off negative energies. The use of magical practices was seen as a way to safeguard oneself and loved ones from harm.

c. Influence on Daily Life: Magic permeated various aspects of daily life in Babylon. It was used to seek guidance on important decisions, to ensure success in endeavors such as agriculture or commerce, and to enhance personal relationships. From matters of love and fertility to business ventures and legal disputes, magic played a role in shaping outcomes and providing a sense of control over one's destiny.

Problems and Exercises:

Reflective Writing: Assign We to write a reflective essay on their personal beliefs and attitudes towards magic. Encourage them to explore their own cultural backgrounds and experiences, and compare them to the beliefs and practices of ancient Babylonians. Prompt them to consider the role of magic in their own lives and its significance within their communities.

Artifact Analysis: Provide We with images or descriptions of Babylonian artifacts associated with magic, such as clay tablets with incantations or engraved amulets. Instruct them to analyze the symbolism, materials used, and the intended purpose of these artifacts. Ask We to discuss the cultural context and beliefs associated with these objects.

Group Discussion: Divide We into small groups and assign each group a different aspect of Babylonian life (e.g., agriculture, family, governance). Instruct them to discuss and analyze how magic might have influenced and interacted with their assigned aspect. Encourage critical thinking and the exploration of potential benefits and limitations of relying on magical practices in different spheres of life.

Comparative Analysis: Guide We in comparing the beliefs and attitudes towards magic in ancient Babylon with those of another ancient civilization, such as ancient Egypt or ancient Greece. Instruct them to identify similarities, differences, and potential reasons for these variations. Encourage them to consider the cultural, historical, and religious contexts that shaped these beliefs.

By understanding the popular beliefs and attitudes towards magic in ancient Babylon, We gain valuable insights into the cultural and social fabric of the time. It allows for a deeper appreciation of how magic was perceived, practiced, and integrated into various aspects of daily life. Furthermore, exploring the similarities and differences between ancient beliefs and contemporary perspectives encourages critical thinking and reflection on the role of magic in today's society.

VI. Legacy and Influences of Babylonian Magic

The practices of Babylonian magic have left a lasting legacy that continues to influence various fields, beliefs, and practices to this day. This section explores the enduring impact of Babylonian magic on the realms of witchcraft, divination, herbalism, shamanism, ecospirituality, and magic itself.

Witchcraft:

Babylonian magic has had a profound influence on the development of witchcraft traditions. Many of the spells, rituals, and magical techniques employed in Babylonian magic form the foundation of contemporary witchcraft practices. Elements such as the use of amulets, divination tools, and incantations have been integrated into modern witchcraft traditions, adapting to different cultural contexts over time.

Divination:

The art of divination, which involves seeking knowledge of the future or hidden truths through supernatural means, has been greatly influenced by Babylonian magical practices. The Babylonians were renowned for their skilled diviners who employed various methods such as astrology, dream interpretation, and reading omens. These techniques have been passed down through generations and continue to be utilized in modern divination practices.

Herbalism:

Babylonian magical practices incorporated the use of herbs and botanicals for their healing and magical properties. The knowledge of herbalism and the use of medicinal plants in Babylonian magic have had a lasting impact on the development of herbalism as a holistic healing practice. The identification of specific plants, their preparation, and their associations with certain magical properties have been carried forward into contemporary herbalism and natural medicine.

Shamanism:

Babylonian magic played a role in shaping the practices and beliefs of ancient shamans. The use of altered states of consciousness, spirit communication, and the ability to access supernatural realms are elements shared by Babylonian magic and shamanic traditions. The legacy of Babylonian magic can be seen in the techniques and spiritual principles embraced by modern-day shamans, who draw inspiration from the ancient Babylonian practices.

Ecospirituality:

The reverence for nature and the interconnectedness between humans and the natural world found in Babylonian magical practices have influenced the development of ecospirituality. Babylonian cosmology viewed nature as a manifestation of divine forces, and rituals were performed to maintain cosmic harmony. This perspective aligns with contemporary ecospiritual beliefs that emphasize the sacredness of the Earth and the need to live in harmony with nature.

Magic itself:

Babylonian magic has had a profound influence on the broader field of magic. Its techniques, rituals, and concepts have been studied and adapted by scholars and practitioners of magic throughout history. The legacy of Babylonian magic can be seen in the foundations of magical systems, such as ceremonial magic, which draw inspiration from the Babylonian magical practices. Concepts like the power of words, symbols, and ritual enactments have been incorporated into diverse magical traditions.

Problems and Exercises:

Comparative Analysis: Instruct We to compare Babylonian magical practices with those of another ancient civilization, such as ancient Egypt or ancient Greece. Ask them to explore the similarities, differences, and potential influences between these cultures, considering historical and cultural contexts.

Contemporary Adaptations: Assign We to research and present on contemporary practices or traditions that have been influenced by Babylonian magic. Examples could include specific witchcraft traditions, herbalism practices, or modern interpretations of divination techniques. Encourage We to discuss how these practices incorporate and reinterpret elements of Babylonian magic.

Reflective Writing: Prompt We to reflect on the enduring legacy of Babylonian magic in their own fields of interest, whether it be witchcraft, herbalism, shamanism, or others. Instruct them to consider the specific aspects or techniques they find most influential and explain how they have been incorporated into their own practices or beliefs.

Group Discussion: Divide We into groups and assign each group a different field influenced by Babylonian magic (e.g., witchcraft, divination). Instruct them to discuss and analyze the specific contributions and influences of Babylonian magic on their assigned field. Encourage critical thinking and exploration of both the positive and negative aspects of these influences.

By examining the legacy and influences of Babylonian magic, We gain a deeper understanding of its lasting impact on various fields. This exploration allows for critical analysis, fostering an appreciation for the historical and cultural contexts that have shaped modern practices. Furthermore, it encourages We to reflect on their own practices and beliefs, promoting a thoughtful and informed approach to their chosen fields of study.

A. Influence of Babylonian magical practices on later civilizations

The magical practices of ancient Babylon have exerted a significant influence on later civilizations throughout history. This section explores the enduring impact of Babylonian magic on various cultures and civilizations, highlighting their adoption, adaptation, and transformation of Babylonian magical concepts and techniques.

Ancient Egypt:

One of the most prominent civilizations that drew inspiration from Babylonian magic was ancient Egypt. The Egyptians incorporated elements of Babylonian magical practices into their own magical traditions. This can be observed in the similarities between Babylonian and Egyptian magical texts, such as the use of spells, rituals, and amulets for protection and healing. The influence of Babylonian magic on Egyptian culture can also be seen in the worship of certain deities and the adoption of specific symbols and motifs.

Greco-Roman World:

The magical practices of Babylon also left a lasting impact on the Greco-Roman world. With the conquest of Babylon by Alexander the Great, the exchange of ideas and cultural assimilation occurred. Greek and Roman scholars studied Babylonian magical texts and incorporated Babylonian magical concepts into their own magical traditions. This fusion of Babylonian and Greco-Roman magical practices laid the foundation for later Western magical systems.

Jewish Mysticism:

Babylonian magical practices had a profound influence on Jewish mysticism, particularly during the time of the Babylonian exile. The Jewish people assimilated certain aspects of Babylonian magic into their religious and mystical traditions. This can be observed in the Kabbalistic texts, where concepts such as divine names, angelic hierarchies, and the power of words and incantations reflect Babylonian magical influences.

Medieval and Renaissance Europe:

During the medieval and Renaissance periods, Babylonian magical practices continued to be transmitted through various channels, including translations of ancient texts and the exchange of knowledge between scholars and practitioners. Babylonian astrology, divination, and talismanic magic found their way into European magical traditions. The grimoires and magical manuscripts of this era often incorporated Babylonian magical techniques and symbols.

Contemporary Occult and New Age Movements:

Babylonian magical practices have also found resonance in contemporary occult and New Age movements. Modern practitioners, scholars, and authors draw inspiration from Babylonian magical texts and concepts, incorporating them into their own magical systems and spiritual practices. Elements such as planetary magic, sigil magic, and the invocation of deities find their roots in Babylonian magic.

Problems and Exercises:

Comparative Analysis: Assign We to compare and contrast the adoption and adaptation of Babylonian magical practices in two different civilizations, such as ancient Egypt and the Greco-Roman world. Instruct them to explore the specific examples, similarities, and differences between the cultures' magical practices.

Research Project: Divide We into small groups and assign each group a specific civilization or time period known to have been influenced by Babylonian magic. Instruct them to conduct research on the specific aspects of Babylonian magic that were adopted and the ways in which they were incorporated into the culture's magical traditions.

Reflective Writing: Prompt We to reflect on the enduring legacy of Babylonian magical practices in contemporary magical and spiritual traditions. Encourage them to discuss the reasons why Babylonian magic continues to be relevant and influential in modern contexts, and to consider the ethical implications of adopting and adapting ancient practices.

Group Discussion: Organize a group discussion where We can share their findings and perspectives on the influence of Babylonian magic on later civilizations. Encourage critical thinking and open dialogue, allowing We to explore counterarguments and dissenting opinions regarding the appropriation and adaptation of ancient magical practices.

By examining the influence of Babylonian magical practices on later civilizations, We gain a deeper understanding of the cross-cultural transmission of magical knowledge and the ways in which ancient traditions have shaped contemporary magical and spiritual practices. This exploration fosters critical thinking skills and encourages We to engage in thoughtful discussions about cultural appropriation, adaptation, and the evolution of magical systems over time.

B. Survival of magical elements in contemporary cultures

Despite the passage of time and the rise and fall of civilizations, certain magical elements have managed to survive and endure in various contemporary cultures around the world. This section explores the ways in which magical practices, beliefs, and traditions have persisted and continue to play a role in the modern era.

Witchcraft and Pagan Traditions:

One notable example is the survival of magical elements within modern witchcraft and pagan traditions. These practices draw inspiration from ancient belief systems and magical techniques, incorporating them into contemporary rituals and spellwork. For instance, the use of herbs, crystals, and divination tools, such as tarot cards, can be traced back to ancient magical practices. Wicca, a modern pagan religion, incorporates elements from diverse ancient traditions, including Babylonian, Celtic, and Norse.

Folk Magic and Hoodoo:

Folk magic, also known as folkloric or traditional magic, is another domain where magical elements have survived. Folk magic encompasses a wide range of practices, often tied to specific cultural or regional contexts. For instance, hoodoo, a form of folk magic originating from African American traditions, incorporates elements such as candle magic, herbalism, and the use of charms and talismans. These practices have been passed down through generations and continue to be practiced in contemporary communities.

Shamanic Traditions:

Shamanic traditions, found in various indigenous cultures worldwide, also maintain magical elements that have been passed down through generations. Shamanic practitioners engage in rituals, spirit communication, and healing practices that involve the use of trance, sacred objects, and plant medicines. These practices connect individuals with the spiritual realm and are deeply rooted in ancient belief systems that have withstood the test of time.

Magical Rituals and Ceremonies:

Certain cultural and religious ceremonies incorporate magical elements that have been preserved over centuries. For example, in some cultures, rituals associated with fertility, protection, or purification involve the use of specific objects, incantations, and gestures. These rituals are often performed during religious or community celebrations and serve as a way to connect with the supernatural forces believed to govern the world.

Contemporary Eclectic Practices:

In addition to the preservation of specific magical traditions, contemporary eclectic practices have emerged that combine elements from various cultural and historical sources. These practices often involve personal exploration and experimentation with different magical systems, drawing inspiration from ancient traditions, mythology, and metaphysical concepts. Such eclectic approaches allow individuals to customize their magical practices based on their beliefs and intentions.

Problems and Exercises:

Case Study Analysis: Assign We to choose a specific magical element or practice that has survived in a contemporary culture. Instruct them to research its historical origins, cultural significance, and its adaptation and integration into modern contexts. We can present their findings in a written report or a class presentation.

Comparative Analysis: Divide We into small groups and assign each group a different surviving magical element or practice from various cultures. Instruct them to compare and contrast the similarities and differences in how these elements are perceived and utilized across cultures, exploring factors such as symbolism, intention, and cultural context.

Personal Reflection: Prompt We to reflect on their own beliefs and practices related to magic and spirituality. Encourage them to explore any magical elements or rituals they incorporate in their lives and to consider the historical and cultural roots of these practices. We can share their reflections in a written journal entry or in a class discussion.

Community Interview: Encourage We to interview members of a community or group that practices a surviving magical tradition. This could include individuals from Wiccan, pagan, or shamanic communities, or practitioners of folk magic. Instruct We to ask questions about the origins, significance, and adaptation of the magical elements within the community.

By exploring the survival of magical elements in contemporary cultures, We gain a deeper understanding of the resilience and adaptability of magical practices across time and space. They also develop an appreciation for the cultural diversity and historical depth of magical traditions. This exploration encourages critical thinking, cultural sensitivity, and a broader perspective on the significance of magical practices in different societies.

C. Relevance and lessons from Babylonian magic in the modern world

Babylonian magic, with its rich history and diverse practices, offers valuable insights and lessons that can be relevant and applicable in the modern world. While the specific beliefs and practices of Babylonian magic may not be directly replicated, the underlying principles and concepts can provide guidance and inspiration for individuals interested in magic and spirituality today. This section explores the relevance and lessons that can be derived from Babylonian magic in the contemporary context.

Connection with Nature:

One of the primary teachings of Babylonian magic is the recognition of the interconnectedness between humans and the natural world. Babylonian magicians believed that nature was filled with divine forces and that working in harmony with these forces was essential for magical practices. In the modern world, this teaches us the importance of reconnecting with nature and developing a deeper appreciation for the environment. Practices such as eco-spirituality and earth-based spirituality draw inspiration from this concept, emphasizing the need for sustainable living and reverence for the Earth.

Personal Empowerment and Responsibility:

Babylonian magic emphasized the empowerment of the individual practitioner. Magicians were seen as intermediaries between the human realm and the spiritual realm, responsible for their own actions and their impact on others. This highlights the importance of personal responsibility and ethical decision-making in magical practices today. Practitioners are encouraged to take ownership of their actions and consider the potential consequences of their magical work.

Ritual and Intention:

Babylonian magic placed great importance on ritual and the use of specific symbols, objects, and incantations to invoke and direct spiritual energies. This teaches us the significance of intention and focused attention in our own magical practices. By crafting meaningful rituals and setting clear intentions, individuals can enhance their magical work and align themselves with their desired outcomes.

Divination and Self-Reflection:

The Babylonians were skilled in divinatory practices, using various techniques to seek guidance and insight into the future. This teaches us the value of self-reflection and seeking guidance in our own lives. Divination practices, such as tarot reading or scrying, can provide valuable insights and help individuals make informed decisions. They serve as tools for self-discovery, personal growth, and understanding the complexities of life.

Cultural Appreciation and Respect:

Studying Babylonian magic encourages cultural appreciation and respect for ancient traditions and belief systems. It reminds us of the rich tapestry of human history and the diversity of magical practices across different cultures. By learning about and respecting the wisdom of ancient civilizations, we can develop a broader perspective on magic and spirituality.

Problems and Exercises:

Reflective Essay: Prompt We to write a reflective essay on the relevance of Babylonian magic in the modern world. Instruct them to consider which aspects of Babylonian magic resonate with them personally and how they can incorporate those principles into their own magical practices or spiritual beliefs.

Comparative Analysis: Assign We to compare and contrast Babylonian magical practices with those of another ancient civilization, such as Egyptian or Greek magic. Instruct them to explore the similarities and differences, considering how these practices have influenced contemporary magical traditions.

Practical Application: Provide We with a list of Babylonian magical techniques or concepts and ask them to create a modern adaptation or variation. For example, they could develop a modern ritual based on Babylonian principles or reinterpret Babylonian divination techniques using contemporary tools or methods.

Community Discussion: Organize a group discussion or debate where We can explore differing viewpoints on the relevance of Babylonian magic in the modern world. Encourage them to consider both supportive and critical perspectives, fostering critical thinking and respectful dialogue.

By studying the relevance and lessons from Babylonian magic in the modern world, We gain a deeper appreciation for the historical and cultural context of magical practices. They also develop a sense of connection to ancient wisdom and can apply these teachings to their own spiritual journeys. This exploration fosters critical thinking, cultural understanding, and personal growth within the field of magic and spirituality.

Chapter 4: Synthesis and Reflection

In the ancient civilization of Babylon, located in Mesopotamia (modern-day Iraq), a diverse array of spiritual and magical practices flourished. Among these practices were witchcraft, divination, herbalism, shamanism, and ecospirituality. While each of these disciplines had its unique characteristics and methodologies, they were interconnected, often influencing and complementing one another. This chapter explores the connections between these practices in ancient Babylon, shedding light on their shared principles, techniques, and the cultural context in which they thrived.

Witchcraft:

Witchcraft in ancient Babylon was a multifaceted and complex system of magical practices that held great significance in the society. Witches, also known as sorcerers or enchanters, were regarded as individuals who possessed extraordinary powers to harness and direct supernatural forces for their purposes.

The practice of witchcraft in Babylon involved a wide range of rituals, spells, and incantations. These practices were conducted with the intent of influencing and manipulating both the natural and spiritual realms. Witches employed various tools and magical objects, such as amulets, potions, and talismans, to enhance their powers and achieve desired outcomes.

One of the key aspects of Babylonian witchcraft was the interaction with spirits and deities. Witches would establish connections with these entities through invocations, offerings, and rituals. By forging relationships with these supernatural beings, witches gained access to their wisdom, assistance, and powers, which they could employ in their magical workings.

Divination was another significant aspect of Babylonian witchcraft. Witches would utilize divinatory practices, such as reading omens, interpreting dreams, and casting lots, to gain insights into the future and receive guidance from the spiritual realm. Divination provided them with valuable information for decision-making, understanding hidden truths, and navigating their magical practices.

Babylonian witchcraft played a vital role in various aspects of society. Witches were sought after for their abilities to influence outcomes, provide protection, and address concerns related to health, relationships, and prosperity. Their services were often sought by individuals, including rulers and commoners alike, who believed in the potency and efficacy of their magical abilities.

It is important to note that witchcraft in ancient Babylon was not limited to a single tradition or practice. It encompassed a diverse range of magical practices, and individual witches may have developed their unique methods and rituals. Furthermore, the practice of witchcraft was not universally accepted or embraced by all members of society. There were varying attitudes towards witches, with some perceiving them as powerful and respected figures, while others viewed them with suspicion and fear.

The study of witchcraft in ancient Babylon provides valuable insights into the rich tapestry of mystical practices and beliefs that shaped the culture of the time. It offers a glimpse into the ways in which individuals sought to harness supernatural forces and exert their influence over the world around them. By exploring the practices of ancient Babylonian witches, we can deepen our understanding of the interconnectedness between magic, spirituality, and the human experience.

Divination:

Divination, the ancient art of seeking knowledge of the future or hidden information, held great significance in Babylonian society. Diviners, known as practitioners skilled in the art of divination, played a crucial role in providing insights and guidance to individuals and the community as a whole.

One of the prominent techniques employed by Babylonian diviners was astrology. They observed celestial patterns, such as the movements and positions of planets and stars, to interpret their influence on human affairs. By analyzing these celestial phenomena, diviners believed they could gain insights into the destiny and fate of individuals and the state. Astrology provided a framework for understanding the interconnectedness between the cosmic realm and human life.

Another method utilized by Babylonian diviners was the interpretation of omens. They closely observed natural phenomena, such as the behavior of animals, the flight patterns of birds, or the appearance of unusual atmospheric phenomena, as signs or messages from the divine realm. These omens were believed to carry symbolic meanings and offered insights into upcoming events or the outcome of specific endeavors. Diviners meticulously analyzed these signs and symbols to decipher their significance and provide guidance.

Dream interpretation was another integral aspect of Babylonian divination. Dreams were considered a means of communication between the divine realm and humans. Diviners were skilled in decoding the symbolic language of dreams, interpreting their meanings, and extracting valuable insights. Dreams were seen as glimpses into the subconscious and were believed to contain messages from the gods or ancestral spirits.

Babylonian diviners also relied on the interpretation of signs and symbols in various contexts. They observed everyday occurrences, such as the behavior of sacred animals, the patterns formed by oil drops in water, or the arrangement of objects, to discern hidden messages and meanings. These signs and symbols were believed to convey divine guidance and offered glimpses into the future or hidden information.

The role of divination in Babylonian society extended beyond personal matters. Diviners were consulted in matters of state, providing insights and predictions that influenced decision-making processes. Kings and rulers sought their counsel to gain a better understanding of potential outcomes, mitigate risks, and shape the course of their reign.

It is important to note that divination in ancient Babylon was not viewed as a purely deterministic practice. Instead, it was seen as a means of gaining insight and understanding the forces at play in the world. Diviners provided advice and guidance, enabling individuals and communities to make informed choices and navigate the uncertainties of life.

The study of divination in ancient Babylon offers valuable insights into the ways in which ancient societies sought to understand the hidden dimensions of reality and gain foresight into future events. By exploring the techniques and practices of Babylonian divination, we can gain a deeper understanding of the interconnectedness between the natural world, human experience, and the spiritual realm.

Herbalism:

Herbalism held a prominent position in the magical practices of ancient Babylon, blending the realms of medicine, spirituality, and magic. Herbalists, who were revered as healers and magicians, possessed a deep understanding of the properties and energies inherent in various plants, roots, and natural substances.

In Babylonian culture, plants were believed to possess potent spiritual qualities and were regarded as conduits to the divine realm. Herbalists recognized that each plant held specific energies, correspondences, and healing properties that could be harnessed for medicinal and magical purposes.

The practice of Babylonian herbalism involved the preparation of remedies, potions, and incense using a wide array of plant materials. Herbalists carefully collected, dried, and prepared plants to extract their beneficial properties. These preparations were used to address various physical, emotional, and spiritual ailments.

Medicinal herbalism played a crucial role in Babylonian society. Herbalists used their knowledge of plants to create remedies and poultices to alleviate illnesses, soothe pain, and promote healing. They recognized the healing properties of plants such as aloe vera, myrrh, and cypress, which were employed to treat a range of conditions, from digestive issues to skin ailments.

Beyond their medicinal applications, plants also held profound significance in Babylonian magical rituals and spellcasting. Herbalists utilized plants to create potions, charms, and incense blends that were believed to enhance their magical intentions. These botanical concoctions were used for protection, divination, love spells, and spiritual purification.

The selection of plants and their incorporation into magical rituals was carefully guided by the correspondences and symbolism associated with each plant. For example, mugwort was considered a powerful herb for divination and lucid dreaming, while frankincense was associated with spiritual purification and connection to the divine.

Babylonian herbalists worked closely with the spirits and deities associated with plants, seeking their assistance in healing and magical endeavors. They would invoke the specific plant spirits during rituals, offering prayers and offerings to establish a connection and harness their energies.

The significance of herbalism in ancient Babylon extended beyond the physical and magical realms. It was intertwined with spirituality and the belief in the interconnectedness of all living beings. Babylonians recognized the sacredness of nature and the inherent wisdom of plants, viewing them as gifts from the divine that could aid in healing, protection, and spiritual growth.

By studying Babylonian herbalism, we gain a deeper appreciation for the ancient wisdom of plant medicine and the profound relationship between humans and the natural world. It offers insights into the use of plants as healing agents, the interplay of spirituality and herbal practices, and the recognition of the inherent spiritual properties of botanical allies. Exploring the magical and medicinal applications of plants in ancient Babylonian culture allows us to connect with the rich traditions of our ancestors and draw inspiration for contemporary herbal practices.

Shamanism:

Shamanism held a significant place in the spiritual fabric of ancient Babylon, where shamans or priests served as intermediaries between the human and spirit realms. These skilled individuals embarked on transformative journeys, utilizing various techniques and rituals to connect with divine entities, spirits, and ancestral beings.

Central to Babylonian shamanism was the practice of ecstatic trance. By entering altered states of consciousness through rhythmic drumming, chanting, or dancing, shamans were able to transcend ordinary reality and venture into the realms of the spirits. In this heightened state of awareness, they forged deep connections and engaged in profound communication with the unseen world.

Shamans in ancient Babylon were adept at performing rituals to facilitate healing, both physical and spiritual. These healing ceremonies addressed a wide range of ailments, including illnesses, emotional imbalances, and spiritual afflictions. Through the invocation of deities, the guidance of spirits, and the utilization of specialized tools and rituals, shamans channeled healing energies and restored balance to the individual.

Soul retrieval was another important aspect of Babylonian shamanism. It was believed that when an individual experienced trauma or distress, fragments of their soul could become lost or dissociated. Shamans would embark on spirit journeys to retrieve these lost aspects of the soul and reintegrate them into the individual, promoting healing and wholeness.

Ritualistic dances were a prominent feature of Babylonian shamanic practices. These dances served as powerful conduits for energy and transformation. Through intricate movements and gestures, shamans engaged in ceremonial dances to honor the spirits, connect with the natural world, and facilitate spiritual communion.

The role of shamans in Babylonian society extended beyond individual healing and guidance. They were often called upon to perform divinatory tasks, offering insights into future events, interpreting omens, and providing spiritual counsel to individuals and communities. Divination, through methods such as dream interpretation, the reading of signs, or the casting of lots, played a crucial role in the Babylonian worldview, and shamans were entrusted with this sacred task.

The practice of shamanism in ancient Babylon was deeply intertwined with the religious and spiritual beliefs of the culture. Shamans acted as conduits for divine wisdom, embodying the bridge between the earthly realm and the realm of the gods and spirits. Their rituals, ceremonies, and journeys served to maintain spiritual harmony, seek guidance, and restore the well-being of individuals and the community.

By studying Babylonian shamanism, we gain insight into the profound role of shamans as spiritual intermediaries and healers. It illuminates the ancient practices of ecstatic trance, ritualistic healing, and divination, highlighting the belief in the interconnectedness of the human and spirit realms. Exploring Babylonian shamanic traditions allows us to appreciate the depth of ancient wisdom, the significance of spiritual journeys, and the timeless role of shamans as facilitators of healing, wisdom, and spiritual transformation.

Ecospirituality:

While the term "ecospirituality" may not have been explicitly used in ancient Babylon, the essence of this concept can be traced in the reverence and deep spiritual connection that Babylonians held with nature and the Earth. The ancient Babylonian culture exemplified a profound respect for the natural world, recognizing the intrinsic divinity and interdependence of all living beings and natural elements.

Babylonians viewed the Earth as a sacred entity, an embodiment of divine forces, and a source of nourishment and sustenance. They understood the intricate web of relationships between humans, animals, plants, and the environment, recognizing the vital role each played in maintaining the balance and harmony of existence. This holistic worldview formed the foundation of their ecological understanding and practices.

Rituals and ceremonies were conducted to honor and align with the natural cycles and rhythms of the Earth. Babylonians celebrated agricultural festivals, such as the Akitu festival, which marked the beginning of the new year and the renewal of life. These rituals acknowledged the cyclical nature of the seasons and the interconnectedness between humans and the Earth's abundance. Through these ceremonies, Babylonians expressed their gratitude, offered prayers, and sought blessings for bountiful harvests and a harmonious relationship with the natural world.

The Babylonians held a deep reverence for specific natural features and elements, such as mountains, rivers, and trees, which they considered sacred and inhabited by spirits and deities. They believed in the presence of divine forces within these natural landscapes, recognizing their spiritual energy and seeking communion with them. This acknowledgment of the sacredness of the Earth and its various manifestations demonstrates an inherent ecospiritual understanding of the interconnectedness and divinity of the natural world.

Furthermore, Babylonians understood the importance of responsible stewardship of the Earth. They recognized that their actions had consequences for the environment and future generations. Practices such as sustainable agriculture, water management, and the preservation of natural resources were integrated into their daily lives as acts of reverence and respect for the Earth.

While ancient Babylon may not have used the term "ecospirituality," their beliefs and practices embodied its essence. The reverence for nature, recognition of the Earth's sacredness, and understanding of the interdependence of all living beings reflect an inherent ecological and spiritual wisdom that aligns with the principles of modern ecospirituality. By exploring the ecological worldview of ancient Babylon, we can gain insights and inspiration for our own spiritual connection with nature, fostering a deep sense of reverence, responsibility, and harmony with the Earth.

Understanding the connections between these practices in ancient Babylon provides valuable insights into the multifaceted nature of spiritual and magical traditions. By examining the interplay between witchcraft, divination, herbalism, shamanism, and ecospirituality, we gain a deeper understanding of the rich tapestry of spiritual beliefs and practices that shaped the lives of the Babylonian people. Furthermore, exploring these connections can inspire contemporary practitioners to draw upon the wisdom and techniques of ancient Babylon in their own spiritual journeys.

Problems and Exercises:

Comparative Analysis: Instruct We to compare and contrast the roles and techniques of witchcraft, divination, herbalism, shamanism, and ecospirituality in ancient Babylon. Ask them to identify similarities, differences, and any shared principles or themes.

Case Study: Assign We to research a specific Babylonian magical practice, such as the use of amulets or the interpretation of dreams, and analyze its connections to witchcraft, divination, herbalism, shamanism, and ecospirituality. Encourage them to discuss the purposes, methods, and cultural significance of the chosen practice.

Group Discussion: Organize a group discussion where We can explore the potential reasons for the interconnectedness of these practices in ancient Babylon. Encourage them to consider cultural, historical, and societal factors that may have influenced their development and symbiotic relationships.

Personal Reflection: Prompt We to reflect on how the interconnectedness of these practices in ancient Babylon can inform and inspire their own spiritual or magical path. Encourage them to identify aspects they find particularly intriguing or relevant and discuss how they can incorporate these elements into their own practices.

By studying the connections between witchcraft, divination, herbalism, shamanism, and ecospirituality in ancient Babylon, We gain a comprehensive understanding of the complexities and synergies within magical and spiritual systems. They develop a broader perspective on the interconnectedness of various practices and can draw upon the wisdom of ancient Babylon to inform and enrich their own spiritual journeys.

A. Exploring the interconnectedness of mystical traditions in ancient Babylon

In the ancient civilization of Babylon, the mystical traditions that flourished were not isolated or independent practices. Instead, they exhibited a remarkable interconnectedness, where various mystical disciplines overlapped and influenced one another. This section delves into the fascinating web of connections between witchcraft, divination, herbalism, shamanism, and ecospirituality in ancient Babylon, highlighting the shared principles, techniques, and cultural influences that shaped these mystical traditions.

Witchcraft and Divination:

In ancient Babylon, witchcraft and divination were closely intertwined mystical practices that often intersected and complemented each other. Witchcraft involved harnessing supernatural powers and manipulating energies to influence outcomes, while divination focused on seeking knowledge of the future or hidden information. Both disciplines shared a common belief in the existence of a spiritual realm inhabited by deities, spirits, and other supernatural entities.

Witches in Babylon were practitioners who possessed the ability to tap into and manipulate supernatural forces. They were sought after for their expertise in casting spells, performing rituals, and working with magical objects to bring about desired outcomes. Witches believed that they could channel and direct spiritual energies to influence events, shape destiny, and even perform acts of healing or harm. Their practices often involved invoking deities or spirits to assist in their magical workings.

Divination, on the other hand, was a practice focused on gaining insights into the future or hidden information through various techniques and methods. Diviners were skilled in interpreting omens, signs, dreams, and other symbolic messages believed to hold clues about future events or divine guidance. They served as intermediaries between the spiritual realm and the human world, offering their services to individuals seeking answers or guidance.

In the context of ancient Babylon, diviners often consulted with witches to gain additional insight or assistance in interpreting the signs and symbols encountered during divinatory practices. The expertise of witches in manipulating energies and working with spirits made them valuable collaborators for diviners in their quest for understanding and interpretation. Likewise, witches might employ divinatory techniques as a means to enhance their magical workings, gaining deeper insights into the spiritual forces at play.

The collaboration between witches and diviners in ancient Babylon showcases the interconnectedness of their practices and their shared belief in the spiritual realm. By combining their knowledge and skills, these practitioners sought to gain a deeper understanding of the forces at work in the universe and to harness that understanding for the benefit of individuals and communities.

The convergence of witchcraft and divination in ancient Babylon highlights the rich tapestry of mystical practices in the culture. It underscores the belief in the existence of supernatural realms and the utilization of spiritual forces to navigate and influence the human experience. The interplay between these disciplines demonstrates the holistic approach to spirituality and the interconnectedness of various mystical practices in ancient Babylonian society.

Herbalism and Shamanism:

In ancient Babylon, herbalism and shamanism were intimately interconnected, as both practices recognized the profound relationship between humanity and the natural world. Herbalists and shamans alike held a deep understanding of the healing properties of plants and utilized them for their medicinal and spiritual applications. This convergence of knowledge and practices further enhanced the efficacy of their healing rituals and magical workings.

Herbalists in ancient Babylon were highly skilled in identifying plants, roots, and other natural substances with medicinal properties. They possessed extensive knowledge of the healing properties and therapeutic uses of various herbs. Through observation and experimentation, they developed a comprehensive understanding of the effects of different plants on the human body and mind. Herbalists were revered for their ability to create remedies, potions, and incenses using these natural substances.

Shamans, on the other hand, were spiritual intermediaries who traversed between the realms of humans and spirits. They incorporated herbalism into their healing rituals, recognizing the intrinsic connection between plants and spiritual well-being. Shamans understood that physical ailments often stemmed from spiritual imbalances, and they employed the healing properties of herbs to restore harmony on both levels. By using herbs in their rituals, shamans sought to address not only the physical symptoms but also the underlying spiritual causes of illness or distress.

The role of herbalism in shamanic practices extended beyond physical healing. Shamans recognized that certain plants had psychoactive properties and could induce altered states of consciousness, which facilitated their spiritual journeys and communication with the spirit realm. Through the careful use of these plants, shamans accessed spiritual wisdom, received guidance, and brought back healing energies to benefit individuals and the community.

Witchcraft, another mystical practice in ancient Babylon, also embraced the use of herbs in its spellcraft and magical rituals. Witches were known to possess extensive knowledge of plants and their magical properties. They employed specific plants, potions, and ointments in their spellcasting, believing that these substances held inherent spiritual powers that could influence outcomes and manifest desires.

The intertwining of herbalism and shamanism, as well as their connection to witchcraft, in ancient Babylon highlights the profound relationship between humans and the natural world. These practices recognized the healing potential and spiritual significance of plants, acknowledging their role in physical well-being, spiritual balance, and magical endeavors. By harnessing the power of herbs, practitioners in ancient Babylon sought to restore harmony within individuals, communities, and the larger ecosystem.

The integration of herbalism and shamanism in ancient Babylon demonstrates the holistic approach to healing and spiritual practices in the culture. It emphasizes the deep reverence for the natural world and the recognition of plants as allies in physical, emotional, and spiritual well-being. The symbiotic relationship between herbalism, shamanism, and witchcraft highlights the interconnectedness of these mystical practices and their shared commitment to utilizing the gifts of nature for the betterment of humanity.

Ecospirituality and Shamanism:

In ancient Babylon, the principles of ecospirituality, although not explicitly labeled as such, found resonance in the shamanic practices of the culture. Shamans served as spiritual intermediaries, connecting the human realm with the spirit realm and recognizing the intrinsic interdependence between humans and the natural world. Through their rituals and ceremonies, shamans honored and celebrated the sacredness of the Earth, aligning with the core principles of ecospirituality.

Shamans in ancient Babylon were deeply attuned to the natural cycles and rhythms of the Earth. They recognized the significance of natural phenomena such as the changing seasons, celestial events, and the movement of celestial bodies. By observing and understanding these natural patterns, shamans harmonized their spiritual practices with the greater cycles of nature. Their rituals and ceremonies were designed to honor and work in harmony with these natural forces.

The shamanic rituals in ancient Babylon often reflected the principles of ecospirituality through their focus on balance, harmony, and interconnectedness. Shamanic ceremonies acknowledged the interconnected web of life, recognizing the spiritual energy and presence in all aspects of the natural world. The Earth, rivers, mountains, forests, and celestial bodies were regarded as sacred manifestations of divine forces, worthy of reverence and respect.

Through their rituals, shamans emphasized the need to live in harmony with the natural environment. They sought to restore and maintain the balance between humans and the Earth, recognizing that human well-being was intimately tied to the well-being of the natural world. By engaging in practices that honored natural cycles and respected the Earth's resources, shamans fostered a deep sense of reverence and stewardship for the environment.

The holistic worldview of ecospirituality, which emphasizes the sacredness of the Earth and the interconnectedness of all life, aligns closely with the spiritual beliefs and practices of ancient Babylonian shamans. The recognition of the Earth as a sacred entity and the need to live in harmony with nature permeated their rituals, ceremonies, and daily lives. Through their practices, shamans embodied the principles of ecospirituality, fostering a spiritual connection and reverence for the natural world.

The integration of ecospirituality principles into shamanic practices in ancient Babylon provides a rich and profound example of the ancient wisdom that still holds relevance today. It reminds us of the importance of recognizing and honoring our interconnectedness with the natural world, cultivating a deep spiritual connection with the Earth, and embracing our role as stewards of the environment. By aligning ourselves with the principles of ecospirituality, we can strive for a harmonious relationship with nature and work towards the preservation and sustainability of our planet.

Exploring the interconnectedness of these mystical traditions in ancient Babylon reveals a rich tapestry of spiritual beliefs and practices. It demonstrates how these traditions informed and influenced one another, creating a cohesive spiritual framework within Babylonian society. By recognizing the interconnected nature of these mystical practices, We gain a deeper understanding of the shared values, principles, and techniques that underpin ancient Babylonian spirituality.
Problems and Exercises:

Comparative Analysis: Instruct We to compare and contrast the interconnectedness of mystical traditions in ancient Babylon with those in another ancient civilization, such as Egypt or Greece. Encourage them to identify similarities, differences, and possible reasons for the variations.

Symbolism and Ritual: Ask We to research and analyze the symbolic significance of specific rituals or objects associated with the interconnected mystical traditions in ancient Babylon. Discuss how these symbols and rituals were used to enhance spiritual experiences and foster a deeper connection with the spiritual realm.

Modern Applications: Prompt We to explore how the interconnectedness of mystical traditions in ancient Babylon can inform and inspire contemporary spiritual practices. Encourage them to identify aspects that resonate with modern concepts, such as holistic healing, ecological consciousness, and the pursuit of spiritual growth.

Group Discussion: Organize a group discussion where We can explore the potential cultural, historical, and societal factors that contributed to the interconnectedness of mystical traditions in ancient Babylon. Encourage them to consider the influence of trade, cultural exchanges, and shared cosmological beliefs.

By unraveling the interconnectedness of mystical traditions in ancient Babylon, We gain a comprehensive understanding of the profound interplay between various mystical practices. This knowledge offers valuable insights into the holistic nature of ancient Babylonian spirituality and can inspire contemporary seekers to embrace a more integrated and interconnected approach to their own spiritual journeys.

B. Overlapping practices and shared beliefs among different traditions

In the mystical landscape of ancient Babylon, we find a remarkable convergence of practices and shared beliefs among different traditions. Despite the diverse nature of disciplines such as witchcraft, divination, herbalism, shamanism, and ecospirituality, there were underlying principles and commonalities that fostered an interconnected web of spiritual understanding. This section explores the overlapping practices and shared beliefs among these traditions, shedding light on the fundamental concepts that bridged their seemingly distinct paths.

Cosmology and the Spiritual Realm:

One of the fundamental shared beliefs among the mystical traditions in ancient Babylon was the recognition of a complex spiritual realm and the existence of higher powers or supernatural entities. Across practices such as witchcraft, shamanism, and astrology, practitioners acknowledged the presence of a divine or transcendent realm beyond the material world. This belief formed the foundation for their rituals, invocations, and spiritual practices.

In witchcraft, practitioners recognized the existence of deities and invoked their assistance in their magical workings. They believed in the presence of supernatural forces that could be harnessed and influenced through spells, rituals, and the use of magical objects. Witches sought to connect with these higher powers and establish a relationship with them, often through offerings, prayers, and incantations. They acknowledged the divine presence and the potential for spiritual interaction in their practice.

Similarly, in shamanism, practitioners communed with spirits, deities, and ancestral beings in order to seek guidance, healing, and resolution of spiritual imbalances. Shamans recognized the existence of a spiritual realm inhabited by these entities and acted as intermediaries between the human and spirit realms. Through ecstatic trance, rituals, and spirit journeys, shamans established a connection with these higher powers and engaged in dialogue and collaboration with them. This recognition of a complex spiritual realm was central to the shamanic practices and beliefs in ancient Babylon.

Astrology, another mystical tradition in ancient Babylon, focused on studying the celestial bodies and their influence on human affairs. Astrologers believed that the movements and positions of the stars and planets held significance and could provide insights into human destiny and events. They recognized the existence of celestial forces and their impact on the world, viewing them as divine entities guiding the course of human life. Astrologers engaged in the interpretation of celestial patterns and alignments, linking them to the unfolding of events in the material world.

The shared belief in a complex spiritual realm and the existence of higher powers or supernatural entities was a cornerstone of these ancient Babylonian traditions. This belief provided a framework for understanding the unseen dimensions of reality and served as a guiding principle in their rituals and spiritual practices. It emphasized the interconnectedness between the material and spiritual realms, as well as the potential for human interaction and communication with the divine. By recognizing the presence of these higher powers, practitioners sought to cultivate a deeper understanding of themselves, their place in the cosmos, and their relationship with the spiritual forces that shaped their lives.

The Power of Intention and Energy:

Another shared belief among practitioners of ancient Babylonian mystical traditions was the understanding that intention and energy play a vital role in shaping reality. Whether they were practicing witchcraft, shamanism, or divination, these ancient mystics recognized the power of focused intention and the manipulation of energy to influence outcomes and gain deeper insights into the unseen realms.

In witchcraft, practitioners believed that their intentions, coupled with the manipulation of energy, could bring about desired changes in the natural and spiritual realms. They understood that by focusing their thoughts, emotions, and willpower, they could direct energy towards a specific goal or outcome. Through the use of spells, rituals, and the invocation of deities or spirits, witches sought to align their intention with the energy of the universe to manifest their desires.

Similarly, shamans in ancient Babylon recognized the power of intention and energy in their healing ceremonies and spirit journeys. They understood that by directing their intention and working with the energetic forces present in the spiritual realm, they could bring about healing, restoration, and spiritual balance. Shamans employed various techniques such as chanting, drumming, dancing, and specific rituals to manipulate and channel energy for the benefit of individuals and the community.

Divination practitioners also acknowledged the influence of intention and energy in their practices. By focusing their attention and intention on the specific question or area of inquiry, diviners sought to tap into the energetic currents of the unseen realms to gain insights and information. Whether it was interpreting omens, analyzing dreams, or studying celestial patterns, diviners understood that their focused intention and connection with the energetic flow could unveil hidden truths and reveal future possibilities.

The shared belief in the power of intention and energy reflected the ancient Babylonian mystics' understanding of the interconnectedness between the human mind, the spiritual realm, and the energies that permeate the universe. It highlighted the idea that thoughts, emotions, and intentions possess a force that can shape reality and influence the outcomes of their endeavors. By harnessing and directing these energies, practitioners sought to align themselves with the natural flow of the universe, tapping into its transformative power and gaining deeper insights into the mysteries of existence.

Overall, the recognition of intention and energy as significant factors in shaping reality was a core belief that permeated the practices of witchcraft, shamanism, and divination in ancient Babylon. It emphasized the active role of the practitioner in co-creating their reality and engaging with the energetic fabric of the universe. By aligning their intentions with the natural and spiritual forces at play, these mystics sought to manifest their desires, bring about healing, and gain profound insights into the hidden aspects of existence.

Nature and Sacred Connection:

A profound reverence for nature and its inherent wisdom was a foundational principle that united the mystical traditions of ancient Babylon. Whether it was the herbalists, ecospiritualists, or shamans, there was a deep recognition of the healing properties and spiritual significance that resided within the natural world. This shared reverence for nature reflected the understanding of the interconnectedness of all living beings and the belief that the Earth itself possessed a sacred wisdom that could guide and nourish the human experience.

Herbalists in ancient Babylon held a deep respect for the power of plants and their ability to heal and restore balance. They recognized that the Earth's abundant flora contained an intricate web of medicinal properties, each plant holding its own unique healing energies. Herbalists cultivated a profound understanding of the properties and uses of various plants, roots, and other natural substances, seeing them as allies in the journey toward wellness and spiritual growth. Their practices emphasized the harmonious relationship between humans and the natural world, acknowledging that by working in partnership with nature, healing and transformation could be achieved.

Ecospiritualists in ancient Babylon went beyond herbalism, embracing a broader spiritual perspective that recognized the interconnectedness of all living beings and the Earth itself. They saw the natural world as a manifestation of divine wisdom, a sacred tapestry in which every element played a vital role. Through rituals, ceremonies, and practices that honored the cycles of nature, ecospiritualists sought to deepen their connection with the Earth and align themselves with its rhythms. They understood that by fostering a sense of reverence and gratitude for the natural world, they could tap into its wisdom, find guidance, and nurture their own spiritual growth.

Shamans in ancient Babylon embodied a profound connection with the natural world. They recognized that nature held a transformative power and a language of its own. By integrating natural elements and environmental symbolism into their rituals and ceremonies, shamans sought to establish a deep communion with the Earth and its spiritual energies. They engaged in practices such as sacred dances, spirit journeys, and invocations, harnessing the power of the elements to access spiritual guidance and facilitate healing. For shamans, the natural world served as a gateway to the divine, a realm where profound wisdom and spiritual insights could be revealed.

The shared reverence for nature among herbalists, ecospiritualists, and shamans in ancient Babylon exemplified the belief in the interconnectedness of all aspects of existence. It underscored the understanding that humans are an integral part of the natural world, deeply interwoven with its cycles and rhythms. This reverence acknowledged the Earth as a sacred source of wisdom, a provider of nourishment and healing, and a reflection of divine harmony. By cultivating a profound respect for nature, these mystical traditions sought to remind individuals of their inherent connection to the web of life and to foster a deep sense of harmony, balance, and spiritual growth.

Overall, the profound reverence for nature within the mystical traditions of ancient Babylon was a testament to the deep understanding of the interconnectedness of all living beings. It exemplified the belief that by honoring and engaging with the natural world, humans could tap into its inherent wisdom, find healing and guidance, and cultivate a profound spiritual connection. This reverence for nature continues to resonate in modern times, inspiring individuals to rekindle their relationship with the Earth and embrace the transformative power of the natural world in their own spiritual journeys.

Personal Empowerment and Spiritual Growth:

The pursuit of personal empowerment and spiritual growth formed a common thread that united the mystical traditions of ancient Babylon. Across various practices, such as witchcraft, shamanism, and divination, individuals sought to cultivate a deeper understanding of themselves, unlock their innate abilities, and embark on a path of self-realization and transformation.

For witches in ancient Babylon, the exploration of their magical abilities was a means to empower themselves and manifest their desires. They believed in their inherent connection to the supernatural realm, harnessing their personal power to influence and shape their reality. Through spells, rituals, and the manipulation of energies, witches sought to tap into their innate magical potential, enhancing their personal power and expanding their consciousness. The pursuit of personal empowerment through witchcraft was rooted in the belief that individuals possess the ability to actively participate in their own destiny and create meaningful change in their lives.

Shamans in ancient Babylon embarked on visionary journeys and engaged in ritualistic practices to facilitate personal transformation and spiritual growth. Through ecstatic trance and communion with the spirit realm, shamans sought to connect with higher realms of consciousness, gain spiritual insights, and heal imbalances within themselves and their communities. The shamanic path was a profound exploration of self-discovery, as shamans delved into their inner landscapes, confronted their fears, and integrated aspects of their psyche to achieve wholeness. By mastering their own spiritual journey, shamans were able to offer guidance and healing to others, serving as catalysts for personal growth and transformation.

Divination practices in ancient Babylon were employed as a means of self-reflection and self-awareness. Individuals sought guidance from the spiritual realm to gain insight into their personal lives, make informed decisions, and navigate their paths with clarity. By consulting oracles, interpreting signs, or analyzing celestial patterns, they aimed to uncover hidden truths and understand the larger tapestry of their existence. Divination provided a framework for individuals to explore their inner depths, gain self-understanding, and align their actions with their highest potential.

The emphasis on personal empowerment and spiritual growth across these traditions underscored the belief in the inherent capacity of individuals to connect with their higher selves and manifest their potential. It reflected the understanding that personal transformation is an ongoing journey, a process of self-discovery and self-mastery. Through the practices of witchcraft, shamanism, and divination, individuals were encouraged to explore their own depths, confront their fears and limitations, and tap into their innate wisdom and power. The pursuit of personal empowerment and spiritual growth was not only seen as an individual endeavor but also as a means to contribute to the well-being of the community and the larger interconnected web of existence.

In summary, the pursuit of personal empowerment and spiritual growth was a unifying goal that permeated the mystical traditions of ancient Babylon. Whether through the exploration of magical abilities, visionary journeys, or divination, individuals sought to cultivate self-awareness, unlock their potential, and align themselves with their higher selves. This shared pursuit reflected the belief in the transformative power of the individual, highlighting the capacity to connect with higher realms, shape personal reality, and contribute to the greater tapestry of existence.

Exploring the overlapping practices and shared beliefs among these traditions offers We a deeper appreciation of the underlying unity that exists within the realm of mysticism. While each tradition may have its unique rituals, techniques, and cultural expressions, they are all rooted in a common pursuit of spiritual understanding, personal empowerment, and connection with the divine. Recognizing these commonalities allows for a more holistic understanding of the mystical landscape and encourages We to seek a broader perspective when exploring their own spiritual paths.

Problems and Exercises:

Comparative Analysis: Instruct We to compare and contrast the overlapping practices and shared beliefs among different mystical traditions in ancient Babylon with those in another culture or time period. Encourage them to identify similarities, differences, and possible reasons for the convergence or divergence of practices.

Ritual Synthesis: Ask We to design a ritual or practice that incorporates elements from multiple mystical traditions, emphasizing their shared beliefs and principles. Prompt them to reflect on the significance of the chosen elements and how they contribute to the overall intention of the ritual.

Case Study: Provide We with a specific historical or mythological figure from ancient Babylon who engaged in multiple mystical traditions. Ask them to analyze how the convergence of practices influenced the individual's role in society, spiritual development, or impact on others.

Panel Discussion: Organize a panel discussion where We can present their research on overlapping practices and shared beliefs among different mystical traditions. Encourage them to explore the implications of these connections for contemporary spiritual seekers and the potential for cross-cultural understanding and collaboration.

By delving into the overlapping practices and shared beliefs among different mystical traditions, We gain a comprehensive understanding of the interconnectedness of spiritual paths. This knowledge fosters an appreciation for the underlying unity that transcends cultural boundaries and encourages a more inclusive and open-minded approach to spiritual exploration.

C. Examples of cross-pollination and integration of various mystical elements

In the realm of mystical traditions, the exchange and blending of different practices and beliefs have played a significant role in shaping spiritual paths throughout history. This chapter explores the fascinating examples of cross-pollination and integration found among various mystical traditions, including Witchcraft, Divination, Herbalism, Shamanism, and Ecospirituality. By examining these examples, we gain insights into the interconnectedness and dynamic nature of mystical practices.

Witchcraft and Divination

Witchcraft, with its rich history of spellcasting and magical rituals, has long recognized the value and power of divination practices. Divination, the art of seeking knowledge of the future or hidden information, serves as a complementary tool that enhances the effectiveness and depth of Witchcraft. By incorporating divination methods such as scrying, tarot reading, and rune casting, witches can tap into hidden knowledge and gain valuable insights to support their magical workings.

Scrying, a form of divination involving the use of reflective surfaces or objects, is a favored method among witches. By gazing into a crystal ball, a black mirror, or a bowl of water, practitioners enter an altered state of consciousness and open themselves to receiving messages and symbols from the spiritual realm. Scrying provides a visual medium through which witches can connect with hidden knowledge, receive guidance, and gain deeper insights into their magical practices.

Tarot reading, another popular divination practice in witchcraft, involves the use of a deck of tarot cards. Each card in the deck carries symbolic imagery and archetypal meanings that can be interpreted to reveal insights into the past, present, and future. Witches utilize tarot cards to explore different aspects of their lives, gain perspective on specific situations, and understand the energies at play in their magical workings. The tarot serves as a powerful tool for self-reflection, offering guidance and illumination on the path of the witch.

Rune casting, derived from ancient Germanic traditions, involves the use of small stones or wooden tiles inscribed with runic symbols. Witches cast or draw runes from a bag and interpret the symbols to receive messages and insights from the spiritual realm. Each rune carries its own meaning and significance, allowing witches to gain guidance, answer specific questions, and tap into the deep well of ancient wisdom. Rune casting provides a direct channel for witches to connect with the spiritual forces and access hidden knowledge.

By integrating divination practices into their craft, witches expand their understanding of the energetic currents at work, gain clarity in their intentions, and make informed decisions in their magical workings. Divination serves as a source of guidance and validation, offering a broader perspective and deeper insight into the complexities of their magical practices. It allows witches to connect with the unseen realms, communicate with spiritual entities, and align their intentions with the flow of universal energies.

The integration of divination practices into witchcraft demonstrates the symbiotic relationship between the two. Divination enriches the craft of witchcraft by providing a means to tap into hidden knowledge, receive guidance, and deepen the practitioner's connection with the spiritual realms. It offers a way to explore the unseen forces at work, gain clarity in intentions, and fine-tune the effectiveness of magical rituals. By incorporating divination methods such as scrying, tarot reading, and rune casting, witches are able to enhance their magical practice and access a greater depth of spiritual insight and understanding.

In summary, divination practices have found a natural place within the realm of witchcraft. Through methods like scrying, tarot reading, and rune casting, witches are able to gain valuable insights, guidance, and hidden knowledge that support their magical workings. Divination serves as a powerful tool for connecting with spiritual realms, aligning intentions, and deepening the practitioner's understanding of the energetic currents at play. By embracing divination alongside their spellcasting and ritual practices, witches enhance their craft and unlock new layers of wisdom and empowerment.

Divination and Herbalism

The integration of divination and herbalism exemplifies the harmonious relationship between these two mystical practices. Herbalism, the ancient art of using plants and natural substances for healing, is enhanced by the intuitive insights and guidance provided by divination techniques. Herbalists, who possess deep knowledge of plants and their medicinal properties, often utilize divination methods such as pendulum dowsing or oracle card readings to enhance their understanding of the energetic qualities and healing properties of specific plants.

Pendulum dowsing is a divination technique in which a pendulum, typically a weighted object suspended on a string or chain, is used to receive answers to questions or gain insights into various aspects of herbalism. Herbalists can hold the pendulum over different plants or herbal preparations and observe the movement and direction of the pendulum's swing. The subtle energy field of the plant interacts with the herbalist's intuition, causing the pendulum to respond in a specific manner. This interaction provides guidance and validation for the herbalist, helping them select the most suitable plants for their healing work.

Oracle card readings, another divination method embraced by herbalists, involve using a deck of cards with symbolic imagery and messages. Herbalists may choose specific oracle cards that correspond to plants or healing themes and draw cards to gain insights and guidance in their herbal practices. The cards act as a conduit for intuitive messages, offering the herbalist valuable insights into the properties, energetics, and healing potentials of different plants. By incorporating oracle card readings into their herbalism practice, herbalists tap into their intuition and receive guidance to support their healing work.

The integration of divination techniques into herbalism empowers herbalists to access intuitive guidance and make informed decisions in their healing practices. By combining their deep knowledge of plants with divination, herbalists gain a deeper understanding of the energetic qualities and healing properties of specific plants. The use of divination allows herbalists to fine-tune their selection of herbs, remedies, and formulations to address the unique needs of individuals or specific health concerns.

This integration of divination and herbalism brings a heightened level of insight and connection to the herbalist's practice. It enables them to navigate the complexities of healing with greater clarity and precision. By consulting divination techniques, herbalists can gain intuitive insights into the underlying causes of illness, identify appropriate remedies, and understand the energetic dynamics at play in the healing process.

Moreover, the integration of divination and herbalism fosters a deeper relationship with the plants themselves. Herbalists develop a profound connection and understanding of the plants as living beings, recognizing their unique qualities and wisdom. By engaging in divination alongside herbalism, practitioners form a co-creative partnership with the plants, honoring their innate intelligence and seeking guidance in utilizing their healing powers effectively.

The combination of divination and herbalism allows for a holistic approach to healing that encompasses both the physical and energetic aspects of well-being. It acknowledges the interconnectedness of the natural world and the intuitive wisdom that guides the selection and application of plant-based remedies. This integration empowers herbalists to embrace their intuition, work in harmony with the plants, and provide holistic healing support to individuals seeking balance and wellness.

In summary, the integration of divination techniques with herbalism offers herbalists a powerful tool to enhance their healing practices. Pendulum dowsing, oracle card readings, and other divination methods provide herbalists with intuitive guidance and insights into the energetic qualities of plants. By combining their deep knowledge of plants with divination, herbalists gain a greater understanding of the healing properties and appropriate applications of specific plants. This integration allows herbalists to work in harmony with the plants, honor their innate wisdom, and provide holistic healing support to those in need.

Shamanism and Ecospirituality

Shamanism and Ecospirituality are two spiritual traditions that share a deep reverence for nature and recognize the interconnectedness of all living beings. Shamanism, with its ancient roots in indigenous cultures worldwide, and Ecospirituality, a modern movement emphasizing the sacredness of the Earth, have found common ground in their shared belief in the intrinsic connection between humans and the natural world.

Shamanic practices have long been intertwined with the natural environment. Shamans, as intermediaries between the human and spirit realms, have traditionally engaged in nature-based rituals and spirit journeys to establish a profound connection with the Earth. Through these practices, shamans deepen their understanding of the interconnectedness of all living beings and gain wisdom from the natural world.

Ecospirituality, on the other hand, is a contemporary spiritual movement that recognizes the inherent value and sacredness of the Earth. It emphasizes the interconnectedness of all ecological systems and seeks to foster a sense of harmony and reverence for the natural world. Ecospirituality recognizes that humans are an integral part of the Earth's ecosystem and encourages individuals to cultivate a deep connection with nature.

The integration of shamanic practices into Ecospirituality serves to deepen the connection between humans and the natural world. Shamanic rituals, such as nature-based ceremonies and spirit journeys, provide individuals with direct experiences of the Earth's wisdom and spiritual energies. By engaging in these practices, individuals gain a profound sense of interconnectedness and develop a heightened ecological awareness.

Nature-based rituals within Shamanism, such as honoring the cycles of the seasons, acknowledging the sacredness of specific landscapes, or engaging in ceremonies to restore ecological balance, have been integrated into Ecospirituality. These rituals allow individuals to connect with the Earth on a spiritual level and develop a sense of responsibility for its well-being.

Spirit journeys, another core practice in Shamanism, involve entering altered states of consciousness to commune with the spirits of the natural world. By journeying into the realms of plants, animals, and natural elements, individuals deepen their understanding of the interconnectedness and interdependence of all living beings. This understanding is fundamental to Ecospirituality, as it recognizes that all life forms are interconnected and that humans have a responsibility to be stewards of the Earth.

The integration of shamanic practices into Ecospirituality enhances the spiritual connection between humans and the natural world. By engaging in nature-based rituals and spirit journeys, individuals develop a sense of reverence and respect for the Earth and its diverse ecosystems. They come to recognize that their well-being is intimately linked to the health and vitality of the natural world.

This integration also fosters a sense of ecological awareness and a commitment to sustainable living. By experiencing the sacredness of nature firsthand through shamanic practices, individuals gain a deeper understanding of the Earth's interconnected web of life. This understanding inspires them to live in harmony with the Earth, making conscious choices that promote ecological balance and sustainability.

In summary, Shamanism and Ecospirituality share a common foundation in their reverence for nature and the interconnectedness of all living beings. By integrating shamanic practices into Ecospirituality, individuals deepen their connection with the natural world, fostering ecological awareness and a sense of harmony with the Earth. This integration encourages individuals to live in reverence and respect for the Earth and inspires them to take actions that promote ecological balance and sustainability.

Shamanism and Healing Practices

Shamanic techniques have indeed had a profound influence on various healing modalities, expanding the spiritual and energetic dimensions of these practices. Incorporating shamanic principles and rituals into healing methods such as energy healing and sound therapy brings a holistic approach to well-being, addressing not only the physical but also the spiritual aspects of healing.

One example of the integration of shamanic practices into healing modalities is the concept of soul retrieval. In shamanic belief systems, it is believed that traumatic experiences or emotional distress can cause a fragmentation or loss of a person's vital essence, often referred to as the soul. Shamanic practitioners, through trance journeys or other techniques, journey to the spirit realm to locate and retrieve these fragmented soul parts, bringing them back to the individual and facilitating their integration. This process can support healing on a deep spiritual and emotional level, restoring wholeness and balance.

Incorporating shamanic techniques such as soul retrieval into energy healing practices expands the scope of healing beyond the physical body. Energy healers who integrate shamanic principles may use techniques such as journeying or guided visualization to access the energetic realm and identify areas where a person's vital energy may be blocked or fragmented. By working with the energetic body and facilitating the retrieval and integration of lost soul parts, energy healers can support the individual in achieving greater well-being and spiritual alignment.

Sound therapy is another modality that has been influenced by shamanic practices. Shamanic cultures have long recognized the power of sound and vibration in healing and spiritual transformation. Shamanic practitioners use various tools such as drums, rattles, or vocal toning to create rhythmic patterns and vibrational frequencies that facilitate healing and induce altered states of consciousness.

Incorporating shamanic sound techniques into sound therapy practices can enhance the therapeutic effects of sound. Sound therapists may use shamanic instruments or vocal techniques inspired by shamanic traditions to create a healing environment that promotes relaxation, emotional release, and spiritual connection. The use of specific rhythms, tones, and harmonics can help restore energetic balance, clear blockages, and support the individual's overall well-being.

The integration of shamanic techniques into healing modalities offers a more comprehensive and holistic approach to well-being. By addressing not only the physical symptoms but also the spiritual and energetic aspects of healing, individuals can experience profound transformation and inner alignment. The incorporation of shamanic practices into energy healing and sound therapy recognizes the interconnectedness of mind, body, and spirit, and acknowledges the importance of working with the subtle energies and spiritual dimensions of health and well-being.

In summary, the integration of shamanic techniques into healing modalities such as energy healing and sound therapy expands the spiritual and energetic dimensions of these practices. Techniques such as soul retrieval and the use of sound and vibration draw upon ancient shamanic wisdom, offering a holistic approach to healing that addresses the physical, emotional, and spiritual aspects of well-being. By incorporating shamanic practices, individuals can access deeper levels of healing and transformation, fostering wholeness, balance, and spiritual alignment.

Summary:

The examples explored In this section demonstrate the dynamic nature of mystical traditions and their capacity for integration and cross-pollination. Through the integration of diverse elements, mystical practices gain depth, effectiveness, and interconnectedness. By understanding the interplay of these traditions, We can appreciate the rich tapestry of mystical paths and find inspiration for their own spiritual journeys.

Review Questions:

How does the integration of divination enhance the practice of Witchcraft?

What role does divination play in guiding herbalists in their healing work?

How does the integration of shamanic practices strengthen the connection between humans and nature in Ecospirituality?

In what ways do shamanic techniques enrich various healing modalities?

Exercises:

Research and discuss a historical figure who exemplifies the integration of mystical elements across different traditions. Analyze the impact of their approach and its influence on subsequent mystical practices.

Reflect on your personal spiritual journey and identify instances where you have experienced the integration of different mystical practices. Share your insights with a study group or in-class discussion.

Compare and contrast two examples of cross-pollination and integration discussed In this section. Analyze the motivations behind these integrations and their impact on the respective traditions or practices.

In a group discussion, explore the potential implications of cross-pollination and integration for contemporary spiritual practice and the broader understanding of interconnectedness.

By studying the examples of cross-pollination and integration in mystical traditions, We develop a deeper appreciation for the interconnectedness of spiritual paths and the potential for personal and collective transformation.

I. Examining the Influences and Legacy of Babylonian Mystical Traditions

The mystical traditions of ancient Babylon have left a lasting imprint on various fields, including Witchcraft, Divination, Herbalism, Shamanism, and Ecospirituality. This chapter delves into the influences and legacy of Babylonian mystical practices, exploring how these ancient traditions have shaped and continue to impact modern spiritual paths.
Babylonian Influences on Witchcraft

The ancient Babylonian civilization indeed played a significant role in the development and evolution of Witchcraft practices. Many elements of Witchcraft, such as spellcasting, ritual magic, and the use of talismans and amulets, find their roots in the magical practices of ancient Babylon. By studying these influences, we can gain a deeper understanding of the origins and evolution of Witchcraft as a mystical tradition.

In ancient Babylon, magic was an integral part of everyday life and permeated various aspects of society. The Babylonians believed in the power of magic to influence and shape reality. They practiced different forms of magic, including both white magic, which aimed to bring about positive outcomes, and black magic, which focused on harmful intentions.

Spellcasting was a central aspect of Babylonian magical practices. The Babylonians used incantations, invocations, and spoken or written spells to manipulate energies and invoke the assistance of deities and spirits. These spells were often specific to particular goals or situations, such as healing, protection, love, or divination. The use of spells in Witchcraft traditions today can be traced back to the incantations and spellcasting practices of ancient Babylon.

Ritual magic was another significant aspect of Babylonian magical practices. Rituals were performed to connect with divine forces, invoke their assistance, and manifest desired outcomes. These rituals involved various symbolic actions, gestures, and offerings to establish a sacred space and engage with spiritual energies. Rituals in modern Witchcraft often draw inspiration from the ceremonial practices of ancient Babylon, incorporating similar elements of symbolism, intention setting, and connection with the divine.

The use of talismans and amulets, objects believed to carry magical powers and provide protection, can also be traced back to Babylonian magical practices. The Babylonians crafted and wore amulets made from various materials, such as stones, metals, or inscribed tablets, to ward off evil, attract good fortune, or enhance their magical abilities. These objects served as symbols of power and spiritual connection. Today, talismans and amulets are still used in Witchcraft as tools for protection, manifestation, and spiritual empowerment.

Studying the Babylonian influences on Witchcraft practices provides valuable insights into the historical and cultural foundations of the tradition. It allows practitioners to connect with ancient wisdom, explore the evolution of magical practices, and understand the rich tapestry of beliefs and techniques that have shaped modern Witchcraft. By delving into the magical practices of ancient Babylon, we can deepen our understanding of the origins and development of Witchcraft, honoring its historical roots while embracing its contemporary expressions.

Divination in Babylonian Mysticism

Divination, the art of seeking insight and guidance from higher realms, played a prominent role in Babylonian mystical traditions. The Babylonians possessed a deep fascination with the unseen realms and believed that divination offered a means to access hidden knowledge and understand the workings of the universe. By studying the techniques and interpretations employed by Babylonian diviners, we can enhance our knowledge of the ancient roots of divination.

Astrology was one of the most prominent divinatory practices in ancient Babylon. The Babylonians meticulously observed and recorded celestial events, believing that the positions and movements of the stars and planets held profound meaning and influence over human affairs. By interpreting these celestial patterns, Babylonian astrologers provided insights into personal matters, predicted the outcomes of events, and offered guidance on important decisions. The rich astrological legacy of ancient Babylon has influenced astrological systems throughout history, and modern astrology owes much to the Babylonian foundations.

Dream interpretation was another significant form of divination in Babylonian culture. The Babylonians believed that dreams were messages from the divine realm, conveying important information and warnings. Babylonian priests and seers were skilled in interpreting the symbols and narratives within dreams, providing individuals with insights into their personal lives, potential outcomes, and even messages from deities or ancestors. The practice of dream interpretation has remained an integral part of divinatory traditions, with various cultures and spiritual traditions continuing to explore the significance of dreams.

Omen reading was yet another divinatory practice deeply embedded in Babylonian mystical traditions. The Babylonians believed that the gods communicated with mortals through signs and omens present in the natural and human world. They observed the behavior of animals, the flight patterns of birds, and the appearance of celestial phenomena, among other things, to discern divine messages and gain insight into future events. Priests and seers possessed specialized knowledge and interpretation techniques to decipher these omens, helping individuals navigate their lives and make informed decisions.

By studying the divinatory practices of ancient Babylon, we can gain a deeper appreciation for the intricate systems of symbolism, interpretation, and spiritual connection that characterized their approach to seeking guidance and insight. Exploring the techniques employed by Babylonian diviners allows us to trace the historical origins and development of divination as a mystical practice, while also recognizing its enduring significance in contemporary spiritual and metaphysical traditions.

Herbalism and Ancient Babylon

The Babylonians were renowned for their extensive knowledge of herbs and their applications in healing practices. Their expertise in herbalism laid the foundation for subsequent traditions, influencing the development of herbal medicine and alternative healing practices that continue to this day. By studying Babylonian herbalism, we can gain valuable insights into the historical and cultural foundations of herbal medicine.

In ancient Babylon, herbalism played a central role in healthcare and was closely intertwined with spiritual beliefs and magical practices. Babylonian healers, known as herbalists or magicians, possessed a deep understanding of the medicinal properties of plants and their applications in treating various ailments. They collected and cultivated a wide range of herbs, roots, and other natural substances, using them to create remedies, poultices, and potions for both physical and spiritual healing.

Babylonian herbalism encompassed not only the knowledge of specific plants and their therapeutic uses but also the recognition of the spiritual properties associated with them. Each plant was believed to possess unique energies and qualities that could be harnessed for healing purposes. Herbalists worked with the inherent energies of plants, incorporating them into rituals and spellcraft to enhance their healing efficacy and promote spiritual well-being.

The legacy of Babylonian herbalism can be seen in modern herbal medicine and alternative healing practices. Many traditional systems of medicine, such as Ayurveda and Traditional Chinese Medicine, incorporate the use of medicinal herbs based on principles and knowledge passed down from ancient civilizations like Babylon. The understanding of the healing properties of plants, the importance of holistic approaches to wellness, and the belief in the interconnectedness of the body, mind, and spirit all find resonance in contemporary herbal medicine practices.

Studying Babylonian herbalism provides us with a deeper appreciation for the historical roots of herbal medicine and the cultural context in which it emerged. By exploring the botanical knowledge and healing practices of ancient Babylon, we can broaden our understanding of the diverse traditions that have contributed to the development of herbal medicine throughout history. Additionally, we can gain valuable insights into the ways in which traditional healing practices can inform and enrich our contemporary approaches to healthcare, emphasizing the holistic nature of well-being and the inherent wisdom of nature.

Shamanism and Babylonian Spirituality

Shamanism, an ancient spiritual practice found in various cultures around the world, shares striking parallels with the mystical traditions of ancient Babylon. Both traditions emphasize the ability to journey to the spirit realm and establish communication with spiritual entities for guidance, healing, and spiritual growth. By exploring these similarities, we can gain a deeper understanding of the cross-cultural connections and universal aspects of mystical practices.

In Babylonian spirituality, shamans played a significant role as intermediaries between the human and spirit realms. They possessed the ability to enter altered states of consciousness through various techniques such as rhythmic drumming, chanting, or ritualistic dances. In these altered states, shamans embarked on visionary journeys to the spirit realm, seeking guidance from deities, ancestral spirits, and other non-ordinary beings.

Similarly, in shamanic traditions, practitioners engage in soul retrieval, a process of retrieving lost or fragmented aspects of the soul, and spirit communication, establishing a connection with spiritual entities for healing and guidance. These practices involve entering altered states of consciousness and utilizing specific rituals, such as drumming, chanting, or the use of ritual objects, to facilitate the journey and establish communication.

The rituals performed by Babylonian shamans, which involved spirit invocation and communication with deities, align closely with the core practices of shamanism. By invoking the presence of spirits and deities through offerings, invocations, and specific rituals, Babylonian shamans sought to establish a channel of communication with the spiritual realm. Similarly, in shamanic traditions, practitioners call upon the assistance of spirit guides, power animals, and ancestral spirits to facilitate healing, gain insights, and receive guidance.

By exploring the similarities between Babylonian spirituality and shamanism, we can recognize the cross-cultural connections and universal aspects of these mystical practices. Despite the geographical and temporal differences, the core principles of journeying to the spirit realm, communication with spiritual entities, and seeking guidance and healing remain consistent. This highlights the underlying human quest for connection with the divine, the recognition of spiritual realms beyond the material world, and the belief in the interconnectedness of all beings.

Studying these parallels broadens our understanding of the rich tapestry of mystical traditions and fosters a deeper appreciation for the universal aspects of human spirituality. It encourages us to explore the common threads that connect diverse cultures and time periods, offering insights into our shared human experiences and the profound quest for spiritual connection and growth.

Ecospirituality and the Babylonian Connection

Ecospirituality, a modern spiritual movement that places emphasis on the interdependence between humans and the natural world, draws inspiration from the ancient Babylonian beliefs that recognized the sacredness of the Earth. The Babylonians held a deep reverence for the natural world and viewed it as an interconnected web of life, where humans and nature were intrinsically linked.

In Babylonian spirituality, the Earth was considered a sacred entity, imbued with divine presence and power. The Babylonians believed that the Earth possessed its own cycles and rhythms, mirroring the celestial movements and influencing human affairs. Rituals and ceremonies were performed to honor and align with these natural cycles, such as the changing seasons, agricultural cycles, and celestial events. Through these practices, the Babylonians sought to establish a harmonious relationship with the Earth and ensure its fertility and abundance.

This profound recognition of the interconnectedness between humans and the natural world resonates deeply with the principles of ecospirituality. Ecospirituality acknowledges the inherent spiritual value of the Earth and advocates for the protection and preservation of the environment. It emphasizes the interconnectedness of all living beings and recognizes that spiritual growth is intimately linked to the well-being of the Earth.

By exploring the connections between ancient Babylonian spirituality and ecospirituality, we gain a deeper appreciation for the ecological wisdom embedded in the beliefs and practices of ancient civilizations. The Babylonians' reverence for the Earth, their recognition of the cycles of nature, and their rituals honoring the natural world offer valuable insights into our own modern-day efforts to cultivate a deeper relationship with the Earth and promote ecological awareness.

Studying the ecological aspects of ancient Babylonian spirituality encourages us to reflect on our own relationship with the natural world and to consider how we can integrate ecological principles into our spiritual practices and daily lives. It invites us to rekindle our connection with nature, to honor the Earth's cycles, and to take responsibility for its preservation and sustainable stewardship.

By deepening our understanding of the ecological wisdom embedded in ancient Babylonian spirituality, we are inspired to cultivate a profound reverence for the Earth, to live in harmony with nature, and to actively engage in the preservation and restoration of the natural world. Through this integration of ancient wisdom and modern ecological awareness, we can forge a path towards a more sustainable and spiritually fulfilling future.

Section Summary:

The influences and legacy of Babylonian mystical traditions can be observed in a range of contemporary practices. From Witchcraft to Divination, Herbalism, Shamanism, and Ecospirituality, the mystical tapestry of Babylon continues to shape and inspire spiritual paths today. By studying these influences, we uncover the rich historical and cultural foundations that underpin modern mystical practices.

Review Questions:

How has Babylonian mysticism influenced the development of Witchcraft practices?

What are some examples of divination techniques employed by Babylonian priests and seers?

In what ways did Babylonian herbalism impact subsequent herbal medicine practices?

What similarities can be observed between Babylonian spirituality and shamanic traditions?

Exercises:

Research and discuss a specific Babylonian ritual or magical practice and its influence on a modern mystical tradition of your choice.

Explore the use of Babylonian symbolism and deities in contemporary magical or spiritual practices. Discuss the reasons for their inclusion and the significance they hold.

Reflect on the ethical considerations and cultural sensitivities when incorporating Babylonian elements into modern mystical practices. Discuss your findings with classmates or in a study group.

Engage in a group discussion on the relevance of Babylonian mystical traditions in addressing contemporary ecological and spiritual challenges.

By examining the influences and legacy of Babylonian mystical traditions, We gain a deeper appreciation for the historical roots and cultural significance of modern mystical practices. This exploration fosters a sense of connection to the ancient wisdom and encourages a thoughtful and respectful approach to incorporating these influences into contemporary spiritual paths.

A. Influence of Babylonian mystical traditions on neighboring cultures

The mystical traditions of ancient Babylon not only had a profound impact on their own civilization but also influenced and shaped the beliefs and practices of neighboring cultures. This chapter explores the influence of Babylonian mystical traditions on the spiritual and magical practices of neighboring societies, shedding light on the interconnectedness of ancient civilizations.

Mesopotamian Cultural Exchange

Mesopotamia, with its vibrant and cosmopolitan city of Babylon, served as a cultural crossroads where diverse civilizations converged. This cultural exchange facilitated the transmission and diffusion of Babylonian mystical traditions to neighboring cultures, leaving a lasting impact on their spiritual practices.

The influence of Babylonian mysticism can be observed in the spiritual beliefs and practices of neighboring civilizations such as Assyria, Persia, and Egypt. The close proximity and interactions between these cultures allowed for the exchange of ideas, rituals, and spiritual concepts, leading to the assimilation and integration of Babylonian mystical elements.

One significant aspect of Babylonian mysticism that influenced neighboring cultures was the belief in a complex spiritual realm and the existence of higher powers or supernatural entities. The Babylonians recognized the presence of divine beings and spirits, and their rituals and invocations sought to establish communication and interaction with these spiritual entities. This belief system, with its pantheon of gods and goddesses, found resonance in the religious practices of Assyria, Persia, and Egypt, shaping their own spiritual landscapes.

Furthermore, Babylonian magical practices, such as spellcasting, divination, and the use of talismans and amulets, permeated the mystical traditions of neighboring cultures. These practices, rooted in Babylonian magical traditions, were assimilated and adapted into the spiritual practices of these civilizations. For example, the Assyrians incorporated Babylonian magical techniques into their rituals, while the Persians drew upon Babylonian astrology and divination in their spiritual and political affairs.

The influence of Babylonian mysticism extended beyond immediate geographical borders. Egypt, with its rich spiritual heritage, also incorporated elements of Babylonian mysticism. The syncretism of Babylonian and Egyptian spiritual beliefs can be seen in the shared use of magical spells, amulets, and divination practices.

Studying the influence of Babylonian mysticism on neighboring cultures allows us to trace the diffusion and adaptation of these mystical traditions across ancient civilizations. It broadens our understanding of the interconnectedness of spiritual beliefs and practices, highlighting the dynamic nature of cultural exchange and the enduring legacy of Babylonian mysticism.

By examining the diverse manifestations of Babylonian mysticism beyond its immediate borders, we gain a deeper appreciation for the cultural and historical interconnectedness of ancient civilizations. We recognize the profound impact of Babylonian mystical traditions on the spiritual landscapes of neighboring cultures, and we uncover the rich tapestry of influences that shaped the ancient world's spiritual beliefs and practices.

The Spread of Magical Techniques

Babylonian magical techniques were not confined to the city of Babylon but spread far and wide, influencing the magical systems of neighboring cultures. The rich and sophisticated magical practices of the Babylonians, which included the use of spells, incantations, and ritual objects, captivated the imagination of neighboring societies, leading to the adoption and adaptation of Babylonian magical elements.

One prominent example of the spread of Babylonian magical techniques can be seen in the magical practices of the Assyrians. As Assyria grew in power and influence, it assimilated many aspects of Babylonian culture, including their magical traditions. Assyrian magical texts and artifacts reveal a significant influence of Babylonian magical techniques, such as the use of written spells and the invocation of deities for magical purposes. The Assyrians recognized the potency and efficacy of Babylonian magical practices and incorporated them into their own magical systems.

Similarly, the Persians, who ruled over a vast empire that encompassed Babylon, were also influenced by Babylonian magical techniques. The Persian magical tradition, known as Avestan magic, exhibited notable similarities to Babylonian magical practices. The use of spells, incantations, and ritual objects in Persian magic mirrored the techniques employed by Babylonian sorcerers. The Persians recognized the power and effectiveness of Babylonian magical practices and incorporated them into their own magical rituals and ceremonies.

Egypt, with its rich magical traditions, also experienced the influence of Babylonian magical techniques. The syncretism between Babylonian and Egyptian magical practices can be observed in the adoption of Babylonian spells and rituals by Egyptian magicians. The famous Egyptian magical text known as the "Greek Magical Papyri" contains numerous spells and incantations that bear similarities to Babylonian magical practices, demonstrating the cross-cultural exchange and the assimilation of Babylonian elements into Egyptian magic.

The spread of Babylonian magical techniques beyond the borders of Babylon underscores the reputation and impact of Babylonian magic in the ancient world. The efficacy and perceived power of Babylonian magical practices attracted the attention and interest of neighboring cultures, leading to their incorporation and adaptation. By studying these cross-cultural exchanges, we gain a deeper understanding of the interplay between Babylonian mysticism and the magical practices of neighboring societies. We witness the diffusion and transformation of Babylonian magical elements, enriching our comprehension of the diverse magical traditions that flourished in the ancient world.

Syncretism and Assimilation

The assimilation and syncretism of Babylonian mystical traditions with the beliefs and practices of neighboring cultures led to the emergence of unique hybrid systems that reflected a fusion of different spiritual and magical elements. The exchange of ideas and the intermingling of cultures in ancient Mesopotamia resulted in the incorporation of Babylonian deities and rituals into the religious systems of neighboring civilizations, giving rise to new forms of worship and magical practices.

One significant example of this syncretism can be observed in the religious practices of the Assyrians. As Assyria expanded its empire and came into contact with Babylonian culture, it adopted and integrated many aspects of Babylonian religious traditions. The Assyrians incorporated Babylonian deities, such as Marduk and Ishtar, into their pantheon, often equating them with their own gods and goddesses. Babylonian religious rituals and festivals also found a place in Assyrian religious observances, resulting in a blending of Assyrian and Babylonian religious practices.

A similar process of syncretism occurred in the religious landscape of ancient Persia. The Persians, who conquered Babylon and ruled over a vast empire, absorbed many elements of Babylonian religion into their own Zoroastrian faith. Babylonian deities, such as Nabu and Nergal, were assimilated into the Persian pantheon, while Babylonian religious rituals and symbolism influenced Persian religious practices. This syncretism created a unique Persian-Babylonian religious tradition that reflected the blending of Babylonian and Persian beliefs.

Even in Egypt, which had its own well-established religious system, elements of Babylonian mysticism found their way into Egyptian religious practices. Babylonian deities, such as Marduk and Ishtar, were occasionally incorporated into Egyptian religious iconography, and Babylonian magical techniques were assimilated into Egyptian magical practices. This syncretism between Babylonian and Egyptian traditions showcased the interplay between different mystical systems and the adaptability of religious beliefs and practices.

Studying these syncretic traditions provides valuable insights into the diverse ways in which Babylonian mysticism influenced the religious landscape of ancient Mesopotamia. It reveals the dynamic nature of religious beliefs and practices, as well as the willingness of different cultures to assimilate and integrate elements from one another. By exploring the hybrid systems that emerged from the assimilation of Babylonian mystical traditions, we gain a deeper understanding of the cultural and religious exchanges that shaped the ancient world.

Cultural and Spiritual Borrowing

Babylonian mystical traditions held a significant allure for neighboring cultures, who recognized the wisdom and power embedded within Babylonian texts and practices. Spiritual leaders, magicians, and healers from surrounding societies actively sought out the knowledge and guidance offered by Babylonian practitioners, understanding the value of incorporating these teachings into their own spiritual and magical practices.

One notable example of this cultural and spiritual borrowing can be seen in the influence of Babylonian astrology on the Hellenistic world. After Alexander the Great's conquests, Greek and Hellenistic scholars eagerly studied Babylonian astrological texts, recognizing their sophisticated astronomical observations and calculations. The Greeks adopted and adapted Babylonian astrological concepts, incorporating them into their own astrological traditions and shaping the development of Western astrology.

Similarly, the influence of Babylonian magical practices extended to ancient Egypt. The Egyptians, renowned for their own magical traditions, recognized the potency of Babylonian magical techniques and rituals. Babylonian magical texts were translated into Egyptian, and Egyptian magicians integrated Babylonian spells and rituals into their repertoire. This blending of Babylonian and Egyptian magical practices created a rich tapestry of magical knowledge and rituals in ancient Egypt.

The impact of Babylonian mysticism was not limited to neighboring cultures alone. The Jewish people, during their exile in Babylon, encountered Babylonian mystical traditions and were influenced by them. Babylonian divination techniques, such as dream interpretation, became part of Jewish mystical practices. The concept of angels and the belief in a heavenly hierarchy, prevalent in Babylonian religious thought, also influenced Jewish mystical beliefs and writings.

By examining these instances of cultural and spiritual borrowing, we gain insights into the enduring influence of Babylonian mysticism on neighboring cultures. It highlights the recognition of Babylonian wisdom and the willingness of these cultures to incorporate and adapt Babylonian practices into their own spiritual and magical traditions. The exchange of knowledge and the assimilation of Babylonian mystical teachings enriched the spiritual landscape of the ancient world, demonstrating the far-reaching impact of Babylonian mysticism beyond its immediate cultural boundaries.

Section Summary:

The mystical traditions of ancient Babylon had a far-reaching impact, extending beyond the boundaries of the Babylonian civilization itself. Through cultural exchange, the spread of magical techniques, syncretism, and borrowing, Babylonian mysticism influenced the spiritual and magical practices of neighboring cultures. Exploring these influences deepens our understanding of the interconnectedness and cross-pollination of mystical traditions in the ancient Near East.

Review Questions:

How did Babylonian mystical traditions influence neighboring cultures such as Assyria, Persia, and Egypt?

Give examples of specific magical techniques or rituals that were adopted by neighboring cultures from Babylonian mysticism.

Discuss the concept of syncretism and its role in the assimilation of Babylonian mystical traditions into neighboring religious systems.

What evidence exists for the cultural and spiritual borrowing of Babylonian mystical practices by neighboring societies?

Exercises:

Research and present a case study on the influence of Babylonian mystical traditions on a specific neighboring culture, highlighting the key elements and practices that were adopted.

Compare and contrast the magical techniques and rituals of Babylonian mysticism with those of a neighboring culture, discussing similarities and differences.

Engage in a group discussion on the implications of cultural borrowing and syncretism in the context of ancient mystical traditions. Analyze the benefits and challenges of such exchanges.

Reflect on the significance of Babylonian mystical influences on neighboring cultures and its relevance in contemporary spiritual and magical practices. Write a short essay exploring your thoughts and insights.

By exploring the influence of Babylonian mystical traditions on neighboring cultures, We gain a deeper understanding of the cultural and spiritual interconnectedness of ancient civilizations. This examination expands their knowledge of the diverse manifestations of mystical practices and fosters an appreciation for the enduring legacy of Babylonian mysticism in the broader ancient Near East.

B. Preservation and transmission of Babylonian knowledge and practices

The preservation and transmission of knowledge and practices were vital in ensuring the continuity and dissemination of Babylonian mystical traditions. This chapter explores the mechanisms through which Babylonian knowledge and practices were preserved, passed down through generations, and ultimately influenced the spiritual and magical landscape of ancient civilizations.

Cuneiform Writing and Textual Tradition

Cuneiform writing, the unique script of ancient Mesopotamia, held immense significance in the preservation and transmission of Babylonian knowledge, including mystical practices. In the temples and scribal schools of Babylon, priests, scribes, and scholars meticulously recorded a wide range of mystical texts on clay tablets using the intricate cuneiform script.

These clay tablets served as a repository of Babylonian wisdom, containing detailed instructions for rituals, spells, incantations, and other mystical practices. They were carefully stored in temple libraries and archives, ensuring their protection and accessibility for future generations of practitioners and scholars.

The meticulous nature of cuneiform writing allowed for the precise recording of complex rituals and incantations, ensuring their accuracy and consistency over time. The texts were transcribed and copied by dedicated scribes, ensuring their widespread dissemination and transmission across different generations.

The temple libraries served as centers of knowledge, where these clay tablets were carefully organized and cataloged. They functioned as repositories of wisdom, accessible to priests, scholars, and those seeking spiritual guidance. The texts were studied, analyzed, and passed down from one generation to another, fostering the continuity and preservation of Babylonian mystical traditions.

The survival of these clay tablets, despite the passage of millennia, is a testament to the enduring value placed on Babylonian knowledge. Archaeological discoveries, such as the famous Library of Ashurbanipal in Nineveh, have unearthed thousands of these clay tablets, providing invaluable insights into Babylonian rituals, incantations, and other mystical practices.

The decipherment of cuneiform writing in the 19th century by scholars such as Henry Rawlinson and George Smith opened a window into the mystical world of ancient Babylon. Their efforts allowed for the translation and interpretation of these clay tablets, shedding light on the intricate rituals, spells, and incantations performed by Babylonian priests and practitioners.

The preservation of Babylonian mystical knowledge through cuneiform writing has provided modern scholars with a wealth of information about ancient practices. It offers a unique glimpse into the beliefs, rituals, and magical techniques employed by the Babylonians, enabling us to study and understand the profound spiritual traditions of this ancient civilization.

Ritual Schools and Oral Tradition

In addition to written texts, Babylonian mystical knowledge was transmitted through ritual schools and oral tradition, ensuring the continuity and practical application of the ancient wisdom. Skilled practitioners, such as priests and experienced mystics, played a vital role in passing down their expertise to the next generation of apprentices.

The transmission of Babylonian mystical knowledge involved a structured system of apprenticeship and mentorship. Aspiring practitioners, often young individuals seeking to become priests or healers, would enter into a formal relationship with a skilled mentor. These mentors, themselves initiated practitioners, possessed deep knowledge and practical experience in the mystical arts.

The apprenticeship process was rigorous and immersive, encompassing both theoretical teachings and practical training. We would spend significant periods of time under the direct guidance of their mentors, living and learning within the confines of ritual schools or temple complexes.

Practical instruction formed a significant component of the apprenticeship. Apprentices actively participated in rituals and ceremonies, observing and emulating the techniques and gestures of their mentors. Through hands-on experience, they learned the intricate nuances of spellcasting, divination, herbalism, and other mystical practices.

Oral tradition played a vital role in the transmission of Babylonian mystical knowledge. Ancient chants, invocations, and prayers were memorized and recited by both mentors and apprentices. The power of these oral recitations lay in the precise intonation, rhythm, and pronunciation of the sacred words, believed to invoke the presence and blessings of deities and spirits.

The oral transmission of knowledge allowed for a direct and intimate connection between the mentor and apprentice. It facilitated the transfer of not only practical skills but also the subtle nuances, insights, and interpretations associated with Babylonian mystical traditions. This direct transmission ensured the preservation of ancient wisdom and prevented the dilution or distortion of sacred knowledge.

The apprenticeship process was often lengthy, spanning several years or even decades. The apprentices underwent a comprehensive education, gradually progressing from basic principles to advanced practices. They were expected to demonstrate mastery of various rituals, incantations, and techniques before being recognized as fully initiated practitioners.

By engaging in the ritual schools and oral tradition, apprentices acquired not only the practical skills but also the spiritual understanding necessary to carry forward the Babylonian mystical traditions. They became the custodians of sacred knowledge, responsible for preserving and transmitting the wisdom of their lineage to future generations.

The combination of written texts, practical training, and oral tradition ensured the continuity and authenticity of Babylonian mystical practices. It fostered a deep understanding of the rituals, symbolism, and spiritual principles embedded within the tradition, ensuring that the essence of Babylonian mysticism endured and evolved over time.

Cultural and Religious Institutions

The preservation and transmission of Babylonian knowledge were deeply intertwined with the cultural and religious institutions of ancient Babylon. Temples, as sacred spaces and centers of spiritual and intellectual activity, played a pivotal role in fostering the preservation and transmission of Babylonian mystical traditions.

Within the temple complexes, priests and scholars dedicated themselves to the study, practice, and teaching of Babylonian mysticism. These learned individuals, often serving as intermediaries between the divine and the human realms, were entrusted with the sacred knowledge and rituals of the tradition. They played a crucial role in preserving and transmitting this wisdom to future generations.

The temples served as vibrant hubs of intellectual and spiritual activity. They housed extensive libraries and archives where written texts, clay tablets, and scrolls containing mystical knowledge were meticulously cataloged and safeguarded. These collections served as invaluable repositories of Babylonian wisdom, ensuring its preservation for posterity.

Priests and scholars within the temples took on the responsibility of imparting their knowledge to aspiring practitioners and We. They established schools and academies where formal education in Babylonian mysticism took place. These educational institutions offered structured programs of study, guiding We through the intricacies of mystical rituals, cosmology, symbolism, and the principles of divination.

We who sought to become practitioners of Babylonian mysticism would enter into these temple schools and undergo a rigorous education. They would learn not only the practical aspects of spellcasting, divination, and ritualistic practices but also the underlying spiritual principles, ethical codes, and cosmological frameworks that shaped the tradition.

The temple schools provided a supportive and nurturing environment for the transmission of knowledge. We received direct guidance from experienced priests and scholars who shared their expertise, insights, and interpretations of the mystical arts. This mentorship ensured the preservation of the tradition's authenticity and allowed for the refinement and evolution of Babylonian mystical practices over time.

Moreover, the temples themselves served as active centers of worship and spiritual practice. Within these sacred spaces, rituals, ceremonies, and festivals were conducted to honor the deities, invoke spiritual blessings, and engage in mystical experiences. Through active participation in these rituals, We and practitioners absorbed the essence of Babylonian mysticism and cultivated a deep connection with the spiritual dimensions of the tradition.

The community of practitioners within the temple complexes provided a supportive and collaborative environment for the preservation and transmission of knowledge. Initiates and experienced practitioners shared insights, exchanged ideas, and engaged in dialogues to deepen their understanding of Babylonian mysticism. This collective engagement fostered a sense of continuity and unity within the mystical tradition.

In essence, the cultural and religious institutions of ancient Babylon, particularly the temples, served as the guardians and custodians of Babylonian mystical knowledge. Through their educational programs, libraries, rituals, and dedicated practitioners, they ensured the continuity and transmission of this sacred wisdom across generations. The temples became the living embodiments of Babylonian mysticism, nurturing a vibrant community of practitioners and preserving the rich tapestry of mystical practices and teachings.

Cross-Cultural Influences and Adaptation

As Babylonian knowledge and mystical practices spread to neighboring civilizations, a process of cross-cultural influences and adaptations took place, resulting in a rich tapestry of mystical traditions. Scholars, practitioners, and spiritual seekers from various cultures were drawn to the wisdom and power of Babylonian mysticism, seeking to understand and incorporate its teachings into their own systems.

This cross-cultural exchange created a fertile ground for the blending and integration of Babylonian mystical practices with the existing spiritual frameworks of neighboring civilizations. As practitioners encountered Babylonian knowledge, they recognized its value and sought to incorporate it into their own belief systems, rituals, and magical practices.

One example of this cross-cultural influence can be seen in the adoption and adaptation of Babylonian deities and cosmological concepts. Neighboring cultures recognized the power and significance of Babylonian gods and goddesses and integrated them into their pantheons, often assigning them new roles and associations that resonated with their own spiritual frameworks. This syncretism resulted in the emergence of hybrid belief systems that reflected the shared influences of Babylonian mysticism.

Additionally, the practical aspects of Babylonian mystical practices, such as spellcasting, ritual magic, and divination techniques, were embraced and adapted by neighboring cultures. These practices were often modified and blended with existing magical traditions, resulting in the development of unique and distinct mystical systems.

The process of cross-cultural adaptation and integration was not limited to the elite or scholarly circles but also extended to the common people. As Babylonian mystical practices spread, they were embraced and adopted by individuals at all levels of society. This grassroots acceptance and adaptation allowed for the widespread dissemination of Babylonian knowledge and practices, further enriching the mystical landscape of the region.

The process of cross-cultural influences and adaptations served to both preserve and disseminate Babylonian knowledge beyond its original boundaries. It contributed to the survival and continuity of Babylonian mystical traditions by embedding them within the spiritual fabric of neighboring cultures. In turn, these adapted practices continued to evolve, influenced by the cultural and spiritual contexts of the adopting civilizations.

This cross-pollination and adaptation of Babylonian mystical practices fostered a dynamic and interconnected mystical landscape, where diverse traditions intermingled, borrowed, and evolved. It resulted in the preservation and dissemination of Babylonian knowledge and wisdom, while also enriching the broader mystical traditions of the ancient Near East.

By studying these cross-cultural influences and adaptations, we gain a deeper understanding of the enduring impact and widespread relevance of Babylonian mysticism. It highlights the interconnectedness of mystical traditions and the fluid nature of knowledge transmission, inspiring us to explore the diverse tapestry of mystical practices and embrace the wisdom of multiple traditions.

Summary:

The preservation and transmission of Babylonian knowledge and practices were achieved through various means, including the use of cuneiform writing, ritual schools, oral tradition, and the support of cultural and religious institutions. These mechanisms ensured the continuity of Babylonian mystical traditions and facilitated their influence on neighboring civilizations. Understanding the methods by which Babylonian knowledge was preserved and transmitted deepens our appreciation for the enduring legacy of these mystical traditions.

Review Questions:

What role did cuneiform writing play in the preservation of Babylonian knowledge?

Discuss the importance of ritual schools and oral tradition in transmitting Babylonian mystical practices.

How did cultural and religious institutions support the preservation and transmission of Babylonian knowledge?

Explain the concept of cross-cultural influences and adaptations in relation to the preservation of Babylonian knowledge.

Exercises:

Analyze a specific Babylonian cuneiform text related to mystical practices and discuss its significance in preserving and transmitting Babylonian knowledge.

Role-play a scenario where a Babylonian priest instructs an apprentice in a mystical ritual, emphasizing the importance of oral transmission and practical training.

Visit a local museum or research online to explore artifacts related to Babylonian mystical practices. Write a reflection on the significance of material culture in preserving ancient knowledge.

Create a timeline showcasing the cross-cultural influences and adaptations of Babylonian mystical traditions in neighboring civilizations. Highlight key events and figures that contributed to the dissemination of Babylonian knowledge.

By delving into the preservation and transmission of Babylonian knowledge and practices, We gain insights into the mechanisms that ensured the continuity and dissemination of mystical traditions. This exploration enhances their understanding of the historical context and cultural significance of Babylonian mysticism while emphasizing its enduring influence on the spiritual and magical landscape of the ancient world.

C. Enduring impact on subsequent mystical and spiritual traditions

The mystical and spiritual traditions of ancient Babylon have had a profound and lasting impact on subsequent belief systems and practices. This chapter examines the enduring influence of Babylonian mysticism on various mystical and spiritual traditions that emerged in later periods, highlighting the ways in which Babylonian concepts, rituals, and beliefs have shaped and enriched these traditions.

Influence on Western Esotericism

The mystical traditions of ancient Babylon left an indelible mark on the development of Western Esotericism. The Babylonians possessed a deep understanding of the celestial realm and recognized the profound influence of celestial bodies on human affairs. Their cosmological beliefs laid the foundation for the astrological systems that later became integral to Western Esotericism.

Astrology, one of the key components of Western Esotericism, can trace its roots back to Babylonian astrology. The Babylonians developed a sophisticated system of celestial observations and interpretations, seeking to understand the patterns and movements of the stars and planets. They believed that these celestial bodies held divine power and influence, shaping human destiny and offering insights into the future.

The Babylonian astrological practices were later adopted and adapted by Greek, Roman, and Hellenistic cultures. These cultures incorporated Babylonian astrological knowledge into their own philosophical and mystical traditions, merging it with their existing belief systems. This syncretism resulted in the development of new astrological systems that integrated Babylonian principles with Greek philosophical concepts, such as the notion of cosmic harmony and the influence of celestial bodies on individual characteristics and events.

In addition to astrology, other Babylonian mystical practices also found their way into Western Esotericism. Divination, for example, was highly regarded in ancient Babylon and was later embraced by Greek and Roman cultures. The Babylonian techniques of dream interpretation, omen reading, and the interpretation of signs and symbols influenced the development of divinatory practices in the Western mystical tradition.

Ritual magic, another significant aspect of Western Esotericism, can be traced back to Babylonian magical practices. The Babylonians employed ritualistic techniques, incantations, and the use of ritual objects to achieve desired outcomes. These practices were later incorporated and further developed in the magical systems of Greek, Roman, and Hellenistic cultures, forming the basis of ceremonial magic and theurgy.

The influence of Babylonian mysticism on Western Esotericism demonstrates the enduring legacy of ancient Babylon in shaping mystical and occult traditions. The concepts, techniques, and philosophical underpinnings of Babylonian mysticism provided a fertile ground for the development of Western Esotericism, which encompasses a wide range of mystical, occult, and spiritual practices.

Studying the impact of Babylonian mysticism on Western Esotericism allows us to trace the historical origins of these traditions and understand the interconnectedness of mystical beliefs and practices across different cultures and time periods. It provides valuable insights into the rich tapestry of Western Esotericism and highlights the enduring relevance of ancient Babylonian wisdom in contemporary mystical and occult traditions.

Impact on Hermeticism and Gnosticism

Babylonian mysticism left an indelible mark on the development of Hermeticism and Gnosticism, two influential mystical and philosophical movements of the Hellenistic period. The ideas and beliefs of ancient Babylonian mysticism, with their emphasis on divine knowledge, the interrelationship between the spiritual and material realms, and the pursuit of transcendent wisdom, profoundly influenced the philosophical and metaphysical concepts embraced by Hermetic and Gnostic thinkers.

In Hermeticism, which originated from the teachings attributed to the legendary figure Hermes Trismegistus, the Babylonian influence is evident in its cosmological and metaphysical framework. The Babylonian cosmology, with its understanding of a complex spiritual hierarchy and the interplay between the divine and the earthly realms, resonated with Hermetic notions of the divine mind, the universal order, and the spiritual ascent of the soul. The quest for spiritual enlightenment, the exploration of hidden knowledge, and the concept of divine revelation all find parallels in the Babylonian mystical traditions.

Gnosticism, another mystical movement of the Hellenistic period, incorporated Babylonian influences into its intricate cosmology and its understanding of the human condition. Babylonian ideas of a divine spark within humanity and the longing for reunion with the spiritual realm resonated with Gnostic concepts of the divine spark trapped within the material world and the quest for gnosis, or experiential knowledge, to liberate the divine essence. The Gnostic emphasis on secret teachings, the illumination of hidden wisdom, and the exploration of the spiritual realm echoes the esoteric nature of Babylonian mystical traditions.

The integration of Babylonian mystical elements into Hermeticism and Gnosticism resulted in a rich synthesis of spiritual and philosophical ideas. The Babylonian concept of divine knowledge, including astrology, magic, and divination, found resonance within Hermetic and Gnostic teachings, shaping their understanding of the cosmos, the nature of the divine, and the path to spiritual transformation. The influence of Babylonian mysticism contributed to the development of intricate mythologies, cosmological frameworks, and ritualistic practices within Hermeticism and Gnosticism.

Studying the impact of Babylonian mysticism on Hermeticism and Gnosticism allows us to discern the cross-cultural influences and shared philosophical threads that shaped these mystical traditions. It reveals the profound legacy of Babylonian wisdom in the development of Western mystical thought and highlights the ongoing exchange of ideas and concepts across different cultures and time periods. By exploring these connections, we gain a deeper understanding of the historical roots and philosophical foundations of Hermeticism and Gnosticism, as well as the broader tapestry of mystical traditions in the ancient world.

Continuity in Middle Eastern Mystical Traditions

The mystical legacy of Babylon continues to resonate within a diverse range of Middle Eastern mystical traditions, reflecting the enduring influence of Babylonian mystical elements on spiritual thought in the region. Babylonian concepts and practices have found expression in mystical strands of Islam, Sufism, and the esoteric dimensions of Jewish Kabbalah.

In Sufism, the mystical branch of Islam, the influence of Babylonian mysticism can be seen in its emphasis on divine union and the quest for spiritual ascension. Sufi practitioners seek a direct personal experience of the divine through practices such as meditation, chanting, and ecstatic dance. The Babylonian idea of seeking a union with the divine, as well as the concept of the mystical ascent of the soul, resonate within Sufi teachings and practices. Sufi poetry often draws upon natural imagery and symbols, reflecting the Babylonian reverence for the interconnectedness of all living beings and the spiritual significance of the natural world.

Similarly, certain strands of Jewish Kabbalah, the mystical tradition within Judaism, incorporate Babylonian mystical elements into their esoteric teachings. Babylonian cosmology, with its layered spiritual realms and the concept of divine emanation, influenced the Kabbalistic understanding of the divine realm and the process of creation. The quest for mystical insight and divine revelation, as seen in Babylonian divination practices, also finds resonance within the contemplative practices and study of sacred texts in Kabbalah.

Through the integration of Babylonian mystical elements, these Middle Eastern mystical traditions have developed unique frameworks for spiritual exploration and personal transformation. While adapting and incorporating Babylonian concepts, each tradition has maintained its distinct characteristics, rituals, and practices. The enduring presence of Babylonian mystical elements in Sufism, Jewish Kabbalah, and Islamic mysticism showcases the cultural and spiritual interplay across centuries, illustrating the richness and adaptability of mystical traditions.

Exploring the connections between Babylonian mysticism and these Middle Eastern mystical traditions deepens our understanding of the historical and cultural roots of mystical thought in the region. It highlights the ways in which Babylonian ideas have been integrated, transformed, and interpreted within diverse spiritual frameworks, fostering a rich tapestry of spiritual practices and beliefs that continue to inspire and guide seekers of divine wisdom.

Influence on Contemporary New Age and Neo-Pagan Movements

The mystical traditions of ancient Babylon have indeed left a lasting impact on contemporary spiritual movements, particularly within New Age and Neo-Pagan contexts. These modern paths draw inspiration from Babylonian practices and incorporate them into their own frameworks, offering a contemporary interpretation of the ancient mystical heritage.

One area where Babylonian influence is evident is in the realm of divination. Modern practitioners of divinatory arts, such as tarot reading, astrology, and rune casting, often explore the ancient Babylonian methods of interpreting signs, symbols, and celestial patterns. By incorporating Babylonian divinatory techniques, these practitioners seek to tap into the timeless wisdom and insights offered by this ancient tradition.

Nature worship and reverence for the Earth are central tenets in both ancient Babylonian mysticism and many contemporary spiritual paths. Neo-Pagan traditions, for example, honor the cycles of nature and hold sacred the natural elements just as the Babylonians did. They recognize the divine presence in the natural world and engage in rituals and ceremonies to connect with the Earth's energies and express gratitude for its abundance.

The revival of magical rituals and spellcraft also reflects the influence of Babylonian mysticism. Modern witches and magicians draw upon Babylonian practices such as spellcasting, ritual incantations, and the use of talismans and amulets to manifest their intentions and work with the subtle forces of the universe. These practices embody the belief in the power of intention, energy manipulation, and the interconnectedness of the spiritual and natural realms.

By incorporating Babylonian mystical elements, contemporary spiritual paths aim to cultivate a deeper connection with the ancient wisdom and spiritual heritage of Babylon. These adaptations allow individuals to explore their own spirituality, engage with the natural world, and develop a profound sense of interconnectedness with both the cosmos and their fellow beings. The resurgence of interest in Babylonian mysticism within modern spiritual movements serves as a testament to the enduring relevance and power of this ancient tradition in inspiring and guiding spiritual seekers today.

Summary:

The mystical and spiritual traditions of ancient Babylon have left an indelible mark on subsequent belief systems and practices. From Western Esotericism to Hermeticism and Gnosticism, Middle Eastern mystical traditions, and contemporary New Age and Neo-Pagan movements, the enduring impact of Babylonian mysticism is evident. By recognizing the influence of Babylonian concepts, rituals, and beliefs, we gain a deeper understanding of the historical and cultural interconnectedness of mystical traditions throughout the ages.

Review Questions:

How did Babylonian mysticism contribute to the development of Western Esotericism?

Discuss the influence of Babylonian concepts on Hermeticism and Gnosticism.

Explore the continuity of Babylonian mystical elements in Middle Eastern mystical traditions.

Explain the role of Babylonian mysticism in shaping contemporary New Age and Neo-Pagan movements.

Exercises:

Compare and contrast Babylonian astrology with its later manifestations in Western Esotericism.

Analyze a specific text or symbol from a Middle Eastern mystical tradition and trace its connection to Babylonian mysticism.

Research the incorporation of Babylonian-inspired rituals and practices in contemporary New Age or Neo-Pagan movements. Discuss the motivations behind their adoption and adaptation.

Engage in a group discussion on the ethical implications of incorporating ancient mystical traditions into modern spiritual practices.

By exploring the enduring impact of Babylonian mysticism on subsequent mystical and spiritual traditions, We gain a deeper appreciation for the interconnectedness of human spiritual experiences throughout history. This exploration fosters critical thinking and a broader understanding of the diverse cultural and historical influences that shape contemporary mystical and spiritual paths.

II. Contemporary Relevance and Adaptation of Babylonian Practices

The ancient mystical practices of Babylon continue to resonate with individuals and communities in the modern world. This chapter delves into the contemporary relevance and adaptation of Babylonian practices, highlighting how these ancient traditions have been reimagined, revived, and integrated into various contemporary spiritual paths.

Modern Babylonian-Inspired Rituals and Magic

Indeed, there has been a notable resurgence of interest in Babylonian rituals and magical practices among contemporary spiritual practitioners. This revival can be attributed to a growing appreciation for the rich mystical heritage of ancient Babylon and a desire to explore its wisdom and transformative potential.

Within the realm of witchcraft, practitioners have delved into the ancient texts and artifacts of Babylonian magic to uncover spells, invocations, and rituals. By studying and adapting these practices, contemporary witches seek to tap into the powerful currents of energy and intention that were integral to Babylonian magic. Through the use of symbolic objects, such as amulets, talismans, and ritual tools inspired by Babylonian artifacts, practitioners aim to connect with the spiritual forces that the ancient Babylonians believed could influence the world around them.

Similarly, pagans and eclectic spiritual practitioners have embraced Babylonian magical practices as a way to deepen their connection with the divine and the natural world. By incorporating elements of Babylonian ritualism, such as invocations of deities and spirits, practitioners seek to establish a direct line of communication with higher realms and tap into the ancient wisdom embedded in these practices. Through spellwork and ritual ceremonies, they aim to manifest their intentions, honor the cycles of nature, and cultivate a harmonious relationship with the spiritual forces present in their lives.

The resurgence of Babylonian magical practices among contemporary spiritual paths reflects a yearning to reclaim and reinterpret ancient wisdom in a modern context. It provides practitioners with a means to engage with the mystical heritage of Babylon, exploring its rituals and teachings as a source of personal growth, spiritual empowerment, and connection with the divine. By incorporating Babylonian elements into their practices, contemporary spiritual seekers honor the legacy of this ancient civilization while forging their own spiritual paths.

Babylonian Divination in the Modern World

The practice of divination, which involves seeking insight and guidance from higher realms, has indeed undergone a resurgence in the modern age. Many individuals are drawn to divination as a means of gaining clarity, connecting with their intuition, and navigating life's complexities. In this revival, Babylonian divinatory techniques have found renewed interest and relevance.

Babylonian divination methods, such as reading omens, casting lots, and interpreting dreams, offer unique insights into the mysteries of the past, present, and future. These ancient practices were deeply rooted in the belief that the natural world and celestial forces held profound wisdom and the ability to communicate messages from the divine realm. Today, contemporary divinatory systems often incorporate Babylonian symbolism, concepts, and interpretations, allowing individuals to tap into the rich mystical heritage of ancient Babylon.

Tarot readings, for example, frequently draw upon Babylonian imagery and symbolism to provide guidance and insights. The archetypal symbols found in the Tarot cards can be traced back to Babylonian iconography and mythological motifs, adding layers of depth and meaning to the readings. Similarly, astrology, which originated in ancient Babylonian astrology, carries echoes of the celestial wisdom that the Babylonians sought in their divinatory practices. The positioning of planets and their influence on human affairs, as understood by Babylonian astrologers, continues to inform modern astrological interpretations.

Rune casting, another divination method popular in contemporary practice, also finds connections to Babylonian mysticism. The use of symbols and the interpretation of their meanings have roots in Babylonian magical traditions and the belief in the power of symbols to reveal hidden truths and provide guidance.

By incorporating Babylonian divinatory techniques and symbolism into modern practices, individuals can tap into the timeless wisdom of this ancient civilization. These ancient methods allow for a deeper connection with the universal forces that shape our lives and offer insights into the spiritual, emotional, and practical aspects of our journey. The revival of Babylonian divination enriches the landscape of modern divination, offering seekers a pathway to connect with the divine and gain wisdom from an ancient tradition that spans across centuries.

Ecospirituality and Babylonian Nature Worship

The ecospirituality movement, with its focus on the profound connection between humans and the natural world, has sparked a renewed interest in ancient Babylonian nature worship. Babylonians held a deep reverence for the Earth and its sacred manifestations, viewing the natural world as imbued with spiritual energy and inhabited by divine forces. In the context of modern ecospirituality, the wisdom and practices of Babylonian nature worship have gained relevance as a means to honor and engage with the Earth and its cycles.

Nature-based rituals, inspired by Babylonian traditions, offer individuals an opportunity to connect with the rhythms of nature and cultivate a sense of harmony and reverence for the Earth. By observing seasonal changes, engaging in ceremonies that celebrate the cycles of growth and harvest, and paying homage to the natural elements, practitioners can deepen their spiritual connection to the Earth and experience a profound sense of unity with the natural world.

Tree and plant symbolism, deeply rooted in Babylonian culture, carries rich spiritual significance in contemporary ecospirituality. Just as the Babylonians attributed divine qualities to specific trees and plants, modern practitioners recognize the inherent wisdom and spiritual energy present in different species. By incorporating tree and plant symbolism into their practices, individuals can cultivate a deeper understanding of the interconnectedness of all living beings and develop a greater sense of responsibility towards the preservation of biodiversity.

Eco-magic, inspired by Babylonian magical practices, focuses on the intentional use of magical rituals and spells to promote environmental consciousness and sustainability. This form of magic encourages individuals to infuse their actions with reverence for the Earth, employing rituals and spells to manifest positive change, healing, and protection for the environment. By drawing from the Babylonian legacy of magical practices, eco-magic practitioners harness the power of intention and energy to create a tangible impact in their relationship with nature.

By embracing Babylonian nature worship within the framework of ecospirituality, individuals can cultivate a deep sense of connection, reverence, and responsibility towards the Earth. The ancient wisdom and practices of Babylonian culture offer valuable insights into our intrinsic interconnectedness with the natural world and provide a profound foundation for nurturing an eco-conscious mindset. Through these practices, individuals are empowered to forge a harmonious relationship with the Earth, promoting environmental stewardship and experiencing spiritual fulfillment in their ecospiritual journey.

Babylonian Mythology and Archetypes in Modern Narrative

Babylonian mythology, with its intricate pantheon of gods and goddesses, has captivated the imaginations of artists, writers, and filmmakers in contemporary times. The epic tales and rich symbolism of Babylonian myths offer a wealth of inspiration for exploring profound themes and universal human experiences. Through adaptations of Babylonian mythology, these creative minds weave ancient wisdom into modern narratives, providing a bridge between the past and the present.

Authors and storytellers incorporate Babylonian myths into their works, reimagining these ancient tales to resonate with contemporary audiences. By drawing upon the archetypal characters, heroic quests, and cosmic conflicts of Babylonian mythology, they delve into the depths of human nature, addressing themes of love, power, destiny, and the human condition. These adaptations breathe new life into ancient stories, inviting readers to explore the timeless lessons and complex emotions embedded within the Babylonian mythic tradition.

Filmmakers and visual artists also find inspiration in Babylonian mythology, utilizing its vivid imagery and dramatic narratives to create compelling visual experiences. Through film, animation, and digital art, they bring the gods, goddesses, and mythical creatures of Babylonian mythology to life, immersing audiences in a world of enchantment, wonder, and awe. By exploring the themes and motifs of Babylonian myths, these visual adaptations invite viewers to contemplate the mysteries of existence and the human connection to the divine.

The popularity of Babylonian mythology in contemporary literature, art, and popular culture reflects the enduring relevance and appeal of these ancient stories. By incorporating Babylonian myths into their creations, artists and storytellers tap into a timeless source of wisdom and symbolism, offering audiences a deeper understanding of the human experience and a glimpse into the mysteries of the cosmos. Through these adaptations, the rich legacy of Babylonian mythology continues to inspire and enchant, connecting the ancient past with the vibrant creativity of the present.

Chapter Summary:

The ancient practices of Babylon have found new life in contemporary spiritual paths, adapting to meet the needs and aspirations of modern individuals. From the revival of Babylonian rituals and magic in witchcraft and paganism to the incorporation of Babylonian divination techniques in modern oracles, the enduring relevance of Babylonian practices is evident. Additionally, the infusion of Babylonian nature worship and mythology into ecospirituality and contemporary narrative demonstrates the adaptability and timeless wisdom of these ancient traditions.

Review Questions:

How have contemporary practitioners adapted Babylonian magical practices for modern witchcraft and paganism?

Discuss the role of Babylonian divination techniques in contemporary divinatory practices.

Explore the connections between Babylonian nature worship and the ecospirituality movement.

Analyze the influence of Babylonian mythology on modern literature and popular culture.

Exercises:

Create a modern ritual based on Babylonian magical practices, incorporating elements such as invocations, symbols, and offerings.

Practice a Babylonian divination method, such as interpreting dream symbols or reading omens, and reflect on its relevance in your life.

Research and discuss contemporary eco-magic practices that draw inspiration from Babylonian nature worship. How do they promote environmental consciousness?

Write a short story or create artwork inspired by Babylonian mythology, incorporating archetypal characters and themes.

A. Revival and reconstruction of Babylonian mystical traditions

This chapter delves into the revival and reconstruction of Babylonian mystical traditions, highlighting the efforts made by scholars, practitioners, and enthusiasts to rediscover and reconstruct the ancient wisdom and practices of Babylon. It explores the motivations behind these revival movements and the methods employed to reconstruct and adapt Babylonian mystical traditions for contemporary spiritual contexts.

Rediscovering Ancient Texts and Artifacts

The revival of Babylonian mystical traditions has been greatly facilitated by the exploration and study of ancient texts and artifacts. Archaeological expeditions to the ancient cities of Mesopotamia, including Babylon, have unearthed valuable relics and cuneiform tablets, shedding light on the beliefs, rituals, and magical practices of the Babylonians. These archaeological discoveries have provided a tangible link to the past, allowing scholars and researchers to delve into the intricate details of Babylonian mysticism.

Scholars specializing in the ancient Near East have dedicated themselves to the decipherment and translation of these cuneiform tablets. Through meticulous analysis, they have been able to unlock the wisdom and knowledge contained within these ancient texts. These texts encompass a wide range of subjects, including religious rituals, magical incantations, divination practices, and cosmological beliefs. By examining and studying these ancient texts, researchers have gained a deeper understanding of the beliefs and practices that shaped Babylonian mystical traditions.

The translation and interpretation of ancient texts have also allowed for the reconstruction of rituals and magical techniques. By piecing together fragments of incantations, invocations, and instructions for spellcasting, scholars have been able to recreate and understand the rituals performed by Babylonian priests, magicians, and healers. This process of reconstruction has provided modern practitioners with valuable insights into the practical aspects of Babylonian mysticism, allowing them to incorporate authentic elements into their own spiritual practices.

The study of ancient texts and artifacts has not only contributed to the revival of Babylonian mystical traditions but has also enriched our understanding of the broader cultural and historical context of ancient Mesopotamia. These texts provide glimpses into the daily life, religious beliefs, and social structures of the Babylonians, painting a comprehensive picture of their civilization. The insights gained from the study of ancient texts have also facilitated comparative studies, highlighting the connections and influences between Babylonian mysticism and other ancient cultures.

The rediscovery and study of ancient texts and artifacts have been invaluable in reviving and understanding Babylonian mystical traditions. They have provided a window into the beliefs, rituals, and magical practices of the ancient Babylonians, enabling a meaningful connection with their wisdom and spirituality. Through the exploration of these ancient sources, the legacy of Babylonian mysticism continues to be rediscovered, celebrated, and incorporated into contemporary spiritual practices.

Reconstruction of Rituals and Ceremonies

Building upon the knowledge gleaned from ancient texts and archaeological discoveries, practitioners and scholars have embarked on the intricate task of reconstructing Babylonian rituals and ceremonies. This endeavor involves a combination of meticulous research, careful interpretation, and creative adaptation to bridge the gap between the ancient world and the present.

The process of reconstructing Babylonian rituals and ceremonies begins with a deep dive into the available ancient texts, such as hymns, incantations, and descriptions of rituals. These texts serve as a guide, providing insights into the specific steps, prayers, and offerings involved in the original practices. By studying the words and instructions left behind by the ancient Babylonians, practitioners and scholars gain a foundation from which to build.

However, due to the fragmented nature of the surviving texts, reconstruction requires a certain level of interpretation and adaptation. Scholars and practitioners carefully analyze the available information, comparing and cross-referencing different sources to piece together a coherent understanding of the rituals. They may consult with experts in ancient languages, history, and archaeology to ensure accuracy in their interpretations.

Experimentation plays a vital role in the reconstruction process. Practitioners test various methods, materials, and techniques, drawing upon their knowledge of ancient practices and contemporary spiritual insights. They seek to capture the essence of the original rituals while also adapting them to the needs and understanding of the modern world. This process involves trial and error, as practitioners assess the effectiveness and authenticity of their reconstructed rituals.

Adaptation to contemporary contexts is an essential aspect of the reconstruction process. While the goal is to remain faithful to the core principles and intentions of the original rituals, practitioners recognize the need to make them accessible and relevant to modern practitioners. This may involve incorporating elements from other spiritual traditions, modifying certain aspects to align with personal beliefs, or finding ways to address the specific needs and concerns of the present-day community.

The reconstructed rituals and ceremonies aim to honor the deities of ancient Babylon, invoke spiritual energies, and create a meaningful connection with the Babylonian cosmology. They serve as a bridge between past and present, allowing practitioners to tap into the wisdom and power of the ancient Babylonians while acknowledging the evolution of spiritual practices over time.

The reconstruction of Babylonian rituals and ceremonies is a dynamic and ongoing process. As new information and insights emerge through ongoing research and archaeological discoveries, practitioners and scholars continue to refine their understanding and adapt their practices. The dedication to this task ensures that the legacy of Babylonian mysticism remains alive and vibrant, offering a window into the rich spiritual heritage of the ancient world.

Adaptation and Integration into Modern Spiritual Paths

The revival of Babylonian mystical traditions has indeed sparked a wave of creative adaptation and integration within contemporary spiritual paths. Modern practitioners, inspired by the wisdom and symbolism of ancient Babylon, have embraced the opportunity to blend Babylonian elements with their existing belief systems, creating unique and personalized spiritual paths.

In this process of adaptation, practitioners carefully select and incorporate aspects of Babylonian cosmology, deities, symbols, and practices that resonate with their spiritual journey. They draw upon the rich tapestry of Babylonian mythology, rituals, and magical techniques, infusing them with their own personal beliefs, values, and experiences. By doing so, they create a spiritual synthesis that is both deeply rooted in ancient Babylonian traditions and relevant to their present-day lives.

For example, in contemporary witchcraft and pagan traditions, practitioners may incorporate Babylonian deities into their pantheons, honoring them alongside other gods and goddesses from various mythologies. They may work with Babylonian symbols and sigils in their rituals, invoking the energies and qualities associated with these ancient archetypes. Additionally, practitioners may adapt Babylonian magical techniques, such as spellcasting or divination methods, to suit their own needs and preferences.

The integration of Babylonian elements into modern spiritual paths goes beyond a surface-level borrowing. It involves a sincere reverence for the wisdom and traditions of ancient Babylon, as well as a deep understanding of the principles and philosophies that underpin these practices. Practitioners engage in research, study, and contemplation to develop a nuanced understanding of Babylonian mysticism, ensuring that their adaptations are informed and respectful.

Moreover, this creative adaptation serves to bridge the gap between the ancient and the contemporary, fostering a connection with the collective human spiritual heritage. It allows individuals to tap into the timeless wisdom of Babylonian mysticism while exploring their own spiritual growth and self-expression.

By integrating Babylonian elements into modern spiritual paths, practitioners find a sense of continuity and resonance with the ancient traditions that have shaped human spirituality for millennia. They honor the lineage of Babylonian mysticism while embracing the ever-evolving nature of spiritual practice. This creative fusion not only breathes new life into ancient traditions but also inspires innovation and personal exploration, fostering a vibrant and diverse spiritual landscape.

The revival and adaptation of Babylonian mystical traditions in contemporary spiritual paths serve as a testament to the enduring relevance and universal appeal of the ancient wisdom. Through the creative synthesis of the old and the new, practitioners find inspiration, guidance, and a deeper connection to the profound mysteries of the universe.

Reimagining Babylonian Magic and Divination

In recent years, there has been a resurgence of interest in Babylonian magical practices and divination methods, as practitioners and scholars delve into the ancient texts and artifacts that provide insights into the mystical traditions of ancient Babylon. This exploration and reconstruction of Babylonian magic and divination have led to the revival and reimagining of these practices in the modern era.

Practitioners, drawing upon the knowledge gleaned from ancient texts and archaeological findings, have embarked on the task of rediscovering and reconstructing Babylonian spells, incantations, and magical techniques. By meticulously studying and analyzing the symbolism, language, and ritual components found in these sources, they have sought to recreate and adapt these ancient practices for contemporary use.

Babylonian spells and incantations, known for their poetic and ritualistic qualities, have captivated modern practitioners. By understanding the underlying principles and intentions behind these ancient invocations, practitioners have reimagined and crafted their own incantations that honor the spirit of Babylonian magic. These newly crafted spells reflect a blend of ancient wisdom and personal spiritual intentions, allowing individuals to connect with the mystical forces that the Babylonians once sought to harness.

Divination methods, integral to Babylonian mystical traditions, have also experienced a revitalization. Omen interpretation, a practice that involves the interpretation of signs and symbols from the natural world, has been revived and integrated into contemporary divination practices. Modern practitioners may draw inspiration from Babylonian omens, such as the flight patterns of birds or the appearance of celestial phenomena, to gain insights into future events or hidden information.

Scrying, another ancient divinatory method, has also found renewed interest among modern practitioners. By gazing into reflective surfaces, such as water or mirrors, individuals seek to access intuitive knowledge and receive guidance from the spiritual realm. Babylonian scrying techniques, such as the use of special bowls or vessels, have inspired contemporary adaptations, allowing seekers to connect with their own inner wisdom and tap into the mystical currents of the universe.

Astrology, a divination method deeply rooted in Babylonian cosmology, has continued to flourish and evolve in the modern era. By studying celestial patterns and planetary alignments, practitioners gain insights into the influences that shape human experiences and destinies. Babylonian astrology, with its emphasis on celestial bodies and their impact on human affairs, has provided a foundation for contemporary astrological practices, allowing individuals to explore their unique cosmic blueprint and navigate the complexities of life.

Through the revival and reimagining of Babylonian magical practices and divination methods, practitioners today seek to connect with the ancient wisdom of Babylon while embracing the transformative power of these mystical arts. By integrating the principles, symbols, and techniques of Babylonian magic and divination into their own spiritual paths, individuals forge a link to the timeless wisdom of the ancient world and find guidance, inspiration, and personal transformation in the modern era.

Chapter Summary:

The revival and reconstruction of Babylonian mystical traditions have allowed contemporary individuals to engage with the ancient wisdom and practices of Babylon. Through the rediscovery of ancient texts, the reconstruction of rituals and ceremonies, and the adaptation and integration into modern spiritual paths, Babylonian mysticism has found new life. These efforts not only honor the rich heritage of Babylon but also provide spiritual seekers with a unique and authentic connection to the wisdom of the past.

Review Questions:

What role do ancient texts and artifacts play in the revival of Babylonian mystical traditions?

How are Babylonian rituals and ceremonies reconstructed in the modern context?

Discuss the process of adapting Babylonian elements into contemporary spiritual paths.

Explore the revival and reimagining of Babylonian magical practices and divination methods.

Exercises:

Conduct research on a specific Babylonian ritual or ceremony and create a step-by-step guide for its reconstruction in a modern context.

Develop an adaptation of a Babylonian magical spell or incantation for a contemporary magical practice.

Engage in a divinatory practice inspired by Babylonian methods, such as omen interpretation or scrying, and reflect on the insights gained.

Write an essay discussing the ethical considerations involved in the revival and reconstruction of ancient mystical traditions.

B. Incorporation of Babylonian elements into modern witchcraft, divination, herbalism, shamanism, and ecospirituality

This chapter explores the incorporation of Babylonian elements into modern witchcraft, divination, herbalism, shamanism, and ecospirituality. It examines how practitioners of these paths draw inspiration from the ancient Babylonian traditions and integrate them into their spiritual practices. Through the exploration of specific examples, this chapter highlights the ways in which Babylonian wisdom and practices enrich and expand the modern mystical landscape.

Babylonian Influence on Witchcraft

Modern witchcraft, as a dynamic and inclusive spiritual path, draws inspiration from a wide array of ancient traditions, and Babylonian mysticism holds a special place in this diverse tapestry. Within the framework of modern witchcraft, practitioners often find resonance with Babylonian mythology, deities, symbols, and spellcraft, integrating these elements to enrich their spiritual practices.

Babylonian mythology, with its rich pantheon of deities and captivating stories, offers a wealth of archetypes and symbols that contemporary witches may explore and incorporate into their rituals and spellwork. The stories of powerful Babylonian gods and goddesses, such as Marduk, Ishtar, and Enki, provide a source of inspiration for invoking and working with specific energies and intentions in modern witchcraft practices.

The practice of spellcasting is an integral part of modern witchcraft, and Babylonian spellcraft techniques offer a unique perspective that practitioners may choose to explore and adapt. By studying ancient texts and artifacts, contemporary witches gain insights into Babylonian spellcraft, which often involved the use of invocations, incantations, and ritual objects to manifest desired outcomes. Incorporating Babylonian spellcraft methods into their own practices allows witches to tap into the potency of these ancient traditions and infuse their spellwork with the wisdom of the past.

Babylonian symbols, such as sacred animals, celestial bodies, and sacred numbers, also find their way into contemporary witchcraft practices. These symbols hold potent meanings and can be used to enhance the intentions and energies in rituals and spellcasting. For example, a witch may work with the symbol of the winged serpent, a significant Babylonian symbol representing the balance between the earthly and celestial realms, to invoke transformative energies in their magical workings.

Rituals in modern witchcraft often draw upon elements from various ancient traditions, and Babylonian rituals offer a rich source of inspiration. Nature-based rituals, seasonal observances, and rites honoring the cycles of the moon are practices that resonate with Babylonian spirituality and can be incorporated into modern witchcraft.

These rituals align with the Babylonian reverence for the natural world and its interconnectedness with the spiritual realm, providing contemporary practitioners with a profound connection to the ancient wisdom of Babylon.

Babylonian correspondences, such as herbs, crystals, and colors associated with specific deities or intentions, also find a place in modern witchcraft. By working with these correspondences, practitioners can tap into the vibrational energies and sacred qualities of these ancient elements, infusing their spells and rituals with the essence of Babylonian mysticism.

The integration of Babylonian mythology, deities, symbols, and spellcraft within modern witchcraft practices serves to enrich the spiritual experiences of practitioners. By exploring and adapting these ancient elements, contemporary witches forge a bridge between the wisdom of the past and the evolving nature of their spiritual paths. Through this synthesis, modern witchcraft continues to evolve as a living, dynamic tradition that honors the ancient roots while embracing the infinite possibilities of the present.

Divination Practices Inspired by Babylonian Traditions

Divination, as a timeless practice, continues to inspire and evolve, drawing upon the ancient wisdom of Babylonian divination techniques to offer modern practitioners a deeper connection to mystical sources.

Omen interpretation, a significant aspect of Babylonian divination, has found its place in contemporary divinatory practices. Modern practitioners may use various tools, such as cards, runes, or even everyday objects, to seek omens and signs that hold symbolic meaning. By studying ancient Babylonian methods of interpreting omens, modern diviners gain insights into the art of reading symbols and messages from the universe.

Astrology, a practice deeply rooted in Babylonian cosmology, has remained a prominent form of divination throughout history. Modern astrologers draw upon Babylonian astrological concepts, such as the zodiac signs and planetary movements, to create natal charts and provide astrological readings. The influence of Babylonian astrological principles allows contemporary practitioners to connect with the ancient lineage of this celestial art and understand the intricate interplay between celestial bodies and human destinies.

Scrying, the act of gazing into a reflective surface to gain insight, also has roots in Babylonian divination. Modern practitioners may use mirrors, crystals, or water as scrying tools, seeking to tap into the spiritual realm and receive intuitive messages. By exploring Babylonian scrying techniques, contemporary diviners deepen their understanding of this ancient method and enhance their ability to receive visions and guidance.

Incorporating Babylonian divination techniques into modern practices provides diviners with unique perspectives and insights. By studying ancient texts and archaeological findings, modern practitioners can access the wisdom of Babylonian diviners and adapt these time-tested methods to suit their own spiritual paths.

The integration of Babylonian divination techniques offers modern practitioners a rich connection to the mystical heritage of ancient Babylon. Whether through omen interpretation, astrology, scrying, or other divinatory methods, the wisdom of Babylonian divination continues to inspire and guide seekers on their spiritual journeys. By honoring these ancient traditions and incorporating them into contemporary divinatory practices, practitioners forge a bridge between the past and the present, creating a living tradition that echoes the timeless quest for insight and guidance from mystical sources.

Herbalism and the Wisdom of Babylonian Plant Lore

Herbalism, as a holistic healing practice, has a deep-rooted connection to Babylonian traditions, where the knowledge of medicinal plants played a vital role in both spiritual and physical healing. Modern herbalists draw inspiration from ancient Babylonian practices, incorporating their wisdom into their own healing work.

In ancient Babylon, herbalists were revered for their understanding of the healing properties of plants and their applications in both spiritual and medicinal contexts. Babylonian texts and clay tablets provide valuable insights into the use of specific plants and botanical remedies for various ailments and spiritual purposes. Herbs were believed to possess spiritual energies and were often used in rituals, spellcraft, and offerings to deities.

Modern herbalists delve into these ancient texts, exploring Babylonian botanical knowledge, and adapt it to contemporary healing practices. By studying the spiritual and medicinal properties of specific plants associated with Babylonian culture, modern herbalists gain insights into their uses and applications.

For example, the use of certain aromatic herbs, like myrrh and frankincense, in Babylonian rituals has inspired modern practitioners to incorporate these herbs into smudging or incense practices for spiritual cleansing and purification. The recognition of sacred trees, such as the date palm, in Babylonian traditions has led to their symbolic use in modern herbalism for enhancing fertility and vitality.

Moreover, Babylonian herbalists often infused their healing practices with rituals and invocations, seeking divine assistance in their healing work. Modern herbalists may choose to integrate similar rituals and affirmations into their healing sessions, emphasizing the spiritual aspect of herbal remedies.

By drawing upon the ancient knowledge of Babylonian herbalism, contemporary herbalists gain a deeper appreciation for the interconnectedness of humans and the natural world. They embrace the concept of herbal remedies as not only physical healers but also spiritual aids, promoting harmony and well-being on multiple levels.

The integration of Babylonian herbalism into modern practices serves as a testament to the enduring wisdom of ancient civilizations and fosters a profound reverence for nature's healing gifts. As modern herbalists continue to explore and adapt Babylonian practices, they contribute to the preservation and evolution of this ancient art, keeping the legacy of Babylonian herbal knowledge alive and thriving in the contemporary world.

Shamanic Practices and Babylonian Shamanism

Shamanism, as a mystical and spiritual tradition, shares profound similarities with the ancient Babylonian shamanic practices. In Babylonian culture, shamans served as intermediaries between the human and spirit realms, engaging in ecstatic trance, rituals, and spirit journeys to seek guidance, healing, and spiritual balance.

Modern practitioners of shamanism draw inspiration from Babylonian shamanic traditions, incorporating their roles and practices into their own spiritual journeys. By studying the roles and techniques of Babylonian shamans, modern practitioners gain valuable insights into the interconnectedness of humans and the spiritual world.

Babylonian shamans were skilled in communicating with deities, spirits, and ancestors to seek guidance and healing. Modern shamans embrace similar practices, seeking to connect with their spirit guides and power animals for insight and support in their spiritual journeys.

In Babylonian shamanic traditions, rituals were performed to honor natural cycles, celestial events, and the sacredness of the Earth. Modern practitioners often integrate nature-based rituals into their practices, aligning themselves with the principles of ecospirituality and deepening their connection to the natural world.

The concept of spirit journeying, which was integral to Babylonian shamanic practices, has found resonance in contemporary shamanism. Modern practitioners embark on visionary journeys to explore the spirit realm, seek answers to life's questions, and retrieve lost aspects of their soul, just as Babylonian shamans did.

Furthermore, the understanding of Babylonian cosmology and its emphasis on celestial bodies and their influence on human affairs has influenced modern shamanic astrology. Practitioners incorporate astrological insights into their shamanic work, recognizing the potential impact of celestial energies on healing and personal transformation.

Modern shamanic healing practices, such as soul retrieval and spirit extraction, draw inspiration from Babylonian rituals involving spirit invocation and communication with deities. These techniques allow practitioners to address spiritual imbalances and facilitate healing on a deeper level.

By exploring the connections between Babylonian cosmology, spirit guides, and shamanic techniques, modern practitioners honor the ancient wisdom while adapting it to contemporary needs. The integration of Babylonian shamanic practices into modern shamanism enriches the spiritual journey, fostering a deeper understanding of the mystical and spiritual interconnections between humans and the spirit world.

Ecospirituality and Babylonian Earth-based Practices

Ecospirituality, with its focus on the spiritual connection with nature and the Earth, can find resonance in ancient Babylonian earth-based practices. The Babylonians held a profound reverence for the natural world, viewing it as sacred and imbued with divine energy. This section explores how modern ecospiritual practitioners can draw inspiration from Babylonian perspectives on nature and integrate these elements into their spiritual path.

Babylonian Perspectives on Nature: In ancient Babylon, nature was considered sacred, and each element held divine qualities. Mountains, rivers, and groves were believed to be imbued with spiritual energy, serving as meeting points between the earthly and divine realms. Modern ecospiritual practitioners can embrace this perspective, acknowledging the sacredness of nature and recognizing the interconnectedness of all living beings.

Sacred Landscapes and Rituals: Babylonian rituals honored natural cycles, such as the changing seasons and celestial events. Modern ecospiritual practitioners can adopt and adapt these rituals, incorporating them into their practices to honor and celebrate the Earth's cycles. By performing rituals in sacred landscapes, practitioners can deepen their connection with nature and experience a sense of unity with the natural world.

Sustainable Living Practices: The Babylonians were adept at utilizing natural resources and maintaining a balance with the environment through their agricultural practices and water management systems. Modern ecospiritual practitioners can learn from these practices and adopt sustainable living habits that minimize harm to the Earth. This includes supporting local and organic food production, reducing waste, and advocating for environmental conservation.

Environmental Activism: Babylonian spirituality involved a deep respect for the natural world and a recognition of the Earth's ability to nurture and provide for humanity. Modern ecospiritual practitioners can draw from this wisdom to become advocates for environmental justice and sustainability. By aligning their spiritual beliefs with environmental activism, they can actively work towards protecting and preserving the Earth.

By exploring Babylonian perspectives on nature, sacred landscapes, and rituals, modern ecospiritual practitioners can deepen their connection with the natural world and foster a sense of responsibility towards the environment. Integrating these elements into their practices, they can align their spirituality with ecological awareness and become stewards of the Earth, embodying the timeless wisdom of ancient Babylonian earth-based practices in a contemporary context.

Chapter Summary:

The incorporation of Babylonian elements into modern mystical practices has enriched and expanded the spiritual landscape of witchcraft, divination, herbalism, shamanism, and ecospirituality. Through the integration of Babylonian mythology, symbols, rituals, and practices, practitioners find new perspectives, wisdom, and connections to the ancient world. This chapter highlights the diverse ways in which Babylonian elements are embraced, honoring the legacy of Babylon while forging innovative paths in the modern mystical realm.

Review Questions:

How does Babylonian mythology influence modern witchcraft practices?

Explore the incorporation of Babylonian divination techniques into contemporary divinatory practices.

Discuss the use of Babylonian plant lore in modern herbalism and healing practices.

How do modern shamans incorporate Babylonian shamanic traditions into their spiritual work?

Analyze the connections between Babylonian earth-based practices and modern ecospirituality.

Exercises:

Create a Babylonian-inspired spell or ritual for a specific intention within modern witchcraft.

Experiment with Babylonian divination methods, such as omen interpretation or scrying, and reflect on your experiences.

Research and cultivate a medicinal plant associated with Babylonian herbalism, exploring its spiritual and healing properties.

Engage in a shamanic journey inspired by Babylonian cosmology, seeking guidance from Babylonian deities or spirits.

Develop an ecospiritual practice that honors the Babylonian perspective on the sacredness of the earth, incorporating rituals and actions to promote environmental sustainability.

C. Challenges and ethical considerations in contemporary adaptations

In the exploration and adaptation of Babylonian mystical traditions in contemporary practices, practitioners encounter various challenges and ethical considerations. This chapter examines the potential dilemmas and issues that arise when working with ancient wisdom in modern contexts. It encourages We to critically analyze the impact and consequences of their adaptations and provides guidance on navigating these challenges with integrity and respect.

Cultural Appropriation and Respectful Adaptation

Incorporating Babylonian elements into contemporary spiritual practices presents practitioners with a responsibility to approach these traditions with cultural sensitivity and respect. Cultural appropriation is a concern that arises when elements from one culture are adopted or used without proper understanding or acknowledgment of their cultural context and significance. This section emphasizes the importance of honoring the cultural heritage of Babylonian traditions and avoiding the commodification or misrepresentation of these practices.

Understanding Cultural Context: Before incorporating Babylonian elements, practitioners should take the time to study the historical and cultural context from which these traditions originated. Learning about the beliefs, rituals, and customs of ancient Babylonians allows practitioners to approach these elements with a deeper understanding and appreciation.

Acknowledging Cultural Heritage: Practitioners should recognize and acknowledge the cultural heritage of Babylonian traditions. This includes recognizing that these practices have deep roots in the history and spirituality of the Babylonian civilization and should not be treated as mere commodities or trendy additions to modern spiritual paths.

Respecting Sacred Knowledge: Babylonian mystical traditions were safeguarded by priests, scribes, and scholars for generations. Practitioners should respect the sacredness of this knowledge and avoid appropriating it for personal gain or profit.

Cultivating Cultural Exchange: Instead of simply borrowing elements from Babylonian traditions, practitioners can seek to engage in cultural exchange. This involves approaching Babylonian elements with humility and a willingness to learn from the wisdom of the past.

Avoiding Misrepresentation: Babylonian practices should not be taken out of context or distorted to fit modern beliefs or agendas. Practitioners should strive to represent these traditions accurately and with integrity.

Collaborating with Cultural Experts: To deepen their understanding of Babylonian practices, practitioners can seek guidance and collaboration with cultural experts, historians, and scholars who have studied ancient Mesopotamia and its mystical traditions.

By approaching Babylonian elements with cultural sensitivity, practitioners can honor the rich heritage of these traditions while incorporating them into contemporary spiritual paths in an authentic and respectful manner. This approach ensures that the wisdom of ancient Babylon is appreciated and preserved without perpetuating cultural appropriation or misrepresentation..

Authenticity and Historical Accuracy

Maintaining authenticity and historical accuracy in contemporary adaptations of Babylonian mystical traditions can indeed be a complex endeavor due to the fragmented nature of ancient texts and artifacts. This section highlights the challenges involved in interpreting these ancient sources and encourages practitioners to approach their adaptations with rigor, critical discernment, and respect for historical knowledge.

Fragmented Nature of Sources: Ancient Babylonian texts and artifacts have often been damaged or lost over time, leaving us with fragmented pieces of information. As a result, some aspects of Babylonian mystical traditions may remain unclear or open to multiple interpretations.

Rigorous Research: To create authentic adaptations, practitioners should engage in extensive research on Babylonian history, culture, and mystical practices. Consulting academic sources, historical records, and scholarly works can provide valuable insights into the context and meaning of Babylonian texts and rituals.

Historical Context: Understanding the historical context in which Babylonian mystical traditions emerged is essential for accurate interpretations. Practitioners should consider the social, religious, and cultural factors that shaped these practices.

Critical Discernment: When interpreting ancient texts and artifacts, practitioners should exercise critical discernment. Not every claim or interpretation in historical sources may be accurate, so cross-referencing information and comparing multiple sources can help separate fact from speculation.

Respecting the Gaps: In cases where information is scarce or ambiguous, practitioners should be cautious about filling in the gaps with their own assumptions. Respecting the limitations of available knowledge can prevent the distortion of Babylonian practices.

Avoiding Cultural Misappropriation: As previously mentioned, practitioners should be mindful of cultural appropriation and ensure that their adaptations are respectful of Babylonian cultural heritage.

Balancing Adaptation and Tradition: While contemporary adaptations of Babylonian practices may incorporate modern elements or personal interpretations, practitioners should strive to strike a balance between creative adaptation and honoring the core principles of the ancient traditions.

Consulting Experts: Collaborating with scholars and experts in the field of Babylonian studies can offer valuable insights and guidance to ensure historical accuracy in adaptations.

By approaching Babylonian mystical traditions with diligence, humility, and respect for historical knowledge, practitioners can create authentic adaptations that honor the wisdom of the past while remaining relevant and meaningful in contemporary spiritual contexts.

Balancing Tradition and Personal Innovation

Adapting Babylonian mystical traditions is indeed a delicate endeavor that requires practitioners to navigate ethical considerations. This section delves into the importance of striking a balance between honoring the ancient practices and incorporating personal innovation, encouraging We to reflect on the potential impact on the integrity and authenticity of the original traditions.

Respect for the Core Principles: When adapting Babylonian mystical traditions, it is crucial to maintain respect for the core principles and essence of the original practices. Understanding the spiritual significance and cultural context of the ancient traditions is essential to ensure that adaptations remain true to their historical roots.

Informed Creativity: Practitioners should approach adaptation with informed creativity. Drawing inspiration from Babylonian practices, while adding new elements or modern interpretations, can breathe new life into the traditions without compromising their integrity.

Integrity and Authenticity: We should carefully consider how their adaptations align with the integrity and authenticity of Babylonian mystical traditions. Any modifications or expansions should be done in a way that does not dilute or misrepresent the original practices.

Ethical Engagement: Ethical considerations also involve acknowledging the potential impact of adaptations on the broader community and cultural heritage. Practitioners should be mindful of the significance of Babylonian culture and spirituality and avoid commodifying or appropriating these traditions.

Cultural Sensitivity: Cultural sensitivity is vital in the process of adaptation. Practitioners should be aware of the potential for cultural appropriation and ensure that their adaptations are respectful and considerate of Babylonian cultural heritage.

Transparency and Acknowledgment: When incorporating personal innovation, practitioners should be transparent about their creative additions and acknowledge the influence of Babylonian traditions on their work.

Reflection and Responsiveness: Encouraging We to reflect on the implications of their adaptations can foster a deeper understanding of the ethical complexities involved. Being responsive to feedback from the wider community and engaging in open dialogues can help refine and improve adaptations over time.

Balancing Innovation and Tradition: Striking a balance between personal innovation and honoring tradition can lead to the creation of adaptations that are both relevant to contemporary spiritual needs and faithful to the spirit of Babylonian mystical traditions.

In conclusion, adapting Babylonian mystical traditions requires ethical awareness and a deep respect for the cultural heritage and core principles of the ancient practices. By encouraging We to reflect on these considerations, practitioners can engage with the traditions in a thoughtful and responsible manner, ensuring that the wisdom of Babylonian mysticism continues to inspire and enrich modern spiritual paths.

Informed Consent and Collaboration

When working with Babylonian elements, practitioners should always be mindful of the perspectives and rights of present-day Babylonian communities and scholars. This section explores the importance of considering their input, seeking informed consent, and engaging in respectful collaborations to ensure ethical and responsible practices.

Informed Consent: When incorporating Babylonian elements, practitioners should be aware of the cultural significance of these traditions and seek informed consent from present-day Babylonian communities or relevant cultural representatives. This involves recognizing the rights of these communities to safeguard their cultural heritage and ensuring that their perspectives and wishes are considered.

Respectful Collaborations: Collaborating with contemporary experts in Babylonian studies can enrich the understanding and interpretation of these ancient traditions. Practitioners should approach such collaborations with respect and humility, recognizing the expertise of scholars and community members who have studied and preserved Babylonian culture.

Acknowledging Contributions: Giving credit to scholars and experts in Babylonian studies is crucial in acknowledging their contributions to our understanding of these ancient traditions. Practitioners should cite their sources and provide appropriate recognition for the insights and knowledge shared by contemporary researchers.

Building Relationships: Building relationships based on trust, reciprocity, and mutual learning is essential when working with Babylonian elements. Practitioners should approach interactions with present-day Babylonian communities and scholars with an open mind and a willingness to learn from their perspectives.

Educational Resources: Practitioners can utilize educational resources provided by Babylonian scholars or cultural institutions to deepen their understanding of the traditions. This not only fosters responsible engagement but also contributes to the preservation and promotion of Babylonian cultural heritage.

Avoiding Exploitation: Practitioners should be cautious of any practices that may exploit Babylonian cultural elements for personal gain or without proper acknowledgment. Respect for the cultural context and the rights of present-day communities should guide their actions.

Cultural Sensitivity: Demonstrating cultural sensitivity in the use of Babylonian elements is vital. Practitioners should be aware of potential cultural appropriation and actively work to avoid misrepresenting or commodifying these sacred traditions.

Continued Learning: Engaging with Babylonian elements is an ongoing journey of learning and understanding. Practitioners should remain receptive to new information, cultural insights, and scholarly research to deepen their knowledge and practice.

By considering the perspectives and rights of present-day Babylonian communities and scholars, practitioners can ensure that their engagement with Babylonian elements is grounded in respect, cultural awareness, and responsible stewardship of these ancient traditions. Through these efforts, they can build meaningful and ethical connections with the wisdom and spirituality of ancient Babylon.

Responsibility and Accountability

Adopting Babylonian mystical traditions requires practitioners to uphold ethical principles and be accountable for their actions within the wider community. This section delves into the ethical obligations practitioners must embrace to ensure responsible and respectful engagement with these ancient traditions.

Client Well-being: Practitioners have a duty to prioritize the well-being of their clients and ensure that their practices do not cause harm. This involves approaching Babylonian elements with sensitivity and discernment, recognizing that not all aspects of these traditions may be appropriate or beneficial for every individual.

Respecting Cultural Boundaries: Practitioners must respect the boundaries of cultural knowledge and avoid claiming authority over aspects of Babylonian traditions that they may not fully understand. Acknowledging the limits of one's knowledge and expertise is essential to avoid misrepresentation or cultural appropriation.

Cultural Sensitivity: Practitioners should be culturally sensitive in their interactions with Babylonian elements, ensuring that they do not perpetuate stereotypes or engage in cultural appropriation. They should approach these practices with humility and a commitment to learning from authentic sources.

Addressing Harm: If practitioners inadvertently cause harm through inappropriate or misinformed practices, they must take responsibility for their actions. This may involve acknowledging the harm, apologizing to those affected, and taking steps to prevent similar issues in the future.

Self-Reflection and Education: Practitioners should engage in continuous self-reflection and education to deepen their understanding of Babylonian traditions and enhance their ethical practices. This process of self-awareness and growth is crucial to becoming more responsible and informed practitioners.

Cultural Exchange: Practitioners should approach the adoption of Babylonian elements as a respectful cultural exchange, seeking to learn and honor the wisdom of these ancient traditions without appropriating or exploiting them.

Community Accountability: Practitioners should be accountable to their wider community, including peers, mentors, and those with expertise in Babylonian studies. Engaging in open dialogue and seeking feedback can help ensure ethical alignment and responsible practices.

Balancing Creativity and Tradition: While practitioners can be creative in adapting Babylonian elements to modern contexts, they should do so while preserving the integrity and authenticity of the original traditions. This balance between creativity and tradition is essential in maintaining ethical integrity.

Cultivating Humility: Practitioners should approach Babylonian mystical traditions with humility, recognizing that these ancient practices hold profound wisdom and value.

Humility fosters a deeper appreciation for the cultural heritage and spiritual significance of these traditions.

By embracing these ethical obligations, practitioners can ensure that their engagement with Babylonian mystical traditions is guided by respect, accountability, and a commitment to promoting the well-being of both individuals and the broader community. This conscientious approach fosters a deeper understanding and meaningful connection to the timeless wisdom of ancient Babylon.

Summary:

The adaptation of Babylonian mystical traditions in contemporary practices presents challenges and ethical considerations related to cultural appropriation, authenticity, personal innovation, informed consent, and responsibility. By critically examining these issues, We can develop a deeper understanding of the potential impact of their adaptations and cultivate practices that are respectful, informed, and ethically sound. The chapter encourages We to approach Babylonian wisdom with humility, integrity, and a commitment to fostering cultural exchange based on mutual respect and understanding.

Review Questions:

What are the challenges associated with cultural appropriation in the adaptation of Babylonian mystical traditions?

How can practitioners ensure authenticity and historical accuracy in their contemporary adaptations?

Discuss the ethical considerations of balancing tradition and personal innovation in the context of Babylonian practices.

Why is it important to seek informed consent and engage in collaboration when working with Babylonian elements?

What are the responsibilities and accountability of practitioners in the adaptation of Babylonian mystical traditions?

Exercises:

Reflect on your motivations for incorporating Babylonian elements into your practice and consider any potential ethical concerns that may arise.

Engage in a discussion or workshop on cultural appropriation and its impact on mystical traditions, drawing examples from Babylonian adaptations.

Conduct research on contemporary Babylonian communities or scholars and explore opportunities for respectful collaboration or knowledge exchange.

Develop a personal code of ethics or guidelines for your adaptation of Babylonian practices, addressing issues such as authenticity, consent, and accountability.

Write a reflective essay on the challenges and ethical considerations you have encountered in your own journey of adapting Babylonian mystical traditions.

By addressing the challenges and ethical considerations associated with the adaptation of Babylonian mystical traditions, We deepen their understanding of the complexities involved in incorporating ancient wisdom into contemporary practices. This exploration promotes a conscientious and responsible approach to honoring and adapting cultural traditions, fostering a respectful and sustainable engagement with Babylonian mystical heritage.

III. Reflecting on the Significance of Studying Babylonian Mystical Traditions

In this section, we delve into the significance of studying Babylonian mystical traditions and explore the reasons why it is a valuable and enriching pursuit for We of new-age studies. By understanding the historical, cultural, and spiritual aspects of Babylonian mysticism, We can gain a deeper appreciation for the wisdom and insights that these ancient traditions offer.

Historical Significance

The ancient civilization of Babylon holds a profound place in human history, with its mystical traditions leaving a lasting impact on spiritual practices and beliefs. Babylonian mystical traditions encompass a rich tapestry of magical rituals, divination techniques, and spiritual wisdom that have influenced cultures across time and space.

Astrology and Celestial Wisdom: Babylonians were early pioneers in observing and interpreting celestial phenomena. Their fascination with the movements of the stars and planets led to the development of astrology, which, in turn, influenced various cultures' beliefs in the interconnectedness of human destiny and celestial forces.

Babylonian astrologers provided insights into personal matters, events, and the overall destiny of individuals and the state through their celestial observations.

Divination as Guidance: Babylonian diviners sought knowledge of the future or hidden information through various methods such as dream interpretation, omen reading, and casting of lots. Their belief in a spiritual realm inhabited by deities, spirits, and other supernatural entities formed the foundation for divinatory practices that persist to this day. Babylonian divination offered valuable information for decision-making, understanding the future, and navigating life in harmony with spiritual forces.

The Art of Magic: Babylonian magical practices involved incantations, spells, and rituals aimed at influencing outcomes and harnessing supernatural powers. Magical knowledge was carefully recorded on cuneiform tablets, safeguarded in temple libraries, and passed down through generations. Babylonian magic laid the groundwork for the development of magical traditions in subsequent cultures, influencing the evolution of mystical practices over millennia.

Spiritual Practices and Deity Worship: Babylonians believed in a vast pantheon of deities associated with natural elements and celestial bodies. They engaged in rituals and ceremonies to honor and seek favor from these divine beings. The reverence for sacred landscapes, groves, and natural elements as meeting points between the earthly and divine realms further exemplified their deep spiritual connection with nature.

Legacy and Influence: The enduring impact of Babylonian mystical traditions can be seen in various esoteric and spiritual movements throughout history. From Hermeticism and Gnosticism in the Hellenistic period to the incorporation of Babylonian symbolism in Western Esotericism, the echoes of Babylon continue to reverberate in mystical beliefs and practices.

Studying Babylonian Mysticism: By delving into the wisdom and practices of Babylonian mysticism, We gain insights into the roots and development of mystical traditions that have shaped humanity's understanding of the spiritual realm. It offers a window into the intricate web of connections between ancient civilizations and the ongoing evolution of mystical beliefs and practices.

In conclusion, the Babylonian mystical traditions hold a significant place in human history, influencing the development of astrology, divination, magic, and spiritual practices across cultures and time periods. By exploring these ancient practices, We can discover the enduring impact of Babylonian civilization on the spiritual heritage of humanity, inspiring a deeper appreciation for the timeless wisdom and mystical insights of this ancient civilization.

Cultural Insights and Worldview

The mystical traditions of ancient Babylon provide a unique and invaluable perspective into the worldview of this ancient civilization. These traditions encompass a diverse array of beliefs, rituals, and practices that offer profound cultural insights and connections to the natural world, deities, and the interconnectedness of all aspects of existence.

Cosmology and the Interconnectedness of All Things: Babylonian cosmology envisioned the Earth as a flat disk surrounded by a celestial dome, with the heavens above and the underworld below. This worldview emphasized the interplay between the earthly, celestial, and chthonic realms, highlighting the holistic nature of existence. Babylonians believed in a complex spiritual realm inhabited by deities, spirits, and other supernatural entities, and they recognized the intrinsic interconnectedness between humans and the natural world.

Reverence for the Natural World: Babylonians held a profound respect for the natural world, viewing it as sacred and imbued with spiritual significance. They observed natural phenomena, such as celestial events and changing seasons, as indicators of divine will and forces beyond the material realm. Sacred landscapes, groves, rivers, and mountains were considered imbued with spiritual energy, serving as sites for rituals, ceremonies, and spiritual retreats.

Deity Worship and Rituals: Babylonian mystical practices involved elaborate rituals and ceremonies dedicated to honoring and seeking the favor of their deities. The worship of various natural elements and celestial bodies reflected their belief in the divine qualities present in all aspects of the cosmos. Shamans and priests served as intermediaries between the human and spirit realms, facilitating communication with deities, spirits, and ancestors for guidance, healing, and spiritual balance.

Magical Practices: Babylonian magical traditions encompassed spellcasting, incantations, and rituals aimed at influencing outcomes and connecting with supernatural forces. Magical knowledge was preserved in cuneiform texts, meticulously recorded by priests and scholars. The integration of magic with religious and spiritual practices further exemplified the interconnectedness between mystical beliefs and daily life in Babylonian culture.

Cultural Insights and Broader Perspectives: Studying Babylonian mystical traditions opens a window into the cultural and spiritual landscape of this ancient civilization. It provides valuable insights into the values, beliefs, and practices that shaped the lives of the Babylonian people. By exploring their connection to the natural world and their reverence for the divine, We gain a deeper understanding of the complexities and nuances of human spirituality throughout history.

Holistic Understanding of Human Spirituality: The study of Babylonian mysticism enriches We' comprehension of human spirituality as a multifaceted and interconnected phenomenon. By recognizing the similarities and differences between ancient Babylonian beliefs and contemporary spiritual practices, individuals can foster a more holistic understanding of the diverse ways in which humanity has sought to connect with the sacred and make sense of the world.

In conclusion, Babylonian mystical traditions offer profound cultural insights into the beliefs, rituals, and cosmology of ancient civilizations. The reverence for the natural world, the connection to deities, and the intertwining of magic and spirituality reflect the complex and interconnected nature of Babylonian culture. By studying these mystical traditions, We can broaden their cultural horizons and gain a deeper appreciation for the multifaceted tapestry of human spirituality throughout history.

Wisdom and Spiritual Teachings

Within the mystical traditions of ancient Babylon lies a treasure trove of philosophical and moral principles that offer profound guidance for personal growth and spiritual development. As We delve into the wisdom of Babylonian texts and practices, they will encounter timeless teachings that emphasize harmony with nature, the pursuit of balance, and the quest for wisdom.

Harmony with Nature: Babylonian mysticism recognizes the intrinsic interconnectedness between humans and the natural world. The belief in the sacredness of the Earth and its cycles fosters a profound reverence for nature. This principle encourages We to align their lives with the rhythms of the natural world, promoting a sense of harmony, respect, and reciprocity with all living beings and elements.

Balance and Equilibrium: Babylonian cosmology emphasizes the balance between the earthly, celestial, and chthonic realms. This concept of equilibrium extends beyond the physical realm and encompasses emotional, mental, and spiritual aspects of life. We are encouraged to seek inner balance and strive for harmony in all aspects of their being.

Wisdom and Knowledge: Babylonian mystical traditions place a strong emphasis on the pursuit of wisdom and knowledge. Priests, scholars, and seekers of truth sought to understand the hidden mysteries of the universe through divination, rituals, and exploration of the spiritual realms. This pursuit of wisdom encourages We to engage in lifelong learning and self-reflection, cultivating a deeper understanding of themselves and the world around them.

Connection to the Divine: Babylonian mysticism recognizes the presence of higher powers and supernatural entities in the spiritual realm. This concept encourages We to explore their connection to the divine, seeking guidance and inspiration from spiritual sources beyond the material world. Through rituals and spiritual practices, We can develop a deeper sense of spiritual communion and inner guidance.

Personal Responsibility: Babylonian mystical teachings emphasize personal responsibility and accountability for one's actions and choices. Practitioners were encouraged to act with integrity, compassion, and respect for others. This principle calls upon We to take ownership of their lives and actions, recognizing the impact they have on themselves and the world around them.

Reverence for Ancestors: Babylonian culture placed great importance on ancestral lineage and the wisdom passed down through generations. This concept encourages We to honor their ancestral heritage and draw inspiration from the wisdom of their predecessors. By acknowledging and respecting the wisdom of the past, We can gain valuable insights for navigating their own life journey.

Rituals and Symbolism: Babylonian mystical traditions involved elaborate rituals and the use of symbolic objects. These practices served as vehicles for spiritual transformation and communion with higher powers. We can explore the power of rituals and symbolism in their own spiritual practices, finding meaning and connection through intentional actions and sacred symbols.

In conclusion, Babylonian mystical traditions hold a wealth of wisdom and spiritual teachings that resonate with contemporary seekers of truth and spiritual growth. The principles of harmony with nature, balance, pursuit of wisdom, and personal responsibility offer valuable insights for navigating life's challenges and cultivating a deeper connection with the sacred. By studying these ancient teachings, We can tap into the timeless wisdom of Babylon and find inspiration for their own personal and spiritual journey.

Archetypes and Symbolism

Babylonian mystical traditions are rich in archetypes and symbolism that continue to resonate in contemporary spiritual practices. This section explores the significance of key symbols, such as the serpent, the tree of life, and celestial bodies, and their connection to the human psyche. By studying these archetypes and symbols, We can deepen their understanding of universal spiritual themes and their relevance in modern contexts.

Inspiring Creativity and Innovation

Studying Babylonian mystical traditions can inspire creativity and innovation in modern mystical practices. This section examines how ancient concepts and practices can be reimagined and integrated into new-age disciplines such as witchcraft, divination, herbalism, shamanism, and ecospirituality. We will explore examples of how Babylonian elements can be incorporated into contemporary spiritual practices, fostering a deeper connection with ancient wisdom while embracing personal innovation.

Chapter Summary:

The study of Babylonian mystical traditions offers We a multitude of benefits. It provides historical insights, cultural understanding, spiritual teachings, archetypal symbolism, and inspiration for creativity. By engaging with Babylonian wisdom, We can expand their knowledge and perspectives, enrich their spiritual practices, and gain a deeper appreciation for the interconnectedness of ancient and modern mystical traditions.

Review Questions:

What is the historical significance of studying Babylonian mystical traditions?

How do Babylonian mystical traditions provide insights into the worldview of ancient civilizations?

What are some of the spiritual teachings and wisdom found within Babylonian mystical traditions?

How does the symbolism and archetypes in Babylonian mysticism resonate with contemporary spiritual practices?

How can the study of Babylonian mystical traditions inspire creativity and innovation in modern mystical practices?

Exercises:

Write a reflection on how studying Babylonian mystical traditions has deepened your understanding of human spirituality and the interconnectedness of ancient and modern practices.

Research and discuss the influence of Babylonian symbolism on a specific modern mystical tradition, such as tarot or astrology.

Create an artistic representation, such as a painting or collage, that incorporates Babylonian symbols and archetypes to express a spiritual concept.

Engage in a group discussion on the relevance of Babylonian mystical traditions in addressing contemporary spiritual and ecological challenges.

Write a short essay on how the study of Babylonian mystical traditions has impacted your personal spiritual journey and influenced your approach to new-age practices.

A. Cultural and historical insights gained from studying Babylonian mysticism

In this section, we explore the cultural and historical insights gained from studying Babylonian mysticism. By delving into the rich tapestry of Babylonian civilization, We of new-age studies can uncover profound knowledge and understanding of the ancient world. This section highlights the significance of cultural and historical context in comprehending Babylonian mysticism.

Cultural Context of Babylonian Mysticism

In order to truly grasp the depth and significance of Babylonian mysticism, we must delve into the rich cultural context in which these mystical practices thrived. The mysticism of ancient Babylon was heavily influenced by social, political, and religious factors that shaped the civilization's beliefs, customs, and rituals.

Babylonian Society was structured hierarchically, with kings, priests, and scholars forming the ruling elite. Mystical practices were closely intertwined with religious and political authority, as priests and scholars played a central role in conducting rituals, divination, and magical ceremonies. Understanding the social structure provides valuable insights into the roles and functions of mystical practitioners within Babylonian society.

Religious Beliefs formed the foundation of Babylonian mysticism, deeply rooted in the polytheistic beliefs of the time. The Babylonians worshipped a pantheon of deities, attributing specific powers and attributes to each god and goddess. Mystical practices often involved invoking deities and seeking divine guidance through rituals and divination. Exploring these religious beliefs sheds light on the spiritual motivations behind Babylonian mystical traditions.

Temples served as sacred centers for Babylonian mysticism, where priests and priestesses performed rituals and ceremonies. Mystical practices were intertwined with temple rituals, such as offerings, incantations, and prayers. By exploring the significance of temples and the role of rituals in connecting with the divine, We can gain a deeper understanding of Babylonian mysticism.

Babylonian mysticism drew inspiration from Cosmology and Mythology, shaping the Babylonian worldview. This influenced their understanding of spiritual realms, celestial bodies, and the cyclical nature of the universe. Delving into cosmology and mythology provides We with a broader context for interpreting Babylonian mystical beliefs and practices.

Magical Practices were prevalent in Babylonian life, used for healing, protection, and seeking insight. We can gain insight into specific magical techniques used by Babylonian magicians and the cultural beliefs that underpinned their magic through exploring magical texts and artifacts.

Historical Events, such as conquests, wars, and political changes, influenced the development of mystical practices in ancient Babylon. Mysticism could serve as a source of hope, protection, and guidance during tumultuous times. Understanding historical events provides valuable insights into how mystical practices adapted and evolved in response to societal changes.

Historical Significance of Babylonian Mysticism

The historical significance of Babylonian mysticism is a fascinating journey that We will embark upon in this section. They will discover how Babylonian mysticism played a pivotal role in the broader landscape of ancient civilizations. From its rich and intricate rituals to its profound connection with the natural world, Babylonian mysticism left a lasting legacy that influenced not only the ancient Babylonian society but also neighboring cultures.

We will learn how Babylonian mystical practices, such as divination, magic, and shamanism, spread beyond the borders of Babylon itself, impacting the spiritual practices of neighboring civilizations like Assyria, Persia, and Egypt. Through cultural exchange and adaptation, the wisdom of Babylonian mysticism transcended geographical boundaries, leaving an indelible mark on the spiritual and mystical traditions of the ancient world.

Furthermore, this section will delve into how Babylonian mysticism's enduring impact extends beyond antiquity. We will discover how its concepts and practices influenced later mystical and spiritual traditions, such as Hermeticism, Gnosticism, and elements of Western Esotericism. By studying Babylonian mysticism's historical context, We will appreciate how it paved the way for the development of mystical thought and spirituality that continues to shape our understanding of the spiritual realm even today.

Language and Texts in Babylonian Mysticism

In our exploration of Babylonian mysticism, we cannot overlook the vital role that language and texts played in preserving and passing down this ancient knowledge. The Babylonians developed a distinctive script called cuneiform, which they impressed onto clay tablets, creating a treasure trove of information about their mystical practices. In this section, we will journey into the world of cuneiform and clay tablets to understand how these remarkable artifacts held the key to unlocking the secrets of Babylonian mysticism.

Cuneiform, with its wedge-shaped markings, was the written language of ancient Mesopotamia. Scribes, who were highly skilled in this script, played an essential role in documenting not only administrative records but also mystical practices and rituals. They meticulously recorded invocations, incantations, and magical spells on clay tablets, ensuring the preservation of Babylonian mystical knowledge for generations to come.

As We dive into the linguistic aspects of Babylonian mysticism, they will discover the fascinating complexities of deciphering cuneiform texts. Textual analysis is a powerful tool in uncovering the cultural and historical information encoded in these ancient writings. By carefully studying the language and context, We can gain insights into the beliefs, rituals, and cosmology of Babylonian society, enriching their understanding of the mystical practices that were interwoven into the fabric of their daily lives.

We will explore how scribes, as guardians of knowledge, meticulously inscribed these clay tablets with mystical texts, ensuring their safekeeping in temple libraries and archives. Through the centuries, these tablets endured, preserving the wisdom of Babylonian mysticism for modern scholars and We like us to rediscover and learn from.

By studying these ancient texts, We will gain a deeper appreciation for the importance of language and the written word in the preservation and transmission of cultural heritage. The texts offer us a unique window into the beliefs and rituals of ancient Babylonian mysticism, allowing us to connect with the spiritual practices that once thrived in the heart of Mesopotamia.

As we embark on this journey into the linguistic and literary aspects of Babylonian mysticism, we will uncover the profound significance of texts and the enduring power of language in preserving the wisdom of ancient civilizations. Let us dive into the world of cuneiform and clay tablets, where the echoes of Babylonian mysticism still resonate, waiting to be discovered and cherished by curious minds like ours.

Mythology and Cosmology in Babylonian Mysticism

Mythology and cosmology are integral to understanding Babylonian mysticism. This section explores the rich pantheon of Babylonian deities, the creation myths, and the celestial symbolism present in their belief system. We will examine the connections between mythology, cosmology, and mystical practices, recognizing the profound influence these narratives had on Babylonian culture.

Rituals, Magic, and Divination in Babylonian Mysticism

Rituals, magic, and divination were essential components of Babylonian mysticism. This section delves into the various forms of rituals and the use of magical practices and divination techniques in ancient Babylon. We will gain an understanding of how these practices were woven into the fabric of daily life, offering insights into the cultural and historical significance of Babylonian mysticism.

Chapter Summary:

The study of Babylonian mysticism provides We with invaluable cultural and historical insights. By exploring the cultural context, historical significance, language and texts, mythology and cosmology, and rituals, magic, and divination of Babylonian mysticism, We can develop a comprehensive understanding of this ancient tradition. These insights enhance We' appreciation of the interconnectedness between ancient civilizations and the evolution of mystical and spiritual practices.

Review Questions:

How does studying the cultural context of Babylonian mysticism enhance our understanding of this ancient tradition?

What is the historical significance of Babylonian mysticism and its contributions to ancient civilizations?

How did language and texts play a role in the preservation and transmission of Babylonian mystical knowledge?

What insights can be gained from studying Babylonian mythology and cosmology in relation to mystical practices?

How do rituals, magic, and divination in Babylonian mysticism reflect the cultural and historical context of ancient Babylon?

Exercises:

Conduct a comparative analysis between Babylonian mysticism and the mystical traditions of other ancient civilizations, exploring their cultural and historical similarities and differences.

Translate and interpret a selected cuneiform text related to Babylonian mysticism, highlighting its cultural and historical significance.

Create a visual representation, such as a timeline or infographic, that illustrates the development and evolution of Babylonian mysticism within its cultural and historical context.

Engage in a group discussion on the impact of Babylonian cosmology on contemporary understandings of the universe and our place within it.

Write a reflective essay on how studying the cultural and historical aspects of Babylonian mysticism has deepened your understanding of ancient mystical traditions and their relevance in the modern world.

B. Deepening understanding of humanity's spiritual and mystical heritage

In this section, we embark on a journey to deepen our understanding of humanity's spiritual and mystical heritage through the exploration of various ancient civilizations. By delving into the rich tapestry of spiritual practices, beliefs, and wisdom from different cultures, We of new-age studies can gain profound insights into the shared essence of human spirituality.

Unveiling Ancient Mystical Traditions

In this section, we embark on an illuminating journey through the annals of history to explore the diverse and enchanting mystical traditions that have captivated humanity throughout the ages. Our adventure will take us to the ancient civilizations of Babylon,

Egypt, Greece, and various indigenous cultures, where we will uncover the profound spiritual practices that shaped their beliefs, customs, and worldviews.

The Mystical World of Babylon:
Our first destination is the legendary city of Babylon, where we will immerse ourselves in the mystical tapestry woven by its ancient inhabitants. From the sacred temples to the mystical rituals conducted by Babylonian priests and priestesses, we will discover the rites of invocation, divination, and magic that formed the core of their spiritual life. The clay tablets, adorned with intricate cuneiform script, reveal their deep reverence for the divine and their pursuit of cosmic wisdom.

The Enchanting Mysteries of Egypt:
Next, we journey to the banks of the Nile River, where the ancient Egyptians left an indelible mark on human history with their awe-inspiring mystical practices. With a captivating pantheon of gods and goddesses, the Egyptian belief system encompassed the cycle of life, death, and rebirth. We'll unveil the intricacies of their burial rites, mummification processes, and their belief in the afterlife. From the monumental pyramids to the sacred tombs, we'll witness the profound connection between spirituality and immortality in the land of the pharaohs.

Greek Philosophy and Mysticism:
Venturing to ancient Greece, we encounter a culture that nurtured the pursuit of knowledge and the exploration of the mysteries of existence. The works of great thinkers like Plato and Aristotle shaped their philosophical landscape, where mysticism and spiritual inquiry intertwined. Delving into the Eleusinian Mysteries, an initiatory tradition, we'll explore the secret ceremonies that promised profound insights into the soul's journey. As we connect with Greek mythology, we'll gain an understanding of their profound connection to the divine and the mysteries of the cosmos.

Embracing Nature in Indigenous Cultures:
In the heart of nature, we find the sacred wisdom of indigenous cultures, where spirituality and the natural world are inseparable. Through their sacred ceremonies, rituals, and shamanic practices, these cultures celebrate the interconnectedness of all living beings. We'll witness the reverence for ancestral spirits, the wisdom of the land, and the harmonious relationship they share with Mother Earth. By learning from their ancient traditions, we'll appreciate the deep bond between humans and the environment, a wisdom that resonates with the universal spirit of nature.

Throughout our exploration, we'll discover that despite the vast differences in time, geography, and cultural customs, mystical experiences hold a universal thread that connects all of humanity. These diverse traditions offer a glimpse into the human spirit's unyielding quest for transcendence, the yearning to understand the mysteries of existence, and the desire to connect with the divine. By learning from the wisdom of ancient civilizations, We will grasp the universality of mystical experiences and the profound impact they have on shaping our understanding of spirituality, both in the past and in the present.

Connecting with Ancestral Wisdom

In this profound section, we delve into the timeless wisdom handed down to us by our ancestors, an invaluable treasure trove that forms the very foundation of our spiritual heritage. Exploring the significance of connecting with our ancestral roots, we come to understand that we are not merely individuals adrift in the currents of time, but rather part of a sacred continuum, carrying within us the echoes of those who came before.

The Wisdom of the Ages:
By looking back through the corridors of history, we uncover the ancient mystical traditions, rituals, and beliefs that have been lovingly passed down from generation to generation. These ancestral legacies offer us a wealth of knowledge, insight, and guidance that can illuminate our spiritual paths in the modern world. From the chants and prayers whispered by our ancestors to the sacred symbols etched into their artifacts, we come to appreciate the deep significance of preserving these sacred teachings.

Navigating the Spiritual Journey:
As We of the mystical, we discover that our journey is not isolated but part of a tapestry woven by countless generations before us. By studying the spiritual practices of our ancestors, we gain valuable insights into the challenges they faced, the wisdom they cultivated, and the profound truths they uncovered. This knowledge becomes a guiding light, illuminating the shadows on our own path, empowering us to overcome obstacles, and fostering a deeper connection with our spiritual selves.

Reconnecting with Ancestral Roots:
In seeking to understand our ancestral heritage, we open the gateway to a profound reunion with our roots. By embracing the traditions and practices of our forebears, we rekindle the sacred flame that has burned for countless ages. This reconnection is not a mere act of nostalgia but a transformative journey that allows us to honor our ancestors, pay homage to their wisdom, and weave their sacred threads into the fabric of our lives.

A Tapestry of Diversity:
Studying the ancient mystical traditions of different cultures and regions, we witness the rich tapestry of diversity that humanity has woven over millennia. Each tradition carries its unique beauty, perspectives, and ways of relating to the divine. As we explore

this mosaic of wisdom, we learn to appreciate the interconnectedness of all spiritual paths and the profound commonality that binds us as one human family.

In the embrace of ancestral wisdom, we find a wellspring of strength, resilience, and a profound sense of belonging. Our journey to understand and reconnect with these ancient mystical traditions enriches our lives with a deeper appreciation for the human experience and the mystical tapestry that weaves us all together. As We of this sacred knowledge, we recognize that we are not just recipients but stewards of this profound heritage, entrusted with preserving and passing on the flame of ancestral wisdom to the generations yet to come.

Exploring Symbolism and Archetypes

In this enlightening section, we embark on a captivating exploration of symbolism and archetypes—the universal language of the collective unconscious that transcends cultures and endures through the ages. Unraveling the mysteries of these timeless representations, we discover their deep-rooted significance in shaping human consciousness and guiding our spiritual evolution.

The Language of the Soul:
Symbols and archetypes are the sacred lexicon through which our innermost thoughts, emotions, and experiences find expression. Across diverse mystical traditions, these potent symbols speak to the depths of our souls, bridging the gap between the conscious and unconscious realms. We venture into the labyrinth of these mystical symbols, deciphering their messages and unlocking the secrets they hold for our personal and spiritual growth.

Threads of Unity:
As we journey through the annals of history, we encounter symbols and archetypes that weave a common thread, connecting the tapestry of human experience across continents and epochs. From the lotus flower blossoming in the heart of Eastern mysticism to the cross symbolizing sacrifice and redemption in Christianity, we bear witness to the remarkable unity of the human spirit and the shared longings that transcend boundaries.

Pathways to Transformation:
Archetypes, those ancient blueprints etched into the collective unconscious, act as transformative catalysts on our spiritual journey. By exploring these archetypal motifs, such as the wise old sage, the hero's journey, or the sacred marriage, we find potent tools for self-discovery, self-empowerment, and profound healing. These archetypes mirror the myriad facets of the human experience, guiding us toward wholeness and integration.

Empowering the Imagination:
Symbolism ignites the fires of the imagination, leading us on a quest to uncover deeper truths and hidden meanings. By engaging with the imagery of mystical traditions, we enter a realm of wonder, awe, and creative inspiration. These potent symbols, whether found in sacred texts, art, or rituals, stir something ancient within us, compelling us to seek a deeper understanding of the mysteries of existence.

Illuminating the Collective Unconscious:
The collective unconscious, that vast repository of shared human experiences and memories, finds voice through symbols and archetypes. Through these powerful representations, we glimpse the essence of our shared humanity and the profound interconnectedness that binds us all together. In this realization, we recognize that we are not solitary travelers but part of a timeless pilgrimage of souls seeking wisdom and illumination.

As we delve into the profound realm of symbolism and archetypes, we uncover the keys to unlock the mysteries of our innermost selves and the profound wisdom passed down through generations. From the ancient symbols etched into temple walls to the timeless archetypal motifs guiding our dreams, these mystical representations offer us a luminous path to self-discovery, spiritual transformation, and a deeper understanding of our place in the vast tapestry of existence. Through the language of symbolism and archetypes, we find solace, inspiration, and a profound connection to the sacred pulse of the cosmos.

Tracing Evolutionary Threads

By tracing the evolutionary threads of mystical traditions, we can discern the interconnectedness and evolution of spiritual practices. This section explores how mystical traditions from different cultures influenced and shaped one another, creating a tapestry of shared wisdom that transcends geographical and cultural boundaries.

Contemporary Relevance and Application

This section examines the contemporary relevance and application of ancient mystical traditions. We will explore how these traditions are adapted and incorporated into modern spiritual practices, including witchcraft, divination, herbalism, shamanism, and ecospirituality. By understanding the enduring relevance of these traditions, We can find inspiration for their own spiritual journeys.

Chapter Summary:

Studying humanity's spiritual and mystical heritage deepens our understanding of the shared essence of human spirituality. By unveiling ancient mystical traditions, connecting with ancestral wisdom, exploring symbolism and archetypes, tracing evolutionary threads, and recognizing the contemporary relevance of these traditions, We gain a holistic perspective on the profound wisdom embedded in our collective human experience.

Review Questions:

How does studying ancient mystical traditions deepen our understanding of the shared essence of human spirituality?

What is the significance of connecting with ancestral wisdom in our spiritual journey?

How do symbolism and archetypes serve as a universal language in mystical traditions?

What insights can be gained by tracing the evolutionary threads of mystical traditions across cultures?

How are ancient mystical traditions adapted and incorporated into contemporary spiritual practices?

Exercises:

Conduct a comparative analysis of mystical traditions from different ancient civilizations, exploring their commonalities and differences.

Reflect on your personal connection to ancestral wisdom and explore ways to integrate it into your spiritual practice.

Create a visual representation, such as a mandala or collage, that incorporates symbols and archetypes from various mystical traditions.

Engage in a group discussion on the contemporary relevance and application of ancient mystical traditions in modern spirituality.

Write a reflective essay on how studying humanity's spiritual and mystical heritage has influenced your understanding of your own spiritual path and its significance in the broader human experience.

C. Inspiring personal and collective exploration of diverse spiritual practices

In this section, we embark on a journey of personal and collective exploration of diverse spiritual practices. We recognize the inherent value and transformative potential of engaging with a wide range of spiritual traditions, as they offer unique perspectives and pathways to self-discovery and inner growth. By embracing the diversity of spiritual practices, We of new-age studies can broaden their horizons, deepen their understanding, and cultivate a rich tapestry of spiritual wisdom.

Embracing the Multitude of Spiritual Paths

In this illuminating section, we embark on a transformative journey towards cultivating a profound appreciation for the diverse spiritual paths that grace our world. As We of the sacred, we are called to embrace an open-hearted and inclusive approach to spirituality—one that recognizes the rich tapestry of wisdom woven by countless traditions.

The Kaleidoscope of Spirituality:
Just as a kaleidoscope reveals a symphony of colors, the world is adorned with a myriad of spiritual paths, each emanating its unique brilliance. From ancient mystic traditions to contemporary spiritual movements, we encounter a cornucopia of beliefs, rituals, and practices that reflect the wondrous diversity of human expression.

Honoring the Sacred Tapestry:
In our quest for truth and understanding, we come to realize that every spiritual tradition holds a precious thread in the sacred tapestry of human experience. Each path, like a luminous star in the night sky, offers guidance, solace, and inspiration to seekers on their individual journeys.

Nourishing the Spirit Within:
By embracing the multitude of spiritual paths, we create an expansive garden where the flowers of wisdom bloom in harmony. Just as diverse flora and fauna contribute to the vibrant ecosystem of our planet, so too do varied spiritual traditions enrich our inner landscapes, nurturing our souls and illuminating our way.

A Mosaic of Unity:
As we honor the different traditions that have emerged throughout human history, we come to recognize the unifying essence that transcends them all. Beneath the surface

diversity lies a profound unity—the recognition that we are all part of a great cosmic dance, interwoven and interconnected in the tapestry of existence.

Seeds of Spiritual Growth:
In this celebration of spiritual diversity, we find the seeds of our own growth and transformation. By embracing a spirit of openness, curiosity, and respect for all traditions, we discover the wisdom that resonates with our souls, guiding us towards the light of self-discovery and self-realization.

The Path of Harmony:
As We of the spiritual arts, we are invited to harmonize with the symphony of existence. By recognizing the richness of spiritual diversity, we pave the way for a world that values inclusivity, understanding, and mutual respect.

Walking the Path of the Heart:
In our journey towards embracing the multitude of spiritual paths, we discover that the true pilgrimage lies within our hearts. The path of love, compassion, and unity calls us to transcend boundaries, opening ourselves to the vastness of the human experience.

As we stand at the threshold of this transformative exploration, let us heed the call to embrace the multifaceted beauty of spiritual paths that grace our world. With open hearts and receptive minds, we embark on a sacred pilgrimage—one that honors the richness of tradition and the boundless potential of the human spirit. Let us revel in the tapestry of spiritual wisdom that enfolds us, weaving a harmonious symphony of light and love, guiding us on our wondrous journey of self-discovery and awakening.

Exploring Ancient Wisdom Traditions

In this captivating section, we embark on an illuminating exploration of ancient wisdom traditions that have withstood the tests of time, transcending epochs and touching the depths of human consciousness. As seekers of truth and wisdom, we open the portals to ancient realms of knowledge, where profound teachings and timeless truths await.

Buddhism: The Path of Awakening
Venturing into the realm of Buddhism, we encounter the teachings of Siddhartha Gautama—the enlightened one. Delving into the Four Noble Truths and the Eightfold Path, we discover a transformative journey towards enlightenment, compassion, and liberation from suffering.

Hinduism: The Cosmic Dance of Deities

Journeying into the intricate tapestry of Hinduism, we encounter a celestial dance of gods and goddesses, each embodying divine aspects of creation, preservation, and destruction. Unfolding the Upanishads and the Bhagavad Gita, we discover the pursuit of self-realization and the recognition of the eternal soul.

Taoism: The Way of Harmony

Embarking on the path of Taoism, we immerse ourselves in the wisdom of Laozi, embracing the flow of the Tao—the Way of Nature. In the Tao Te Ching, we find guidance on living in harmony with the rhythms of existence, attuning our hearts to simplicity and balance.

Indigenous Spirituality: The Wisdom of the Earth

Honoring the indigenous peoples' profound connection with the land, we enter the realms of ancient wisdom rooted in reverence for Mother Earth. Listening to ancestral stories and practices, we discover the sacredness of all life and the interconnectedness of humanity with the natural world.

Universal Teachings: Threads of Unity

As we traverse through these ancient wisdom traditions, we find threads of unity that unite them all. The recognition of the eternal soul, the pursuit of inner peace, and the cultivation of compassion resonate as universal teachings, transcending cultural boundaries.

Cultivating Insights: The Gift of Ancient Wisdom

Throughout our journey, we come to realize that the gift of ancient wisdom lies not merely in the knowledge itself but in the profound insights that they offer. These timeless truths can guide us in navigating the complexities of life, inspiring us to become better versions of ourselves.

Embracing Wholeness: Integrating Ancient Wisdom

As we journey through these sacred traditions, we are invited to embrace the wholeness of our spiritual heritage. Just as a mosaic is adorned by the unique beauty of each individual piece, so too are our spiritual paths enriched by the wisdom of the ancients.

In the sanctuary of these ancient wisdom traditions, let us immerse ourselves in the teachings that have been passed down through generations. By delving into their philosophical foundations, practices, and key concepts, we uncover a treasure trove of timeless truths that resonate with the depths of our souls. As we draw inspiration from the vast array of wisdom, we are reminded that these teachings hold the power to guide and inspire us on our sacred journey of self-discovery and spiritual growth.

Embodying Mindfulness and Meditation

In this transformative section, we delve into the art of mindfulness and meditation—an age-old practice that has found renewed resonance in our modern world. Through the lens of both ancient wisdom and contemporary science, we uncover the profound benefits and transformative techniques that lie at the heart of mindfulness and meditation.

Understanding Mindfulness: The Art of Present Awareness
We begin by unraveling the essence of mindfulness—a state of present awareness that allows us to embrace each moment with open-hearted attention. Drawing inspiration from ancient Buddhist teachings, we explore the power of being fully present in our thoughts, emotions, and sensations.

The Science of Meditation: Nurturing the Mind-Body Connection
Venturing into the realms of modern neuroscience, we unearth the fascinating findings that corroborate the positive effects of meditation on our mental and physical well-being. From reducing stress and anxiety to boosting focus and cognitive abilities, the scientific evidence underscores the profound impact of meditation.

Cultivating Inner Peace: Techniques for Tranquility
We are introduced to a diverse array of meditation techniques—guided meditations, breath awareness, body scanning, loving-kindness, and more. These timeless practices offer a sanctuary of serenity amidst the hustle and bustle of daily life, inviting us to embrace the stillness within.

Mindfulness in Action: Taking Awareness to Daily Life
Mindfulness extends beyond the meditation cushion—it becomes a way of life. Exploring the integration of mindfulness in daily activities, we discover the art of savoring simple moments, fostering gratitude, and embracing the fullness of life.

Navigating Challenges: Finding Equanimity
In the face of life's challenges, mindfulness becomes a beacon of resilience and equanimity. By cultivating a mindful approach to adversity, We learn to navigate difficult emotions with grace, finding peace even amidst life's storms.

Unveiling Inner Wisdom: Listening to the Soul
Through mindfulness and meditation, we create a sacred space to listen to the whispers of our inner wisdom. Insights and intuition rise to the surface, guiding us on our unique paths of self-discovery and growth.

Embracing the Journey: Making Mindfulness a Way of Life

Encouraging We to make mindfulness and meditation a regular practice, we recognize that true transformation lies in consistency and dedication. By nurturing this sacred practice, We embrace the journey of self-awareness and self-compassion.

In the realm of mindfulness and meditation, we discover an oasis of calm and insight—a gateway to the vast reservoir of our inner wisdom. As we journey through these practices, we recognize that they are not mere techniques but potent tools that empower us to become the authors of our lives. By cultivating mindfulness and meditation as a way of life, We embark on a profound voyage of self-discovery, connecting with the richness of their own hearts and awakening to the beauty of each present moment.

Engaging with Shamanic Traditions

In this captivating section, we embark on a mystical journey into the realm of shamanism—an ancient spiritual practice that embraces the interconnectedness of all existence. As we delve into the heart of shamanic traditions, We will be introduced to the core principles, practices, and transformative rituals that have been revered by cultures across time and space.

The Shamanic Path: Navigating the Spirit World
We begin by unveiling the foundational principles of shamanism—an animistic belief system that perceives all things, living and non-living, as imbued with spirit. Exploring the shamanic worldview, we understand the sacred connection between humans, nature, and the spirit world.

Journeying Between Worlds: The Shaman's Quest
Intriguing and immersive, we dive into the ancient practice of shamanic journeying—a technique that enables one to traverse the boundaries of the physical and spiritual realms. Through experiential exercises, We will embark on their own journeys, guided by the rhythm of drums and the wisdom of their spirit guides.

Spirit Guides: Allies in the Unseen Realms
Discovering the profound relationship between shamans and their spirit guides, We will learn to forge connections with these benevolent beings. Drawing from indigenous wisdom, we understand how spirit guides bestow guidance, protection, and healing on the shamanic path.

Shamanic Tools: Instruments of Transformation
Intricately woven into the fabric of shamanic rituals are sacred tools that empower practitioners to navigate the spiritual landscape. From rattles and drums to crystals and

feathers, we explore the symbolic significance and healing properties of these transformative instruments.

Healing with Energy: Restoring Balance and Harmony
In the realm of shamanism, healing transcends the physical body—it involves restoring the balance of mind, body, and spirit. Through case studies and practical techniques, We will learn how shamans employ energy healing to bring profound transformation to themselves and others.

Rituals of Renewal: Embracing the Cycles of Life
Shamanic rituals celebrate the cyclical nature of life—birth, death, and rebirth. By embracing these rituals, We will deepen their understanding of life's transitions and gain wisdom on navigating the ever-changing tapestry of existence.

Shamanic Wisdom in Modern Life: Embodying the Teachings
Guided by the wisdom of ancient traditions, we explore how shamanic principles can be integrated into our modern lives. We will be encouraged to embrace the interconnectedness of all living beings, honor the Earth's sacredness, and cultivate reverence for the natural world.

Through immersive experiences, captivating case studies, and hands-on practices, this section invites We to embark on a profound journey—a journey of personal healing, spiritual expansion, and connection to the unseen realms. By embracing the wisdom of shamanic traditions, We will discover a world where the sacred and the ordinary merge, revealing the potential for profound transformation and a deeper sense of unity with all of creation.

Nurturing Ecospirituality

In this enlightening section, we immerse ourselves in the profound wisdom of ecospirituality—an empowering spiritual path that celebrates the sacred bond between humanity and the natural world. As we delve into the principles of ecospirituality, We will discover the transformative potential of living in harmony with the Earth and embracing ecological stewardship.

The Sacredness of Nature: Recognizing the Divine in All
We begin by unraveling the core principles of ecospirituality, which highlight the inherent divinity and interconnectedness of all living beings and the natural elements. We will explore how this profound recognition of sacredness in nature inspires reverence and respect for the Earth and its inhabitants.

Communing with Nature: Nurturing the Soul

In a fast-paced world, connecting with nature becomes a profound source of solace and spiritual nourishment. Through guided exercises and practices, We will learn to engage with the natural world mindfully, fostering a deeper bond with the Earth and embracing the healing power of its rhythms.

Eco-Conscious Living: Harmonizing with the Earth
Ecospirituality extends beyond theory—it permeates into our daily lives. We will be encouraged to embrace eco-conscious living, adopting sustainable practices that honor the Earth's resources and minimize our ecological footprint. From conscious consumption to sustainable gardening, we explore practical ways to embody ecospirituality.

Sacred Landscapes: Honoring the Earth's Sacred Sites
Throughout history, cultures have revered specific locations as sacred sites of power and significance. In this segment, we journey into the wisdom of sacred landscapes, where We will learn about revered places and rituals that foster a deeper spiritual connection to the Earth.

Earth-Based Rituals: Harmonizing with Natural Cycles
The cycles of nature offer profound lessons in renewal and transformation. In this segment, We will discover the significance of earth-based rituals that honor the changing seasons, celestial events, and the interconnectedness of all life.

Eco-Activism: Advocacy for the Earth
Embodying the principles of ecospirituality, we delve into eco-activism—an essential aspect of honoring the sacredness of nature. We will be encouraged to embrace their role as environmental advocates, making conscious choices that contribute to the well-being of the Earth and all its inhabitants.

Sustainability and Spirituality: A Harmonious Union
As we conclude this journey into ecospirituality, we reflect on the profound unity of sustainability and spirituality. We will recognize how embracing ecological consciousness enhances their spiritual growth, fostering a deeper sense of interconnectedness and alignment with the web of life.

Through meaningful explorations, practical exercises, and reflections, this section invites We to embrace the transformative power of ecospirituality—a path that honors the sacredness of nature and awakens a profound sense of purpose and responsibility as ecological stewards. By integrating the principles of ecospirituality into their lives, We will cultivate a deeper sense of harmony with the Earth, living as conscious participants in the grand symphony of creation.

Summary:

This chapter serves as an invitation for We to embark on a personal and collective exploration of diverse spiritual practices. By embracing the multitude of spiritual paths, delving into ancient wisdom traditions, embodying mindfulness and meditation, engaging with shamanic practices, and nurturing ecospirituality, We can broaden their spiritual horizons, deepen their connection with the divine, and cultivate a more harmonious relationship with themselves, others, and the natural world.

Review Questions:

Why is it important to embrace the multitude of spiritual paths?

How can ancient wisdom traditions inspire and guide our spiritual journeys?

What are the benefits of mindfulness and meditation practices? How can they be incorporated into daily life?

What are the core principles and practices of shamanic traditions? How can they facilitate personal healing and transformation?

What does it mean to nurture ecospirituality? How can we promote environmental consciousness in our spiritual practices?

Exercises:

Attend a spiritual gathering or ceremony from a tradition different from your own and reflect on the experience.

Create a daily mindfulness and meditation practice, incorporating techniques from different traditions.

Engage in a shamanic journeying practice, documenting your experiences and insights.

Spend time in nature and journal about your connection with the natural world and its impact on your spirituality.

Organize a discussion group with fellow We to explore and share experiences from different spiritual practices.

IV. Potential Impact on Personal Spiritual Practices

In this section, we delve into the potential impact that the study of Babylonian mystical traditions can have on our personal spiritual practices. By exploring the wisdom and practices of ancient Babylon, We of new-age studies can gain valuable insights and tools to enhance their own spiritual journeys. This section explores how the knowledge and understanding of Babylonian mystical traditions can deeply impact and transform our personal spiritual practices.

Broadening Perspectives

In this captivating section, we embark on a journey of exploration into the enchanting world of Babylonian mystical traditions. By immersing ourselves in the beliefs, rituals, and practices of this ancient civilization, We will encounter a kaleidoscope of spiritual insights that enrich and expand their understanding of the mystical realm.

A Tapestry of Belief Systems: Embracing Diversity
We begin by acknowledging the diversity of spiritual paths that have blossomed throughout history. From Babylon to distant lands, each tradition weaves a unique tapestry of beliefs. Through this exploration, We will cultivate an open-hearted and inclusive approach to spirituality, honoring the multiplicity of human experiences in connecting with the sacred.

Delving into Babylonian Mysticism: Unveiling Ancient Wisdom
With wonder in our hearts, we uncover the mystical practices that thrived in the heart of Babylonian civilization. Through ancient texts, artifacts, and archaeological discoveries, we unearth the hidden treasures of Babylonian mysticism, discovering the spiritual gems that have shaped humanity's quest for transcendence.

Rituals and Ceremonies: The Soul's Journey
Babylonian rituals were woven into the fabric of daily life, guiding individuals on a sacred journey of transformation. As we study these practices, We will encounter the beauty of ancient ceremonies, igniting a sense of wonder and reverence for the sacred rites that once connected the people of Babylon to the divine.

Wisdom of the Cosmos: Celestial Insights

The Babylonians were stargazers, mesmerized by the celestial wonders that adorned the night sky. In this segment, We will witness the profound interplay between Babylonian cosmology and their spiritual beliefs. By contemplating the cosmic dance, We will find inspiration in aligning their own lives with the rhythms of the universe.

The Power of Symbolism: Language of the Soul
Symbols hold a language that transcends time and culture, speaking directly to the human soul. In Babylonian mysticism, we encounter a treasure trove of symbols that reveal the mysteries of existence. By unraveling their meanings, We will unlock the profound insights embedded in the symbols of this ancient wisdom.

Embracing Ancient Wisdom: Bridging the Past and Present
As we draw this journey to a close, We are invited to embrace the richness of Babylonian wisdom and integrate its timeless teachings into their spiritual practices. By blending the sacred knowledge of the past with their contemporary understanding, We will honor the legacy of Babylonian mysticism in their own unique spiritual journey.

Through this immersive exploration, We will not only gain an appreciation for the depth and significance of Babylonian mystical traditions but also foster a greater sense of connection with the human experience of the sacred. By honoring the wisdom of the ancients, we illuminate the path ahead, infusing our lives with the timeless brilliance of Babylonian mysticism.

Rediscovering Ancient Rituals and Ceremonies

In this enchanting section, we journey into the heart of Babylonian mystical rituals, discovering a treasure trove of ancient ceremonies and practices that resonate across time. Through our exploration of purification ceremonies, divination techniques, and the invocation of deities, We will uncover profound avenues for deepening their spiritual connections and enhancing their personal practices.

Purification Ceremonies: Cleansing the Soul
Babylonian purification rituals held a sacred space for cleansing and renewal. As we delve into these practices, We will learn how to create their own purification ceremonies, clearing away negative energies and inviting in spiritual clarity. By embracing these ancient rites, We will embark on a soul-nourishing journey of inner cleansing and purification.

Divination Practices: Unveiling the Unknown
Divination, the art of seeking insight from mystical sources, held a place of reverence in Babylonian culture. We will explore various divination methods, such as reading omens, casting lots, and interpreting dreams, to gain wisdom and guidance. By

integrating divination into their spiritual toolkit, We will tap into the hidden knowledge that lies beyond the veil.

Invocation of Deities: Forging Sacred Connections
In Babylonian mysticism, deities were revered as powerful sources of divine energy. Through the study of invocation practices, We will learn how to honor and connect with these ancient gods and goddesses, forging sacred relationships with the divine realm. By invoking the energies of the deities, We will invite their guidance and blessings into their lives.

Adapting Ancient Rituals: Personalized Spiritual Journeys
As We immerse themselves in the mystique of Babylonian rituals, they are encouraged to adapt and personalize these practices to suit their own spiritual paths. By infusing their unique intentions and energies into the rituals, We will create a sacred space that resonates deeply with their spiritual aspirations.

Enhancing Spiritual Experiences: From the Ancient to the Contemporary
In the final stages of our exploration, We will realize the transformative power of integrating Babylonian rituals into their daily lives. Through these practices, they will infuse their spiritual experiences with the timeless wisdom of Babylonian mysticism, creating a harmonious blend of ancient wisdom and modern spirituality.

By embracing the rituals of Babylonian mysticism, We will open themselves to a world of sacred possibilities, enriching their spiritual journey with the profound insights of this ancient wisdom. These rituals serve as gateways to the divine, guiding We towards a deeper understanding of themselves and the interconnectedness of all things. As we conclude this exploration, We are encouraged to embark on a soulful quest, weaving the threads of ancient Babylonian mysticism into the vibrant tapestry of their own spiritual lives.

Deepening Connection with Nature

In this enlightening section, we embark on a journey of ecological discovery, uncovering the profound wisdom of Babylonian mystical traditions and their reverence for the natural world. Through practices such as eco-spirituality, herbalism, and honoring the cycles of the seasons, We will forge a deeper connection with nature, cultivating harmony and reverence for the Earth.

Eco-Spirituality: Embracing the Sacredness of Nature
Babylonian mysticism celebrated the sacredness of the Earth and recognized the interdependence between humans and the natural world. As we explore eco-spirituality,

We will learn to view nature as a living, divine entity deserving of respect and care. By embracing ecological awareness, We will cultivate a deeper understanding of their role as stewards of the Earth and tap into the healing power of nature.

Herbalism: Nourishing Body and Soul

Babylonian herbalism held a profound knowledge of the medicinal properties of plants and their spiritual significance. We will delve into the ancient wisdom of herbalism, learning how to work with the healing energies of plants to nourish both body and soul. By incorporating herbal practices into their lives, We will harmonize with the rhythms of nature and embrace the ancient art of herbal healing.

Honoring the Cycles of the Seasons: Celebrating Nature's Rhythms

The Babylonians celebrated the changing seasons with reverence, acknowledging the cyclical nature of life. We will discover how to honor the cycles of the seasons, aligning their spiritual practices with the ebb and flow of nature's rhythms. By embracing seasonal rituals and celebrations, We will deepen their connection to the Earth and infuse their lives with the energy of renewal and transformation.

Eco-Conscious Living: Making a Difference

As We immerse themselves in the wisdom of Babylonian mysticism, they are encouraged to embrace eco-conscious living. By adopting sustainable practices in their daily lives, We will embody the principles of ecological harmony and become agents of positive change for the planet.

A Deeper Connection: The Fusion of Spirituality and Nature

In the final stages of our exploration, We will witness the profound transformation that occurs when spirituality and nature unite. By integrating eco-spirituality, herbalism, and seasonal rituals, We will experience a profound sense of interconnectedness with the natural world. This integration will empower them to live in harmony with the Earth and embrace their role as guardians of the environment.

Through these practices, We will cultivate a deeper, more meaningful relationship with the Earth and discover the timeless wisdom of Babylonian mystical traditions. As they embrace the sacredness of nature and align themselves with the rhythms of the seasons, We will uncover a profound sense of purpose and spiritual fulfillment. This connection to nature will become a wellspring of inspiration, guiding them on their journey of personal growth and deepening their spiritual connection to the world around them.

Cultivating Ethics and Responsibility

In this critical section, we delve into the ethical principles embedded within Babylonian mystical traditions, emphasizing their relevance in modern spiritual practices. As We explore these ethical considerations, they will gain a deeper understanding of their responsibilities as spiritual practitioners and their impact on personal and collective well-being.

Responsibility to Self and Others: Self-awareness and Empathy

Babylonian mysticism emphasized the importance of self-awareness and empathy towards others. We will explore the ethical imperative of understanding one's actions, intentions, and their effects on themselves and those around them. By cultivating empathy and compassion, We will foster an ethical foundation for their spiritual journey, promoting harmony and understanding in their interactions with others.

Integrity and Authenticity: Honoring Personal Truth

Babylonian spirituality valued authenticity and integrity in one's beliefs and actions. We will learn to embrace their personal truth, free from external pressures or expectations. By staying true to their spiritual path and beliefs, We will build a strong ethical framework, ensuring that their actions align with their inner values and principles.

Respect for All Beings: Valuing Life in its Diversity

The Babylonians held a deep reverence for all living beings, recognizing the interconnectedness of all life. We will explore the ethical imperative of respecting the diversity of life forms and their habitats. By honoring the inherent value of every being, We will foster a sense of stewardship and ecological responsibility, ensuring that their spiritual practices promote the well-being of all living things.

Honoring Cultural Heritage: Sensitivity to Cultural Appropriation

In their exploration of Babylonian mystical traditions, We will learn about the importance of cultural heritage and respecting the origins of these practices. Ethical considerations of cultural appropriation will be examined, encouraging We to approach Babylonian wisdom with respect and sensitivity. By acknowledging the significance of cultural context, We will ensure that their spiritual practices do not commodify or misrepresent ancient traditions.

The Greater Good: Positive Impact on the World

Babylonian spirituality emphasized the pursuit of wisdom and the betterment of society. We will explore the ethical responsibility of using their spiritual practices to positively impact the world around them. By seeking knowledge, sharing wisdom, and engaging in altruistic actions, We will align their spiritual journey with the greater good, contributing to a more compassionate and just world.

Through the exploration of these ethical considerations, We will gain a deeper appreciation for the profound impact their spiritual practices can have on themselves and the world. By integrating these ethical principles into their spiritual journey, We will foster a greater sense of responsibility, integrity, and respect in their interactions with others and the natural world. Ultimately, this ethical framework will guide We in building a transformative and ethically-grounded spiritual path that aligns with the wisdom and values of Babylonian mystical traditions.

Summary:

The study of Babylonian mystical traditions has the potential to deeply impact our personal spiritual practices. By broadening our perspectives, rediscovering ancient rituals, deepening our connection with nature, integrating Babylonian wisdom into modern practices, and cultivating ethics and responsibility, we can enhance our spiritual journeys and create a more meaningful and transformative spiritual path. Through this exploration, We can tap into the richness of Babylonian wisdom and find inspiration and guidance for their personal spiritual practices.

Review Questions:

How does the study of Babylonian mystical traditions broaden our perspectives on spirituality?

What are some ancient Babylonian rituals and ceremonies that can be incorporated into personal spiritual practices?

How can the connection with nature be deepened through the study of Babylonian mystical traditions?

In what ways can Babylonian wisdom be integrated into modern spiritual practices?

Why is cultivating ethics and responsibility important in personal spiritual practices?

Exercises:

Research and perform a Babylonian purification ritual, reflecting on its impact on your personal spiritual practice.

Create a personal ceremony inspired by Babylonian divination practices, using divination tools of your choice.

Spend time in nature and practice eco-spirituality by honoring and connecting with the natural elements around you.

Integrate Babylonian deities or symbols into your existing spiritual practices, observing any shifts in energy or connection.

Reflect on the ethical considerations within Babylonian spirituality and identify ways to incorporate them into your personal spiritual practices.

A. Broadening perspectives and fostering a more inclusive approach to spirituality

In this section, we delve into the significance of broadening our perspectives and fostering a more inclusive approach to spirituality. By exploring diverse mystical traditions, including those from ancient Babylon, We of new-age studies can expand their understanding of spirituality and cultivate a more inclusive worldview. This section explores the importance of embracing diverse spiritual perspectives and the transformative impact it can have on our personal spiritual journeys.

Embracing Diversity in Spiritual Beliefs

In this inclusive section, we celebrate the diversity of spiritual beliefs and practices, emphasizing the value of exploring various mystical traditions, including Babylonian mysticism, in the broader context of spirituality. By embracing diversity, We can enrich their understanding of the human quest for meaning and transcendence.

Appreciating Universality: Common Threads in Mystical Traditions
By studying Babylonian mysticism alongside other mystical traditions, We will discover common threads that unite humanity's spiritual experiences. They will explore shared themes such as the search for divine wisdom, connection with the sacred, and the pursuit of inner transformation. Through these explorations, We will gain a broader perspective on the universal nature of spiritual yearnings.

Recognizing Cultural Uniqueness: Embracing Spiritual Diversity
In exploring various mystical traditions, We will learn to appreciate the richness of cultural expressions in spirituality. They will encounter the distinct beliefs, rituals, and symbols that reflect the unique heritage and worldview of different cultures. By honoring cultural uniqueness, We will cultivate a spirit of respect and inclusivity, celebrating the beauty of diverse spiritual paths.

Nourishing Individual Exploration: Finding Personal Meaning

Encouraging We to explore multiple mystical traditions empowers them to find resonance and meaning in diverse teachings. As We draw from various sources, they can tailor their spiritual practices to align with their personal values and spiritual needs. This individualized approach fosters a sense of authenticity and empowers We to craft a meaningful and transformative spiritual journey.

Learning from Different Perspectives: Expanding Spiritual Horizons

By embracing the multiplicity of mystical traditions, We can gain new perspectives on spiritual truths and practices. They will recognize that various traditions offer unique insights and approaches to spiritual growth. Engaging with diverse perspectives broadens their spiritual horizons, enabling them to deepen their understanding and enrich their own spiritual paths.

Fostering Interconnectedness: Unity in Diversity

As We explore Babylonian mysticism and other mystical traditions, they will understand that, despite cultural differences, all paths share a common goal of seeking spiritual truth and connection. By appreciating the interconnectedness of spiritual beliefs, We cultivate a sense of unity and shared purpose with people of various faiths and practices.

Cultivating Open-Mindedness: Embracing Growth and Learning

Encouraging open-mindedness and curiosity, this section emphasizes the importance of continual growth and learning in spiritual exploration. We are invited to approach different mystical traditions with humility and a willingness to learn from diverse sources of wisdom. This open-minded attitude fosters personal growth and a deeper appreciation for the tapestry of human spirituality.

Through this exploration of diverse mystical traditions, We will gain a broader and more inclusive understanding of spirituality. By appreciating the universality and cultural uniqueness of spiritual beliefs, they will cultivate respect, curiosity, and an open heart towards different paths. In embracing diversity, We can enrich their own spiritual journeys and contribute to a world where compassion, understanding, and interconnectedness thrive.

Cultivating Empathy and Interconnectedness

In this section, we delve into the transformative power of empathy and interconnectedness, fostered through the study of Babylonian mystical traditions. By recognizing the shared human experience and interconnectedness with the natural world, We can cultivate empathy and compassion in their spiritual journeys.

Understanding the Human Experience: Connecting Through Shared Wisdom
Through the study of Babylonian mysticism, We encounter the collective human quest for meaning, transcendence, and connection with the divine. By exploring the struggles, hopes, and aspirations of ancient civilizations, We gain a deeper understanding of our shared human experience. This understanding fosters empathy as they recognize the universal desire for spiritual growth and fulfillment.

Honoring the Interconnected Web of Life: Nature as a Source of Unity
Babylonian mystical traditions celebrate the interconnectedness of humans with the natural world. By studying the reverence for nature and the cycles of life present in these traditions, We develop a sense of unity with the environment and all living beings. This appreciation for nature nurtures empathy for the Earth and a commitment to environmental stewardship.

Recognizing the Sacred in Others: Empathy as a Path to Compassion
As We explore the rituals and ceremonies of Babylonian mysticism, they encounter a profound reverence for the sacredness of life. This recognition of the divine in all beings lays the foundation for empathy and compassion. By acknowledging the sacred spark within others, We can extend kindness, understanding, and support, fostering a more inclusive and compassionate spiritual community.

Bridging Cultural Differences: Embracing Diversity with Empathy
Studying Babylonian mysticism allows We to encounter diverse cultural beliefs and practices. By approaching these traditions with empathy, We develop the ability to respect and appreciate different worldviews. This skill of empathetic understanding bridges cultural differences and promotes a sense of unity among diverse spiritual paths.

Cultivating Active Compassion: Empowering Positive Change
Inspired by the ethical principles within Babylonian mystical traditions, We are encouraged to translate empathy into action. By advocating for social justice, environmental sustainability, and the well-being of all beings, We become agents of positive change. Compassion becomes a driving force in their spiritual practice, fostering a deeper connection with the world around them.

Fostering Inclusivity in Spiritual Communities: Creating Safe Spaces
By embracing empathy and interconnectedness, We contribute to the creation of inclusive and welcoming spiritual communities. In these spaces, diverse beliefs and perspectives are respected, and compassion becomes the guiding principle in interactions. This inclusive approach to spirituality strengthens the collective journey towards harmony and understanding.

Through the study of Babylonian mystical traditions, We develop empathy, compassion, and a sense of interconnectedness with all beings and the natural world. These transformative qualities enrich their spiritual journeys, empowering them to extend kindness and understanding to others. By fostering an inclusive approach to spirituality, We become advocates for positive change and contributors to a more compassionate and harmonious world.

Challenging Assumptions and Stereotypes

In this section, we explore the transformative power of critical self-reflection when studying Babylonian mystical traditions. By challenging assumptions and stereotypes, We can cultivate an open-minded and inclusive approach to spirituality.

Unraveling Preconceived Notions: Embracing Intellectual Curiosity

Studying Babylonian mysticism encourages We to approach their exploration with intellectual curiosity. By questioning their preconceived notions and opening their minds to new perspectives, We embark on a journey of self-discovery. This process fosters a deeper understanding of their own beliefs and creates space for the appreciation of diverse spiritual traditions.

Acknowledging Cultural Biases: Embracing Cultural Humility

Babylonian mystical traditions offer an opportunity to confront cultural biases that may unconsciously influence our understanding of spirituality. We are encouraged to embrace cultural humility, recognizing that their own cultural lens shapes their interpretations. By acknowledging these biases, We become more receptive to diverse spiritual practices and traditions.

Breaking Free from Stereotypes: Recognizing the Complexity of Spirituality

The study of Babylonian mysticism challenges stereotypes about ancient civilizations and their spiritual beliefs. By delving into the nuanced and multifaceted nature of these traditions, We learn to recognize the complexity of spirituality across cultures and time periods. This newfound perspective fosters a more inclusive and respectful approach to spiritual exploration.

Fostering Respect for Diversity: Embracing the Tapestry of Beliefs

Studying Babylonian mysticism invites We to embrace the diversity of spiritual beliefs and practices. By appreciating the richness and variety of human spirituality, We develop a profound respect for the tapestry of beliefs woven throughout history and across cultures. This respect lays the foundation for a more inclusive and accepting spiritual outlook.

Addressing Cultural Appropriation: Cultivating Ethical Awareness

As We engage with Babylonian mystical traditions, they learn about the ethical implications of cultural appropriation. They are encouraged to approach these traditions with sensitivity and respect, acknowledging the importance of understanding and honoring the cultural context from which they emerged. This awareness fosters a responsible and ethical approach to spiritual exploration.

Embracing the Unknown: Finding Freedom in Uncertainty
Studying Babylonian mysticism may challenge We to embrace uncertainty and ambiguity. In the face of ancient texts and practices that may have fragmented over time, We learn to appreciate the beauty of mysteries yet to be fully uncovered. This willingness to embrace the unknown nurtures a sense of humility and openness in their spiritual journey.

By critically examining assumptions and biases, We foster an inclusive and open-minded approach to spirituality. The study of Babylonian mystical traditions provides a platform for challenging stereotypes and embracing the diversity of human spiritual expression. Through this process of self-reflection, We lay the groundwork for a more accepting and respectful spiritual exploration, fostering a harmonious connection with themselves, others, and the mystical wisdom of the ages.

Exploring Intersections of Spiritual Traditions

In this section, we delve into the power of recognizing intersections and shared elements among different spiritual traditions, particularly through the study of Babylonian mysticism. By identifying these common threads, We can enrich their spiritual journeys and foster a more holistic and inclusive approach to spirituality.

Unearthing Universal Themes: Recognizing Shared Wisdom
Studying Babylonian mysticism allows We to unearth universal themes present in various spiritual traditions. From concepts of divinity and sacred rituals to the pursuit of wisdom and transcendence, We discover shared wisdom that transcends cultural and historical boundaries. These universal themes provide a foundation for building bridges between different spiritual paths.

Bridging the Ancient and Modern: Integrating Ancient Wisdom
Through the study of Babylonian mysticism, We encounter ancient practices and insights that can be integrated into their modern spiritual practices. The timeless wisdom of these traditions can offer fresh perspectives and guidance in navigating the complexities of contemporary life. By embracing this ancient knowledge, We create a bridge between the past and the present, enriching their spiritual experiences.

Embracing Cultural Diversity: Celebrating Unity in Multiplicity

The exploration of Babylonian mysticism alongside other spiritual traditions encourages We to embrace cultural diversity. By recognizing the unity that exists within multiplicity, We foster a sense of global interconnectedness. This celebration of diversity enhances their appreciation for the richness of human spirituality and promotes a more inclusive and compassionate worldview.

Integrating Rituals and Practices: A Tapestry of Spiritual Expression

The shared rituals and practices found in Babylonian mysticism and other traditions offer a tapestry of spiritual expression. We are invited to draw inspiration from different practices, blending elements to form a unique spiritual path that resonates with their individuality. This integration promotes a sense of empowerment and authenticity in their spiritual journey.

Finding Unity in Core Principles: Shared Ethical Foundations

As We explore the moral and ethical principles of Babylonian mysticism, they discover shared values that align with those found in other traditions. Concepts of compassion, respect for nature, and social responsibility are emphasized in both ancient and contemporary belief systems. This recognition of shared ethical foundations fosters a sense of unity among diverse spiritual paths.

Encountering Sacred Symbols: A Language of Unity

Babylonian mystical traditions, like other spiritual paths, are rich with symbolic representations. As We study these symbols, they gain insights into the collective unconscious and its shared language across cultures. This universal symbolism reinforces the interconnectedness of humanity and serves as a unifying force in their spiritual exploration.

By identifying intersections and shared elements among different traditions, We cultivate a more inclusive and holistic approach to spirituality. The study of Babylonian mysticism serves as a gateway to recognizing universal themes, embracing cultural diversity, and integrating shared wisdom into their spiritual practices. This inclusive perspective fosters a profound sense of interconnectedness, unifying diverse spiritual paths and weaving a beautiful tapestry of human spiritual expression.

Building Bridges and Creating Dialogue

In this section, we highlight the significance of fostering an inclusive approach to spirituality through respectful communication and collaboration with individuals from diverse spiritual backgrounds. By engaging in meaningful conversations and sharing experiences, We can broaden their perspectives and create a more inclusive and supportive spiritual community.

The Power of Respectful Dialogue: Creating Understanding

Respectful dialogue is at the core of fostering an inclusive spiritual community. Encouraging We to engage in open conversations with others from different spiritual backgrounds helps create a deeper understanding of diverse beliefs and practices. This dialogue fosters empathy, compassion, and a sense of interconnectedness among individuals, transcending differences and promoting unity.

Embracing Different Perspectives: Expanding Horizons

By welcoming diverse perspectives, We can broaden their horizons and enrich their spiritual journey. Encountering varied beliefs and practices helps challenge preconceived notions and allows for personal growth. The willingness to embrace different viewpoints cultivates a more tolerant and accepting spiritual environment.

Collaboration and Learning: A Journey Together

Collaboration with individuals from diverse spiritual backgrounds offers a unique opportunity for mutual learning. By sharing experiences, practices, and rituals, We can glean insights from others and incorporate these learnings into their own spiritual path. This collaborative spirit fosters a sense of unity and cooperation within the spiritual community.

Building Bridges, Not Walls: Breaking Barriers

Encouraging We to build bridges with individuals from diverse spiritual backgrounds breaks down barriers that may exist between different belief systems. Through shared experiences and respectful communication, We realize that, despite unique expressions of spirituality, they are all united by a common quest for meaning and transcendence.

Nurturing an Inclusive Environment: Empowering All Seekers

An inclusive spiritual community empowers all seekers, regardless of their spiritual background, to participate and contribute. We are encouraged to create spaces where everyone feels welcome and valued. This nurturing environment allows individuals to explore their spirituality freely, fostering personal growth and self-discovery.

Celebrating Diversity: A Tapestry of Unity

Diversity within the spiritual community is celebrated as a tapestry of unity. We are inspired to embrace the myriad expressions of spirituality as threads that weave together to create a beautiful mosaic of human spiritual exploration. This celebration of diversity strengthens the sense of interconnectedness and mutual respect among individuals.

By emphasizing the importance of respectful communication and collaboration with diverse spiritual perspectives, We learn to build bridges and create a more inclusive and supportive spiritual community. Through meaningful conversations and shared experiences, they gain a deeper understanding of different beliefs and practices, cultivating empathy, tolerance, and unity within the spiritual landscape. This approach fosters personal growth, strengthens the sense of interconnectedness, and enriches the spiritual journey of all seekers.

Summary:

The exploration of Babylonian mystical traditions provides an opportunity to broaden our perspectives and foster a more inclusive approach to spirituality. By embracing diverse spiritual beliefs, cultivating empathy and interconnectedness, challenging assumptions and stereotypes, exploring intersections of traditions, and building bridges through dialogue, We can develop a more inclusive and expansive understanding of spirituality. This inclusive approach promotes respect, compassion, and unity within the realm of spiritual exploration.

Review Questions:

How does embracing diversity in spiritual beliefs contribute to a more inclusive approach to spirituality?

What are the benefits of cultivating empathy and recognizing interconnectedness in our spiritual journeys?

How can studying Babylonian mystical traditions help challenge assumptions and stereotypes in spirituality?

Why is it important to explore the intersections and shared elements among different spiritual traditions?

How can building bridges and creating dialogue contribute to a more inclusive spiritual community?

Exercises:

Engage in a respectful conversation with someone from a different spiritual background to learn about their beliefs and practices.

Reflect on your assumptions and biases about certain spiritual traditions and challenge them through further research and education.

Attend a workshop or event that explores the intersections of different spiritual traditions, and reflect on the insights gained from these shared elements.

Write a journal entry describing how studying Babylonian mystical traditions has expanded your perspective and understanding of spirituality.

Organize a group discussion or study circle to explore the concept of inclusivity in spirituality and share personal experiences and insights.

By embracing diverse spiritual beliefs, cultivating empathy, challenging assumptions, exploring intersections, and fostering dialogue, this chapter encourages We to develop a more inclusive and expansive approach to spirituality. By doing so, We can deepen their understanding of the diverse spiritual heritage of humanity and contribute to a more inclusive and harmonious world.

B. Drawing inspiration from Babylonian practices to enhance personal rituals and ceremonies

In this section, we explore the ways in which We of new-age studies can draw inspiration from Babylonian practices to enhance their personal rituals and ceremonies. By studying the rituals and ceremonies of ancient Babylon, We can gain insights into the symbolism, intention, and transformative power of these practices. This section encourages We to incorporate elements of Babylonian traditions into their own spiritual rituals, fostering a deeper connection with the ancient wisdom and enhancing the efficacy of their personal practices.

Understanding Babylonian Rituals and Ceremonies

In this section, we delve into the fascinating world of Babylonian rituals and ceremonies, offering We an overview of their significance and purpose. By exploring various types of rituals, such as purification ceremonies, offerings to deities, and rites of passage, We will gain a deeper understanding of their cultural and historical context, appreciating their relevance and adaptability to their own spiritual journey.

Purification Ceremonies: Cleansing the Body and Soul
Purification ceremonies were an integral part of Babylonian mysticism, aimed at cleansing the body and soul from impurities and negative energies. We will learn about the different purification rituals, their practices, and the symbolic significance of each step. Understanding the purpose of these ceremonies can help We incorporate cleansing practices into their spiritual routines, fostering a sense of renewal and spiritual clarity.

Offerings to Deities: Honoring the Divine

Babylonian rituals often involved offering sacrifices and gifts to various deities, honoring their power and seeking their favor. We will explore the diverse deities and their associated offerings, understanding the spiritual connection between humans and the divine. This exploration can inspire We to develop their own rituals of gratitude and devotion, strengthening their connection with the spiritual realm.

Rites of Passage: Marking Life Transitions

Babylonian culture celebrated significant life events through rites of passage, such as birth, marriage, and death rituals. We will discover the symbolic importance of these rites and their role in acknowledging life's milestones. Understanding rites of passage can inspire We to create meaningful ceremonies for their own life transitions, infusing them with spiritual significance and personal growth.

Seasonal Celebrations: Honoring Nature's Cycles

The Babylonians marked the changing seasons with joyous celebrations, acknowledging the cyclical nature of life and the interconnectedness with the natural world. We will explore the significance of these seasonal rituals and how they deepened the bond between humans and the Earth. This understanding can encourage We to develop their own rituals, aligning their spiritual practices with the rhythms of nature.

Invocations and Blessings: Seeking Divine Guidance

Babylonian mysticism involved invocations and blessings to seek divine guidance and protection. We will learn about the practices and words used to invoke the presence and blessings of deities. Understanding these invocations can inspire We to create their own prayers and affirmations, establishing a direct connection with the spiritual forces they resonate with.

Adaptability and Personalization: Honoring Individual Paths

One of the most valuable lessons from studying Babylonian rituals is the adaptability and personalization of spiritual practices. We will discover that rituals can be tailored to suit individual beliefs, preferences, and needs. This understanding empowers We to create rituals that align with their unique spiritual journey, fostering a sense of authenticity and empowerment.

By providing an overview of Babylonian rituals and ceremonies, this section equips We with insights into the significance and purpose of these practices. As they explore the diverse rituals of purification, offerings, rites of passage, seasonal celebrations, invocations, and blessings, We will be inspired to adapt and integrate these meaningful practices into their own spiritual journey. Emphasizing the adaptability and personalization of rituals, We will discover the beauty of crafting their unique spiritual path while honoring the wisdom and heritage of ancient Babylonian mysticism.

Symbolism and Sacred Objects

In this section, we delve into the fascinating symbolism behind common objects used in Babylonian rituals, providing We with insights into their spiritual significance. By exploring the meanings behind objects like incense, candles, and sacred amulets, We will discover how to incorporate these symbols into their own rituals, enriching their practices with deeper meaning and intention.

Incense: Purification and Connection
Incense has been a significant element in Babylonian rituals, symbolizing purification and connecting with the divine. We will learn about the various types of incense used and their associations with specific deities or spiritual intentions. Understanding the symbolism of incense can inspire We to incorporate its use in their rituals, enhancing the atmosphere of sacredness and creating a link between the physical and spiritual realms.

Candles: Illumination and Invocation
Candles have a profound symbolism in Babylonian rituals, representing illumination, transformation, and the presence of divine energies. We will explore the meanings of different candle colors and how they correspond to specific intentions or spiritual forces. Embracing the symbolism of candles, We can infuse their rituals with focused intention, invoking spiritual energies and seeking guidance from higher realms.

Sacred Amulets: Protection and Empowerment
Sacred amulets were treasured objects in Babylonian rituals, believed to offer protection and empowerment. We will discover the symbolism of these amulets and the deities they were associated with. Understanding their significance, We can create their own sacred objects or wear amulets with personal meaning, inviting protection and empowerment into their spiritual practices.

Offerings: Gratitude and Communion
Babylonian rituals often involved offerings of food, drink, or precious items as symbols of gratitude and communion with deities. We will explore the symbolism of different offerings and how they express respect and appreciation for the spiritual forces. By incorporating offerings into their rituals, We can cultivate a sense of gratitude and deepen their spiritual connection with the divine.

Altars: Sacred Space and Focus
Altars held a central role in Babylonian rituals, serving as sacred spaces for spiritual practices. We will learn about the symbolism of altars and how they anchor spiritual

energies and intentions. Creating their own altars, We can establish a dedicated space for their rituals, enhancing focus and intention in their spiritual practices.

Symbolic Gestures: Ritual Actions with Meaning

Babylonian rituals often involved symbolic gestures and movements to invoke spiritual energies or mark transitions. We will explore the symbolism of these ritual actions and their significance in enhancing the overall experience of the ritual. Incorporating symbolic gestures into their own practices, We can amplify the power of their intentions and create a deeper sense of connection with the spiritual realm.

By delving into the symbolism behind common objects used in Babylonian rituals, this section empowers We to infuse their spiritual practices with deeper meaning and intention. As We explore the symbolism of incense, candles, sacred amulets, offerings, altars, and symbolic gestures, they will gain a profound appreciation for the richness of Babylonian rituals. By incorporating these symbols into their own rituals, We can create a sacred space where intention and symbolism converge, inviting spiritual energies and divine blessings into their spiritual journey.

Invocation and Chanting

In this section, we delve into the profound practices of invocation and chanting, which were integral to Babylonian rituals. These sacred arts served as potent means of connecting with deities and harnessing spiritual energies. By introducing We to the art of invocation and chanting, we offer examples of Babylonian invocations and their purposes, empowering We to create their own invocations and chants, infusing their rituals with the vibrational energy and spiritual resonance of ancient Babylon.

The Art of Invocation: Connecting with Deities

Invocation is a powerful practice of calling upon specific deities or spiritual forces to seek their guidance, protection, or blessings. We will learn about the significance of invocation in Babylonian rituals, understanding how it forged a connection between the human and divine realms. By studying ancient invocations and the deities they invoked, We can gain insights into the language and symbolism used to establish a profound connection with the spiritual forces.

Chanting: Vibrational Energy and Resonance

Chanting involves repeating sacred words or sounds, generating vibrational energy that resonates with the spiritual realms. We will explore the role of chanting in Babylonian rituals, recognizing its ability to elevate consciousness and evoke a deep sense of unity with the divine. By studying examples of Babylonian chants and their intentions, We can understand the power of sound in spiritual practices and its potential to uplift and transform.

Creating Personal Invocations and Chants

We will be encouraged to craft their own invocations and chants, drawing inspiration from Babylonian traditions while infusing their unique intentions and personal connection to the divine. They will explore the use of specific words, phrases, and sounds that resonate with their spiritual path, deepening their understanding of the spiritual power inherent in language and sound.

Intentions and Purposes of Invocations

We will learn about the various intentions and purposes behind invocations, including seeking guidance, expressing gratitude, or invoking protection. By understanding the different aspects of intention in invocations, We can personalize their practices and align them with their spiritual goals and aspirations.

The Role of Sound in Chanting

This section will explore the significance of sound and its transformative effect in chanting. We will learn about the rhythm, cadence, and harmonics of chanting that create a powerful resonance in both the individual and the surrounding environment. By studying the impact of sound in Babylonian rituals, We can harness the potential of sound in their own spiritual practices.

Ritual Timing and Astrology

Babylonian rituals were often performed at specific times aligned with celestial events and astrological influences. This section explores the concept of ritual timing and astrology in Babylonian practices, highlighting the significance of lunar phases, planetary alignments, and astrological symbolism. We will learn how to incorporate astrological considerations into their own rituals, aligning their intentions with cosmic energies for enhanced potency.

Personalizing Babylonian Rituals

This section encourages We to personalize Babylonian rituals and ceremonies according to their own spiritual beliefs and needs. We will learn how to adapt and modify Babylonian practices to align with their unique spiritual paths. By infusing their personal rituals with elements of Babylonian wisdom, We can create a harmonious blend of ancient and modern practices that resonate with their individual spiritual journeys.

Chapter Summary:

Drawing inspiration from Babylonian practices allows We to enrich their personal rituals and ceremonies with the wisdom and symbolism of ancient Babylon. By understanding Babylonian rituals, incorporating sacred objects and symbols, exploring invocation and chanting, considering ritual timing and astrology, and personalizing these practices, We can deepen their connection to the ancient mystical traditions and enhance the transformative power of their spiritual rituals.

Review Questions:

What is the significance of understanding Babylonian rituals and ceremonies for personal spiritual practices?

How can the symbolism of sacred objects enhance the meaning and intention of personal rituals?

What role does invocation and chanting play in Babylonian rituals, and how can We incorporate these practices into their own rituals?

Why is ritual timing and astrology important in Babylonian practices, and how can We align their rituals with celestial influences?

How can We personalize Babylonian rituals to create a meaningful and authentic spiritual practice?

Exercises:

Research and select a specific Babylonian ritual or ceremony to study and incorporate into your personal practice.

Create a sacred space for your rituals by incorporating Babylonian symbols and sacred objects.

Practice an invocation or chant inspired by Babylonian traditions and integrate it into your regular rituals.

Explore the astrological influences on your own spiritual journey and align your rituals with celestial energies.

Reflect on how incorporating elements of Babylonian practices has enhanced your personal rituals and ceremonies, and write a journal entry documenting your experiences.

C. Nurturing a deeper connection with nature and the cosmos through Babylonian wisdom

In this section, we delve into the profound relationship between Babylonian wisdom and the natural world. By exploring the teachings of ancient Babylon, We of new-age studies can nurture a deeper connection with nature and the cosmos. This section emphasizes the importance of understanding Babylonian perspectives on nature, celestial bodies, and the interconnectedness of all living beings. Through this exploration, We can expand their awareness and develop a more harmonious and reverential relationship with the natural world.

Babylonian Cosmology and Nature

In this section, we explore the captivating realm of Babylonian cosmology and its profound connection with nature. We will gain insights into the Babylonian worldview, which perceives nature as a divine creation intricately woven with the fabric of human existence, animals, plants, and celestial bodies. By studying Babylonian cosmology, We can cultivate a sense of awe and respect for the natural world, fostering a deeper understanding of their place within it and the spiritual significance it holds.

Babylonian Worldview: Nature as a Divine Creation
We will be introduced to the core tenets of the Babylonian worldview, which perceives nature as an awe-inspiring manifestation of divine creation. They will explore the belief that the gods and goddesses played integral roles in shaping the cosmos, imbuing nature with their wisdom and life force. By recognizing nature's intrinsic sacredness, We can develop a profound appreciation for the interconnectedness of all living beings and their relationship with the divine.

Interconnections in Babylonian Cosmology
This section will delve into the intricate web of interconnections within Babylonian cosmology. We will learn how the Babylonians perceived a harmonious relationship between humans, animals, plants, and celestial bodies. By studying the symbolism and significance of these connections, We can gain a deeper understanding of the unity that underpins the cosmic tapestry.

Nature and Spirituality: The Sacred Landscape

We will explore how Babylonian spirituality integrated with the natural world, recognizing that sacredness resided in every aspect of the environment. They will learn about sacred landscapes, such as temples and natural sites, where rituals were conducted to honor the gods and connect with the divine energies present in the natural realm. By understanding the rituals and practices associated with these sacred spaces, We can appreciate the profound spiritual significance of the natural world.

The Cycles of Nature: Celestial Bodies and Seasons

Babylonian cosmology acknowledged the celestial bodies and the cyclical nature of the seasons as powerful forces governing life on Earth. We will learn about the significance of celestial bodies like the moon and stars in shaping agricultural practices, calendars, and spiritual observances. By studying the cycles of nature, We can gain a deeper awareness of the interconnectedness of the cosmos and the rhythms that govern life.

Cultivating Respect and Awe for the Natural World

Throughout this section, We will be encouraged to reflect on the wisdom of Babylonian cosmology and its relevance in contemporary times. By understanding the deep reverence that the ancient Babylonians held for nature, We can draw inspiration to foster their own sense of awe, respect, and care for the natural world. By integrating this awareness into their daily lives, We can embark on a journey of spiritual growth and ecological consciousness.

Sacred Landscapes and Sacred Ecology

In this section, we delve into the profound concept of sacred landscapes in Babylonian culture, where specific natural features held deep spiritual significance. We will gain insights into the Babylonian reverence for sacred rivers, mountains, and groves, and how these natural spaces were considered portals to the divine. By studying sacred landscapes, We can learn to recognize and honor the sacredness of their own environments, fostering a deeper connection with the land and its inherent spiritual energies.

The Sanctity of Sacred Rivers

We will explore how Babylonian culture attributed divine significance to certain rivers, such as the Euphrates and Tigris. These rivers were not only sources of life-giving water but were also believed to be pathways connecting the earthly realm to the spiritual realm. By studying the rituals and practices associated with sacred rivers, We can reflect on the symbolic importance of water as a conduit of spiritual energy and renewal.

The Majesty of Sacred Mountains

Babylonian cosmology regarded mountains as sacred sites where the gods and goddesses resided. We will learn about the symbolism of mountains as bridges between heaven and earth, representing the meeting point of the divine and the terrestrial. By exploring the practices and beliefs tied to sacred mountains, We can gain a deeper appreciation for the spiritual significance of mountainous landscapes and their role in ancient rituals.

The Tranquility of Sacred Groves

In Babylonian culture, certain groves and forests were considered sacred spaces where the energies of the natural world and the divine converged. We will delve into the symbolism of groves as places of spiritual contemplation and communion with nature. By studying the rituals and offerings performed in sacred groves, We can contemplate the sacredness of nature and its potential for spiritual connection.

Honoring Sacred Landscapes in Modern Times

Throughout this section, We will be encouraged to draw parallels between Babylonian sacred landscapes and the natural spaces in their own surroundings. By recognizing the sacredness of their local rivers, mountains, and groves, We can cultivate a deeper connection with the land and its inherent spiritual energies. They will explore practices to honor and protect these landscapes, fostering ecological consciousness and a sense of stewardship for the earth.

Embracing the Sacredness of Nature

By reflecting on Babylonian wisdom and its reverence for sacred landscapes, We can gain a heightened appreciation for the interconnectedness of humanity and the natural world. This section aims to inspire We to recognize the sacredness of nature in all its forms and to cultivate a spiritual connection with the land. By doing so, We can embrace the sacredness of their own environments and embark on a journey of eco-spirituality, promoting harmony, respect, and reciprocity with the earth.

Through the exploration of sacred landscapes in Babylonian culture and their significance, this section encourages We to recognize the spiritual essence present in their own natural surroundings. By honoring and connecting with sacred spaces, We can deepen their spiritual experiences and develop a profound sense of reverence and gratitude for the interconnected web of life that surrounds them.

Celestial Influences and Natural Cycles

In this section, we delve into the fascinating realm of Babylonian celestial observations and their profound impact on their spiritual beliefs and practices. We will gain insights into how the Babylonians closely observed celestial bodies, such as the moon, planets, and stars, and recognized their influence on natural cycles and human affairs. By studying Babylonian cosmology, We can learn how to attune themselves to these cosmic rhythms and incorporate them into their own spiritual practices, deepening their connection with the celestial energies of the universe.

The Phases of the Moon
We will explore the Babylonian understanding of the lunar phases and their significance in marking time and natural cycles. The moon played a crucial role in their calendar and religious observances, guiding rituals and agricultural practices. By studying the lunar calendar and its connection to spiritual celebrations, We can learn how to attune themselves to the ever-changing energies of the moon and its impact on their own spiritual journey.

Planetary Alignments and Cosmic Influences
Babylonians believed that the movements of planets and celestial bodies had direct influences on human destinies and events on Earth. We will explore Babylonian astrology and its role in guiding decisions and understanding the interconnectedness of cosmic energies and human affairs. By studying the Babylonian approach to astrology, We can gain insights into how celestial alignments can be integrated into their own spiritual practices for guidance and self-awareness.

Seasonal Changes and Nature's Rhythms
In Babylonian culture, the changing seasons were intricately linked to agricultural practices and spiritual rituals. We will learn about the Babylonian festivals and ceremonies tied to seasonal changes, acknowledging the cyclical nature of life and the interconnectedness between human life and the natural world. By embracing the wisdom of these ancient practices, We can deepen their connection with the Earth's rhythms and find resonance with their own spiritual journey.

Attuning to Cosmic Rhythms in Modern Times
Throughout this section, We will be encouraged to contemplate the ways they can integrate celestial observations and natural cycles into their modern spiritual practices. By aligning with the cosmic rhythms of the universe, We can foster a deeper connection with the divine and gain a profound sense of harmony with the cosmos.

Finding Spiritual Meaning in Celestial Observations
By exploring Babylonian insights into celestial phenomena, We can discover a wealth of spiritual meaning and connection in the vastness of the cosmos. This section aims to inspire We to embrace the wisdom of ancient Babylonian observations and recognize the celestial influences in their own lives. By attuning themselves to the cosmic rhythms, We can infuse their spiritual practices with a deeper understanding of their place in the universe and cultivate a sense of wonder and reverence for the celestial dance that surrounds them.

Through the study of Babylonian celestial observations and their connection to natural cycles, this section encourages We to explore the profound impact of cosmic rhythms on human spirituality. By incorporating these insights into their own spiritual practices, We can deepen their connection with the universe and embrace the timeless wisdom of Babylonian mysticism, finding solace, guidance, and inspiration in the celestial wonders that continue to illuminate our lives.

Nature-Based Rituals and Practices

In this section, we embark on a journey through the nature-based rituals and practices of ancient Babylon, revealing their profound reverence for the Earth and celestial phenomena. We will gain insights into how Babylonians celebrated the cycles of nature, connected with nature spirits, and engaged in rituals to heal and honor the land. By studying Babylonian nature-based practices, We can learn how to adapt and incorporate these ancient traditions into their own spiritual routines, fostering a greater sense of connection with nature and the cosmos.

Seasonal Celebrations and Festivals

We will explore Babylonian seasonal celebrations, marking the changing rhythms of the Earth and the agricultural cycles. These festivals were times of joy and gratitude, offering offerings and rituals to honor the gifts of the land and the blessings of the seasons. By understanding the significance of these festivals, We can adapt them to their own lives, celebrating the changing seasons and finding meaning in the cyclical nature of life.

Offerings to Nature Spirits

Babylonians believed in the presence of nature spirits, guardians of the land and its inhabitants. We will learn about the rituals and offerings made to these spirits as a way of showing respect and seeking their blessings. By studying these practices, We can connect with the spirits of nature around them and deepen their appreciation for the unseen forces that shape our world.

Land Healing and Blessings

Ancient Babylonians engaged in land healing rituals to restore balance and harmony to the Earth. We will explore these practices and learn how to adapt them to their own environments, infusing their spiritual practices with a sense of responsibility for the well-being of the land. By honoring the Earth in this way, We can foster a greater connection with the planet and actively contribute to its healing.

Embracing the Cosmos in Nature

Throughout this section, We will be encouraged to contemplate the interplay between celestial events and the natural world. Babylonians recognized the interconnectedness of the cosmos and nature, and We will learn how to observe celestial events as a way of attuning to the greater cycles of the universe. By embracing the cosmos in nature, We can develop a profound sense of wonder and awe for the interconnectedness of all things.

Personalizing Nature-Based Rituals
In this section, we will explore the beauty of adapting and personalizing Babylonian nature-based rituals to suit our individual spiritual paths and the unique environments in which we live. By doing so, we can forge deep and meaningful connections with nature, infusing our spiritual routines with a profound appreciation for the Earth and all its wonders.

Understanding the Essence of Babylonian Nature-Based Rituals
Before we begin adapting these rituals, we will delve into the essence of Babylonian nature-based practices. We will study the intention behind their rituals, the symbolism they used, and the principles that guided their interactions with the natural world. Understanding the underlying philosophy of these rituals will help us grasp their significance and enable us to personalize them with authenticity.

Observing Our Local Environment
We will then turn our attention to the landscapes and ecosystems of our own local environment. By observing and appreciating the unique features of the land, weather patterns, and seasonal changes, we can align our rituals with the natural rhythms of our surroundings. Connecting with the flora, fauna, and geographical elements will enrich our spiritual experiences and foster a deeper sense of belonging to our ecosystem.

Adapting Rituals to Personal Beliefs
While honoring the wisdom of Babylonian traditions, we will also embrace our own spiritual beliefs and practices. This section will encourage us to explore how Babylonian rituals can harmonize with our personal cosmology, beliefs about the divine, and spiritual goals. By blending elements from various traditions, we can create rituals that resonate deeply with our hearts and minds.

Infusing Intentions and Personal Meaning
Infusing our rituals with personal intentions and meaning is key to making them our own. We will learn how to incorporate our aspirations, gratitude, and desires into the rituals, making them more powerful and relevant to our lives. By doing so, we can cultivate a stronger connection with the natural world and align our actions with our spiritual values.

Building a Sustainable Practice
Creating a personalized nature-based practice is a journey that requires adaptability and growth. We will explore ways to make our rituals sustainable and respectful of the Earth's resources. This includes using environmentally friendly materials, treading lightly on the land, and giving back to nature through conservation efforts.

Nurturing a Spirit of Exploration
Throughout this section, we will foster a spirit of exploration and experimentation. Each individual's journey is unique, and we encourage students to try new rituals, adapt existing ones, and be open to new insights and discoveries. We will celebrate the diversity of our spiritual practices, recognizing that there is no one-size-fits-all approach to connecting with nature.

By adapting and personalizing Babylonian nature-based rituals, we open ourselves to a deeper and more intimate relationship with the Earth and its wonders. Embracing the essence of Babylonian wisdom while integrating our own beliefs and values allows us to create rituals that are not only meaningful but also relevant to our modern lives. Through this process, we can cultivate a profound appreciation for the interconnectedness of all life and find solace, wisdom, and inspiration in the embrace of nature's ever-changing beauty.

By delving into the nature-based rituals and practices of ancient Babylon, this section aims to inspire We to connect with the natural world and find spiritual significance in the cycles of the Earth and cosmos. By incorporating these rituals into their own spiritual routines, We can foster a greater sense of harmony with nature and the universe, embracing the wisdom of Babylonian traditions and cultivating a profound connection with the sacredness of the Earth.

Environmental Stewardship and Ecospirituality

The wisdom of ancient Babylon emphasizes the importance of environmental stewardship and ecospirituality. This section explores the ethical and practical aspects of living in harmony with nature and taking responsibility for the well-being of the Earth. We will learn how to integrate these principles into their daily lives, promoting sustainability, and fostering a sense of reverence for the natural world.

Summary:

By delving into Babylonian wisdom, We can nurture a deeper connection with nature and the cosmos. Understanding Babylonian cosmology, recognizing sacred landscapes, attuning to celestial influences, practicing nature-based rituals, and embracing environmental stewardship, We can cultivate a profound reverence for the natural world and develop a harmonious relationship with the interconnectedness of all life.

Review Questions:

How does Babylonian cosmology emphasize the interconnectedness of nature and the cosmos?

What are sacred landscapes in Babylonian culture, and how can we honor the sacredness of our own environments?

How do celestial influences impact natural cycles and human affairs, according to Babylonian wisdom?

What are some nature-based rituals and practices in Babylonian traditions, and how can we incorporate them into our spiritual routines?

Why is environmental stewardship important in Babylonian wisdom, and how can we practice ecospirituality in our daily lives?

Exercises:

Spend time in nature, observing and reflecting on the interconnectedness of all living beings.

Research and create a personal ritual that honors a specific landscape or natural feature in your environment.

Observe and document the celestial influences in your surroundings, such as moon phases or seasonal changes.

Explore and adapt a Babylonian nature-based ritual to celebrate a seasonal change or natural event.

Engage in an environmental stewardship activity, such as participating in a local cleanup or implementing sustainable practices in your daily life.

www.ingramcontent.com/pod-product-compliance
Lightning Source LLC
Chambersburg PA
CBHW082139120626
46553CB00010B/2710